HEGEL'S
POLITICAL
WRITINGS

HEGEL'S POLITICAL WRITINGS

TRANSLATED BY
T. M. KNOX

WITH AN INTRODUCTORY ESSAY BY
Z. A. PELCZYNSKI

OXFORD
AT THE CLARENDON PRESS

Oxford University Press, Great Clarendon Street, Oxford OX2 6DP
Oxford New York
Athens Auckland Bangkok Bogota Buenos Aires Calcutta
Cape Town Chennai Dar es Salaam Delhi Florence Hong Kong Istanbul
Karachi Kuala Lumpur Madrid Melbourne Mexico City Mumbai
Nairobi Paris São Paolo Singapore Taipei Tokyo Toronto Warsaw
and associated companies in
Berlin Ibadan

Oxford is a registered trade mark of Oxford University Press

Published in the United States by
Oxford University Press Inc., New York

© Oxford University Press 1964

Special edition for Sandpiper Books Ltd., 1998

British Library Cataloguing in Publication Data
Data available

ISBN 0-19-827148-4

1 3 5 7 9 10 8 6 4 2

Printed in Great Britain
on acid-free paper by
Bookcraft (Bath) Ltd.,
Midsomer Norton

CONTENTS

PART I

AN INTRODUCTORY ESSAY

Z. A. PELCZYNSKI

PREFACE

VERY few students of political thought are aware that Hegel was the author of a number of pamphlets and commentaries dealing with various topical political issues. These political writings are a most valuable supplement to the *Philosophy of Right* and the *Philosophy of History*, and being relatively free from speculative elements and philosophical jargon they provide in some ways a clearer insight into Hegel's basic political ideas than the major works. They also show that this perhaps most metaphysical of political thinkers kept a firm eye on facts, past and present, and could pursue the smallest details of political arrangements with the passion of an empiricist.

The author of this study of Hegel as a political writer owes a great debt to the late Michael Foster, Student of Christ Church, Oxford, for his unfailing interest, stimulus, and assistance as a supervisor of the research originally undertaken for a doctoral thesis at Oxford. He is also indebted to Sir Malcolm Knox for his generous help in revision as well as for his criticisms and suggestions. Professor John R. Rodman of Harvard and Dr. Andrzej Walicki of Warsaw University also read the whole text and made valuable comments, and Mr. Michael Rogers of Pembroke College, Oxford, helped to clear up a number of points in Chapters II and III. None of them is in any way responsible for the faults that remain.

The essay is intended to be read in conjunction with the political writings, most of which have been translated into English by T. M. Knox and form the second part of this volume. The passages quoted in the essay are from that translation, but page references (in square brackets) are to the Georg Lasson edition of Hegel's political and juristic writings, published by Felix Meiner (second edition, Leipzig, 1923).

Z. A. PELCZYNSKI

Pembroke College, Oxford
June 1962

I

HEGEL AS A POLITICAL WRITER

What, then, does a rational writer want? What can he
want? Nothing but to intervene in the universal and
public life, and to shape and transform it in his image.
If he does not want to do that, all his speech is but an
empty sound to gratify idle ears.

J. G. FICHTE, *Reden an die deutsche Nation.*

IT was perhaps a mere coincidence that the first and last works
actually published by Hegel in his life were not philosophical
works in any sense of the word. They were both popular,
political writings—a pamphlet and a newspaper article—and represented Hegel's reaction to two immediate political situations. The
coincidence in fact is not fortuitous; at any rate, two things follow
from it. First, that politics was an abiding, lifelong interest of
Hegel's; and second, that political philosophy as found in the
Philosophy of Right and the *Philosophy of History* was not the only
expression of that interest. Before we introduce Hegel the publicist and his works, the background of his political interest must
be briefly considered.

Broadly speaking, there were three sources of that interest:
his family and friends; his school, university and private studies;
and contemporary events. Many of his ancestors had been in the
civil service. His father was an official in the government of
the Duke of Wurtemberg,[1] and living in Stuttgart, the seat of the
Court and the capital of the Duchy, maintained a close touch with
men more highly placed than himself. Hegel must have heard
politics discussed at home as early as he could remember, and
there is a tradition that son and father had heated arguments after
the outbreak of the French Revolution. These early contacts with

[1] Wurtemberg was one of the most constitutional states in Germany at the
time, characterized by 'a strong parliamentary and liberal tradition, distinguishing Wurtemberg from most other parts of Germany. . . . In the later eighteenth
century it inspired Charles James Fox to the remark that there were only two
constitutions in Europe, the British constitution and that of Wurtemberg.'
F. L. Carsten, *Princes and Parliaments in Germany: from the Fifteenth to the
Eighteenth Century* (Oxford, 1959), p. 5.

politics and government continued after Hegel left home. In Frankfurt he was friendly with Sinclair, a counsellor and confidant of one of the smaller German rulers. Later on, when Bavaria was being reorganized from top to bottom, his friend Niethammer kept him informed of the moves of the government, in which he himself had an official position. Hegel was hoping to obtain a governmental post for himself at that time, but had to be satisfied with the headmastership of a royal secondary school in Nuremberg. Later, when he resigned his Heidelberg chair in order to accept one at Berlin, he gave the possibility of 'a more practical activity' as a reason to the Government of Baden. He may have hoped even for a place in the Prussian government, but he succeeded only in becoming a member of a Royal Examination Commission of the Province of Brandenburg, and later on a counsellor in the Ministry of Education. Nevertheless, in Prussia he stayed near the centre of public affairs, and enjoyed the confidence of his Minister Altenstein.[1] These contacts and aspirations not merely sustained his lifelong interest in politics, but also account for the strong governmental and bureaucratic bias which is evident in his political works.

His principal means of keeping in touch with the deliberative and representative aspects of government were the press and reports of parliamentary proceedings. Hegel had been an avid and regular reader of periodical literature from his youth, and throughout his life he read German, French, and English periodicals and parliamentary reports; in an aphorism of the Jena period he called newspaper reading 'a kind of realistic morning prayer. One orientates one's attitude to the world by God or by that which the world itself is.' In 1807 he decided to try his hand at journalism and became editor of a Bavarian newspaper called *Die Bamberger Zeitung*. He started with high hopes but resigned after a year without regret; difficulties in collecting information and the strict Napoleonic censorship made editing a rather unrewarding task.[2]

---

[1] Altenstein belonged to a group of leading Prussian administrators who had introduced many liberal reforms in Prussia, but lost the King's support after the fall of Napoleon. See W. Simon, *The Failure of the Prussian Reform Movement, 1807–1819* (Cornell University Press, 1955). Many of Hegel's mature political ideas bear a close resemblance to those of the Altenstein circle.

[2] Hegel's first reaction to the offer of editorship is interesting, as the following extract from a letter to Niethammer, quoted by K. Rosenkranz in his *Georg Wilhelm Friedrich Hegels Leben* (Berlin, 1844), p. 231, shows: 'The work itself will interest me since, as you know, I follow world affairs with curiosity, and as

His wide contacts and a long practice of corresponding with friends and acquaintances on political matters served him well during the year. Published posthumously, these letters are a most valuable source of insight into his political opinions, indeed the main one for the period between the publication of the *Phenomenology of Mind* and the *Science of Logic*. It is only from his letters that we learn the full extent and nature of the enormous fascination and influence which Napoleon exercised over his mind.[1] Of various types of political action only what may be called the popular or party activity remained largely alien to Hegel; apart from belonging to a pro-revolutionary club in his student days at Tübingen and to an anti-court faction during the 1798 conflict in Wurtemberg, he appears to have kept deliberately aloof from all such activity. This fact, too, is not without consequence for his political thought,

far as this side of the work is concerned I have to fear its attraction rather than repulsion . . .' (20 February 1806). Rosenkranz, like other commentators, tended to dismiss that episode in Hegel's life as unimportant. But W. R. Beyer in his *Zwischen Phänomenologie und Logik; Hegel als Redakteur der Bamberger Zeitung* (Frankfurt-on-Main, 1955) maintains the contrary. He sees in Hegel's early life a strong desire to influence political events, a practical political interest, and concludes that, as distinct from his philosophical achievements, 'Hegel's political career . . . reached its peak in Bamberg in his journalistic work'. (p. 86.)

[1] Here are some examples of Hegel's references to Napoleon in his letters to Niethammer, quoted from K. Hegel, *Briefe von und an Hegel* (Leipzig, 1887), vol. ii:

'I saw Napoleon, the soul of the world, riding through the town on a reconnaissance. It is indeed a wonderful sensation to see, concentrated in a point, sitting on a horse, an individual who overruns the world and masters it.' Jena, 13 October 1806. (p. 68.)

'Everybody here is waiting for the organization which is to start soon. I have announced in my paper that the country [i.e., Bavaria] is to be divided into prefectures. There is talk of some other great congress of the [former] Imperial Estates. The crucial decision will certainly come from Paris. The multitude of small princes left in Germany alone makes some closer bond between them necessary. German jurists go on writing heaps of works on the concept of sovereignty and the meaning of the Acts of Union. The great constitutional jurist sits in Paris.' Bamberg, 29 August 1807. (p. 130.)

'They write of another book too, the *Code Napoléon*, and though it is merely an invitation [to adopt it] it carries a *compelle* with it. . . . But the Germans are still blind—just as they were 20 years ago. The merit, the *grace*, which could have been acquired is now wholly lost.—But the importance of the *Code* is incomparably smaller than that of the hope one may now entertain that other parts of the French or the Westphalian Constitution will also be introduced [in Germany]. Nothing happens spontaneously and as a result of one's own judgement, for where is it to be found? And so Heaven's, i.e. the French Emperor's, will must decree it.' Bamberg, 11 February 1808. (pp. 158, 159.)

although it has to be remembered that party politics in Germany had not developed very far before Hegel's death.

His education—the second mainspring of his political interest—consisted of the formal instruction he received at the Royal High School in Stuttgart and at the Tübingen Theological Seminary, and also of his own private studies begun there and continued in Berne and Frankfurt, where afterwards he acted as private tutor to sons of wealthy bourgeois families. Of the two it was his own studies which were by far the more important factor. He was under the spell equally of classical antiquity and contemporary Enlightenment and he steeped himself in their literature. Mainly during those early years he devoured, digested, and assimilated the works of Plato, Aristotle, Thucydides, and Cicero; Hobbes, Locke, Hume, and Gibbon; Spinoza, Montesquieu, Rousseau, and Voltaire; Leibniz, Mendelssohn, Kant, and Fichte—not to mention a host of other, minor, and mostly German writers. The beauty of Greek and early Roman political life overwhelmed Hegel, as it had so many other thinkers, and left a permanent mark on his political philosophy. The concept of the state as an integral part of the ethical life of a people Hegel owes to the classical studies of his youth, as to some extent he does his belief in government by an intellectual *élite* or politics as education.[1] But equally, and for his popular political writings more, important was his reading of the great authors of the Enlightenment, especially their political and historical works. At first, German Enlightenment, unlike the French and the British, was largely non-political in character, but the American and French Revolutions and their repercussions in Germany and the rest of Europe stimulated a vigorous political literature. Kant, for instance, wrote practically all his political works after the outbreak of the Revolution, and Fichte's first political work was a vindication of 1789. This makes Hegel's familiarity with non-German writers all the more significant. He owed to them a lifelong preference for reflective or 'pragmatic' history, although historical literature of the more narrative, 'empirical' kind seems to have figured quite prominently on his reading list. And 'history', in his day, meant very largely 'political history'.

Political thinking thrives on upheavals, crises, and rapid political changes. They force man to take sides, undermine old assumptions

---

[1] Hegel's debt to ancient political thought is brilliantly discussed in M. B. Foster, *The Political Philosophies of Plato and Hegel* (Oxford, 1935).

and beliefs, excite passions, and stimulate curiosity. Such were the times in which Hegel lived, and we can see in them the third main cause for his absorption in politics. The French Revolution and its aftermath dominated Hegel's formative years: he was just under nineteen when the Bastille fell, and under forty-five at the time of the battle of Waterloo. He died a year after the July Revolution. Thus he witnessed the destruction of the *ancien régime*, the restoration and the second overthrow of the Bourbons; the foundation of the Republic and its degeneration into the Terror; the rise, apogee, and fall of Napoleon; the collapse and reconstruction of Prussia; the death of the Holy Roman Empire of the German Nation. Underlying these 'tremendous political experiments' and 'colossal spectacles'[1] were a number of permanent and radical changes in European polity and society. New states had been created; some of the old ones had changed their dynasties and a few their forms of government; large-scale reforms of constitutional, administrative, and legal systems had taken place; the middle classes rose to a position of equality with or even superiority to the nobility; and the urban industrial proletariat was born. It is not surprising that during this period all sorts of people took to the pen in Germany; philosophers, poets, and politicians became publicists overnight; articles, pamphlets, and books on political subjects appeared and multiplied in spite of censorship and publishing difficulties.

1. *Vertrauliche Briefe* (*Confidential Letters*)

In 1798 the Jägersche Buchhandlung in Frankfurt-on-Main published a small booklet of about 200 pages under the title: *Confidential letters upon the previous constitutional relation of Wadtland (Pays de Vaud) to the City of Berne. A full unmasking of the former oligarchy of the Bernese Estate. Translated from the French of a deceased Swiss with additional comments.* While the name of the author was mentioned in the preface, it took over a hundred years to discover that the anonymous translator and commentator was young Hegel.[2] It was his first political work, and his first published work at all.

---

[1] The first phrase comes from *The German Constitution* [26], the second from *Briefe von und an Hegel*, vol. i, p. 371. 'Great things have happened around us; it is a colossal spectacle to see an enormous genius destroying himself.' (To Niethammer. Nuremberg, 29 April 1814.)

[2] See Hugo Falkenheim, 'Eine unbekannte politische Druckschrift Hegels', *Preussische Jahrbücher*, vol. cxxxviii, 1909.

Hegel had spent the years 1793–6 in Berne as tutor to the son of a leading patrician of the city, Carl Friedrich von Steiger of Tschugg. His relations with the Steiger family were coldly official and he remained an outsider in Berne, but he was close enough to the centre of the political scene to observe and form his judgement on the politics of the city and the canton. Disgusted with manifest abuses he decided to expose the misrule of Berne to the German public. In the same year in which Hegel went to Berne, Jean-Jacques Cart, an exiled barrister from Vaud, published in Paris a series of letters on the political situation of his country, and the book became an instrument of Hegel's purpose.[1] He omitted two of the letters and some particularly personal and emotional passages, translated the rest, added some comments of his own— based on his own reading about the legal, constitutional, and financial position of Vaud—and finally wrote a preface to the whole work.

The book begins with a description of the political condition of Vaud under the rule of the House of Savoy, when it enjoyed extensive liberties and privileges. In 1536 the canton came under the suzerainty of the City of Berne, but all its rights were solemnly confirmed, and it is Cart's claim in his letters that they are still the only valid basis of the constitution. Nevertheless by a series of encroachments the rule of Berne has degenerated into an arbitrary and oppressive oligarchy, which Cart examines and castigates in detail. His main charges are that (1) the Estates of Vaud have been allowed to lapse and the powers to legislate and tax wholly arrogated by Berne; (2) there has arisen a glaring inequality of civil and political rights between the citizens of Berne and the inhabitants of Vaud; (3) the ordinary judicial procedure has been modified to the advantage of the government and their agents; and (4), since the outbreak of the French Revolution, a policy of persecuting the 'Patriots' or sympathizers with the new order in France has been set on foot.

In general, Cart's attitude may be summed up as the championship of constitutionalism and the rule of law against unfair privi-

[1] The title of the original was as follows: *Lettres à Bernard de Muralt, trésorier du Pays de Vaud, sur le droit de ce pays, et sur les événements actuels; par Jean-Jacques Cart. A Paris 1793.* F. Rosenzweig, who makes a detailed comparison between the original and the translation, concludes that 'Hegel is not merely a translator but, within narrow limits, an adapter of Cart's work'. (*Hegel und der Staat* (Munich and Berlin, 1920), vol. i, p. 51.)

leges, arbitrariness, and centralization. Like a typical lawyer he defends the case of Vaud by quoting documents and precedents, written statutes, and unwritten customs, and by drawing inferences and deductions from them. He specifically refuses to consider the law of nature or the rights of men, and bases himself solely on established, positive laws, sanctioned by time and tradition. He does, however, show strong sympathy for the revolution across the border, draws examples and parallels from other countries, notably Britain, and to clinch two arguments frequently appeals to the authority of *L'Esprit des Lois*.

Unfortunately the more interesting question of Hegel's political attitude at the time cannot be answered easily, since he has kept his own personality carefully out of the work. His comments tend to be factual, and merely underline Cart's points, although once or twice he criticizes him.[1] Their tone, however, shows him siding whole-heartedly with Vaud, and it is a fair presumption that without some agreement with the general attitude of Cart he would not have chosen to translate his work. Hegel's preface implies that his purpose was wider than the 'unmasking of oligarchy' in a particular country; it was to be a censure of oppression everywhere, and a warning that injustice brings its own punishment. For between the translating and the publishing of the work French troops had marched into the country to liberate Vaud. A number of useful lessons, writes Hegel in the preface, could be drawn from the comparison of the contents of these letters with the recent events in Vaud, from the contrast between, on the one hand, the peace apparently imposed in 1792 and the pride of the government in its victory, and, on the other, its real weakness in the country and sudden downfall. But the events speak for themselves loudly enough; all that remains is to learn from them in all their fullness. They cry loud over the earth,

Discite justitiam moniti,

and the deaf will be hard smitten by their fate.[2]

[1] Here is an example of Hegel's comments: 'It is a very great mistake to measure the goodness of a constitution by whether the taxes paid under it are high or low. In this case the constitution of England would be the worst of all because nowhere else does one pay so many taxes. And yet there is no nation in Europe which enjoys a greater apparent prosperity or more individual and national respect. This is because the Englishman is free, because he enjoys the rights inherent in freedom, in one word because he taxes himself.' *Vertrauliche Briefe über das vormalige staatsrechtliche Verhältnis des Waadtlandes (Pays de Vaud) zur Stadt Bern*, p. 71.
[2] Ibid., pp. 7, 8.

The refusal to make timely reforms, the insistence on unjust privileges, and the flouting of the consciences and sympathies of the people necessarily undermines a régime and prepares a catastrophe —this is the moral of *Confidential Letters*.

2. *Innere Verhältnisse Württembergs* (*Wurtemberg's Domestic Affairs*)

In the same year in which *Confidential Letters* appeared in print Hegel wrote his first original political work. On the way to Frankfurt to take up another tutorship, which his seminary friend the poet Hölderlin had procured for him, Hegel stopped for a few months at home in Stuttgart. He found the Province in considerable turmoil and exitement. For years Duke Frederick had been governing Wurtemberg despotically, his power limited only by· an oligarchic Permanent Committee of the Provincial Diet, which was important because it controlled the treasury of the Province. To break an impasse in foreign policy, caused by a pro-French attitude of the Committee, the Duke had summoned the Estates of the Province, which had not met as a Diet for a quarter of a century. The Estates proved themselves as intractable as the old Committee and were eventually dissolved,[1] not to meet again till 1815, but their brief life stirred up political thinking in Wurtemberg, and produced a flood of pamphlets with varying proposals. Hegel decided to make a contribution to the discussion with a pamphlet of his own, hastily written and bearing the title *On the recent domestic affairs of Wurtemberg, especially the inadequacy of the municipal constitution*.[2] From Frankfurt he sent it to some friends in Stuttgart, but they—for reasons not entirely clear— advised against publication.[3] The work remained in manuscript

---

[1] Hegel's contemporary comment is interesting: 'In Berg the Diet still exists. When it was abolished in Wurtemberg Napoleon said severely to the Wurtembergian minister, "I have made your master a sovereign, not a despot". German princes have not yet grasped the concept of a free monarchy or attempted its realization. Napoleon will have to organize it all.' Bamberg, 29 August 1807. (To Niethammer.) *Briefe von und an Hegel*, vol. i, p. 130.

[2] *Über die neuesten innern Verhältnisse Württembergs, besonders über die Gebrechen der Magistratsverfassung.* The fragment of this essay printed in Lasson [150–3] is translated below.

[3] Rosenkranz, op. cit., p. 91, publishes an extract from a letter written by an anonymous friend of Hegel, which ends with the words, 'Under these circumstances the publication of your essay would be for us more an evil than a benefit'. The circumstances in question are somewhat cryptically stated in the letter. Rosenzweig, op. cit., pp. 62, 63, suggests that they refer to the *Realpolitik* of France at the Congress of Rastatt; it seemed to discredit the principles of 1789

till the middle of the nineteenth century, and subsequently vanished except for a few fragments and a brief summary in Rudolph Haym's *Hegel und seine Zeit.* The pamphlet opens with a long and stirring introduction. Hegel asserts that the constitutional structure of Wurtemberg is widely thought to be untenable and in urgent need of fundamental reform. What Wurtembergers lack, however, is courage—courage to examine the faults and to set them right, even though some private interests and sectional privileges may have to be sacrificed for the sake of justice. Hegel condemns the absolutism of the Duke, the narrow-minded traditionalism of his officials (perhaps echoing here discussions with his own father), and the activities and procedure of the old Permanent Committee. He welcomes the convening of the Estates, on whom he pins his hopes of reform. But the method of election to the Diet seems to him no less faulty than the rest of the constitution. He is not opposed in principle to the system of indirect election through town councils, but he wants to see the latter popularly elected rather than co-opted. Yet he also perceives the difficulty and the danger of granting suffrage to 'an unenlightened multitude, used to blind obedience [towards the Duke] and dependent on the impressions of the moment',[1] and so the pamphlet ends with a confession of ignorance how a good electoral body can be secured in Wurtemberg. The very inconclusiveness of the work may have been one of the factors which eventually deterred Hegel from publishing it.[2]

3. *Verfassung Deutschlands* (*The German Constitution*)

At the beginning of 1801 Hegel moved to Jena, where he became a *Privatdozent* at the University. But before leaving Frankfurt he had begun working on a new political work, an analysis and critique of the constitution of the German Empire. He seems to have written the earliest version in 1799 and revised and rewritten it intermittently till the spring of 1802. Then the work was abandoned, when almost but not quite complete, and left in manuscript till after Hegel's death.[3] It is the most serious and substantial

for which Hegel and his friends stood, and which they sought to propagate in Wurtemberg.   [1] Haym, op. cit. (Leipzig, 1927), p. 66.
   [2] This is suggested by Haym: 'Such a work, so exciting in its premises and so unsatisfactory in the inconclusiveness of its results might well have remained unpublished.' Ibid., p. 67.
   [3] The composition of the various drafts and manuscripts of the work (which,

of his early political writings, and marks the rapid widening of his political horizon. After the politics of a Swiss canton and a German Province, he tackles the complex problem of the Holy Roman Empire, to some extent considering it in a still wider context of a constitutional evolution common to the whole of Western Europe.

Several factors combined to focus his attention on the subject. In Frankfurt, where emperors had been crowned, he was reminded of the past glory and the empty ceremonial of the contemporary Empire. An imperial congress held at Rastatt in 1799 suggested that there was still a flicker of life in the body politic, but the loss of the left bank of the Rhine to France and the separate peace treaty which the North, under Prussian leadership, concluded with the French, proved more convincingly that it had begun to decompose. The study of German political and constitutional history seemed to Hegel to confirm this conclusion by showing the main stages and turning-points in the weakening of the imperial power and the disintegration of its sovereignty.

The fact which strikes Hegel most forcibly, and which forms the fundamental theme of the work, is the sharp cleavage between theory and practice, law and fact, the ideal and the actual in the German constitution. Imperial institutions supposedly exist, jurists write volumes about imperial public law, people keep talking as if the Empire really meant something. But, Hegel maintains, 'Germany is no longer a state'; it is not even (as Voltaire maintained) a 'constitutional anarchy'; it is a multitude of independent political units, and their mutual relations have all the marks of a state of nature rather than a civil state. The greatest political vice of the Germans is refusing to admit the facts, valuing forms without substance, and pretending to themselves and others that they are German patriots. One of Hegel's purposes in writing *The German Constitution* was to expose that hypocrisy and to make his countrymen face reality.

He begins by discussing the concept, the essential nature, of the state in a long theoretical chapter.

incidentally, was not given any title by Hegel himself) has been the subject of considerable controversy among Hegel's biographers. Rosenkranz suggested the period 1806–8, but this was disproved by subsequent writers. Rosenzweig, who discusses the matter thoroughly, decides on 1799–1802. The dating of other writers (Dilthey, Nohl, Haering) falls substantially within those years, but is generally somewhat shorter. See Rosenzweig, op. cit., vol. i, pp. 231–3.

A multitude of human beings can only call itself a state if it be united for the common defence of the entirety of its property. What is self-explanatory in this proposition must none the less be stated, namely that this union has not merely the intention of defending itself; the point is that it defends itself by actual arms, be its power and its success what they may. [17]

Incidentally he stresses that effective organization for defence, or 'public authority', does not imply absolute or even highly centralized government. The autonomy of various bodies—cities, corporations, provinces—within the state is not only possible, but highly desirable; a public authority is immensely strong when 'it can be supported by the free and unregimented spirit of its people'. [31]

Two powers indispensable to defence are armed forces and finances, yet, as Hegel shows in detail, the Empire has none in effect; as a result its territory has been steadily contracting through foreign conquests and internal aggrandizement. The Empire has no real legislative power; the Imperial Diet cannot alter by one jot any of the meticulously defined rights and duties of the various political units or 'estates', which are protected by the constitution and supported by a general but false concept of 'justice'. The judicial process is so organized that it can be paralysed at every stage by the guilty party, quite apart from the fact that the courts are wholly incapable of coping with the enormous number of disputes between the multiplicity of authorities. In any case, all really important disputes are settled by force.

To explain the causes of this state of affairs Hegel examines the normal pattern of political evolution in Western Europe from a primitive Germanic warrior community through feudalism to constitutional monarchy with representative institutions. Two factors, according to him, had prevented Germany from following the same path: the rise of a powerful and individualistic burgher estate, which sought to protect itself against medieval lawlessness by its own independent efforts rather than by supporting the central public authority, and the religious split caused by the Reformation. A statesman of genius, such as Machiavelli postulated for Italy in his *Prince* and such as Richelieu actually was in France, might have saved German statehood by a policy of cunning and force, but Germany was not fortunate enough to produce one.

At the end of the work Hegel raises the question if and how the

Holy Roman Empire can become a real state once again. The ultimate end is the creation of an effective common public authority, with the Emperor at the head of the government and the army, and a Diet with financial and legislative powers to represent the provinces by their princes and the people by deputies. This is the 'principle' of the modern world, the principle of monarchy, as applied to Germany, and the Germans must learn this. They must realize that true civil and political freedom lies in such organization and not in the independence of the 'estates'. Even if the truth were universally known and accepted, however, something else would still be necessary, namely force, for men do not surrender power and privilege voluntarily. Austria and Prussia are the two German countries strong enough to undertake unification by conquest, and though there are passages in the work that read like a prophecy of Bismarck and the policy of *Blut und Eisen*, Hegel actually favours Austria, on the ground that her constitution is more liberal and provides a better guarantee that the reconstructed Empire will be a free state. But in his concluding remarks he reiterates that the salvation of Germany really depends on something not far short of a political miracle: a statesman of genius, a Machiavellian 'Theseus'.

This hopeless and impractical conclusion, so reminiscent of the uncertain conclusion of his previous work, seems to suggest a fundamental defect in Hegel's talent for *Publizistik*: his mastery of facts and the acuteness of his theoretical analysis are not matched by practical wisdom and a realistic political sense. Hegel seems to do brilliantly up to the moment when a bold, constructive proposal seems to be forthcoming, but none actually follows.[1] The source of Hegel's uncertainty, however, at least in this work, should probably be sought elsewhere. As a fervent German patriot, he hopes against hope that his country's low fortunes will after all be restored; as a detached academic observer he realizes that the process of disintegration has probably gone too far to be reversed. He is thus torn between faith and fatalism; he chides his compatriots for dishonesty, but himself yields to wishful thinking. Also on another ground one should not be too severe upon Hegel. How could a young man of thirty, without a shred of power or influence, without any first-hand political experience, offer a workable solution of a problem of such immense magnitude as

[1] This was in particular Haym's criticism. Cf. op. cit., pp. 75, 76.

the reunification of Germany? To have seen the problem, to have attempted to clarify muddled thinking on the matter, was surely already an achievement in itself.

Hegel himself is only too conscious of his own impotence, as the following passages show.

Those who so act in the midst of these great affairs that they could themselves direct them are very few; but the others have to wait on events with understanding and insight into their necessity.

The thoughts contained in this essay can have no other aim or effect, when published, save that of promoting the understanding of what is, and therefore a calmer outlook and a moderately tolerant attitude alike in words and in actual contact [with affairs]. [5]

He makes it clear that he is not composing a manual for statesmen, which would be a profitless and presumptuous task. Public men do not need private men to tell them what they ought to do; they have a better insight into history and can draw their own lessons. But the case is different with the masses of the people or rather their more educated section, and they need someone to explain the meaning of events, and help them to acquire a sort of vicarious 'understanding and insight'. And, as Hegel shows elsewhere in the work, a publicist can also achieve at least one practical result: he can prepare others for what is to follow and perhaps pave the statesman's way a bit.

Nevertheless this Spinozistic preface seems not wholly consistent with the Machiavellian conclusion of the work. The discrepancy can partly be removed by recalling the origin of *The German Constitution*. Hegel conceived it in Frankfurt, and it was also there that he discovered his vocation for speculative philosophy and made the first sketch of his system, in which the concept of *Schicksal*— an inevitable fate or destiny—played a dominant role. Some parts of *The German Constitution* reflect this philosophical interest and clearly foreshadow his mature philosophy of the state and of history. This essay thus stands at the parting of Hegel's two approaches to politics; the thorny path of a publicist, followed only occasionally from then on, and the approach of a philosopher, which proved to be a royal highway to success and fame.

The three writings dealt with so far followed each other rapidly and were produced in a comparatively short time—between 1796 and 1802. It seems more than likely that at that stage Hegel had serious ambitions as a political publicist. But fate was unkind to him; the problems he tackled were unusually difficult; his words were outstripped by events; history found in Napoleon an obvious genius to guide her. Probably with regret, Hegel had to confine himself to philosophy and to give up for the time being all direct influence on public opinion.[1]

4. *Württembergische Landstände* (*The Wurtemberg Estates*)

Apart from the short and disappointing experience with *Die Bamberger Zeitung*, the opportunity did not occur again for fifteen years. In 1817 the *Heidelbergische Jahrbücher* published a long essay by him under the title: *Proceedings of the Assembly of Estates of the Kingdom of Wurtemberg in the Years 1815 and 1816*.[2] It was Hegel's commentary on the first thirty-three sections of the official report of the proceedings in the Diet of Wurtemberg, centring mainly on a constitutional conflict between the King, the former Duke Frederick, and the newly convened Estates. The King, who by a clever *Realpolitik* and with Napoleon's support, had succeeded in doubling the size of his dominions and becoming a sovereign monarch, attempted in 1815 to legitimize his position by summoning an Assembly of Estates of the Kingdom and presenting them with a constitutional Charter. The Estates, however, refused to accept it and demanded the restoration of the old, i.e. pre-revolutionary, constitution. It was their contention that the latter was still in force, since it could not be unilaterally abrogated by the monarch, and they proceeded with the utmost caution in order to avoid a *de facto* recognition of the King's right. The King offered various concessions, but would not abandon his Charter. Eventually the Estates set up a committee, which prepared the project of 'a new constitutional contract', which was based on the old constitution. Here the matter rested, and new elections to the Diet, the death of King Frederick, and the accession of his son William failed to break the impasse. Not until two years after the publication of *The Wurtemberg Estates* was a compromise achieved and a new constitution brought into force.

[1] In an unfinished early draft of the introduction to *The German Constitution*, published as an appendix to the work by Lasson, Hegel refers to the dilemma of 'the man whom the time has banished to an inner world'. His alternatives are either ' a lasting death' if he does nothing or 'a striving to cancel the negative in the existing world' in order to make it worth living in, but this transcends the power of an individual. [139]

[2] *Verhandlungen in der Versammlung der Landstände des Königreichs Württemberg im Jahre 1815 und 1816. XXXIII Abteilungen. 1815–16.* [155–323]

It has been suggested, but not actually proved, that the real motive behind Hegel's commentary was a desire to obtain an official position in his native land by winning the favour of the government. He is supposed to have been in touch with the Prime Minister, Freiherr von Wangenheim, about the chancellorship of Tübingen University, and certainly the post, which carried with it a seat in the Diet, would have satisfied both the academic and the political ambitions of Hegel. The hypothesis would also help to explain the extremely partisan tone of the work, which consistently takes the side of the King and praises him while the Estates are scathingly censured. One can, however, interpret the work simply as a natural expression of an interest in his country, and in a subject which had once before led him to compose a political pamphlet, and its partisan character may thus be a result of his personal temperament and ideological engagement.[1]

In the preface to *The Wurtemberg Estates* Hegel justifies his new work on the ground that 'the task begun two and a half years ago, of completing, by the introduction of a representative constitution, a German monarchy . . . has aroused from its start . . . a universal interest in the German public . . .'. [157]

The fact that the transactions can be studied only from the official, public side, and that nothing can be learned about the subjective motives and behind-the-scene manœuvres, Hegel actually welcomes as being in accordance with the true nature and dignity of history. Another reason for examining the report of the proceedings is that the subject is fresh and belongs to contemporary history.

The concepts concerning the matter at issue which we must bring with us to this event we may not cull from any more remote age, especially not from the civilized age of Greece and Rome: they are peculiar to our own day. Thus these ideas on a political constitution, and especially on the inclusion of a part whereby the people is conceded an influence on it and a public life, are not seen here as the thoughts of

---

[1] Haym, op. cit., p. 350, was the first to put forward the view that Hegel had an ulterior motive for writing the commentary, and based his account of negotiations between Hegel and Wangenheim on an oral report of a contemporary witness. M. Lenz, in *Geschichte der königlichen Friedrich-Wilhelms-Universität zu Berlin* (Halle, 1910–18), vol. ii, pt. i, p. 203, repeats that view without producing any evidence. Rosenzweig discusses the evidence for and against and decides that the story is without substance. He also mentions that Haym withdrew the accusation of servility against Hegel in his autobiography at the end of his life. See op. cit., pp. 51, 251.

one essayist compared, e.g., with the thoughts of another; on the contrary what we see is a German government and a German people engaged in an intellectual (*geistige*) labour on these matters, and thoughts employed in the rebirth of an existent reality. [158]

The fact that the concepts used in the debates of the Wurtemberg Diet are so new and that they have practical consequences gives Hegel the opportunity and the excuse for a discussion of a good many of them. 'State', 'constitution', 'law', 'monarchy', 'Assembly of Estates', 'civil service', 'electoral system', 'people', and others are critically analysed in the course of the commentary. This does not mean that the work has a primarily theoretical character. On the contrary, what strikes one about it after *The German Constitution* is precisely its non-theoretical, unsystematic, almost untidy character.

Hegel more or less follows the order of the proceedings, summarizing important parts of the report and commenting on them at various lengths. He begins with a summary of the Royal Charter, then analyses the attitude of the Estates to it, and finally traces the course of the proceedings of the Diet and its inconclusive negotiations with the King, which terminated with the latter's death. At many points, however, he interrupts the commentary and indulges in long digressions. These are sometimes of a philosophical, but more often of an historical kind. The history of Wurtemberg, of other German provinces, of the Empire, and occasionally of France and Britain is adduced to support his arguments or to throw light on the tendencies of the present. Hegel's passion for history and the thoroughness with which he approaches facts reaches its peak in the analysis of what he calls the *Schreiberei-Institut*, a monopolistic system of official clerkship, peculiar to Wurtemberg. More than one-tenth of *The Wurtemberg Estates* is devoted to this subject and forms what is really a brilliant and learned socio-historical monograph.[1]

So far as Hegel's own attitude to his main subject-matter is concerned, he welcomes 'the end it deserved' of the 'nonsensical arrangement called the *German Empire* . . . an ignominious end suited to it even in externals', and he approves the establishment of a sovereign Kingdom of Wurtemberg, 'one of the actual *German realms* which are taking the place of the nonentity which had

---

[1] Most of it is translated.

borne only the empty name of an "Empire" ' [159]. Just as strongly he approves the summoning of the Estates and the introduction of representative institutions.

There surely cannot be a greater secular spectacle on earth than that of a monarch's adding to the state's power which *ab initio* is entirely in his hands another foundation, indeed *the* foundation, by bringing his people into it as an essentially effective ingredient. [163]

The constitutional Charter itself appears to Hegel to have some defects but on the whole to be immensely more liberal and rational than the old constitution of Wurtemberg or the actual constitutions of many other countries. This is the background against which one ought to consider his attack on the summoned Wurtemberg Estates on the score of their political hostility to the Royal Charter.

One might have expected the further course of history to show how this new creation, the Estates, operated within the sphere granted to it and how there worked in it this important vital element grafted on to the organism of the state. But it is not the history of such an assimilating and vitally active operation that unfolds before our eyes. On the contrary, the members summoned to the Assembly decline to allow themselves to be incorporated into the state as one of its limbs; they declare themselves indeed to be Estates, but Estates of another world, of a time long past, and demand that the present be changed into the past and reality into unreality. [186]

Though Hegel finds plenty of fault with the behaviour of the Estates, his criticism is centred on one fundamental point: their irrational, traditionalist, and formalistic attitude to the constitutional Charter and to laws and institutions in general. Thus, once again, the theoretical bias of Hegel's political writings becomes evident. He is not primarily concerned with the constitutional conflict itself or the best ways of ending it; he aims at correcting what he regards as an outdated, false, and pernicious attitude to politics.

Nevertheless it was exactly this commentary which became the one great and unqualified success of Hegel's publicistic activity. Though it offended many people and alienated some friends, *The Wurtemberg Estates* was certainly widely read and commented on in Wurtemberg because a royalist newspaper in Stuttgart reprinted it in instalments. It is even thought that the work contributed to the eventual settlement of the conflict by inducing a more compromising attitude in a section of the Assembly of Estates and helping a pro-government party to crystallize.[1]

5. Englische Reformbill (*The English Reform Bill*)

Almost fifteen years were to pass before Hegel again turned political writer, and on this occasion his luck deserted him once more. In 1831 he wrote a long article or essay *On the English Reform Bill* for the official *Preussische Staatszeitung*. The work began to appear in instalments, but about two-thirds of the way through the King of Prussia intervened and forbade the continuation. The explanation of the article's fate is to be found in a letter of Hegel's widow (he himself died of cholera shortly after the last part of the article had been suppressed) to Niethammer.

His Majesty had nothing against it as such, only the concern that a ministerial newspaper contained a censure of English affairs. By command the continuation was printed separately and distributed secretly, and Hegel, who did not want to be mentioned at all, nevertheless received the greatest eulogies for it *privatim*.[2]

Hegel had always been interested in England, and considered himself something of an authority on English politics. In *Confidential Letters*, for instance, he questioned some of Cart's remarks in the light of recent history[3] and in *The Wurtemberg Estates* he corrected some misconceptions about English parties. In the Reform Bill controversy, coming as it did during a wave of revolutions which had disturbed Hegel, he perceived an event of the first importance, a shock to the English devotion to positive law,

[1] The name of the newspaper, *Württembergischer Volksfreund*, and the account of the influence of Hegel's commentary is to be found in Rosenkranz, op. cit., pp. 57–60.

[2] *Briefe von und an Hegel*, vol. ii, p. 378.

[3] Cf., e.g., the following note by Hegel:

'The author has not lived to see how [in England] in recent years security of property has been endangered in many respects and domestic rights diminished by the powers granted to the collectors of still more taxes; how personal freedom has been restricted by the suspension of the fundamental law, and the rights of citizens by positive statutes. It has become obvious that the minister [i.e. Pitt], having provided himself with a majority in Parliament, is in a position to defy public opinion, while the nation is so incompletely represented that it cannot assert its voice in Parliament. Its security depends more on the threat of its unconstitutional power, the prudence of ministers or the discretion of the higher estates. The respect for the English nation, even among its strongest admirers, has sunk as a result of those facts and their recognition.' *Vertrauliche Briefe*, pp. 81, 82.

'which in England is quite new and unheard of' [290]. The Bill, in other words, seemed to have consequences far transcending its immediate object, and this was his justification for dealing with it.

There are numbers, localities, private interests, which are to be ordered differently; nevertheless, it is on the nobility, the very heart and vital principle of the constitution and condition of Great Britain, that this alteration presses in fact. This is the aspect of the present Bill which deserves special notice. And the aim of this essay is to put together here these higher aspects of the matter which have been discussed in the parliamentary debates up till now. [283]

As a matter of fact the essay goes far beyond this purpose. Having outlined the case for a reform of the English suffrage, Hegel embarks on a survey of some of the major political and social evils plaguing the country. He then considers the question how far the provisions of the Bill are likely to facilitate further reforms and decides that, as they do not sufficiently modify the fundamental balance of political power, their immediate effect will be negligible. The situation might, however, become dangerous if the Bill opened the way into the House of Commons to large numbers of 'new men'—demagogues and radical politicians—and led to a struggle for power between them and the traditional ruling class. A certain safeguard against this he sees in the good sense of the English people, its distrust of abstract principles, and its as yet slight awareness of the need for reforms.

Hegel's analysis, faulty at times and wrong in some of its predictions, is yet remarkably incisive and penetrating. Once again an impressive amount of empirical material is blended with more theoretical passages, although the latter are less frequent than in some of the earlier writings. Hegel's knowledge of English conditions is so detailed that it must have been based on a very assiduous reading of current English newspaper articles and parliamentary reports. What mars the work is its strongly anti-English flavour and a tone of patronizing superiority. Just as in *The Wurtemberg Estates* Hegel was far from being fair to both sides in the constitutional controversy, so now he disparages the English and exalts the continental, especially German, achievements with an equal lack of moderation. His particular scapegoat seems to have been, oddly enough, the nationalism of the English.

National pride in any case keeps the English back from studying and understanding the progress made by other nations in the development of their legal institutions. The pomp and display of the formal freedom to discuss public business in parliament and in other assemblies of all classes and groups . . . prevents the English from or at least does not encourage quiet reflection on and penetration into the essence of legislation and government. Few European nations are dominated by such dexterity of reasoning in terms of their prejudices and by such shallowness of principle. [302–3]

The extremely critical tone of *The English Reform Bill* lends plausibility to the hypothesis that one of the objects of the article was to counteract a current wave of Anglomania in Prussia, but even so the work remains something of an enigma.[1]

After this brief survey of the contents of Hegel's minor political works we may draw a few conclusions about their general character and about Hegel as a political writer. We must of course remember that they belong to different periods in Hegel's life and are often widely separated from each other.

In the youthful works the style is amazingly clear and lively. The parallel draft versions of *The German Constitution* which Lasson publishes show Hegel's great concern for perfection of expression, and the later drafts are consequently superior to the earlier. This care seems to have decreased somewhat in his middle age and after, but though the style becomes more involved, there is nothing even remotely resembling the schematism, abstractness, and technicality of the *Philosophy of Right*. It is obvious that, when he chose, Hegel was capable of writing fresh, vigorous, and readable prose. The tone is on the whole evenly pitched, though from time to time, and particularly in the early writings, it rises to a flourish of rhetoric. Only seldom does one find a really striking epigram, aphorism, or dictum. Wit is completely absent. Hegel's main literary weapon is irony, which often becomes sarcastic and occasionally descends to ridicule and invective.

There is little sustained argumentation or logical demonstration in the writings. Most of the time Hegel describes or criticizes attitudes and institutions. When he does resort to argument this takes one of two forms: 'pragmatic' or 'conceptual'. In the former

[1] Some of the expressions in the article were considered so abusive that they were left out or toned down by the editors of the *Preussische Staatszeitung*. Rosenkranz suggests that the tone was due to incipient cholera. 'One senses in the essay the bad temper of illness, however thorough the work is and however interesting the turn of phrase was for the purpose of opposing the blind admiration of England and the blind contempt for Germany in respect of politics.' Op. cit., p. 419.

case he adduces a number of historical instances and draws a general lesson valid for a particular instance or he appeals to an accepted rule applicable to the instance. Even when Hegel invokes the 'nature', 'essence', or 'concept' of a thing to clinch the argument, these are seldom abstract, *a priori* ideas, dogmatically introduced. They tend to be justified historically, by reference to the evolution of the thing in question; alternatively he appeals to 'universal conviction' of their validity, their 'general acceptance', and their being 'principles of sound common sense' or 'parts of public opinion'. This seems to suggest that Hegel held public opinion in unexpectedly high esteem, but this is not quite the case. Although in *The German Constitution* and in *The Wurtemberg Estates* he appeals to public opinion on such important issues as the necessity of a representative assembly or the nature of monarchy, he does so because opinion is on his side. At other times he does not hesitate to brand public opinion as mistaken and to denounce what he regards as popular misconceptions; in *The English Reform Bill* he also points out that it is fickle and mischievous on occasions.

But even if public opinion in Great Britain were almost always for reform . . . we would still have to be allowed to examine the substance of what this opinion desires, all the more so because in recent times we have not infrequently experienced that its demands have proved to be impracticable, or, if practicable, pernicious, and that public opinion has now turned just as vigorously against what immediately before it had vigorously demanded and appeared to welcome. [284]

Hegel was too much of a thinker to accept public opinion unquestioningly at any time. He saw that on many issues it needed enlightening, especially in Germany where even the middle class had no political experience, not to mention the masses of the people. Moreover time was moving fast—old attitudes and institutions, and the ideas bound up with them, were losing validity. Here was the publicist's task and opportunity. But while he had to instruct and correct, he could be effective only if he communicated with his public. If he used concepts they could not understand or strayed too far from their familiar ideas, he would cease to be read and to have any influence. However magisterial he might occasionally become, Hegel never lost sight of that essential truth.

The place of the political writings in Hegel's thought as a whole has not been appreciated properly. The fame—and infamy—he has won as a political philosopher has blinded commentators to the importance or even existence of the more modest achievement. Recently the minor political works have received rather more attention. H. Marcuse has rightly stressed[1] that

. . . the connecting of his philosophy with the historical developments of his time makes Hegel's political writings a part of his systematic works, and the two must be treated together, so that his basic concepts are given philosophical as well as historical and political explanation.

He also writes that '. . . the elaboration of Hegel's philosophic system is accompanied by a series of political fragments that attempt to apply his new philosophical ideas to concrete historical situations'. As it stands the assertion is somewhat misleading. It suggests that Hegel's political writings were more or less an incidental by-product of his philosophical activity, so to speak working sketches preparatory to the great canvases of the *Philosophy of Right* or the *Philosophy of History*. This view does not do justice to the passion with which Hegel threw himself into political pamphleteering and journalism and the undoubted talent which he displayed there. The suggestion of an earlier writer that he originally intended to combine the vocations of philosopher and publicist seems much more apposite.[2] The most hostile of his German commentators has to acknowledge that 'Hegel was an excellent publicist before he had written the *Phenomenology*: . . . he remained an able publicist still after he had written it'. While another biographer of Hegel calls *The Wurtemberg Estates*, written *after* the *Phenomenology*, 'one of the best pamphlets that came from a German pen'.[3] But in the history of German political literature, as probably of any other, quantity must count no less than quality, and the one and a half original political writings published by Hegel during his lifetime entitle him to but a modest place in its pages.

---

[1] *Reason and Revolution: Hegel and the Rise of Social Theory* (Oxford, 1954), p. 29. Another author who takes account of the minor works is C. J. Friedrich in G. W. F. Hegal, *Lectures on the Philosophy of History*, trans. by J. Sibree (New York, 1956).

[2] 'The work on Berne is the first proof of his endeavour to pursue the careers of philosopher and publicist side by side. If we add to the work on Berne the two political projects which he partly executed and partly prepared in Frankfurt —on the recent domestic affairs in Wurtemberg, especially on the inadequacy of the municipal constitution, and on the constitution of Germany—we have a planned publicistic programme before us.' Falkenheim, op. cit., pp. 204, 205.

[3] The first quotation is from Haym, op. cit., p. 269; the second from Lenz, op. cit., p. 203.

II

REASON AND TRADITION

> Most observers of the Revolution, especially the clever
> and the refined, have declared it to be a fatal and con-
> tagious disease. They have gone only as far as the
> symptoms, and have analysed and expounded them
> in the most diverse ways. Some have regarded it as a
> merely local ailment. Those of most genius among the
> opponents, on the other hand, have pressed for castra-
> tion. They have perceived correctly that the alleged
> disease is nothing but the crisis of incipient puberty.
>
> NOVALIS, *Blütenstaub*.

IN one of his rare but striking aphorisms Hegel defines political
genius as 'identifying oneself with a principle' [108]. Admittedly
he had in mind the genius of a statesman rather than that of
a thinker, but a desire to champion a principle or to serve a cause
is not restricted to men of action.[1] It is frequently also the motive
that impels a man of letters to become a political pamphleteer or
commentator. Hence we may ask whether in Hegel's case we can
discern a central, fundamental issue which underlies and unifies
his various political writings, and what the principle with which
he identifies himself is.

It seems that one can discover such a principle or issue. It is
something which pervades Hegel's writings and is implicit in a
number of passages but which he himself nowhere explicitly states
or fully elaborates. The nearest he comes to doing so is perhaps
in the following passages of *The Wurtemberg Estates*:

What we see in the behaviour of the Estates summoned in Wurtemberg
is precisely the opposite of what started twenty-five years ago in a neighbouring realm and what at the time re-echoed in all heads, namely that

---

[1] This usage of 'principle' was common in the nineteenth century. Cf. the
following passage from Cobden's letter to Peel, 23 June 1846: 'It is necessary
for the concentration of a people's mind that an individual should become the
incarnation of a principle. It is from this necessity that I have become identified
. . . as the exponent of Free Trade. You, and no other, are its embodiment among
statesmen. . . . You embody in your person the idea of the age.' J. Morley, *The
Life of Richard Cobden*, 1883 ed., pp. 252–3 and 254.

in a political constitution nothing should be recognized as valid unless
its recognition accorded with the right of reason. . . . The Wurtemberg
Estates wanted to resume the standpoint of the old Estates. They have
not concerned themselves with the content of the King's constitutional
charter; they have not asked or sought to prove what rational law is or
what accords with it. Instead they have simply stuck to the formalism
of demanding an old positive law on the ground that it was positive and
in accordance with the contract. . . .

One might say of the Wurtemberg Estates what has been said of the
returned French *émigrés*: They have forgotten nothing and learnt
nothing. They seem to have slept through the last twenty-five years,
possibly the richest that world history has had, and for us the most
instructive, because it is to them that our world and our ideas belong.
There could hardly have been a more frightful pestle for pulverizing
false concepts of law and prejudices about political constitutions than
the tribunal of these twenty-five years, but these Estates have emerged
from it unscathed and unaltered.

'Old rights' and 'old constitution' are such fine grand words that it
sounds impious [to contemplate] robbing the people of its rights. But
age has nothing to do with what 'old rights' and 'constitution' mean or
with whether they are good or bad ([197–9] cf. also [160–1]).

We find in these passages two different and opposed attitudes.
The one regards constitutional and other law as beyond criticism
because it is based on a good 'positive' title—in this case antiquity
or a contract of government once made by the prince and the
provincial estates. Having positive legal validity it refuses to consider whether in some other sense law or the constitution may not
be invalid. The opposite attitude ignores antiquity and all other
'positive' grounds. According to it the determining factor is the
rationality of the content of the law, its agreement with 'the law of
reason'.

But Hegel does not merely describe and contrast the two attitudes; he argues that the former rests on a 'fundamental mistake'
and is false, absurd, and pernicious. First of all Wurtemberg has
become a sovereign state; hence the circumstances of the country
have changed so much that most of the old concepts, attitudes, and
institutions no longer apply. Secondly, the old constitution was
a confused tangle of customary laws and privileges unworthy of
a civilized country. Thirdly, an event of extraordinary importance
has changed the whole basis of politics in Wurtemberg and elsewhere in Europe, and inaugurated a new era of human relations,

a new system of institutions, attitudes, and concepts, a new social and political order or 'world'. This event is the French Revolution and the period up to 1815 which Hegel regards as its continuation. These 'richest' and 'most instructive' years have taught mankind the lesson that 'nothing in a state constitution shall be deemed valid that has not been sanctioned by the law of reason'. The Wurtemberg Estates have failed to learn the lesson; they have forgotten the French Revolution; they have been thinking and acting as if nothing had happened, as if they still lived in the good old pre-revolutionary days; they have taken a stand on tradition when tradition has ceased to be universally regarded as a sufficient basis of law and in any case has been rendered questionable by the new political circumstances of Wurtemberg.

It is this new attitude to politics, born during the French Revolution, that is the cause which Hegel's political writings ultimately propagate. All his political writings show him imbued with it, and in revolt against his rival, the reactionary traditionalist or 'positivist' attitude. We can call it the Principle of Rational Law as opposed to the Principle of Positive Law which Hegel is anxious to condemn. The belief in rational law as the only legitimate and tenable criterion of laws, institutions, and constitutions is the first basic article of Hegel's political faith.

There is no doubt as to the origin of the belief in rational law, which may loosely be called 'political rationalism'; all the biographers of Hegel agree on this point, and a reading of his own works amply confirms their views. Stated most briefly their views amount to this: certainly the French Revolution acted as a spark, but it struck flame only because Hegel's mind was already thoroughly imbued with the spirit of the Enlightenment. Hegel became familiar with the principal writers of the Enlightenment already at school in Stuttgart, and he was engrossed in the reading of Kant at the seminary in Tübingen when the French Revolution broke out.[1]

[1] Its impact on Hegel and his fellow students (who included the poet Hölderlin and the philosopher Schelling) has been thus summed up by Dilthey: 'It was just during those years 1788 to 1793, which Hegel spent at Tübingen, that there occurred the two world-historical events which at one and the same time brought the age of Enlightenment to a close and opened the gates of a new era: Kant completed the recasting of German thought, and the Revolution in France destroyed the old state and undertook the establishment of a new order of society. The young men embraced with enthusiasm both these mighty manifestations of the great century that was passing. . . . Hegel himself was considered

That the young Hegel felt great enthusiasm for the French Revolution and believed that 1789 marked the beginning of a new epoch in world history should not surprise us; many of his contemporaries in Germany and abroad fully shared this belief at the time.[1] What is, however, remarkable is that, unlike most of them, he retained it throughout the intervening period of the Terror, the Consulate, and the Empire. In the passage quoted at the beginning of this chapter we saw Hegel reiterating his early credo in 1817, at the mature age of 47, after he had published his greatest philosophical work, the *Science of Logic*, and been appointed to a chair at Heidelberg.

The question arises, however, whether Hegel's ardent championing of political rationality did not become modified or even reversed when, shortly after writing *The Wurtemberg Estates*, he moved to Prussia. In *The English Reform Bill* we can find an answer to the question. The fact that Hegel was sufficiently interested in the Reform Bill controversy to write an article about it is in itself significant. At the beginning of the nineteenth century Britain was almost the only major country unaffected by the French Revolution. Her attachment to traditional institutions and her belief in their superiority had been, if anything, intensified. By 1830, however, the position had altered fundamentally; the introduction of a Reform Bill by the Whig ministry reflected widespread discontent with the *status quo* and the desire for change. Hegel saw in England the same influence at work which had permeated Wurtemberg fifteen, and France forty-five, years earlier. And so we find Hegel using this opportunity to reaffirm his old belief in the cause of rational law and to attack the attitude opposed to it.

On the other hand another legal principle especially characteristic of England is attacked by the Bill. This is the character of positivity which preponderates in the institutions of English law, public and private alike. It is true that every right and its corresponding law is in *form*

one of the most zealous spokesmen for freedom and equality by his comrades of those days. Sovereign, advancing Reason, which constituted the soul of the Kantian philosophy, seemed to him to be realizing its rule at last in the work of the Revolution.' Wilhelm Dilthey, *Die Jugendgeschichte Hegels* (Berlin, 1905), pp. 13, 14. Cf. also K. Rosenkranz, op. cit., pp. 32, 33; R. Haym, op. cit., pp. 32, 33; F. Rosenzweig, op. cit., vol. i, pp. 18, 19. A recent study specifically concerned with the impact of the Revolution on Hegel is J. Richter, *Hegel und die französische Revolution* (1957).

[1] This is fully shown in G. P. Gooch, *Germany and the French Revolution* (London, 1920), *passim*. (Pp. 295–302 deal with Hegel.)

something positive, ordained, and instituted by the supreme power in
the state, something to which obedience must be given just because it
is a statute. But at no time more than the present has the general
intelligence been led to distinguish between whether rights are purely
positive in their material content or whether they are also inherently
right and rational. In no constitution is judgement so strongly induced
to attend to this distinction as in the English, now that the continental
nations have allowed themselves to be imposed on for so long by
declamations about English freedom and by England's pride in her
system of law. It is well known that the latter rests entirely on particular
rights, freedoms, privileges conferred, sold, presented by or extorted
from kings and Parliament on special occasions. [288-9]

Hegel distinguishes two meanings of the word 'positive'—formal
and material—but shifts his argument from one to the other without warning. He implies that continental countries have long
abandoned the rigid 'positivist' attitude and have, on the one hand,
transformed their private and public law into something rather
more rational than a heap of rules, dating from different periods
and without internal coherence, and on the other hand they have
purged the law of absurd, iniquitous, and outdated provisions.
The British, however, have hitherto adhered rigidly to the 'positive' principle in theory and practice, with the result that their law
is chaotic and full of injustices. Too many Englishmen, Hegel
believes, still accept the uncivilized and reactionary belief that
a statute or charter is sacrosanct because it was once granted—
perhaps for quite accidental reasons—and has since been confirmed by usage and tradition. It is clear from the passage just
quoted that even at the end of his life Hegel strongly believed that
the rationality of the content of a law was a better ground, a more
satisfactory basis, than the 'positive' title of prescription or an
ancient fundamental law. He does not appear to have in the least
modified his original standpoint, which in 1817 he summed up as
the supreme lesson of the French Revolution—'nothing in a state
constitution shall be deemed valid that is not sanctioned by the
law of reason'. Nor has any of his early enthusiasm for political
rationalism waned significantly in the intervening years, for he
writes of the Bill elsewhere in *The English Reform Bill*:

What rouses the greatest interest is the fear in some quarters, the
hope in others, that the reform of the franchise will bring in its train
other reforms of substance. The English principle of positivity on which,

as I have said, the whole of English law rests, does through the Bill actually suffer a shock which in England is entirely new and unheard of, and one instinctively suspects that more far-reaching changes will issue from this subversion of the formal basis of the existing order. [290]

The whole article on the Reform Bill is in fact a renewed attack on Hegel's *bête noire*, the 'positive principle', even though this is partly disguised as an attack on the national pride of the British and on their uncritical admirers in Germany.

It has been argued in this chapter, first, that Hegel's career as a political publicist should be conceived as a desire to serve the cause of Political Rationality, and secondly, that his belief in Political Rationality dates back to the impact of the French Revolution on a youthful mind imbued with the ideas of the Enlightenment and extends in time until his death. Hence we would expect the Principle of Rational Law to have dominated the earliest group of Hegel's writings and to have been asserted there with even greater vigour. With some qualifications this is in fact the case.

The first concerns the pamphlet by Cart. Although *Confidential Letters* is not Hegel's own work, there is a marked inconsistency between its spirit and that of Hegel's later writings, and the matter is worth examining. Admittedly Cart bases his case for the removal of abuses and restoration of justice in Vaud on the ancient charters and privileges of the land, in short, on positive law. But one has the impression that he does so for the sake of expediency rather than on principle. Any arguments other than those of the 'positivist' kind would have found no response among the ruling class, perhaps none even among the people of Vaud. An appeal to the law of reason would have branded him from the start as a revolutionary and destroyed any possibility of persuading the Bernese oligarchy to grant reforms. There is no doubt at all that his sympathies, like those of his young translator, are all with the French Revolution.[1] But he prefers to fight reaction with the weapons of reaction and to condemn abuses of many years' standing by invoking rights several centuries old.[2] Finally, were Cart's

---

[1] In his letters Cart consistently defends the supporters of the French Revolution in Switzerland, the 'Patriots', and shows hostility towards its opponents, the 'Aristocrats'. In one place he refers to the years since 1789 as 'the most critical epoch which ever convulsed Europe and in which all feelings were stirred up by the most stupendous of revolutions'. (Op. cit., p. 66.)

[2] 'I shall not look for the principles of our state in Nature. Not that I do not feel that she alone is the true source from which all of them must be deduced,

'positivism' genuine, it still would not follow that Hegel shared it at the time. He was, after all, only the translator and editor of the work, which he chose because it suited his purpose, not because he was completely in agreement with its author.[1]

The preface to Hegel's own *Wurtemberg's Domestic Affairs* is so imbued with political rationalism that it is impossible to quote from it; the whole of it should be consulted. In *The German Constitution*, however, Hegel's advocacy of rational law takes on a subtler form. The 'positivism' or traditionalism he attacks consists in the attitude, typical of the great majority of her inhabitants, of regarding Germany as a real state, since allegedly she has a constitution, a crowned emperor, an imperial diet, and so on. Hegel maintains that such obstinate clinging to positive constitutional forms which have long lost any meaning is more than absurd. It is basically immoral since it hides unwillingness to do anything for the country's welfare. Thus Hegel's rationalism expresses itself in two main ways. He counters the woolly thinking of his compatriots by applying to the German Empire the concept of the state as an effective union for the defence of the totality of the inhabitants' property. Secondly, he insists that if the Germans are earnest about wanting to be a state, they must set about constructing or reconstructing an effective central public authority.

In Hegel's detailed analysis of the constitution of the German Empire there is more than a hint that it is thoroughly 'positive' and irrational. Like the British constitution, which in an earlier passage we have seen Hegel condemn, it is a product of a haphazard evolution, a creature of force, accident, and caprice, an aggregate rather than a system. In *The English Reform Bill* Hegel specifically com-

---

and that one cannot depart from her without creating force on the one hand and compulsion on the other. Such a condition, incidentally, makes every agreement between prince and people invalid and gives the people a right to revoke it at any moment. But I will not go quite so far to prove what the rights of my country are; far from demanding the repeal of a contract, I merely demand its observance.' (Ibid., p. 2.) Here Cart explicitly acknowledges Nature as the ultimate source of law and right, and the law of nature is merely another name for the law of reason, a name which Hegel himself occasionally uses.

[1] H. Glockner in his *Hegel* (Stuttgart, 1929), vol. i, p. 364, suggests that Hegel's stay in Berne contributed to his understanding of the essential difference between rationalism and 'positivism' in politics. 'Here Hegel lived in the realm of the old-fashioned conservative political attitude, as yet hardly affected by the Revolution. Only in the midst of this living past incapsulated in the present, which he had closely observed, did he really learn to grasp the meaning of the Revolution.' It was in Berne that Hegel began working on Cart's letters.

pares the two in respect of their irrationality.[1] The crucial difference, however, was that Britain had never ceased to be a state. Although at one time she too was subject to various disintegrating tendencies, she had managed to preserve her political unity.

Thus France, England, Spain, and the other European countries have succeeded in pacifying and uniting the elements which fermented within the state and threatened to wreck it. . . . They have succeeded in attaining a centre in which all power is concentrated. . . . From this epoch of the development of countries into states there dates the period of the power and the wealth of the state and the free and lawful prosperity of individuals. [109]

A large part of *The German Constitution* is merely an elaboration of this basic theme. Hegel surveys the whole course of modern European history to show that without a centralized public authority or political power, a 'central point', a country cannot remain a state. He calls this the Principle of Monarchy, and claims that it was given to the world by the Teutonic tribes who conquered and destroyed the Roman Empire. He believes that it existed in an embryonic form in the tribal and military organization of the various Germanic peoples who became the forerunners of modern European states. In the first phase of the development of these states public authority was on the whole weak, and a number of strongly entrenched particular authorities came into being; this was the stage of feudalism. In the second phase the central public authority proceeded to assert itself against the peripheries and to subordinate them to itself; this was the stage of monarchy. Germany, in Hegel's view, shared with the rest of Western Europe the first half of constitutional evolution, but the country considered as a whole had failed to traverse the second.

The principle of the original German state, a principle spread from Germany over the whole of Europe, was the principle of monarchy, a political power under an overlord for the conduct of national business with the co-operation of the people through its representatives. The form of this principle survives in what is called the Diet; but the thing itself has vanished.

In Europe's long oscillation between barbarism and civilization, the

---

[1] 'To counter the Englishman's pride in his freedom, we Germans may well cite the fact that even if the old constitution of the German Empire had likewise become a formless aggregate of particular rights, it was only the external bond of the German states. . . .' [286]

German state has not completely made the transition to the latter; it
has succumbed to the convulsions of this transition; its members have
torn themselves apart to complete independence; the state has been
dissolved. The Germans have failed to find a middle way between subjection, despotism, what they called universal monarchy, on the one
hand, and complete disintegration on the other. [131]

A point of great importance emerges from this discussion of
The German Constitution. Hegel's rejection of the positive principle
—of traditionalism in politics—and his championing of political
rationalism is in fact less sweeping than appears at first sight. What
he unconditionally condemns is the traditionalist *attitude* to law
and constitution; he is very far from condemning all traditional
political *institutions* of contemporary Europe. The demand that
'nothing in a state constitution shall be deemed valid that has not
been sanctioned by the law of reason' meant something different
to Hegel from what it meant to some of his contemporaries. To
them it meant that reason should supply actual political schemes
and devices, independent of history and experience and deduced
purely from first principles by logical thinking. Fichte's idea of an
ephorate and his project of an exclusive commercial state are probably classical German examples of this kind of political rationalism,
while in France Abbé Siéyès is the main representative of such
rational constitution-mongering. In *The German Constitution* Hegel
refers with scorn to 'the political theories . . . partly propounded
by would-be philosophers and teachers of the rights of man and
partly realized in tremendous political experiments' [26]. He
opposes the traditional freedom of civil society characteristic of
'the old states of Europe' and hereditary monarchies to the new
idea of centralized government. He calls 'the silliest conceit' the
notion that representation is an invention of recent origin and
traces it to feudalism and the rise of a burgher estate in the Middle
Ages. Almost invariably Hegel invokes history rather than reason
whenever any institutional questions in the modern state—the
union for the defence of property—are involved, and he adheres
to this historical approach to the basis of the state throughout his
career as a publicist. By 'history', however, is meant not the detailed
account of events, the chronicle type of history, but the wider and
more speculative approach typical of the pragmatic historians of
the Enlightenment. If one was to single out one thinker to whom
Hegel's institutional ideas owe more than to anybody else, it would

be Montesquieu.[1] Although *The German Constitution* stands some-what apart from the rest of Hegel's political writings, it does not invalidate the generalization that political rationalism is the out-standing cause which his writings champion. Political rationalism, however, now appears in a new light. It has been said earlier that Hegel regarded the French Revolution as the beginning of a new era of human political relations, the dawn of a new epoch, the birth of a new legal and constitutional world. But also it must be stressed that to Hegel the state of his day was the result of a develop-ment as long as the history of modern Europe itself. Its roots extended to the time of the Germanic invasions and each of the subsequent stages of its growth had left an imprint on it and deter-mined its present shape. The French Revolution was a new and important stage in the evolution of this ancient structure, but it was only a stage. It shook the structure to its foundations, destroyed much that was useless and outdated, introduced desirable changes, and so on. Its real importance, however, was that it brought to light the underlying plan and symmetry of the whole, and taught men to act consciously and thoughtfully in politics. In other words the Revolution did not proclaim completely new principles of human political existence; rather it made men aware of the ones which had already been implicit but not fully appreciated and of the necessity to guide actions by reference to them. The French Revolution did not so much attempt to *revolutionize* political life as *rationalize* it. The epoch which began with it was a genuine, but not a total, break with the past; it affected not so much its sub-stance as its form; it altered not the basic outline of the structure but only man's attitude to it, its intellectual foundation.[2]

We thus come back to the original thesis of this chapter that Hegel the political writer must be considered first and foremost as a champion of political rationality, i.e. a certain attitude to the state, its constitution, and laws. Only in the second place is he a champion of a concept of the modern state, based on a theory of its historical evolution out of the embryonic political organization

[1] In the major works Hegel frequently praises Montesquieu. Cf. *Philosophy of Right*, paras. 3, 261, 273. In the minor works direct references to him are rather few, but his influence is unmistakable.

[2] See [159–60] where the typical pre-revolutionary constitution is compared to 'an old house' which 'has come into being like an aggregate' and is 'a formless and unintelligible whole'. 'The intellectual culture of our time', Hegel concludes, 'has given us the idea of the state and hence its essential unity. . . .'

of a primitive Teutonic community. He has definite views about many constitutional and political problems, but his chief enemy is not a definite type of constitution or any specific abuses but the attitude towards the state and its laws which we have called traditionalism or 'positivism'. This consists in accepting the existing, established laws and institutions as they have historically evolved because they are established, traditional, customary, and 'positive', without regard to the unsystematic, planless, aggregate-like character of the whole and despite the absurdities and wrongs which lurk behind them.

Hegel has often been compared to Burke, and indeed there are many similarities and parallels in their political thought. Nevertheless it is not so much the details of their views as the similarity of their general position that has struck many students of politics. And yet, if the interpretation put on Hegel's writings in this chapter is correct, it would be difficult to find two thinkers whose basic political beliefs and preferences were more opposed or whose mutual opposition went deeper. Hegel never mentions Burke in any of his writings and there is no conclusive evidence that he had ever read him. But had he come face to face with his writings, his first reaction would have been one of utter hostility and disapproval. Burke not only glorifies the British constitution which we have seen Hegel condemn in no uncertain terms; he is probably the greatest and certainly the most eloquent apologist for the very political attitude which Hegel is concerned to combat in his writings. The spirit which pervades all of Burke's political writings and becomes most explicit in his works on the French Revolution is the spirit of traditionalism and 'positivism', the respect for the established institutions of the country, the veneration of antiquity, precedent, and prescription.[1]

[1] One passage may be quoted by way of illustration; it would be difficult to improve on it as a statement of the opposite of political rationalism in Hegel's sense. 'In this enlightened age I am bold enough to confess, that we are generally men of untaught feelings; that instead of casting away all our old prejudices, we cherish them to a very considerable degree, and, to take more shame to ourselves, we cherish them because they are prejudices; and the longer they have lasted and the more generally they have prevailed, the more we cherish them. . . . Many of our men of speculation, instead of exploding general prejudices, employ their sagacity to discover the latent wisdom which prevails in them. If they find what they seek, and they seldom fail, they think it more wise to continue the prejudice, with the reason involved, than to cast away the coat of prejudice, and to leave nothing but the naked reason.' *Reflections on the Revolution in France*, Works of the Rt. Hon. Edmund Burke, The World's Classics, vol. iv, pp. 94, 95.

If we may resort to a religious analogy, we might say that political rationalism and its opposite, which Burke represents, differ as much as orthodoxy and heresy. In fact one can gain additional insight into the gap that separates the two if one thinks of the Revolution as a kind of political Reformation engaged in a struggle with established orthodoxy, a political Catholicism.[1] Let us imagine a Protestant publicist living and writing about the middle of the sixteenth century. He would most certainly regard Catholicism as an outdated approach to Christianity and the Catholic Church as a reactionary institution. He would have little doubt that eventually the new faith or the new interpretation of the Faith would spread to most other Christian countries and to all parts and sections of his own country. Though his pamphlets and commentaries might ostensibly deal with specific issues, his antipathy to Catholicism would be something more fundamental and profound than disagreement over a particular dogma or disgust with the corruption of the clergy. What would anger, irritate, and repel him would be the whole Catholic attitude to religion. He would resent what he considered the spirit of servility to an external religious authority and the blind worship of tradition. The former seemed to involve the abdication of one's conscience and judgement in favour of the fiat of another man; the latter—the absence of any discrimination between the chaff and the grain, religious superstition and true faith. The attitude of a Catholic publicist fighting Protestantism can easily be imagined. Though ostensibly in the same camp as far as religion was concerned, Hegel and Burke belonged to opposing camps in the political struggle of attitudes and principles.

Their assessment of the French Revolution, though strikingly similar in one respect, differs completely in others. They are merely agreed on the symptoms of the complaint, not its character or cure.

---

[1] Burke clearly perceived the 'religious' character of the Revolution and the parallel between it and the German Reformation. 'There have been many internal revolutions in the government of countries, both as to persons and forms, in which the neighbouring states have had little or no concern. . . . The present revolution in France seems to me quite of another character and description; and to bear little resemblance or analogy to any of those which have been brought about in Europe, upon principles merely political. *It is a revolution of doctrine and theoretic dogma.* It has a much greater resemblance to those changes which have been made upon religious grounds, in which a spirit of proselytism makes an essential part. The last revolution of doctrine and theory which has happened in Europe is the Reformation.' *Thoughts on French Affairs*, ibid., p. 238.

For Hegel it was like a fever accompanying a stage of rapid development of the organism towards a new and higher life; this development was beneficent and should not be interfered with. For Burke
it was like a dangerous, infectious disease, to be checked by all
possible means including amputation in the best interest of both
the patient and his neighbours. Whatever other similarities there
may be, their views on the French Revolution and the proper
attitude to the state and law are divided by an unbridgeable gap.

III

REFORM AND REVOLUTION

> If it became a fact, if the extraordinary eventuality
> really occurred that political law-making was vested in
> reason, that man was respected and treated as an end
> in himself, that law was raised to the throne and true
> freedom made the foundation of state structure, then
> indeed would I take leave of the Muses for ever and
> devote all my activity to the most splendid of all works
> of art—the rational monarchy.
>
> FRIEDRICH SCHILLER, *Briefe.*

THE principle of political rationalism is summed up by Hegel
as 'nothing in a state constitution shall be deemed valid that
has not been sanctioned by the law of reason'. The attitude
which refuses to acknowledge the legitimacy of any law or institution that cannot stand up to reason forms, so to speak, one pole of
political reality as Hegel conceived it. The mass of traditional laws
and institutions of a particular country, 'the disconnected aggregate
of positive provisions' as he calls the English constitution, the
rambling, sprawling, planless constitutional structure the evolution
of which he compares to the growth of an old mansion—this is the
other pole of the politics of his time. The two may either clash
violently or be more peacefully reconciled by transforming the
aggregate of positive rules into a coherent system of public and
private law based on rational principles.

The tension or opposition between rationalist attitude and
irrational institutions, which ideally ought to lead to their reconciliation in a system of rational law, finds many illustrations in
Hegel's writings. His first original political work, written under
the stimulus of a temporary immersion in the public affairs of his
province, bears striking testimony to the fact that the conflict of
reason and tradition was something which he deeply felt and
experienced and which, perhaps rashly, he believed his contemporaries felt also. *Wurtemberg's Domestic Affairs* thus opens with
the avowal of a universal experience of the conflict.

Calm satisfaction with the present, hopelessness, patient acquiescence in a fate that is all too great and powerful have changed into hope, expectation, and a resolution for something different. The picture of better and juster times has become lively in the souls of men and a longing, a sighing for purer and freer conditions, has moved all hearts and set them at variance with the actuality [of the present]. [150]

Clearly 'the picture of better, juster times' and 'a longing for a purer, freer condition' represent to Hegel the beginning of an impact of rational ideas on the minds of Wurtembergers who no longer can find satisfaction in the existing 'institutions, constitutions, and laws' [151]. At the moment, its result is simply disgust and an indefinite dream of something better, but he goes on to warn that it may harden into an active hostility and lead to the overthrow of the constitution. Hopeless waiting for the breakdown of the existing institutions or the toleration of abuses until they produce a revolutionary ferment is thoroughly repugnant to Hegel, and he insists that a radical reform of the *status quo* is the only wise and honourable course of action. Hegel, who specifically accuses the Duke of Wurtemberg of absolutism and his officials of a thoroughly 'positivist' attitude,[1] addresses himself primarily to the members of the newly convened Provincial Diet, but also to the more enlightened section of the population in general.

For men of nobler wishes and purer enthusiasm it may above all be time to focus their will, so far lacking a definite object, on those parts of the constitution which are based on injustice and to direct their energies to the necessary alteration of these parts. [150]

Hegel thus insists, first, that there must be a reform in Wurtemberg and, secondly, that the reform must be thorough and radical. Elsewhere in the same work he makes it clear that it must also be cautious and gradual. As long as customary institutions, however defective, maintain a hold on the population, they should not be abolished too sweepingly. New institutions, however perfect in theory, will not at first command the same allegiance, and the country may find itself without any effective governing arrangements at all. One can say that there is a sense in which he equates the rational and the reasonable.

---

[1] Hegel says of the officials that they have lost 'all consciousness of the inborn rights of men' and when their office and conscience conflict they look round for 'historical reasons for the positive'. R. Haym, op. cit., p. 87. See also *Wurtemberg's Domestic Affairs* [151].

As long as it is not in one's power to introduce reforms and to with-draw them when they have been tried and found harmful, one would do well to stop at changes the consequences of which, in all their ramifica-tions, can be foreseen and calculated, and to be satisfied with the block-ing of the sources of abuse. [153]

The type of reform, then, which Hegel advocates for Wurtemberg as an alternative to actual present inaction and possible future revolution is one of 'piecemeal social engineering'[1] by the estab-lished public authority. Since from the outset Hegel rejects violent popular action as a satisfactory method of rationalizing the legal and constitutional structure, he has to seek the mainspring of re-forming activity in either the Government or the Estates Assembly, the two main parts of the supreme public authority.

Hegel's belief that organic but gradual reform of private and public law by constitutional means is the best method of recon-ciling existing institutions and the law of reason gains in strength with the passage of years. *The Wurtemberg Estates*, for instance, reflects it quite clearly. Incidentally it implies that in his first work on Wurtemberg he greatly over-estimated the strength of the rationalist attitude among his contemporaries.

We might have feared that the leaven of the revolutionary principles of that period, of abstract concepts of freedom, had not yet fully fer-mented or been digested in Germany and that Estates Assemblies there might take the opportunity to make similar experiments and so give rise to disturbances and dangers. Wurtemberg at any rate has provided a comforting demonstration that this evil spirit does not walk there: but [it is also clear] that the portentous experience in France and out-side it, in Germany as well as there, has been lost on these Estates—the experience that at one extreme the rigid adherence to the positive constitutional law of a bygone situation and, at the other extreme, abstract theories and shallow chatter, have both alike been the bulwarks of selfishness and the source of misfortune in France and outside it. [198]

Here Hegel admits that, in Wurtemberg at any rate, the principles of the French Revolution have had remarkably little influence on the people and their representatives. Twenty-five years afterwards they are still immersed in the positive attitude, as if they had spent the whole intervening period in deep slumber. This has its advan-tages since it obviates the dangers that are liable to arise when the

---

[1] A phrase used in K. R. Popper's 'The Poverty of Historicism', *Economica*, 1944, though not with reference to Hegel.

rational ideas of freedom and justice are conceived by the masses in an abstract, one-sided way. Hegel seems to imply that exasperation with bad positive laws and institutions, if it persists for long, hardens into hostile opposition to *all* laws and institutions. In this situation, political rationalism degenerates into 'an abstract theory and a silly prattle' and reforms, however thorough and desirable, will not be accepted wholeheartedly because they do not correspond to some Utopian ideas. On the other hand 'stubborn persistence in the positive public law of a past condition' is equally a false extreme since here the claims of reason go quite unheeded. The 'immense experience' gained through the French Revolution is that both extremes must be avoided, the law of reason must be given a firm institutional embodiment, and existing positive law must be examined and revised in the light of reason.

Towards the end of his life Hegel seems to have become convinced that of the major European countries Germany alone had profited by experience and learned the secret of combining theoretically rational principles with practical governmental wisdom. In *The English Reform Bill*, written under the influence of the July Revolution, Hegel explicitly contrasts France, England, and Germany in this respect. The first seems to him to be ridden with abstract ideals of freedom, equality, and so on, and hence a prey to periodic instability. The second has remained firmly wedded to the positivist principle, although the Reform Bill controversy is a sign that, there too, political rationalism has begun to produce a ferment. Only the third has known how to preserve stability and order while progressing towards rationality.

In France [rational] ideas have been intermixed with many further abstractions and bound up with the violent upheavals familiar to us all. But unalloyed, they have for long past in Germany become fixed principles of inner conviction and public opinion, and have brought about the actual peaceful gradual and legal transformation of the [old feudal] rights. The result is that here we have already made great progress with the institutions of real freedom; the most important of them we have established and enjoy already, while the governing power of [the English] Parliament has scarcely yet brought them seriously to mind. . . . In England the contrast between prodigious wealth and utterly embarrassed penury is enormous; just as great, perhaps still greater, is that between on the one hand the privileges of its aristocracy and, in general, the institutions of its positive law and, on the other, the rights and laws as reconstituted in the civilized states of the Continent and the principles which, being grounded on universal reason, cannot always remain so foreign even to the English understanding as they have been hitherto. [317-18]

Discounting a certain amount of national pique against the English and the French, and making allowances for the concern which a new wave of revolutions seems to have caused Hegel, his last views on reform are both clear and consistent with his early ones. Legislative quiescence and the veneration of traditional laws and institutions are irrational and in the long run impossible. Trivial and occasional patching up to meet this or that emergency may do for a period of time, but, when reason has been awakened, this must give way to thorough, organic reform.[1] The only satisfactory way to transform the body of positive private and public law of a country into a rational system is through the existing governmental machinery, and this requires a degree of political rationalism among those with political power. When, as in pre-revolutionary France and in Britain at the time of the Reform Bill, the governing classes have a vested interest in preserving the *status quo* and are thoroughly imbued with the 'positivist' attitude, a crude kind of rationalism may first of all affect the masses of the people or at any rate their politically inexperienced middle-class section, and lead to conflict between them and the rulers.[2] The more intransigent the latter are the more violent the clashes are liable to become and the more complete will be the eventual change of the *status quo*. Once the old order has been destroyed, the new one, however rational it appears to be in theory, is unlikely to prove completely stable and lasting in practice. The ferment left behind by the Revolution, the distorted and oversimplified principles which for years have circulated among the common people, the presence of demagogic politicians ready to exploit them to gain power over their opponents, all these evils are likely to plague

[1] In one passage in *The English Reform Bill* Hegel suggests that the awakening of reason may be delayed by prosperity. 'Fame and wealth [in England] make it superfluous to go back to the foundations of existing rights, a process to which external need, and the need of reason thereby aroused, has driven peoples who have felt existing rights oppressive.' [303]

[2] *Wurtemberg's Domestic Affairs* clearly implies that the possibility of such conflict in Germany was weighing on Hegel's mind. But apparently the rulers were converted to rationalism long before the people acquired a revolutionary mood. Nowhere was this more true than in Prussia, changed out of recognition by the Stein Ministry. Cf. Gooch, op. cit., Simon, op. cit., and E. Weil, *Hegel et l'Etat* (Paris, 1950).

a country for years. They certainly did so in France after Hegel's death, but his assessment of the German and British situation proved less correct. It was Germany which was to experience a profound upheaval in 1848 despite her apparent stability and the reforms which had been introduced there by monarchs and their governments. In Britain, on the other hand, the ruling class gradually modified its 'positivist' attitude, and, without losing governmental power, undertook a host of necessary reforms in a piecemeal, haphazard fashion. The country's stability was never seriously endangered, but neither did a radical transformation of her public and private law into a rational, coherent system ever take place.

It has been argued in this chapter that in Hegel's view political rationalism is not merely something intellectual, but an essentially active and practical attitude, the outcome of which, granted favourable circumstances, is to transform the positive laws and institutions of a country in such a way that they approximate to the law of reason. There is a hint of a causal mechanism which Hegel does not develop but which can be stated as follows. The dissatisfaction with or alienation from the given, the existing, the positive, leads men to take refuge in the realm of ideal, rational relations. But this only accentuates unhappiness because the given is no longer seen to be necessary. When the tension persists too long it tends to generate violence. Timely reform bridges the gap between ideal and existing reality and reconciles men's hearts, minds, and wills to the laws and institutions they have to live under. We must now examine the nature of this process more thoroughly, in particular trying to gain a more precise and definite idea of what Hegel means by 'reason' and 'rational'.

The difficulty of understanding Hegel is very largely due to his preference for complex rather than simple political concepts. Terms which other thinkers would be inclined to regard as different though perhaps related, appear to Hegel to be merely parts or aspects of a single all-embracing idea. Thus, for example, 'licence' becomes 'abstract freedom', 'freedom under the law' becomes 'concrete freedom', and a system of 'just law' becomes 'rational freedom', all three being elements of the idea of 'freedom'. Rationality itself seems to have two separate and distinct senses in Hegel's political writings: the material and the formal. A materially rational law or institution means one which is based on or can be justified by some universal principle of reason. The principle, however, may be present implicitly rather than explicitly, i.e. it may be discovered after an examination of the law or institution concerned instead of being more or less obvious to every intelligent mind. Hence a relationship or arrangement will be formally rational when the inner or inherent rationality of it is easily apparent. In Hegel's opinion, custom or a charter granting particular privileges necessarily lacks the form of rationality even if it is substantially rational; only general statutes or *Gesetze* possess rational form.[1]

When discussing Hegel's concept of material rationality, i.e. the universal principles of reason which should govern laws and institutions, a sharp distinction should be drawn between the private and the public law of a country. So far as private law or rules regulating relations between private individuals are concerned, Hegel believes that the guiding principle of reform ought to be justice or *Gerechtigkeit*. In *Wurtemberg's Domestic Affairs* Hegel calls justice 'the sole criterion' in the examination of the legal system and maintains that 'the courage to do justice is the one power which can completely, honourably, and peaceably remove the tottering edifice and produce something safe in its place' [151]. Immediately afterwards he identifies justice with equality.

Let every individual, every class, start of its own accord to weigh its position and its rights before beginning to make demands on others and before trying to find the cause of the ill outside itself, and if it finds itself possessed of inequitable rights, let it strive to redress the balance in favour of others. [152–3]

Though Hegel is not primarily concerned with civil rights in *The German Constitution*[2] he does at least in one one place [95, 96] strongly criticize the unjust exclusion of burghers from military and civil service in some countries. In *The Wurtemberg Estates*, as

---

[1] None of these and the following concepts are specifically discussed in the minor works. Some more light is thrown on them in Chapter VIII below in the section on the *Philosophy of Right*.

[2] In fact Hegel is inclined to minimize the importance of civil equality in order to emphasize the essential conditions of political unity (cf. [20]). Elsewhere in the same work, however, he maintains that in civilized states the public authority functions through universal, equally applicable, statutes (cf. [71] footnote). He clearly accepts Rousseau's (and Kant's) view that laws are universal conditions of political society and bind all citizens equally.

we shall presently see, he singles out for praise the part of the Royal Charter where equality of rights is guaranteed to all subjects. A whole section of *The English Reform Bill* [292–303] is devoted to the exposing of various unjust privileges and unequal relations in Britain. Hegel, who sees in the Reform Bill a shock to 'the English principle of positivity on which the whole of English law rests', expects the electoral reform to lead to 'other reforms of substance' [290].

. . . As a result of reform the route to Parliament may be open to ideas which are opposed to the interest of this class and which therefore have not yet entered its head. Ideas, I mean, which make up the foundations of a real freedom and which affect the matters above mentioned— ecclesiastical property and organization, duties of the clergy—as well as the manorial and other bizarre rights and property restrictions derived from feudalism, and further sections of the chaos of English laws. [317]

The stress on legal equality confirms Hegel's debt to the ideas of the Enlightenment and the French Revolution discussed in the last chapter.[1]

When we come to the fundamental principle of constitutional law, i.e. the law governing the relations between public authorities, defining their rights and duties, their jurisdiction and the mode of their operation and so on, we find that Hegel recognizes a different rational principle. The central normative concept of public law, which is the measuring-rod in the examination, revision, and reform of a constitution, is not *Gerechtigkeit* but *das Allgemeine*, not justice or equality but the common good, general interest, or public welfare (literally 'the universal').

The fullest discussion of the point is to be found in *The German Constitution*.[2] Hegel opens the work by contrasting the procedure of two generations of German constitutional jurists.

The older professors of constitutional law had the idea of a science before their minds when they were handling German constitutional law and consequently they did set out to establish a concept of the German

[1] The conflict between the 'positive' legal order and the spirit of egalitarianism, fostered among others by the *philosophes* and the *physiocrates* in pre-revolutionary France, was stressed in A. de Tocqueville, *L'Ancien Régime et la Révolution*, passim.

[2] In *Wurtemberg's Domestic Affairs* there is a passage which anticipates the later discussion, and implies that the common good may on occasions require the sacrifice of unequal *political* privileges, though this is not realized by the politically privileged [152].

constitution. But they could not become of one mind about this concept before the modern professors gave up trying to find it. They now no longer treat constitutional law as a science but only as a description of what exists empirically and not conformably with a rational idea. . . . [3]

The contrast here drawn between the two approaches to the constitution is reminiscent of that between natural and positive jurisprudence, which Hegel draws elsewhere. The older jurists attempted to subsume the constitution of the Empire under the general categories and principles elaborated by the natural jurists. The abandoning of this approach by the younger jurists was not accidental, Hegel implies; it rather reflected the fact that the constitution itself had gradually become more and more irrational and was now purely positive. Hence all that could profitably be done was to collect and classify the various powers possessed by the many different authorities within the Empire at any given time (see [11]). In two other passages of *The German Constitution* this point is elaborated still further. In the course of history, Hegel writes,

the branches of the state's universal power became a multiform exclusive property, independent of the state and distributed without rule or principle.

Political powers and rights [in the Empire] are not offices of state devised in accordance with an organization of the whole. The burdens and duties of individuals are not determined by the needs of the whole. [9–10]

The last passage contains the crux of the matter. The state for Hegel is an organization with a definite purpose—in *The German Constitution*, it will be remembered, he defines it as 'a union of men for the defence of the totality of their property' although in later works a broader concept is implied. Consequently the organization of the various departments, agencies, or branches of government must be purposeful; their structure, composition, powers, and duties must be determined consciously and deliberately adapted to the end or ends of the state.

The strength of a country consists not in the number of its inhabitants and troops, nor in its fertility, nor in its size, but solely in the manner whereby all these things can be used for the great end of common defence as a result of the rational association of its parts in a single public authority. [57]

Throughout *The German Constitution* Hegel insists the German Empire is far from being such a rational union. The union is thoroughly positive in character since the relations of the parts to the whole, the distribution of functions and powers among the various authorities in the Empire, reflect not any present needs of the country but the result of past political upheavals, conflicts, and agreements.[1] If one examines the powers, one finds not only that there is the greatest diversity and asymmetry but also that certain authorities have too little power while others have too much—and some so much that the amount contradicts the fundamental purpose of the state. Moreover, this haphazard, unplanned distribution of power has been sanctified by usage and tradition to such an extent that public authority has become analogous to private property and any attempt at a more rational redistribution or reform is resented as an unjust interference with a prescriptive right.[2]

It seems to have struck Hegel that the principle of justice, which he himself regards as supremely valid when applied to private law, has been given a very different meaning in the German Empire. 'Justice' there means the sanctity of all positive titles to parts of public authority acquired in the past as a result of temporary contingencies. This kind of positive 'justice' is of course the antithesis of the justice which Hegel puts forward as the fundamental principle of civil rights. In the latter case it is a rational ideal, serving as a measuring-rod of actual laws; in the former case it is a positive concept justifying and upholding the *status quo*, the disintegration of Germany into a number of almost sovereign states. Hence it clearly contradicts the fundamental rational principle of constitutional law, namely that the good of the state as a whole should be the criterion of all public rights.

The German political edifice is nothing but the sum of rights which the individual parts have wrested from the whole, and this [system of] justice, which carefully watches to see that no power is left over to the

---

[1] Cf. [7].

[2] The distinction between public authority and private property Hegel regards as absolutely fundamental. In one of the parallel drafts of *The German Constitution* he puts it as follows: 'Public authority cannot be private property. It flows from the state and only the state can have right to it. Its extent and possession depend on the state and are valid only in relation to the state. . . . The state is the highest commander, if only in one respect—the defence of laws and foreign defence. In this respect decision lies with it and not with chance or documents or other legal titles.' ([63] footnote.)

state, is the essence of the constitution. . . . [Whatever the consequences of the conduct of the parts] nevertheless constitutional law proves that they had the right to behave in this way, the right to bring the whole into the greatest danger, harm, and misfortune. Because there are rights, the individual Estates and the whole must most strictly preserve and protect rights of this kind, the right to total destruction. For this legal edifice of the German state there is perhaps no more appropriate super-scription than *Fiat justitia, pereat Germania.* [13–14]

Even when the historical evolution has less disastrous conse-quences than it has had in the German Empire, the result is not likely to be satisfactory to reason. The 'positive' differentiation, which takes place in the course of a long historical evolution, is no substitute for a conscious and deliberate differentiation by means of constitutional reform. Thus in *The Wurtemberg Estates* Hegel compares 'the historical origin of differentiated constitutions' to the growth of an old house full of useless nooks and annexes which are intelligible in the light of past rather than present needs. This he contrasts with the situation after 1789 when the state has been organized in the full consciousness of its unity.

The intellectual development of the age has afforded the *idea* of a state and therewith of its essential unity. Twenty-five years of past and mostly terrible history have given us a sight of the numerous attempts to grasp this idea and a costly comprehensive experience [of their out-come]. [160]

In *The Wurtemberg Estates* and *The English Reform Bill* Hegel applies the idea of rational public law to various specific institutions such as the power of the Estates or the privileges of the nobility, and uses it to condemn abuses such as rotten boroughs and elec-toral corruption. The Reform Bill, in so far as it attempts to change established institutions and rationalize an aspect of the constitu--tion, seems to Hegel to represent an awakening of reason in Eng-land.

. . . we can see that the right way to pursue improvement is not by the moral route of using ideas, admonitions, associations of isolated in-dividuals, in order to counteract the system of corruption and avoid being indebted to it, but by the alteration of institutions. *The common prejudice of inertia, namely to cling always to the old faith in the excellence of an institution, even if the present state of affairs derived from it is altogether corrupt, has thus at last caved in* [in England]. ([287] My italics.)

The conviction that nothing ought to be left to chance; that the goodness of a law or institution should not be taken for granted despite its halo of antiquity; that reforms must take the form of conscious and deliberate changes of those laws and institutions; and that the guiding principles of reform should be justice or equality between individuals and classes and the primacy of the common good over any vested interests or prescriptive rights of public bodies—all this constitutes the material aspect of political rationality. A short remark in *The Wurtemberg Estates* sums it up admirably: 'in political institutions, as in any rational organization, *chance* is not to be reckoned on' [170].

What gives Hegel's political thought its peculiar rationalist flavour is even more his conviction that material rationality in the sphere of private and public law ought to be supplemented by changing the form of the law from a positive into a rational one, and thereby making explicit the material rationality inherent in it. In *The Wurtemberg Estates* we find the fullest discussion of formal rationality, mainly with reference to fundamental civil rights, but also with a bearing on political rights. In both instances Hegel asserts the extreme importance and desirability of giving all such rights a rational form appropriate to their rational content.

Having discussed at length the part of the Royal Charter dealing with the representative assembly, Hegel turns to the bill of rights which the Charter contains. He quotes some of them, e.g. 'All subjects are equal in the eyes of the law; they are eligible for all official positions; from these they are excluded neither by birth nor by membership of any of the Christian denominations' [184]. Then he goes on to make some general comments (see [185]).

But Hegel does not waste time discussing the royal bill of rights in detail as he regards it as self-evident that these rights 'are simple organic provisions, which . . . form the rational basis of constitutionalism' [184]. In other words, no constitution can, in his opinion, be considered rational unless it is substantially based on those rights. In most constitutions, developed as they have in a haphazard fashion, the rights (if they are present at all) are implicit rather than explicit, and the knowledge of them is confined to a narrow group of men—public-law theorists, lawyers, politicians, and the like. In the Royal Charter, however, they are 'expressly' stated and formulated 'in simple sentences like an elementary catechism' [185]—they can be taught even to the young and certainly understood by all adults. This advance in constitutional drafting Hegel hails as an extremely important cultural event. Equally important is the fact of the open and general recognition of civil rights by the government, facilitated by their embodiment in one set of universal principles of rights and duties. A particularly significant point, so far as this chapter is concerned, is Hegel's belief that these rational principles can and ought to be the basis for the transformation of all established law. They are 'the permanent regulators, which must underlie any revision or extension of what already exists, whenever revision or extension be necessary' [185].

We see that Hegel seems to postulate a kind of hierarchy of rules of increasing concreteness:

1. The fundamental rational principle of justice and equality ('absolute right');
2. a number of general principles, suitable for formulation in a bill or declaration of rights ('organic constitutional provisions');
3. a much larger number of specific legal rules ('laws proper'), covering different aspects of social life and representing the application of general principles to concrete circumstances.

While the general principles can be laid down once for all, the task of enacting specific laws is a continuous one. At any given time there will be a whole mass of positive rules in existence—the product of the whole previous legal evolution of a country. They will not have to be repealed *in toto* since some of them are likely to be rational, at least in substance, but they will have to be examined in the light of the basic rights, and revised whenever necessary. Similarly all claims for new laws regulating private relations must be tested against the declaration of rights. Perhaps even the basic rights themselves may have to be changed with the change in social relations. The process of testing and adjusting laws by reference to general principles, and general principles by reference to absolute justice, constitutes reform, and it is the primary expression of political rationality in practice.

Hegel's insistence on the necessity of a rational transformation of 'positive' constitutional law as well as private law is strikingly illustrated by another passage in *The Wurtemberg Estates*. The original attitude of the Wurtemberg Estates was to demand a return to the old constitution as it stood or rather had stood before the

Revolution on the ground that it was the legitimate and valid constitution.[1] After a time, however, they abandoned this negative and formalistic standpoint, and appointed a committee to put the old constitution into writing and to modify it where circumstances had made it necessary. The result was published in 1816 under the title 'Project of a New Wurtemberg Constitutional Contract', and was applauded by Hegel as a tremendous advance on the old constitution and as a sign of a more rationalist attitude on the Estates' part. But even more revealing is Hegel's following comment:

> The project had attached to it a general clause, on which the Diet had earlier set its heart, to the effect that all fundamental provincial and dynastic laws continue to retain their binding force in so far as they have not been changed by the project. Such a clause must always be conceded, partly as an innocent sop to a formalistic conscience, and partly because a constitution is in general something firm but not wholly static; it is chiefly the work of a Diet in session, which furthers its constant, quiet development. This is the true, general clause, which the spirit of the world itself appends to every existing constitution. [275–6]

Hegel's preference for peaceful, gradual, and constitutional reform finds here another striking expression. However strongly he may condemn the irrationality of positive law, he is against sweeping it away at one stroke and starting with a *tabula rasa*. As long as they have not been altered or repealed by the legislature, all established laws and institutions retain provisional validity until they have been examined; 'this is the general clause which the spirit of the world itself appends to every existing constitution'. The purpose of the examination is not merely to approve, reject, or alter the substance of the rules, but to change their form as well —to generalize, unify, and systematize the complex aggregate of positive provisions. It is clear that this cannot be achieved without

[1] When challenged to declare what the old constitution consisted of the Estates replied that they could not say because they had been denied access to the Provincial Archives. Cf. Hegel's comment: 'That an academic scholar is somewhat in distress when he has lost the key to his library is understandable. But what a musty concept of the constitution is implied when the Estates find it impossible to adduce their constitution because they cannot use the Archives.' [221] Hegel calls the old constitution a 'paper labyrinth' and 'an armoury of lawyers' and asks sarcastically: 'How can an Estates Assembly be afraid of reason, the source of the so-called natural public law, and seek help and security against such fear by plunging into a paper labyrinth? . . . [The Estates] wished to assert also that this [i.e. the old constitution] was the will of the people, yet how can a people possibly know a constitutional structure which the Estates themselves were unable to adduce?' [222]

a written constitution and legal codes, and Hegel is obviously committed to advocating the ultimate replacement of all custom, precedent, charter, and agreement by statutory public and private law.

Although Hegel maintains that the fundamental principle of public law is different from that of private law, he believes that political rights no less than civil rights ought to be clearly and expressly formulated—that they too ought to be given a rational form. Such political rights were contained in the first part of the Royal Charter, which dealt with suffrage and the powers of the Estates Assembly, and which Hegel emphatically approves (cf. [166]).

Hegel's attitude towards political as opposed to civil rights in the constitution is thus the same. He praises 'the simplicity and the straightforwardness of these provisions' and 'the open and determinate way' in which political rights are expressed. He stresses that they are stated as general principles and not just as a collection of particular privileges—'formless', 'illiberal', and 'obscure'. At the same time because they are general they leave room for further development, for additions of more specific provisions, 'which yet would accord with these universal truths of constitutionalism' [166]. Hegel is far from regarding the rights as complete innovations; it is true that in some respects they are more liberal than political rights before the French Revolution, but their real novelty lies in the explicit, general, rational form in which they are expressed. Even if the Royal Charter had not enlarged them, but merely stated them clearly, it would still have been a great advance on the old positive constitution because at least the rights of the people would not have been 'stunted, restricted, and made ambiguous'. There can be no arguments about them, and the least infringement or restriction can be immediately recognized and branded as unconstitutional by public opinion. The greatest guarantee of constitutional procedure in the relations between different public authorities among themselves and towards the people consists for Hegel essentially in the clearness, definiteness, and simplicity of the constitution itself.

The formal rationality of public law, on which Hegel lays such great stress, thus turns out to be not merely intrinsically right but also historically necessary as well as politically expedient. In the new era inaugurated by the French Revolution public law must be purged of any 'positive' form and given an intellectually more satisfactory expression. But, in addition, at all crucial points in his justification of reform practical expediency supports and strengthens the case for rationalization. Unequal legal relations and privileges are inherently wrong since they infringe the rational principle of justice; they are also inexpedient since they cause resentment and may lead to popular disturbances and upheavals. The sacrifice of the common good for the sake of particular interests, in addition to its irrationality, weakens the strength of the public authority and undermines the unity and independence of the country. In this as in other respects Hegel refuses to accept dichotomies, and while his theory of reform is grounded in, and a logical extension of, his concept of rationality, expediency plays a necessary part in the justification of reason in practice.[1]

[1] Hegel's dislike of lawyers and the common law is one of several points of contact between his and Bentham's thought. We find in both the same stress on the virtues of certainty and intelligibility in law and the belief in the necessity of codification. On that ground Bentham denies that England has a constitution at all: 'The Anglo-American United States have a constitution. They have a constitutional code; the constitution is a system of arrangements delineated in that code. . . . The French and Spanish nations have constitutions. The English monarchy has no constitution, for it has no all-comprehensive constitutional code, nor in general any constitutional code whatsoever generally acknowledged as such. . . . England, having no constitution at all, has no excellent, no matchless constitution; for nothing has no properties.' (*The Constitutional Code* in *The Works of Jeremy Bentham*, published by John Bowring, 1843, vol. ix, p. 9.) In another work of Bentham (*View of a Complete Code of Law*, op. cit., vol. iii, p. 203) we find the following eulogy of codes in general: 'A code formed on [scientific] principles would not require schools for its explanation, would not require casuists to unravel its subtilties. It would speak a language familiar to everybody: each one might consult it at his need. It would be distinguished from all other books by its greater simplicity and clearness. The father of a family, without assistance, might take it in his hand and teach it to his children, and give to the precepts of private morality the force and dignity of public morals.' This passage bears a striking similarity to that in *The Wurtemberg Estates* where Hegel praised the simplicity of the bill of rights of the Royal Charter and wanted it impressed on the minds of the young [185]. There is little doubt that Bentham was a champion of political rationality in the same sense as Hegel. On the other hand his moral utilitarianism distinguishes him sharply from Hegel. Bentham has no use for 'natural rights' or 'the law of reason', and in this respect Hegel is much nearer Paine than Bentham.

IV

THE NATION AND CIVIL SOCIETY

A state is such a complex and intricate machine that its laws, which must always be few in number and simple and general in nature, cannot possibly prove adequate to the full accomplishment of its ends. The great essentials of social welfare are always left to be secured by the voluntary and harmonious endeavours of its citizens.

WILHELM VON HUMBOLDT,
Ueber die Grenzen der Wirksamkeit des Staates.

THE French Revolution and the quarter-century following it, which *The Wurtemberg Estates* calls 'possibly the richest [years] that world history has had, and for us the most instructive, because it is to them that our world and our ideas belong' [199], appeared in somewhat different light to Hegel from that in which it appeared to many of his contemporaries. To him the fundamental issue of those years was whether the state should be based on positive law or on the law of reason or, more specifically, whether the rational attitude and the reforming activity resulting from it should prevail over the positive attitude and its practical consequences—the preservation of the *status quo* and legislative quiescence. We have seen that the constitutional conflict in Wurtemberg, and the Reform Bill controversy in Britain, also represented in Hegel's opinion the continuation of the struggle of rational law against positive law and privilege. To other observers, however, the Revolution seemed rather to concern the basic political relationship in the state, the relation of the people to the government, and the form of the government itself. Hegel's pamphlets and commentaries do not ignore those issues. One cannot write about the form of political life without revealing something of one's attitude to its substance. Hegel, moreover, believed that several constitutional concepts current since the Revolution were false or inadequate. Sometimes this was due to the continuing hold of tradition, but more often the cause was to be found in one-sided, abstract interpretations of rationality. The first to be examined will be his views on a nation or people (*Volk*) and its public authority (*Staatsgewalt*), which in a sense concern the most fundamental political relationship.

The concept of the nation is treated fully in *The German Constitution* and it is intimately linked with Hegel's discussion of the concept of the state. In order to emphasize the minimum which would have to be done in Germany to re-establish an effective public authority, he is concerned to distinguish between the universal or common interests of the nation, for which such authority is necessary, and all other interests. The latter, he maintains, may be furthered by particular authorities and bodies of the most diverse kind, related to the central public authority in countless different ways. The central authority itself may be internally organized as it likes provided it is effective.

If a multitude is to form a state, then it must form a common military and public authority. . . . In dealing with this topic we must keep two things distinct: first, what is necessary if a multitude is to be a state and a common authority, and, secondly, what is only a particular modification of this authority and what belongs not to the sphere of the necessary but, as regards theory, to the sphere of the greater or lesser good, and, as regards actuality, to the sphere of chance and caprice. [18–19]

Hegel goes on to mention specifically such things as the diversity of legal status, property rights, political privileges, the administration of justice, and the inequality of taxes.[1] All these belong to the accidental characteristics of a state and should be carefully distinguished from its necessary feature—the existence of a supreme public authority.

This distinction has an aspect very important for the peace of states, the security of governments, and the freedom of peoples. If the general public authority demands from the individual only what is necessary for itself, and if it restricts accordingly the arrangements for ensuring the performance of this minimum, then beyond this point it can permit the living freedom and the individual will of the citizens, and even leave considerable scope to the latter. [19]

[1] One of these accidental characteristics is cultural, social, and national homogeneity [24]. Although in another place Hegel calls the suzerainty of the Holy Roman Empire over Hungary, Poland, Prussia, and Naples 'an unnatural union of territories, separated by both geographical situation and national individuality' [50–51] he is far from postulating national unity as a basis of the state. Hence it seems wrong to regard Hegel as a *nationalist* political thinker.

It turns out, then, that, in addition to the problem of restoring effective central government, the concept of the state has another practical application. It serves Hegel as a criterion for distinguishing what can and ought to come under the direct control of the government (as the executive branch of the public authority) and what the latter can and ought to leave alone. The rest can then be left to 'the individual will of the citizens' and provides 'considerable scope for their living freedom'. Freedom, in the sense in which Hegel thinks of it here, finds its expression in the organs of local and sectional autonomy. He sets out to argue in detail that this course of action is justified by expediency as well as being the logical consequence of a rational concept. In the passage last quoted, he has already mentioned one reason for confining the activity of central government to the indispensable minimum, and he pursues the utilitarian argument further by mentioning the relative advantages and disadvantages of leaving large areas of administration in the hands of non-central authorities [29]. Hegel admits that efficiency and uniformity are great gains of centralization, but he believes that they are counterbalanced by the material advantage of a saving in government expenditure and the spiritual benefit of 'vitality, the contented mind, and free and self-respecting self-awareness' conferred on the people by a local and sectional self-government. A completely centralized government shows by its organization and operation that it has no confidence whatever in the public spirit and self-help of the people, and thus inevitably strengthens a passive, submissive attitude.[1]

An active, self-reliant population is of great advantage to the state since 'a public authority is infinitely strong if it can be supported by the free and unregimented spirit of its people' [31]. Hegel, however, goes one step further and stresses that freedom from unnecessary central control is not only expedient but absolutely right and a duty.

This is no place to argue at length that the centre, as the public authority, i.e. the government, must leave to the freedom of the citizens whatever is not necessary for its appointed function of organizing and maintaining authority and thus for its security at home and abroad. Nothing should be so sacrosanct to the government as facilitating and

---

[1] Cf. the passage in *The German Constitution* where Hegel talks of 'a mechanical hierarchy highly intellectual and devoted to noble ends, [which] evinces no confidence whatever in its citizens' [30].

protecting the free activity of the citizens in matters other than this. This is true regardless of utility, because the freedom of the citizens is inherently sacrosanct. [29]

Having justified the restriction of governmental activity to its minimum—external and internal security—on three separate grounds, Hegel proceeds to attack what may be called a theory of *étatisme*. He regards it as a false, extreme deduction from the concept of the state he has discussed. Since the state is a union for the defence of property it must be appropriately organized to achieve this purpose. This, however, Hegel argues, involves neither a complete control of all social relations nor a system of a single centralized and hierarchical public administration. Because the supreme authority of the state must be strong enough to maintain independence and order, it does not follow that it may turn all bodies and authorities into cogs of a vast bureaucratic machine and deprive its citizens of the opportunity of governing themselves. But this is exactly what some recent theories by men whom Hegel contemptuously calls 'would-be philosophers and teachers of the the rights of man' have suggested.

[Their] fundamental presupposition is that a state is a machine with a single spring which imparts movement to all the rest of the infinite wheelwork, and that all institutions implicit in the nature of a society should proceed from the supreme public authority and be regulated, commanded, overseen, and conducted by it. [28]

The disastrous results of such theories, when put into effect, are seen by Hegel in some of the contemporary states. Although the 'monstrous political experiments' which he mentions in this connexion obviously refer to France, he believes that the Prussia of Frederick the Great provides a better example of the evils of state centralization (see [31]).

These passages clearly imply that Hegel regards the theory and practice of *étatisme* as false and dangerous innovations. Moreover the evolution of modern Europe furnishes him with the idea of the supreme public authority as something essentially narrow and limited in scope. He visualizes it as something so to speak superimposed on society, a system of institutions which the people evolve to protect their property, an organization which claims their allegiance as far as its purpose is concerned, but apart from that leaves them in a state of great freedom. The starting-point of this evolution is the prehistoric Teutonic or Germanic community, a situation 'in which the nation was a people without being a state'. The remark implies that society, the nation, or the people is something prior to the state. In another passage [8–9] he implies that it is also a condition of extreme individualism. The fragmentation of political power characteristic of medieval feudalism Hegel regards as an expression of this Germanic 'drive to freedom'.

> Out of this arbitrary activity, which alone was called freedom, spheres of power over others were built by chance and character, without regard to a universal and with little control by what is called the public authority, since this authority scarcely existed at all in opposition to individuals. [9]

Nevertheless, as Hegel goes on to say, despite the paucity of constitutional bonds and the weakness of the central public authority the whole was a unity because it was bound by 'an inner connexion of dispositions'.

> When religion was uniform and when the still embryo *bourgeoisie* had not introduced a great heterogeneity into the whole, princes, dukes, and lords could regard one another more easily as a whole and accordingly could act as a whole. [73]

It was the rise of the *bourgeois* class and the religious split which doomed Germany's political unity.[1]

We are not concerned in this chapter with the most important result of the historical evolution Hegel is describing, the disintegration of the German Empire, or with the validity of his notions of the Germanic community or medieval feudalism. But the passages are of interest because they throw light on the nature of what Hegel later was to call a Civil Society. The result of the evolution from prehistoric people has been, first, the creation of a multitude of particular authorities and privileged classes, which form a closely interwoven network, an 'organic' unity. These authorities and estates can possess varying degrees of independence from the supreme public authority, and we have already seen that Hegel favours the maximum of autonomy compatible with the existence of the state.

The estate of burghers (*Bürgerstand*), however, presents a special

---

[1] Hegel believes that the Reformation has made an important contribution to the disintegration of the German Empire by alienating individual burghers from the central authority. Cf. [74] where Hegel anticipates later theories of the connexion between capitalism and Protestantism.

problem. They are 'by far the greater number of free men' [93] and are 'often simply called "the people" ' though they are really 'the third Estate' of it [160]: Because the estate is so large, it is still further differentiated into a number of authorities, areas, and groups, which taken together form a distinct type of society, a burgher, civic, or civil society (*bürgerliche Gesellschaft*), and this civil society increasingly dominates national life and imposes on it its own needs and problems.

The most important characteristic which distinguishes the burghers from the other sections of national community is their individualism. To this extent the burgher resembles somewhat the ancient Teuton—'the individual who stood on his own feet in his life and activity' [8]. But the burgher, even more than the ancient Teuton, is primarily concerned with his 'own wants and livelihood', interested in his private affairs far more than in public ones and apt to minimize his dependence on the whole. Although the institutions of civil society do much to curb the self-interest and private point of view of the burghers, it remains basically a multitude of self-seeking individuals, impatient of customs, traditions, and privileges, and apt to conceive freedom as the absence or at least the minimum of political obligations.

Such a society threatens not merely the rest of the nation but the supreme public authority itself, and calls for consciously created laws and political institutions to control and confine its expansion. 'External legal bonds were necessary if Germany was to be united in a state after its inhabitants had ceased to be one people and become just a mass' [82], writes Hegel of a point in the evolution of the Empire. Nevertheless, within the limits imposed by the necessity of having a strong and effective public authority and protecting the rest of the nation, both types of freedom—corporate self-government and individual self-assertion—are intrinsically good in Hegel's opinion. Far from being suppressed, they should be carefully safeguarded by the central government of the state.

The scope of governmental activity implied in *The German Constitution* is confined within extremely narrow limits. Earlier on we have seen Hegel insist that 'the government must leave to the freedom of the citizens whatever is not necessary for its appointed function of organizing and maintaining authority and thus for its security at home and abroad' [29]. Elsewhere in the same work Hegel writes apropos the nature of state sovereignty:

'The state is the highest commander, if only in one respect—*the
defence of the laws and external defence.*' ([63] footnote. My italics.)
What then are the grounds on which central government can control society in Hegel's view? The government may and should
intervene when its own stability is at stake, when law and order
are endangered at home or national independence threatened from
outside; otherwise it must respect the freedom of the nation [26–27].

The common good in this narrow sense, then, is the first ground
on which the supreme public authority may interfere with and
curb the freedom of groups within the nation. The second ground,
which Hegel adds shortly afterwards, is justice or equality. He
seems to see two main ways in which the latter principle may be
infringed in society: first by the establishment of an oligarchy
within a particular class of the people, and, secondly, by the
domination or oppression of one or more classes by another class.

A nation is free in Hegel's opinion when it is self-governing, in
other words when the central government leaves full scope to the
citizens' own activity in details of the administration of justice,
civil administration, &c. In contrast to the state proper, the nation,
and especially that part of it which forms the burgher estate, might
be called in a sense democratic. The people govern themselves by
electing officers or appointing responsible officials, who transact
the current business of the estate, corporation, or authority, handle
its laws and customs, raise and disburse funds, and soon.[1] As long as
the nation is truly self-governing, central government remains inactive, but, when the officers or officials of local other authorities
emancipate themselves from popular control and become a self-
perpetuating oligarchy, the case for central intervention arises and
grows stronger with the abuses to which such an oligarchy leads.
Hegel illustrates this point by an example drawn from the experience of German Imperial cities, which he claims sank to the lowest
level of corruption under their oligarchic government when the
authority of the Emperor over them had declined and then vanished
altogether. (Cf. [129, 130].)

If oligarchy destroys equality *within* a particular section of the
nation, oppression or domination destroys equality *among* its several

[1] In this connexion Hegel praises the financial autonomy which exists in
Germany. '. . . there is no superfluous meddling by the state in every public
expenditure; on the contrary, a village, a city, a city guild, &c., itself looks after
financial matters which are its concern alone, under the general oversight but
not at the command of the state.' [40–41]

sections. Hegel sees society as a network of institutions spontaneously evolved in the past to meet the needs of various groups and classes. These groups coexist side by side, interact, and mutually affect each other.[1] From time to time, however, one of them may gain so much power that it threatens the independence or welfare of other groups, and then again the duty of the central government is to intervene and restore equality [28].

It is fairly obvious that by insisting on the limits to the freedom of the nation Hegel implicitly asserts the principle of political rationality discussed in the two previous chapters. The institutions of the nation are a product of an unplanned, haphazard historical development. They are the result of chance and past arbitrariness, created by spontaneous action of citizens. They form a network developed under its own impulse, which has grown up independently of any regulation and control. Precisely because the development is blind, it may have various undesirable effects—it may obstruct the work of the government and also harm society itself. 'The exuberant development' of one part may impede the work of other parts. The implicit conclusion is clearly that things cannot be left completely to chance. Freedom and spontaneity are necessary and desirable, but they must be curbed if they lead to hardship, injustice, inequality, and so on. In other respects, however, because the common good is not at stake, mistakes and failures may and should be tolerated, for they are the price the nation has to pay for spontaneity and experimentation.

Because Hegel's primary concern in *The German Constitution* is the re-establishment of some degree of effective central authority, he does not advocate the thorough revision of all laws and institutions which dominates his other writings.[2] His later political writ-

---

[1] Rosenkranz (op. cit., pp. 85–86) reports that Hegel was at that time greatly interested in Britain and made excerpts from British newspapers about current poor-law debates in Parliament. He also wrote a commentary on a German translation of Sir James Steuart's *An Inquiry into the Principles of Political Economy* (London, 1767), in which he criticized the mercantilism of the Scotsman and defended the principles of free competition. This confirms the impression one gets from reading *The German Constitution* that Hegel's concept of an autonomous civil society was strongly influenced by British experience.

[2] It is worth recalling that in both *Confidential Letters* and *Wurtemberg's Domestic Affairs* Hegel is preoccupied with justice. In the former he exposes the civil and political inequality as between the citizens of Berne and the inhabitants of Vaud and attacks the principle of oligarchy. In the latter work Hegel is against the oligarchic composition of town councils in Wurtemberg and advocates their election by the people.

ings stress more strongly the necessity for a thorough rationalization of the relations and institutions within society. Also the extent of social autonomy which he believes to be desirable seems to be somewhat more narrowly conceived. Nevertheless, Hegel's basic ideas of the nation and civil society do not appear to change significantly through time. He remains a resolute opponent of bureaucracy, centralism, and *étatisme* and a champion of local and sectional freedom and self-government.

The Wurtemberg Estates resumes the discussion of oligarchy in the Imperial cities, but instead of advocating the reintroduction of some form of central supervision, Hegel accepts the suppression of many of the previous functions of these authorities or rather their transfer to the central government. The evidence of maladministration and neglect of duties by city councils seems to him a proof of their basic inability to cope with at least some of the affairs of civil society. Matters such as the provision of legal justice, education, or the support of churches and the poor, he now regards as legitimate functions of central government. The supreme public authority is viewed as playing a more active and direct part in the affairs of civil society, as well as furthering the universal interests of the population. The former functions remain in one sense within civil society since they concern the particular rights and interests of individuals and groups. It is their promotion which ceases to be voluntary and autonomous and becomes a matter for the civil servants or the king's judges. Nevertheless the government does not wholly supersede the independent authorities of civil society; it merely *restricts* their scope. Hegel thus abandons the minimalist position he took up in *The German Constitution* without at the same time going over to the extreme of centralism he himself condemned in that work.

... From one end of Germany to another there has been such a loud complaint about the incompetence, laziness, and indifference of local administrations. ... The right of the [town] councillors themselves to appoint to vacancies in their number will certainly have been a principal reason for their having sunk so far.[1] What otherwise might be called despotism, i.e. the fact that many governments have deprived town councillors and other local officials of the administration of the locality's

---

[1] It will be remembered that in *Wurtemberg's Domestic Affairs* Hegel also criticized the co-optation of town councillors. In both cases he supports a measure of democracy in local government.

property and the other foundations and institutions concerned with churches, schools, and the poor, may not only find its justification in this incapacity but may even have appeared as an inescapable duty. It is on this same ground of incompetence that often nothing but a pure formality has been left to town councillors, as justices, of the share they were supposed to have in the administration of justice. . . . Governments thus found themselves induced to take out of the hand of town councillors their former share in the administration of justice. [174]

In another part of *The Wurtemberg Estates* Hegel discusses at length a social phenomenon peculiar to Wurtemberg which he calls the 'Writers' Institute' (*Schreiberei-Institut*). 'Writers' (*Schreiber*) were clerks who possessed a virtual monopoly of official clerical work in each district of the country and formed a privileged and oppressive class. The evidence produced in the Wurtemberg Diet showed that the writers were able to exercise such a degree of influence over the local authorities within civil society that the latter's independence had practically vanished. In Hegel's opinion the case for the intervention of the government and the reform of the Writers' Institute was crystal-clear, and he blames the Ministry for failing to advise the king on the necessity of 'the regeneration of the blighted constitutional position of the masses of the people' [259]. Thus Hegel shows great sensibility to the danger of oligarchy, whether it is an open one as in Berne or a hidden one as in Wurtemberg.

The English Reform Bill confirms this general interpretation and adds some interesting new illustrations of Hegel's position. His views on English civil society are mixed. On the one hand he sees—and praises—the existence of much more freedom and autonomy in the United Kingdom than on the Continent. On the other hand he emphasizes that its benefits are cancelled by the evil of a large number of ancient abuses and inequalities as between different sections of the nation.

. . . It also lies in the character of their constitution that the government as good as does not encroach at all on the particular circles of social life, on the administration of counties, cities, &c., on ecclesiastical and educational establishments, and even on other public concerns such as road-making. [323]

Hegel calls this a 'freer and more concrete condition of civic life' than is to be found on the Continent, and mentions some of the advantages that result from it: a greater degree of political consciousness, a feeling of national pride, and a practical attitude to politics. On the debit side of the balance sheet, however, are innumerable wrongs and evils crying out for remedy.

In England a broad field for reform is open, comprising the most important aims of civil and political society. . . . Something of what has been indicated [above] on this subject may serve as an example of the amount of work which is over and done with elsewhere and which still waits to be done in England. [291]

A large part of *The English Reform Bill* is taken up with the review of those abuses, which Hegel discusses under three main headings: the Anglican Church, the landlord's privileges, and Ireland (see [293–5], [297–300], 296–8]).

Hegel sees Britain differentiated into more sections than any other modern nation. Several distinct ethnic groups, a large number of trades and professions, an upper, middle, and lower economic class, and a host of particular autonomous authorities make up a complex and impressive web of national life. In other respects, however, Britain is not unique; the inequalities which exist within the country make it analogous to, for example, Wurtemberg. In both countries one class has acquired preponderance at the expense of just rights and legitimate interests of other classes. In Wurtemberg that class was the burgher aristocracy of writers, while in Britain it is the landed aristocracy, squirearchy, and the Established Church which, though a separate estate, is bound up with the landed interest politically, socially, and economically. Both cases are good instances of what in *The German Constitution* Hegel calls 'the exuberant growth of (one) part that (oppresses) other necessary parts'. Here, however, the analogy ends. Hegel blamed the Wurtemberg Ministry for its omission to intervene in order to further rational reforms, because he knew it had the necessary power and merely lacked foresight or courage. But in Britain it was neither the foresight nor the courage of the government that was lacking. The basic trouble in Britain was that the government lacked the necessary *power* to interfere since it depended on the support of a Parliament largely composed of deputies or spokesmen of the privileged class. Since he believed that the Reform Bill would not significantly alter the domination of that class, Hegel was naturally sceptical about the various reforms which the British had promised themselves from the Bill.

The other striking feature of Britain, which Hegel implies rather than states explicitly in *The English Reform Bill*, is the presence of a dynamic civil society within the British nation. When referring to one of the sections of a continental nation Hegel generally uses the term 'estate' (*Stand*), and hardly ever the term 'class' (*Klasse*) with its economic implications of income or wealth or the relations to the means of production. On the contrary, in *The English Reform Bill*—Hegel uses the term 'class' almost exclusively. He distinguishes 'the lower' class, which in England is extremely numerous [323], from the important middle class and (by implication) from the dominant upper class, comprising the aristocracy, the squires, and the Anglican clergy. The lower class consists apparently of labourers as well as tenants and domestic servants. Hegel repeatedly draws attention to the extremes of wealth and poverty in Britain; he also argues that the problem of alleviating misery has transcended the resources of civil society and might have been tackled by the supreme public authority long ago if it had been impartial. The widespread poverty among the lower classes seems, in Hegel's view, to make England a fertile ground for the abstract, revolutionary ideas of freedom, equality, popular sovereignty, and so on which have been mentioned before.

It is evident that Hegel's views on the limits of state activity undergo an evolution between *The German Constitution* and *The English Reform Bill*. At first he is prepared to see the scope of central government confined to external defence, internal security, and a general oversight of national life. At the end of the Napoleonic era he accepts the administration of justice, the provision of education, the support of religious institutions, and the care for the poor as legitimate functions of the central public authority. Towards the end of his life Hegel admits the necessity of considerable governmental interference with property relations in order to provide employment and subsistence to whole classes of the population. This change of view reflects to a large extent the changes in national life itself; clearly a slowly evolving complex of self-governing corporate bodies raises fewer problems and difficulties than a dynamic *bourgeois* society engaged in the production, distribution, and exchange of wealth.

Hegel is not dogmatic about the limits of state activity and he forgoes the laying down of any rigid and absolute principles in that sphere. He argues the value of autonomy in general, and leaves it to the conditions of a particular country to determine the exact amount of freedom. In the last resort it is a matter of expediency, the outcome of balancing the gain in efficiency, uniformity, and certainty with the loss in self-reliance, spontaneity, and diversity. But expediency, now as previously, does not exclude rationality. Central supervision of, and interference with, national life is called for because of three main tendencies: towards oligarchy, towards class domination, and towards pauperization, and each of them may be conceived as an infringement of equality. The principle of formal rationality also requires intervention since it demands 'purging of privileges and wrongs' and the transformation of a positive aggregate into a rational system. Finally, the requirements of the common good, the strength and stability of the public authority, set a limit to the freedom of civil society and autonomy in the national life. Hegel emphatically condemns anarchy, but equally emphatically he condemns the other extreme to which the notion of the common good has been pressed by some of his contemporaries—the complete bureaucratization of national life or 'statocracy' as a recent writer[1] has strikingly called it. All in all, the scope of free activity which an individual, a locality, or a sectional interest should enjoy in Hegel's view can stand comparison with that assigned to them by many liberal thinkers of the age.

[1] B. de Jouvenel in *Power: the Natural History of its Growth* (London, 1945).

V

THE PEOPLE AND THE STATE

Democracy, in the proper sense of the word, is of
necessity despotism.

IMMANUEL KANT, *Zum ewigen Frieden.*

In fact and in right the people is the highest power,
above which there is none, and it is the source of all
other power and responsible only to God.

J. G. FICHTE, *Grundlagen des Naturrechts.*

PERHAPS the greatest virtue of Hegel's political writing consists in their non-technical language and common-sense
argumentation. Another, closely related, merit lies in the
wealth of all kinds of concrete details and historical references with
which he supports and illustrates his more theoretical points. The
question how far and in what form the nation (people or population) of a country should participate in its central government
seems to have offered particularly ample scope to Hegel's empirical interest and talent. And yet, paradoxically, it is precisely
here that he plumbs depths of mysticism rare among political
thinkers, and in a few bold sentences anticipates his future speculative philosophy of history.

The German Constitution, among its many reflections on history,
includes a sketch of the evolution of the central political power in
modern European states. Hegel maintains that such a power did
not exist as a separate, established institution in the early states
founded by the Germanic tribes. However, the evolution of a
'third estate' of burghers and the necessity of a division of labour
gradually concentrated the management of common affairs in 'a
centre consisting of the monarch and the Estates' [92, 93]. This
is the origin of representation which, as a system of government,
'marks an epoch in world history' and forms a 'middle-term'
between the despotism of the Orientals and the republic of the
Greeks and Romans. 'The Germans are the people from whom
this third universal form of world spirit was born' [93].

Nobody can accuse Hegel of under-estimating the significance of
representation in this early political work. He regards it as something

so fundamental that a whole new epoch of world history derives
its character from it. He sees the germ of the institution in the
primeval right of every free man among the ancient Teutons
(of whom, he implies, Germans are the most direct descendants)
personally to participate in the public affairs of his people. The
modern European nations have lost their primitive equality and
homogeneity and have become differentiated into subordinate communities, associations, and classes. While some of these (e.g. nobility
and clergy) are small enough to make personal participation of their
members in the supreme public authority possible, 'the numerically
preponderant part of freemen, the estate of burghers', is too large
for that and has to be represented by deputies. But the representative principle is also implicit in the relationship of lord and vassal
or suzerain and feudatory [94]. Hence Hegel sees the origin of
representation in the feudal system, its development, and the rise
of an estate of burghers [96].

The strength of Hegel's conviction that popular participation in
the supreme public authority through a system of representation
is a necessary feature of the constitutional structure of the modern
state is illustrated by another passage in *The German Constitution*.
He argues that, as a result of the French Revolution, mankind has
learned a lesson about freedom and become immune to demagogic
slogans. On the other hand the lesson has also been learned that
despotic government is untenable. Freedom has acquired the 'concrete' meaning of popular participation in government through a
representative body (see [128–9]).

In *The Wurtemberg Estates* Hegel makes a similar appeal to
enlightened public opinion except that he links representation
with the concept of the monarchical state, not just the modern
European state in general. But the difference is less important than
it appears, for, in his view, monarchy and a representative body are
both indispensable parts of the modern supreme public authority.
The state which has a strong executive without a representative
body has 'force' but no 'will', an external but not an internal
constitution. The King of Wurtemberg had summoned a representative assembly in the fulfilment of an earlier promise, but
something more than that was at stake.

. . . A necessity higher than that lying in the positive bond of a
promise lies in the nature of the concepts which have arisen to become
a universal conviction and which attach to monarchy, as essential

characteristics, the formation of a representative constitution, the rule of law (*eines gesetzmässigen Zustandes*), and popular influence on legislation.—Frederick II [of Wurtemberg] now took this second step as well, the step of fashioning the monarchical state *internally*. [161]

A little farther on Hegel adds:

There surely cannot be a greater secular spectacle on earth than that of a monarch's adding to the public authority, which *ab initio* is entirely in his hands, another foundation, indeed *the* foundation, by bringing his people into it as an essentially effective ingredient. [163]

Finally, in *The English Reform Bill* we find a passage which shows that, even at the end of his life, Hegel's ideas on representation had not undergone a substantial change.

. . . It is in this right [to elect Members of Parliament] that there lies the right of the people to participate in public affairs and in the highest interests of the state and government. The exercise of this right is a lofty duty, because there rests on it the constituting of an essential part of the public authority, i.e. the representative assembly, because indeed this right and its exercise is, as the French say, the act, the sole act, of the 'sovereignty of the people'. [309]

Besides showing the persistence of Hegel's belief in representation, the passages give us also a partial insight into why he regards it as necessary and desirable. We have seen that he views representation as an essential part of the traditional structure of the supreme public authority, the result of a development with roots going back to the ancient Germanic community. But to accept tradition without any further reason would clearly be contrary to his fundamental attitude to politics. On examination a double justification of representation seems to emerge: from the standpoint of the nation and the standpoint of the public authority itself. For the nation it is the guarantee that the government is conducted according to law and that the general will co-operates in the most important affairs concerning the general interest [128]. 'The formation of a representative constitution, the rule of law and popular influence on legislation' [161] are organically bound up with and mutually support one another. The existence of representative institutions ensures that law is not merely the will of the monarch, but also the general will, or, in other words, that the nation shares in the deliberation on, and the determination of, the requirements of the common good.

But for the very same reason a system of national representation is of advantage to the central government itself. Hegel is profoundly convinced that a modern state, in normal circumstances,[1] cannot be based on force alone. The government, as the central point of public authority, is inherently insecure as long as the nation is not associated with its operation. This seems to be the reason why Hegel calls the establishment of a representative system in Wurtemberg the internal creation of the state and why he says that bringing the people in as 'an essentially effective ingredient' of the public authority adds 'another foundation—indeed *the* foundation' to the monarch's power [163].

It is characteristic that Hegel often stresses the intensity of national pride in England and points out that taxes—one of the chief sacrifices which the government demands from the population—are particularly high in that country because of representative institutions. The practical absence of any link between the mass of the German people as represented by provincial estates and their nominally supreme authority, the Emperor and the Imperial Diet, is in Hegel's view the basic cause of the unpatriotic attitude of most Germans to the Empire.

For it lies deep in human nature to interest oneself only in something for which one acts, something with which one can co-operate in resolve and deed, something into which one can put one's will. [132]

The re-creation of an effective supreme public authority in Germany, like the foundation of a sovereign Wurtemberg state, could come about only by Machiavellian means of force and cunning. But, as in Wurtemberg, the task would have to be completed by the addition of a machinery for free consent and voluntary co-operation (see [135]).

Before passing on to the question *how*, in Hegel's view, the nation should be represented, we may pause to note a parallelism between this and the previous chapter. In that chapter Hegel was shown to be a believer in an unregimented society; in this he can be seen to believe in a government subject to popular influence and co-operation. However, in both cases he takes a moderate position. Previously we saw him arguing against both extreme centralization and feudal anarchy; now we find him rejecting direct popular participation in government as well as condemning the absence of

[1] See below, Chapter VII.

any popular influence. The concept of the nation composed not of individuals but of subordinate areas and authorities was a traditional one, and while Hegel accepted it, he also urged that the underlying reality should be subjected to rational re-examination and reform. Similarly now we find Hegel rejecting the idea of representation based on equal, individual suffrage and numerical geographical constituencies in favour of the traditional idea of representation by sectional interests, occupational groups or estates, but at the same time stressing the necessity of rational revision of the existing positive representative institutions.

Hegel's preoccupation with the best representative system goes back to his earliest writings, namely to *Wurtemberg's Domestic Affairs*.[1] In this work Hegel severely criticizes the arrangement according to which the members of the Provincial Diet of Wurtemberg were appointed by various town councils, which themselves were filled by co-optation, and advocates the popular election of the councils. So much is evident from the original title of the work, viz. 'Town councillors ought to be elected by the people' (later altered to 'citizens'), and from the dedication of the pamphlet 'To the people of Wurtemberg'. But the democratic character of the pamphlet should not be exaggerated. Hegel not only accepts the indirect election of the Provincial Diet through the reformed town councils; he asks whether it is safe, even to this limited extent, to enfranchise 'an unenlightened multitude, used to blind obedience [towards the prince] and dependent on the impressions of the moment'.[2] In other words Hegel doubts whether the two stages of the electoral process are a sufficient bulwark against the ignorance and selfishness of the multitude, and he concludes on a note of deep pessimism.

The essential thing is to place suffrage in the hands of a corps of enlightened and honest men, independent of the court. But I do not see what method of election could guarantee such an electoral assembly, no matter how carefully the active and the passive voting qualifications were determined.

The German Constitution is not very specific on the subject. In one passage, where the evolution of representative institutions is

[1] The fourth of the *Confidential Letters* condemns the fact that legislative and taxing powers over Vaud are exercised by the city council of Berne and not by a body representing the people of the canton, but offers no specfic reform proposals.

[2] Haym, op. cit., p. 67. The next quotation is from the same work, p. 66.

discussed, Hegel talks of the three estates of clergy, nobility, and the burghers, only the last of which is represented by deputies. One would expect Hegel to advocate the indirect representation of the burghers through the existing town councils, perhaps themselves made elective, but, oddly enough, a different scheme is in fact put forward, which, vague though it is, implies direct election (see [133, 134]).

The three early works give us relatively less insight into this part of Hegel's political thought than *The Wurtemberg Estates*. Here Hegel discusses at length the principles of the representative system laid down in the Royal Charter. He shows himself extremely critical of the proposal that the non-hereditary and non-official members of the Diet should be elected by all male citizens over twenty-five years of age, owning a certain minimum of property. Such an arrangement, he maintains, 'has more in common with the democratic, even anarchical principle of separatism than with that of an organic order'. It turns electoral assemblies into 'unordered inorganic aggregates'; 'the people as a whole is dissolved into a heap' [175–6]. Hegel grants that the fabric of German society contained much unpromising material for the establishment of a scheme of indirect and functional representation, but he argues that it was wrong to ignore it completely. Both from the standpoint of the state and that of the people, the proper way of organizing a new representative system was to reform the old guilds, corporations, estates, and associations, purge them of privileges and wrongs, and make them elements of the political structure of the state.

A living inter-relationship exists only in an articulated whole whose parts themselves form particular subordinate spheres. But, if this is to be achieved, the French abstractions of mere numbers and quanta of property must be finally discarded, or at any rate must no longer be made the dominant qualification or made all over again the sole condition for exercising one of the most important political functions. Atomistic principles of that sort spell, in science as in politics, death to every rational concept, organization, and life. [177]

His opposition to voting qualifications based on age, property, and residence is, however, not extreme as he admits that they have their legitimate place at a lower level of political organization, in determining the conditions of membership of various local and sectional bodies which serve as electoral colleges (see [178]).

In this part of the work Hegel is concerned not only with a proper representation of the nation in the Diet but also with the presence there of members possessing the necessary ability to govern, since the Diet is part of the public authority of a country. He believes that the system he is advocating does in fact secure both ends—good national representation and the selection of able deputies—but at the moment we are primarily interested in the former.[1] Quite clearly what underlies his concept of representation is the concept of a nation organically articulated into a number of smaller groups, not the different concept of a civil society consisting of a multitude of individuals. In actual fact even civil society is not a wholly 'atomistic' condition, but 'a civic order'. Each burgher is an inhabitant of a particular city or commune; he has a certain trade or profession; he may be a member of a guild or corporation. These social factors, which determine men's interests and opinions, should be fully recognized and allowed for in the representative system. It is true, of course, that a system of direct election in numerical constituencies will tend to reflect the social structure of the population and that sectional interests will play a certain role and express themselves indirectly. But this, Hegel points out, like the other objective of securing able deputies, thus becomes a matter of chance, accident, and caprice, and he condemns it on the ground of irrationality (see [179]). Hegel is a little vague in his positive suggestions about how the representative system in Wurtemberg could be improved, but it seems that he would retain the principle of direct election only within the smaller corporate bodies composing civil society, and vest parliamentary suffrage primarily in their councils and officials.[2]

In *The English Reform Bill* we find the same double emphasis on indirect representation and the representation of interests, and on the necessity of providing institutions consciously and deliberately designed to facilitate it. Hegel notices that the chief consideration in English parliamentary debates on the reform of the franchise has generally been the representation of great social interests rather than of individuals as such. This system is the old, traditional one and is 'opposed to the modern principle in accordance with which

---

[1] Hegel's distinction between 'representative' and 'governmental' functions of a legislative assembly bears some resemblance to that made by J. S. Mill in Chapter V of *Representative Government*.

[2] Hegel visualizes the rest of the nation being represented by certain hereditary nobles and *ex officio* members.

only the abstract will of individuals as such is to be represented'
[304]. He grants that the existing system is tolerable, as the rotten
boroughs serve as a channel through which new and formally un-
recognized interests in fact acquire representation. It is the
irrationality of the method which he criticizes (see [304–5]). He is
also aware that the system as it exists, e.g. in Britain and Sweden,
cannot be wholly justified, since it no longer corresponds to the
actual condition of those states. But, instead of the destruction of
the positive, he suggests a thorough revision and re-examination
in order to make it more rational. Hegel goes on to point out that
the measures proposed in the Reform Bill in fact depart from his
own suggestions. The Bill represents a partial concession to the
'individualist' principle since it fixes a general property qualification for voters.

In fact the Bill is a hotchpotch of the old privileges and the general
principle of the equal entitlement of all citizens (except for the external
limitation of a freehold of £10) to vote for those by whom they are to
be represented. Thus the Bill contains an internal contradiction between positive rights and an abstract and theoretical principle. Therefore the illogicality of what is derived from the basis of the old feudal
law is shown up in a cruder light than if all entitlements to voting had
been put on one and the same footing of positive rights. [306]

Nevertheless, though the Bill seems imperfect to Hegel from
many points of view, he welcomes it on the ground of justice,
believing that it will remove the most glaring inequalities between
localities. But another serious defect of the existing representative
system seems to him less affected by the reform. A large proportion
of seats are controlled directly or indirectly by the landed aristocracy
and gentry, and a further proportion is purchasable by the wealthy.
Thus 'the democratic element, which in the English constitution
has an important sphere in the people's participation in the election
of members of the Lower House' [286] is overshadowed by the
aristocratic. Hegel again agrees that the Bill will do something to
modify the domination of the landowning class over the rest of the
nation, at least in respect of representation, but he is sceptical as
to the extent of change. He thinks that even after the reform the
real power will remain in the hands of the privileged aristocracy
and squirearchy.

Hegel is thus aware that a rational, thorough-going reform of
the representative system cannot limit itself to the establishment

of formally equal suffrage among 'the different classes and divisions of the people'. As long as there are sections of the population which are privileged and powerful the system will continue to be biased in their favour and the nation will not be fairly represented. Already in *The Wurtemberg Estates* Hegel pointed out that truth. This realistic point of view, reminiscent of Rousseau and strikingly anticipating the later Marxist strictures of *bourgeois* representative institutions, certainly does credit to Hegel. On the other hand Hegel glosses over or does not seem to be aware of the practical difficulties inherent in any scheme of functional representation. Questions such as what interests should be represented, how many seats they should have, and so on, are highly controversial.

That Hegel's idea of representation would not be called democratic today is perhaps too obvious a point to make. And yet it would be wrong to regard him as being opposed to democracy in any sense. On the contrary, he may be said to welcome popular influence as long as it forms only one element of the constitutional structure of the modern state, or, in other words, as long as the constitution as a whole is not based on the principle of democracy. Democracy in the ancient and literal sense of the word Hegel believes to have been possible in the small city state of Greece or Rome or the primitive Germanic warrior-community; this is why he generally uses it together with some such adjective as 'formless' or 'crude'. In *The German Constitution* he says that 'a democratic constitution like the one Theseus gave to his own people is self-contradictory in modern times and large states' [135]. The modern democratic institutions of constitutional and legislative referenda get an equally short shrift from Hegel. The former he at least thinks worth considering even if in the end both theory and practice convince him that 'nobody can have less skill to make the constitution than the so-called people'.[1] The latter—ordinary

---

[1] Cf. the following passage from *The Wurtemberg Estates*: 'It seems not only a fair but also an absolutely just demand that the people should examine the constitution it receives, and that nothing can give it validity except the people's acceptance of it with their whole will and insight. If it were not so, one could add, despotism, tyranny, and infamy could put any chains it liked on the people. And yet, to look at the thing from no other side than that of experience, two points may be invoked. First, the peoples themselves, indeed the most liberal (*freisinnigste*) among them, have recognized their lack of ability to give themselves a constitution and have entrusted the task to a *Solon* or a *Lycurgus*, who used cunning to overcome the so-called will of the people and the declaration of its will on the matter of constitution. Secondly, men like *Moses* or *Louis XVIII*

legislative referendum—he dismisses as an aberration of the revolutionary period in France (see [310–11]). Only democracy in a third and still more attenuated form—wide suffrage and direct elections to the central legislative assembly—seems to Hegel to have sufficient plausibility to be dangerous, and to be worth refuting at length. These practical arguments based on expediency supplement the case against the principle of individual representation to which Hegel opposed the concept of representation by estates and corporations.

It is worth stating at the outset that Hegel never contemplates extending suffrage farther than the urban middle class or burghers, and when he talks of 'the people' in this connexion it is this class that he has mainly in mind. He would probably consider small rural landowners and independent peasant proprietors, at least those with holdings of a certain size, to belong to the same category. But he never entertains the idea that the classes below them, e.g. domestic servants, industrial proletariat, tenants-at-will, agricultural labourers, and so on, have any claims to be represented separately. In Hegel's opinion democracy, or excessive democracy, means direct election by the middle classes on the basis of equal individual suffrage with at most a certain age and a property qualification.

Three separate, though interconnected, lines of argument against democracy in this sense can be distinguished in his political writings. The first applies to Germany where the mass of the people has for centuries lived in what he calls 'political nullity' (*politische Nullität*), i.e. without any direct contact with, and consequently experience of, central state government and its problems. To make a legislative assembly *directly* elected by a multitude suffering from an *incivisme* due to age-long political impotence, might have all sorts of disastrous practical consequences for the state. This is the danger of which Hegel is particularly acutely aware in *The Wurtemberg Estates* though there are hints that it preoccupied him already in the first work on Wurtemberg. This situation Hegel

granted a constitution *by themselves*, and based its validity not on the will of the people but on divine or royal authority. . . . The result of experience is easily confirmed by insight into the nature of the thing, namely that nobody can have less skill to make the constitution than the so-called people or the Assembly of its Estates, quite apart from the fact that the existence of the people and an Estates Assembly already presupposes a constitution, an organic condition, an ordered popular life.' [219–20] specifically contrasts with that of the English nation where 'the sense of national honour has permeated the different social classes more generally' [182].

The second ground on which Hegel condemns democratic suffrage is the general ignorance, lack of political education, and irresponsibility characteristic of most contemporary countries. In *The Wurtemberg Estates* Hegel is critical of any references to 'the people' in the deliberations of the Estates Assembly and writes on one occasion:

In this case the Assembly should all the more have left the people and its existing opinions out of it because of the prevailing conditions of disquiet in France, because of the usual lack of understanding of the so-called people when it comes to speak about public affairs, even if it wills the best, still more because of the novelty of its position and the natural lack of concepts about a state constitution in a people which has never had the thing, and finally because of the [sudden] transition from its political nullity into a still unknown participation in and influence on the whole of the state. [223]

This 'lack of understanding of public affairs and the natural lack of [true] concepts' showed itself in Wurtemberg chiefly in wide popular support for the restoration of the outdated, pre-revolutionary constitution. In England, on the other hand, the popular misconception that franchise is property lies at the root of widespread electoral corruption and irresponsibility (see [309]).

In France, Hegel believes, popular political ignorance finds its chief expression in the circulation of abstract 'universal notions of freedom, equality, the people, its sovereignty. &c.', and also of the 'abstractions of mere number and a quantity of property', which are thought to be the only qualifications for suffrage. This exposes France to the activities of all sorts of demagogues and doctrinaires, and leads to periodical popular restlessness, disturbances, and revolutions.

The third main argument, which Hegel puts forward against the introduction of such suffrage, is electoral apathy and indifference to voting. The value of one's vote, he believes, varies inversely with the size of the electorate one belongs to, and in a large geographical constituency (as opposed to one's local authority or professional organization) it becomes so small that one is easily tempted not to use the vote at all. Moreover, elections are usually infrequent and absorb one's interest occasionally, while the membership of some local or professional body which meets, deliberates, and decides fairly often develops one's permanent interest and capacity for political activity. It is therefore better to have two stages in election instead of one, and to associate the people only with the former since the vote will mean more to them and be exercised with greater intelligence and zeal.

Already in *The Wurtemberg Estates* we find Hegel discussing the topic of electoral apathy and stressing the insignificance of one vote among many hundreds or thousands (see [177–8]). It must have greatly puzzled Hegel why voters are so indifferent to suffrage since almost one-tenth of *The English Reform Bill* is concerned with the question. He even toys with the idea of a statistical inquiry into the relative levels of absenteeism in central and local elections to see what light they throw on the matter [311].

We are offered a new explanation of the phenomenon, not in terms of the number of voters or the kind of issues, but of the attitude towards the function of voting. In the sphere of elections Hegel sees the same influence at work that he has seen in other areas of contemporary political life, namely individual freedom conceived abstractly as caprice, arbitrariness, or 'sovereignty of the will'. This feeling of irresponsibility militates against both taking seriously the duty to vote and exercising this important political function with circumspection and patriotism. Strangely enough instead of condemning this attitude as contradicting the true concept of political obligation, Hegel prefers to use it as an argument against a wider individual suffrage and direct election. Having criticized the English people for so many political defects, Hegel makes a volte-face and praises them for their sound common sense of which electoral apathy is but one expression (see [312]).

The dangers of wide direct franchise were often perceived by Hegel's contemporaries; they were obviously much more real and serious in his own time than in ours. There was no sustained and organized party activity among the electorate to stimulate the latter's interest, to clarify political issues, and to simplify political decisions. Afraid of an uneducated and unorganized mass electorate, Hegel sought both to restrict it in number and to filter its influence through the existing institutions of local and professional self-government. He did not consider the counter arguments, which have often been used since the spread of party politics to local government, namely that they tend to subordinate and ultimately to sacrifice local to national interests, and to make local institutions an appendage of national government. If one remembers how much the preservation of civic autonomy mattered to Hegel, one may doubt whether he would have been happy about such results. One cannot help feeling, too, that Hegel was over-pessimistic about the political capacity of the electorate. Though he realized and admitted the fact, he failed to allow sufficiently for the educational effect of suffrage and elections. He may have also under-estimated the masses usual conservatism, which in most cases prevents sudden and frequent political fluctuations. Perhaps he was unduly influenced by the peculiar circumstances of France and Germany—in the former the revolutionary aftermath of 1789 and in the latter the long-standing exclusion of the middle class from any participation in politics. It is at any rate certain that he exempted Britain from some of his criticism and specifically ascribed the practical political sense of the British to their civic liberty.

But though preoccupied with the dangers of popular influence when exercised through the wrong kind of channels, and though severe on the ideas and institutions we nowadays identify with democracy, Hegel nowhere abandons the principle of popular influence itself. Within what he calls the people or civil society that influence is paramount and primary since the people actually administer or control local and sectional affairs. Within the state proper, i.e. the sphere of national, central government, the people's influence is not so decisive, but it none the less makes itself felt through the electoral system and representative institutions. Hegel is admittedly concerned to limit that influence, but he does so on grounds of expediency rather than principle and of temporary rather than permanent necessity. His views do not exclude the possibility that one day, with a higher level of general and political education and a more highly articulated society, the people may rightly acquire a degree of political importance in national affairs far greater than could be contemplated in his own time.

VI

THE ASSEMBLY OF ESTATES

The Constitution of this country [i.e. Britain] is a
monarchy, modified by the co-ordinate authority of
Estates of the Realm. An Estate is a political order
invested with privilege for a public purpose.

BENJAMIN DISRAELI.

'ESTATE', as a name of a class of men, sounds quaint and antiquated in English, and (*pace* Disraeli) this may have been so already in Hegel's time. *Stand*, its German equivalent, however, is still a living word. Its most general connotation is that of a place, position, or standing. A second, closely related, sense is that of a group or class of men having a similar profession or occupation or enjoying the same legal, economic, or social status; this is the sense in which the term has normally been used in the preceding chapters. When the word is used in the plural and in combination with the word 'assembly' (*Ständeversammlung*) or 'country' (*Landstände*) or 'realm' (*Reichsstände*), it denotes a representative body—a part of what Hegel calls the supreme state power or public authority (*Staatsgewalt*). Although the Estates in this sense are something different from the various groups within the nation, the etymological affinity is significant. Not only does it suggest that there must have been a close connexion between the two in the past, but it also makes it plausible to believe that the connexion is still valid and important, and that (social) estates should be the ground and basis of representation in the (political) Estates of the Realm.

The term 'Assembly of Estates' could in Hegel's time often be met as the official title of various German representative bodies, just as 'Parliament' or 'National Assembly' were the official names of their British or French counterparts. Hegel, however, tends to use it as a general term covering similar bodies in all countries, although occasionally he replaces it by 'representative assembly', 'diet', or even 'legislature' and 'legislative assembly'. But the last two terms are infrequent, probably because they give a wrong impression of the character of such bodies. It is an important element in Hegel's political thought (1) that representative bodies *share* legislative power with the monarch, and (2) that they vote taxes just as much as they vote laws.

Two passages in *The German Constitution* show clearly what Hegel's view of the nature of the Assembly of Estates is. Owing to a number of historical causes, he writes, in Europe

the management of national affairs became more and more closely concentrated in a centre consisting of the monarch and of the Estates, i.e. of one part of the nation consisting of (*a*) the nobility and the clergy speaking personally in discussion on their own account, and (*b*) the third Estate, [speaking] as representative of the rest of the people. The monarch manages national affairs, especially in so far as they concern foreign relations with other states; he is the centre of the state's power; from him everything issues which requires legal compulsion. The legal power is thus in his hands; the Estates participate in legislation and they pass the budget which supports the state's power. [93]

In another passage Hegel specifies the function of the Estates Assembly from the standpoint of the people.

The guarantee that the government will proceed in accordance with law, and the co-operation of the general will in the most important affairs of state which affect everyone, the people finds in the organization of a body representative of the people. This body has to sanction payment to the monarch of a part of the national taxes, but especially the payment of extraordinary taxes. Just as in former days the most important matter, i.e. personal services, depended on free agreement, so nowadays money, which comprises influence of every other kind, is equally so dependent.

Without such a representative body, freedom is no longer thinkable. Once freedom is so defined, all vague ideas vanish, along with all the emptiness of the clamour for freedom. This notion of freedom is not something, like a scientific concept, which individuals come to know by learning; on the contrary it is a fundamental principle in public opinion; it has become part of sound common sense. [128]

It is obvious that the Estates in Hegel's view are an essential partner of the monarch in the conduct of the government of the country. Although the monarch may have the last word before enactment, they must give their consent to bills; in this sense they 'participate in legislation' and 'share in the making of laws'. Similarly, although the monarch conducts foreign relations and ultimately controls the whole governmental machinery, the Estates Assembly provides the funds for the carrying on of government. These take the form of taxes, especially taxes to cover extraordinary war-time expenditure; in peace-time the narrow scope of governmental activities envisaged by Hegel may make other sources of public revenue (e.g. from royal domains) almost sufficient.[1] By consenting to taxes the Estates provide the means 'which support the public authority', and the grant of money, 'which comprises influence of every other kind', is thus made dependent on 'the free agreement' between the representatives of the nation and the king.

If one goes beyond the powers of the Estates Assembly and asks what its purpose is, Hegel's answer is that it is a guarantee of freedom and an organ of the general will. Without such an assembly the government could impose restrictions on property or on traditional liberties, which had no justification from the point of view of either justice or the common good, and which might be merely arbitrary fiats of the King or his officials. Hegel explicitly condemns Prussian arbitrariness in matters of taxation and rejects the possibility of Prussia's leading the rest of Germany towards free unity (cf. [129]).

His theory of safeguarding freedom, however, is not a theory of checks and balances. If some such checking has to take place, its purpose is not to oppose the arbitrary power of one institution to that of another. The role of the Assembly of Estates is to enlighten the government about the nation's attitudes and desires, and at the same time to be enlightened by the government about the state's requirements. The rational concept of the Assembly is thus that of a meeting-ground between the general and the particular interests of the country, where each can state and argue its own case and where, after deliberation, a mutually acceptable decision is reached. The Estates and the government are not antagonistic bodies; they are complementary organs of one and the same body politic.

In the second of the two passages quoted above Hegel expresses this in terms of the general will. The existence of a representative assembly, he writes, ensures 'the co-operation of the general will in the most important affairs of state which affect everyone' [128]. By this he does not mean that the actual will of the people or the

---

[1] But never *wholly* sufficient. Cf. [23–24].

nation always constitutes the general will; this, for him as for
Rousseau, is something reasonable or rational, a will enlightened
about, and guided by the desire for, the general interest. The
existence of an Assembly of Estates merely guarantees that the
nation, through its representatives, shall participate in the formation of such a general will; the Assembly's financial and legislative
powers are a necessary safeguard that the nation will be duly consulted. But though Hegel accepts Rousseau's concept of the general
will, he differs from him profoundly about the process of its formation or emergence. For Hegel the 'people' are not the only or even
the main channel of the general will. On the contrary, the general
will, as the rational deliberation and decision on matters of public
concern, has several different organs or stages. Its formation begins
with the nation divided into various localities and sections, who,
through the system of indirect representation discussed in the last
chapter, elect an Assembly of Estates. From the other end the
king's ministers and officials contribute their knowledge, experience, and professional concern for the public interest. The Estates,
mirroring the diversity of particular interests in the country, may
be hostile or indifferent to the government's demands. The latter,
based on theoretical perfectionism or an exaggerated national pride,
may be harsh and excessive. By a process of give and take, an
agreed policy eventually emerges; the general interest becomes
'concrete' instead of abstract. The final step in the process is the
signature of the monarch which enacts a bill or a budget and con-
verts the general will of the nation into the official will of the state.

The Wurtemberg Estates does not contain a systematic, theoretical
justification of a representative assembly and its powers. Hegel
takes the necessity of representation in a monarchical state for
granted and regards the summoning of the Wurtemberg Estates
as the completion of the internal structure of the state. He calls it
the incorporation of the Estates into the organism of the state and
the bringing to life of the *will* in addition to the *power* of the state
(cf. [186] and [160, 161]). The work nevertheless contains some
valuable illustrations of theoretical points and throws light on the
conditions which produce a wise and responsible Estates Assembly.

It would be a mistake to expect the Wurtemberg Diet of 1815
to resemble a contemporary representative assembly at all closely.
In some respects it bore the marks of pre-revolutionary native
institutions; in others it followed the pattern of the various

Napoleonic assemblies. By our standards the Diet seems to have been only moderately powerful and not very representative, but Hegel, who remembered the long period of absolutism and semi-absolutism in his native land, hailed its powers with enthusiasm.

> The infinite importance and liberality of the rights . . . conceded to the Estates and likewise the simplicity and straightforwardness of these provisions, examined impartially and without regard to anything except their content, undoubtedly do the greatest honour to the Prince who gave them and to the age in which constitutional law has been purged of privileges and matured into [a set of] principles. [166]

He himself summarizes them fully and a further summary seems superfluous (cf. [164–5]). Let us hence examine what Hegel's own comments are, grouping his remarks under the headings of (1) taxation, (2) legislation, and (3) administration.

(1) The first point to notice about taxation is that Hegel does not expect the Assembly of Estates to provide the whole of the public revenue. A part of it, admittedly progressively decreasing, will come from sources which are under the direct control of the government. Thus for a time, and particularly in periods of peace, the government enjoys a certain financial independence of the Estates, which Hegel not only approves but regards as a positive advantage. Moreover, even when taxes are unavoidable, he does not believe that all of them must be consented to annually. A certain established level and variety of taxes may safely be conceded to the government, as long as 'extraordinary' taxes to meet particular emergencies or a permanent increase in the existing level are subject to the Estates' approval. This limitation on the power of the Estates seems to Hegel a useful and legitimate safeguard of a measure of executive independence, and later on he was to show regret that the British Crown had lost all vestige of such financial autonomy (see [319]). The independent sources of revenue, and expedients to fix the height of taxes, to some extent weaken the financial power of the Estates but do not undermine it. Particularly in war-time, and increasingly in all the other spheres, the Wurtemberg Estates were bound to exert great influence on the government.

One must remember that the whole discussion of the powers of the Wurtemberg Estates takes place against the peculiar historical background of Hegel's country, and that his conclusions are not necessarily valid for other countries, least of all Britain.[1] Hegel maintains that the previous German Provincial Diets tended to leave foreign policy to the Princes and the Emperor, and to adopt what he calls a policy of 'passive neutrality', devoid of decision, action, and pride. Some Diets went further and took advantage of temporary difficulties to extort concessions which led to the permanent weakening of the government. The result was universal 'political nullity', an engrossment in private affairs, and an indifference towards any idea of national honour. But, while in the former Empire the Princes could at least appeal to the Emperor, in the new condition of sovereignty such safeguards have completely fallen away. The taxing power has thus acquired a new and tremendous importance.

The right of participating in fixing public taxation, whatever its form in the past, is now, when the Estates have no superior except the government of their state, which they confront on equal terms, inherently an infinitely higher and more independent sphere of authority than it was before. It has given them a connexion with and an influence on war and peace, on foreign politics generally, and on political life at home. [182]

(2) In his political writings Hegel stresses that legislative power must not be regarded as belonging solely to the Assembly of Estates. In the last resort it belongs rather to the monarch, since his signature is necessary for the enactment of any bill; the Estates, however, should share in this power. *The Wurtemberg Estates* illustrates how the power may in fact be divided between the two: the Estates had the right of consenting to new general statutes and could submit legislative proposals, the king had the right of initiating and promulgating statutes and consenting to the bills proposed by the Estates. Hegel believes that the amount of control over legislation which the Estates possessed was sufficient to achieve 'the rule of law and the influence of the nation on legislation' which characterize a true monarchy.

(3) The third group of rights granted to the Wurtemberg Diet by the Royal Charter concerned administration. They comprised

---

[1] Hegel had always been impressed with the high level of taxes in Britain. It will be remembered that in *Confidential Letters* he took Cart to task for equating low taxes with good government, and used the example of Britain to prove that the freest country could also be the most highly taxed. The connexion between political liberty and high taxation is mentioned again in *The English Reform Bill*. Cf. [292-3].

the rights of making suggestions, lodging complaints, and calling civil servants to account. Since the Charter permitted ministers to be present in the Diet, it is possible that it also implicitly granted the right of questioning the political heads of departments. In any case the monarch and his government could not easily ignore the pressure of the Assembly for changes in the administration, exercised through those rights, since the Assembly could retaliate by refusing to co-operate in fiscal and legislative matters, and thus hamper the conduct of the government.

One would have thought that from this position there was only a short step to the doctrine of parliamentary responsibility of the government, but Hegel refuses to take this step. One could say that he favours the Assembly of Estates having as much *influence* as possible on the government; he is resolutely opposed to the influence becoming a *control*. In *The Wurtemberg Estates* this attitude is still largely implicit, but it becomes explicit in *The English Reform Bill.* Here Hegel makes the point that the constitutional right of the monarch to appoint Ministers, civil servants, and other officials is a formality because the substance of power lies elsewhere.

> To the power of the Crown [in England] there belong the most important branches of the supreme control of the state. . . . Yet it is to Parliament that there belongs the sovereign decision on the budget (including even the sum allowed for the maintenance of the King and his family), i.e. on the entire range of the means for making war and peace and having an army, ambassadors, &c. Moreover, a Ministry can only govern, i.e. exist, in so far as it falls in with the views and the will of Parliament. [313–14]

For reasons to be discussed in the next chapter, Hegel strongly deplores the passing of all effective power from the British king to Parliament, and the elimination of all his influence on legislation.

We have noticed before that Hegel tends to be rather critical towards contemporary political innovations. On issues such as centralization, representation, and the electoral system he consistently defends the more traditional institutions. His insistence that the proper function of the Assembly of Estates is deliberative, that it may influence but must not control the government, and that the latter should be dependent on the head of the state are all further instances of this traditionalism. We shall now briefly examine some of the consequences which follow from the deliberative character of the representative body.

The most unexpected of these is Hegel's strong defence of political parties. By parties, of course, he means groups of politicians within the representative body, not the modern mass organizations of the electorate, though he is aware of the popular type of party activity.[1] The first reference to parliamentary parties occurs in *The Wurtemberg Estates*. The Estates refused even to discuss the Royal Constitution and, in order to exert all the more pressure on the king, the Assembly aimed at complete unanimity. Hegel comments ironically that the Estates should have not only allowed dissent but even appointed an *advocatus diaboli* to challenge their own tacit decision to oppose the Royal Charter root and branch.

> Whoever has reflected a little on the nature of an Assembly of Estates and is familiar with its manifestations cannot fail to see that without an opposition such an assembly is without outer and inner life. It is precisely this antagonism within it that forms its *essence* and *justification*, and it is only when it has engendered an opposition within itself that it is properly constituted. Without it it has the appearance of only *one party* or of just a clump. [205–6]

In his opinion, then, the division of an Assembly of Estates into a pro-government party and a party of opposition is an essential precondition of deliberation, and the latter is fruitful and successful only when it takes the form of a debate between rival and conflicting viewpoints.

Closely connected with the last point is a belief, implied rather than stated by Hegel, that party opposition is fruitful only when it is an opposition *within* an accepted framework of ideas and institutions. The opposition of the Wurtemberg Estates was a total one; they did not question this or that part but rejected the whole of the constitutional system proposed by the king; consequently, it was difficult to find any ground for compromise or reconciliation. In another part of *The Wurtemberg Estates* Hegel illustrates this point by reference to Britain, where party strife and opposition were particularly fierce and where they even transcended the

---

[1] In *The English Reform Bill* Hegel mentions a recent election in Paris, 'where the parties seem to have shown no lack of zeal in summoning the electors to cast their votes'. On the same page he writes: 'In the earlier years of the French Revolution the zeal and the behaviour of the Jacobins at elections disgusted peaceful and decent citizens and even made it dangerous for them to cast their votes. So faction alone held the field' [311].

immediate purpose of parliamentary debate, i.e. deliberation, and yet remained fully within the bounds of a common ground and hence were beneficial.

It is a mark of the uneducated to regard the English opposition as a party against the government or against the ministry *as such*; even if the opposition does not limit its attack to individual ministerial measures only (as happens with the independent members, though otherwise they vote as a rule with the ministry) but fights the ministry at any and every point, still the fight is only against *this* single ministry, not against any and every ministry or against the government as such. What it is often charged with, as if with something bad, namely that all it wants is to form a ministry itself, is in fact its greatest justification. [170]

Hegel implies here that in Britain both parties, by striving to control the ministry, prove that they really accept the governmental system. The question of its character is never for a moment at stake; it is taken for granted by both parties. Their contention centres on relatively minor issues of the personnel of the ministry or a particular policy. The result of party strife is not only a lively discussion of national affairs, but also a detailed criticism of legislation and administration, which keeps the government up to scratch.

Despite his various criticisms of Britain, Hegel seems to regard the British Parliament as a model of rational organization and procedure also in another respect. Invoking the British example, Hegel condemns the practice of reading written papers in the Wurtemberg Diet.

The nation is the essential public of Estates Assemblies. How can the former take an interest in and advance through such paper proceedings and pedantic deductions? Its representatives rather isolate themselves from each other and from the nation itself in this way, and conduct the affairs of the nation with the latter effectively excluded, even if sittings are public. [207–8]

In this passage Hegel points out that the deliberations of the Estates are of interest not merely to themselves or the government, but also to the nation at large. A representative assembly is a mediating organ, through which the nation gains an insight into the work and the needs of the government, and they can do that only when their representatives express themselves in a lively, interesting, and intelligible way. The cut and thrust of an oral debate seems to Hegel the best way of attracting the interest and attention of the people, and the English ban on written speeches seems to him thoroughly justified. It is obvious, though he does not point it out explicitly, that the publicity of debates and the freedom of the press are equally indispensable requirements for the fulfilment of the Estates Assembly's function.

In *The English Reform Bill* Hegel develops the view that British parties are groups within a single political class, connected by all sorts of economic, social, family, and other bonds, and possessing a uniformity of maxims and motives.

However much it [i.e. the British Parliament] is divided into parties and however great the passion with which they confront one another, still equally so little are they factions. They stand within the same general interest, and hitherto a change of ministry has had important consequences rather in relation to foreign affairs, to war and peace, than in relation to domestic affairs. [319]

In this kind of situation not merely does deliberation thrive, but even the dependence of the government on a temporary majority in Parliament loses a good deal of its disadvantage. Thus Hegel's critical attitude to Parliament's direct control over the executive seems to be unfounded, since he himself admits that no disastrous consequences need follow from such control. However, he points out the danger to the system of a new kind of M.P.s recruited from outside the traditional ruling class. The entry of these new men into politics would almost certainly upset the stability of the government and alter the working of the party system (see [321]). The new opposition

erected on a basis hitherto at variance with the stability of Parliament, might feel itself no match for the opposite party in Parliament, could be led to look for its strength to the people, and then introduce not reform but revolution. [323]

To be fruitful and constitutional, party activity must presuppose a bond between the rival groups, some 'universal interest' such as an agreed form of government, a body of political conventions, or a common class background. Such parliamentary parties are an indispensable help to the Estates in fulfilling their fundamental purpose; as Hegel says, an Assembly of Estates is not properly constituted without them.

Although Hegel fully recognizes the importance of political parties, they are not, in his view, the primary factor in the composition of the Estates Assembly. This, of course, consists of a number of separate orders representing the various sections of the nation; the problem which of the many interests ought to be represented in the Assembly and in what proportions was considered in the last chapter. One has the impression that Hegel gradually abandons his early standpoint of treating estates as historically evolved privileged orders, and adopts a position much more consistent with his general political rationalism, according to which not past evolution but present importance is the decisive factor in representation. Nevertheless, to the end of his life, he seems unwilling to question the place of nobility in the Assembly of Estates, whether as forming part of a one-chamber legislature or as having a separate hereditary chamber of its own. And yet the presence of nobility seems anomalous on two grounds. First, while other estates, especially the burghers, are represented in the Estates Assembly by deputies, nobility frequently has the right of appearing there in person. Secondly, it is difficult to see what interest, *qua* nobility, it represents. If it is the ownership of land, then clearly it is landowners as such (who may well be non-noble) who should be represented. If nobility forms the most educated section of the population, then surely education, not birth, should form the basis of representation in this case.[1]

The answer, perhaps, lies in the other aspect of the Assembly; since it mediates between the prince and the nation and forms a part of the public authority, it has also a governmental aspect. This makes it necessary to balance the democratic by an aristocratic element, in the broadest sense of aristocracy, in other words to infuse wisdom, enlightenment, and experience into a predominantly popular Assembly where these qualities may be deficient. One can almost say that Hegel's ideal is an Assembly which, without ceasing to be representative, should be as aristocratic as possible. This can be realized in his view by ensuring that men of the highest calibre become elected to the Estates Assembly, but also by supplement-

---

[1] Hegel's way out of the difficulty in *The German Constitution* is to argue that nobility normally does have a representative character and that it is the natural spokesman for certain sections of the people who would otherwise be unrepresented. Cf. [94–95]. In *The Wurtemberg Estates*, however, his main consideration seems to be expediency. The estate of nobles, he implies, is too important and too powerful to be ignored, and it has enjoyed its privilege for too long to be deprived of it all at once; the latter should be merely restricted and reformed by statute, not abolished altogether [166].

ing the elective by non-elective members, recruited from the hereditary nobility, in order to make up for deficiencies of the representative system.

Hegel's 'aristocratic' attitude to representation is well illustrated by a comment he makes about the phrase 'the will of the people', used on one occasion in the proceedings of the Wurtemberg Diet.

This is a great word, and the representatives of the people should take the greatest care not to profane it or use it light-heartedly. . . . To say 'he knows what his will is' is one of the most difficult, and hence most noble, things one can say of a man. People's representatives must not be picked at random, but rather one should choose the wisest from among the people, since not everyone knows, as it is his duty to know, what one's true and real will is, i.e. what is good for one. [218]

It has been said at the beginning of the chapter that Hegel regards the representative body as essential to the formulation of the general will of the country. The general will is not a temporary, ephemeral whim of the people or its deputies, but the result of careful reflection and mature deliberation. It is a matter of knowing or rather discovering what is good for the country, what is in the public interest. Hence not everybody is fit to be a representative of the nation, and measures should be taken to ensure that the wisest are in fact elected.

Consequently a large number of passages in Hegel's political writings deal with qualifications for the membership of the Estates Assembly, and with the various practical, intellectual, and moral qualities necessary in representatives. Topping the list is something he calls a 'political consciousness' or political sense.

A political consciousness is principally acquired in habitual pre-occupation with public affairs. By this means not only is the infinite intrinsic worth of the general [weal] felt and recognized, but experience is gained of the resistance, hostility, and dishonesty of private interest, and the battle with it, especially with the stubbornness which results from its having been established in the form of law, is fought to the end. [170]

Hegel maintains that as deputies of different sections of the country the members of the Assembly of Estates tend to be primarily concerned with the protection of their sectional rights and interests, and only secondarily and indirectly with the needs of the state and the government. Were this disposition to become predominant, it would, as he says in another place, lead to 'the most dangerous evil that can arise in a state' [169] because the Estates have the power of slowing down or even paralysing the course of the government if they choose. The opposite disposition, without which a representative body cannot function well, is in his opinion 'principally acquired in habitual occupation with public affairs'. Hence the problem of infusing 'a political consciousness' into the Estates Assembly becomes one of ensuring that its members have had some experience of public life.

In this connexion Hegel makes one of his few criticisms of the Wurtemberg Constitutional Charter. He regards as wrong and unwise the disqualification of civil servants, physicians, and surgeons from being members of the Diet. The case against excluding civil servants, he maintains, is that they are precisely the people whom experience of public life and of state service has given most political sense. In a small country like Wurtemberg they are almost the only men with any higher education and administrative experience, and in any case it seems to Hegel unfair that such a large section of the people should be deprived of a political right which others, less well qualified, enjoy (see [168]). He brushes aside the objection that civil servants would naturally favour the government and the monarch. That may have been true before, when they were royal servants, without independence and security of tenure, but it is invalid today. If the civil servants are excluded, he goes on to ask, who else is left?

The class of advocates, which of the remaining classes is the one that may demand first consideration in this connexion, is tied in its concepts and activities primarily to the principles of private and *positive* law. . . . The legal exclusion of this class might well be contested from the point of view of abstract right, but no more so than the exclusion of physicians and surgeons; the organization of a state rests, however, on a concrete wisdom totally different from a formalism derived from private rights. [168–9]

Lawyers, then, are no more fit to be deputies than the other sections of the middle class because they have no more public experience; they are almost less fit because one of the duties of the Diet is to revise and reform the positive law of the country, and the lawyers, by their position and 'habitual occupation', are stubborn supporters of the legal *status quo*.

The constitutional exclusion of civil servants from the Wurtem-berg Estates makes Hegel look for another source of political sense in the officers of local self-government. He admits that, as they have been constituted up to the present, local authorities are not a promising breeding-ground for deputies, but that should be a reason for reorganizing rather than ignoring them. His case for drawing deputies to the Diet from among town councillors or magistrates rests on an already familiar ground.

To be a city councillor is no bad preparatory school for functioning in the Estates. City councillors, like civil servants, spend their lives in the daily activity of helping to administer the civil order. They know by experience how laws and institutions work and what counter effects of evil passions they have to fight and withstand. Further, they are them-selves drawn from the citizenry, they share its more limited interests, and may enjoy its closer confidence. [174]

One only needs to add that Hegel disapproves of the payment of salaries to members of the Estates, apparently in order to exclude men without property and a stake in the country, who might be inclined to act irresponsibly,[1] and this will complete the account of what he regards as a rational composition of the Estates Assembly in *The Wurtemberg Estates*. Had he been entrusted with the draft-ing of the constitution for his native country he would have made sure that the legislature consisted of well-to-do burghers and land-owners, judicial and administrative officers of local government, civil servants, and nobles. Nothing could illustrate better the strength of Hegel's underlying attitude—the fear of political irresponsibility or in his terminology the lack of 'a political consciousness'.

Although *The English Reform Bill* is highly critical of the Eng-lish representative system, the major fault of the British Estates Assembly, or Parliament, is not, in Hegel's view, the absence of political sense or of patriotism. Apart from the unbalanced and

---

[1] Cf. the following passage in the *The Wurtemberg Estates*. 'There is something inherently very distasteful in members of the Estates drawing salaries or allow-ances. The matter is of the highest importance since it alters something essential in the whole character and position of such a system of representation. It is one of the things which give preponderance in elections to property, apart from the fact that it vitally affects the honour of such an Assembly. The Estates, when they are remunerated, can never escape the suspicion and objection that, if not to all, then at least to many or some of their members the salary is an important consideration.' [234]

haphazard representation of various interests, it is the low intellectual standard of the average British M.P. and the total lack of any
provisions to remedy it that seem to Hegel the greatest vices of
the parliamentary system (see [301]). While Hegel realizes that in
the British Parliament birth and wealth have undue or excessive
weight, his main complaint is that in the case of the majority of
M.P.s the two are not accompanied by 'profound insight and
true knowledge'. The Reform Bill fails to impose any academic
qualifications or do anything to obtain 'proofs of capacity from
candidates for the legislature and political administration' [302].
The situation could also have been improved by giving the franchise
to those most likely to elect enlightened men as representatives,
but as he points out 'the new Bill . . . sanctions the principle that a
free income of £10 drawn from property in land is a full qualification for the task of judging and deciding on a man's capacity for
the business of government and financial administration which lies
with Parliament' [302].

With this deplorable state of affairs he contrasts the situation in
his own country.

The qualifications required in Germany even from the well-born and
from wealthy landowners if they are to take part in public administration or politics either in general or in special spheres, [are] theoretical
study, scientific education, practice and experience in affairs. [301]

The point that strikes one here is that Hegel is contrasting two
apparently different institutions: a representative assembly in
Britain and a public administration in Germany. It is quite
plausible to require theoretical and practical qualifications from
candidates for the latter, but a Parliament, or Assembly of Estates,
consisting of intellectuals or even academically educated men
would in a real sense be most unrepresentative. As against this
objection, however, one can remind oneself that a legislature to
Hegel is never merely a representative body. It is also in a sense
a governmental one, and nowhere more so than in Britain where it
is vested with effective governmental power and where it controls
the executive. Hence, on his own premisses, he is fully justified in
demanding a higher standard of enlightenment from it than he
seemed prepared to accept in Wurtemberg. His condemnation of
the intellectual quality of the British Parliament turns out, however, to be less sweeping than the above passages suggest. It is,

he implies later in the work, only the rank and file of M.P.s who are ignorant or half-educated fox-hunters and country squires. There are also others, members of the government and chief opposition leaders, who are men of ability, even if mainly practical political ability and even if no regular and determinate channel of recruiting and promoting such men exists (see [316]).

But while Hegel finds so much fault with British politicians, he is not at all anxious to see them superseded by new men. The greatest and perhaps only virtue of the old Parliament is the high degree of 'political consciousness' among its members. This is due to the fact that so many of them are men with actual public experience, that they form a closely knit and homogeneous clique, and that they have wielded power for generations and know what is required. The Reform Bill may undermine the whole system by introducing a new type of politician, a doctrinaire middle-class radical. Its result is likely to be not only that

many other individuals will appear in place of those belonging to the present circle of those devoted to the interest of the national government; but it is likely to bring as its sequel a disturbance of the uniformity of the maxims and considerations of that class, and these constitute the brains of parliament. [317]

Worse still, as has already been touched upon in connexion with parties, Hegel fears that the middle-class M.P.s finding themselves out of power inside Parliament, may seek to win power by appealing to the people in the name of abstract principles (see [318]).

Thus one can see that throughout Hegel's career as a political writer he was greatly preoccupied with the problem of how to ensure that a representative assembly shall be sufficiently government-minded or shall have enough political sense to exercise the power it has responsibly and to facilitate rather than to hamper government. In the early writings, thinking chiefly of Wurtemberg and the other German countries, he saw the main danger to that attitude in private and group selfishness owing to defective or insufficient political experience; in his last work, with France and Britain chiefly in mind, he regards doctrinaire and demagogic radical politicians—*les hommes à principes*—as the greatest threat to government. This danger was in no doubt real, but one wonders if Hegel did not exaggerate it too much. He himself, towards the end of *The English Reform Bill*, admits that the political abstractions which have wrought havoc in France are not likely to have the same dire consequences in Britain.

The members of the English Parliament under the existing system, and Englishmen in general, have a more practical political sense [than the French] and they have an idea of what government and governing is. [323]

One could also use against Hegel his own observation that parliamentary experience tends to have a sobering effect, especially when it leads to ministerial experience, and that real governmental responsibility is one of the best ways of curing politicians of doctrinairism (see [318]). But by the end of his life this seemed a small consolation to Hegel. He had become convinced that the proper guarantee of governmental stability as well as rationality in law and administration was not to be sought in the composition of the Assembly of Estates. No doubt one should have sought to improve the latter, but the only real safeguard of both order and progress was to be found in the other part of the public authority—the independent monarchical executive.

VII

THE MONARCH AND THE GOVERNMENT

> While it is a noble and elevating spectacle to see a people breaking its chains in the full consciousness of its human and civil rights . . . the spectacle of a prince unlocking the chains and bestowing freedom must be infinitely more noble and elevating, all the more so if he regards the action not as a fruit of his benevolence but as a fulfilment of his primary, unavoidable duty. Because the freedom for which a nation strives by changing its constitution is to the freedom which an already organized state can give as hope is to enjoyment or plan to fulfilment.
>
> WILHELM VON HUMBOLDT,
> *Ueber die Grenzen der Wirksamkeit des Staates.*

PROBABLY no part of Hegel's political thought has given rise to more divergent interpretations than the position of the government in the state. According to a common view Hegel's ideal is government by an absolute king; according to a rival interpretation it is a limited, constitutional monarchy. Even the most impartial reader is bound to concede a certain amount of ambiguity in Hegel's attitude towards the government and the monarch. There are many passages in his works where their power and role are maximized, almost exalted, but there are also others where they are given a more modest place. One of the aims of this chapter is to remove, or help to remove, this discrepancy by analysing what Hegel has to say about government in his minor political works.

For Hegel the monarch is the keystone of the governmental structure, so we may begin by discussing a passage in *The German Constitution* where his character and place in the state are most explicitly stated.

The condition of barbarism consists in this, that the multitude is a nation without at the same time being a state, and that the state and the individuals exist in opposition and separation. The ruler, in his personal capacity [als eine Persönlichkeit], forms the public authority, and the only remedy against his personality is the juxtaposition of the personality of his subjects. In a civilized state laws or the universal stand between the personality of the monarch and that of the individuals; a single act of the monarch affects all, burdens or injures all, benefits all.

The phrases 'the monarch is the public authority', 'he has the supreme power', 'there is a state' mean one and the same thing. The force of laws solves the conflict between the state having supreme power and the individuals not being oppressed by it. . . . All wisdom in the organization of states depends on the solution of this [conflict]. [70-71 footnote]

The fundamental role of the monarch according to Hegel emerges quite clearly from this passage. He is the individual in whom the sovereignty of the state is vested and from whom it devolves on all subordinate authorities. As Hegel says elsewhere in the same work, the monarch is 'the centre of the state's power; from him everything issues which requires legal compulsion' [93]. But from the fact (or the theory) that he is sovereign it does not follow that the exercise of supreme authority is his own personal concern and that his subjective opinion and arbitrary will determines what should and what should not be done in the state. This, Hegel says, is true only of primitive, barbarian states, where rulers are essentially despots whose oppression is checked only by the threat of their people's rebellion. In a civilized country the monarch exercises authority through universal statutes and not *ad hoc* commands. These statutes are the result of complex processes which, so to speak, neutralize the personal influence of any one man. They are normally drafted by Ministers or officials; they have to be submitted to the Assembly of Estates for its debate and vote; the monarch, when they have reached him, may have no more to do with them than add his signature to a final document. A civilized nation does not exist outside the state, 'in opposition and separation'; it is connected with the state and associated with the government in an organic way. The legislative power, says Hegel, is in the monarch's hands, but it is shared with the Estates. It is the function of the other authorities—the Assembly of Estates, but also the Ministers and officials advising the monarch—to reconcile the needs of a strong supreme public authority with the freedom and welfare of the individuals. The monarch and the government are limited by universal laws; these laws are made through constitutional channels to which the nation's representatives contribute; on this 'all wisdom in the organization of states depends'.

It will be remembered that this view of sovereignty does not, for Hegel, imply a highly centralized government. On the contrary, he states emphatically that the monarch is a supreme commander only in respect of universal interests of the country—its external and internal security. So far as particular interests are concerned, they are only under the indirect supervision of the government and are autonomous within their own sphere. In one passage in *The German Constitution* Hegel links such autonomy with the existence of hereditary monarchy, and argues that the latter is the best guarantee of the former.

The public authority must be concentrated in one centre for deciding these matters and, as government, for executing these decisions. If this centre is secure on its own account in virtue of the awe of the masses, and is immutably sacrosanct in the person of a monarch appointed in accordance with a natural law and by birth, then a public authority may without fear or jealousy freely hand over to subordinate systems and bodies a great part of the relationships arising in society and their maintenance according to the laws. [27]

Hegel, it will be remembered, goes on to point out that it is the newly founded monarchy of Prussia and the even newer French Republic that have pushed centralization to unusual and excessive extremes.[1]

In the preceding chapter we have examined Hegel's views on the division of legislative power between the monarch and the Assembly of Estates. But the monarch's more immediate concern is with the executive functions of the supreme public authority; he 'manages national affairs, especially in so far as they concern foreign relations with other states' [93]. In the actual discharge of this task the monarch acts through the government consisting of the Ministry and the higher state officials, and the means by which he controls the government is his power of appointment and dismissal.

[1] In deference to the French Republic Hegel concedes that the modern state need not be headed by a crowned hereditary king, but he still insists that it must have *one* man at its head, 'a centre in which all power is concentrated'. '. . . It does not matter in this connexion whether this centre has a strictly monarchical or a modern republican form, since the latter also falls under the principle of a limited monarchy, i.e., one bound by law' [109]. In the subsequent political writings of Hegel the hereditary character of monarchy is always taken for granted. Another passage in *The German Constitution* suggests, however, that though a single head is desirable, it is not absolutely necessary [20].

Throughout his political writings Hegel assumes that the monarch is assisted and advised by a Ministry or a Cabinet, but the exact nature of this institution is nowhere specifically discussed. We do not know, e.g., how large it should be or from whom it should be recruited. Similarly we are left in the dark about Hegel's views on the relations between the first minister, if any, and the rest of the Cabinet, or between Ministers and officials. Although Hegel is against the responsibility of the Cabinet to the Estates Assembly he fully allows the latter the right to question, criticize, and impeach Ministers and in fact, if not in form, to share in the monarch's control over them.

His views on the civil service are stated in the minor works more explicitly than his views on the Ministry. Though civil servants, like Ministers, are appointed to their office by the monarch, Hegel believes that they should not be dismissible at pleasure but on the contrary should enjoy full security of tenure. He points out that they are servants of the state and not of the king personally, and thus their position is fundamentally different from that of the members of the king's household. To illustrate the distinction he draws a parallel with the property of princely families in Germany, which at first had the legal form of their own private property, but gradually took on the character of public property and became state domain. Such a corps of public servants, independent of the good will of the monarch and his Ministry, dedicated to the interest of the state, and with a loyalty transcending that to any particular person, forms in his opinion an essential feature of a rational state (see [172–3]).

Reflecting the prevailing practice of his time, Hegel originally assumed that the higher civil servants would be recruited from the estate of nobility.[1] But already in the same work, i.e. *The German Constitution*, he argues that the estate of burghers should be allowed to compete freely with the nobility, incidentally giving us a glimpse of his ideal of a civil servant (see [95–96]). He thinks the broader horizon and a more independent outlook of the nobility are a great asset in the work of public administration, but maintains that the ordinary educated burgher has also something to contribute.

---

[1] He refers to the increase in the number of those who devoted themselves professionally to state service and to the multiplication of 'the mass of things needed by the free man, or by the noble, who had to maintain themselves in their social position respectively by industry or by work for the state' [93].

This stress on education as a necessary qualification for public service is particularly marked in *The Wurtemberg Estates* and even more so in *The English Reform Bill*. In the former work, e.g., Hegel refers to the young men of Germany as those who

have shed their blood together that the German provinces might acquire free constitutions. They have brought back from the field of battle the hope of working some day or other towards that end and of participating in the political life of the state. Their academic education has equipped them for this purpose and destined them in the main for the public service. [172]

And in another place, comparing the opportunities which an individual has of 'working and acting' for 'more general interests' than those of himself and his family in a large state like France or Britain and in the small German states, he says:

In such smaller countries the large majority of those who acquire an academic or any more general culture find themselves induced to seek their living and their social ties in some public service. [168]

The passages are extremely revealing. While Britain in the early nineteenth century was governed by amateur politicians assisted by an ill-organized civil service, based on patronage, Germany (and France) already had a corps of professional administrators with high academic qualifications. The absence of any educational qualifications for public service in contemporary Britain fills Hegel with astonishment, and he ridicules the prejudice 'nowhere more than in England . . . so fixed and so naïve that if birth and wealth give a man office they also give him brains' [301]. He contrasts the ignorance and lack of formal preparation among the 'members of an asssembly in whose hands lies the most extensive power of government and administration' with the situation in Germany where all public servants are required to have qualifications in 'theoretical study, scientific education, and practice and experience in affairs' (ibid.). More strongly than in *The German Constitution* Hegel insists that nobility and wealth are not a sufficient title to public office. Hegel confuses the issue, however, by treating representatives as if they were civil servants and requiring the same educational standards from both.

The high academic calibre of civil servants that Hegel assumes has also an important bearing on the exercise of the monarch's legislative prerogative of initiation. It is now clear that by being educated at universities they can profit from 'centuries of quiet academic work' in the sphere of legislation and learn the principles of 'the scientific remodelling of law whereby on the one hand general principles have been applied to and carried through the particular specifications [of law] and their complexities, while on the other hand concrete and special cases have been reduced to simpler provisions' [289]. The civil service, then, is an essential channel through which rational ideas on legislation reach the government, and the main instrument for their practical application to the existing constitutional and juridical order.

The nature of universally accepted concepts links monarchy with the provision of 'a representative constitution, the rule of law, and popular influence on legislation', writes Hegel in *The Wurtemberg Estates* [161]. It follows clearly from the passages quoted in this and in previous chapters that for him monarchy means essentially limited monarchy. But this is not to say that the role of the monarch in the state is or should be a purely formal one, and that he must never exercise his own judgement or take an independent decision.[1] In continental terminology, Hegel's monarchy is constitutional rather than parliamentary. The king may more or less withdraw from active political life and leave the day-to-day conduct of government to a chancellor or a Cabinet. He may even choose to be guided by the views of the majority of the Estates Assembly and dismiss the Ministry who have lost the former's confidence. On the other hand he may also take an active part in the government, exercise his royal prerogatives according to his personal views, and, like the President of the United States, combine in himself the roles of the head of the state and the head of the government.

It is likely that in the long run Hegel's preference was for an inactive monarch. What is certain, however, is that he did not regard his own times as justifying a complete withdrawal of the monarch from the political scene. Three separate reasons for that, most of which have already been touched upon in different contexts, can be discerned in the minor works.

First of all, Hegel is convinced that some nations, and his own Germany in particular, are basically devoid of patriotism, national pride, or 'state consciousness'. The roots of this Hegel sees in the

[1] In *The English Reform Bill* Hegel in fact ridicules the idea of such a purely formal monarch (cf. [314]).

past. The persistence of old forms of political unity and Imperial government persuaded many provincial diets to refuse supplies to their local princes although in fact the provinces were becoming more and more sovereign, and independent policy was impossible without such supplies. Hegel brands their attitude as 'passive neutrality' and 'political nullity', and points out its harmful consequences (see [181]). A good example of such an attitude, which had survived the disappearance of the German Empire, occurred in Wurtemberg. In order to force the monarch to restore the old constitution and all their former privileges the Estates refused him all co-operation and supplies for nearly two years. Even the return of Napoleon from Elba and the renewed threat to the security of Europe and of Wurtemberg failed to move them to action. Hegel does not fail to point out the moral of it in *The Wurtemberg Estates*.

The whole merit for Wurtemberg's joining the ranks of the other European powers thus accrued to the King, the then Crown Prince, the Ministry, and the army.

In fulfilment of its general, moral, and positive obligations the government pursued its path with honour and glory, and it appears that the refusal of the Estates' co-operation did not hold it up in the slightest. The Estates, on the other hand, achieved nothing apart from having demonstrated their malice, the failure to appreciate the splendour of their position, and the superfluity of their co-operation. [212]

We know from another part of the work that the King of Wurtemberg was to some extent financially independent of the Diet and this enabled him to fulfil his international military commitments without bowing to the will of the Estates. Thus where the feeling of patriotism is weak or absent the dynastic interest of the monarch can supply the mainspring of foreign policy, provided he is in a constitutional position to act independently.

Hegel's second reason for believing in the necessity of a strong monarchical power is an extension of the first. He seems to believe that while the interests of the people and of the government are generally identical in foreign affairs, the people's representatives are often too narrow-minded, too selfish, too much concerned with the defence or the extension of privileges to realize that and to act accordingly. In other passages Hegel generalizes the situation and maintains that in domestic affairs the spokesmen of the people have often betrayed their trust as well.

In most cases of great political upheaval prince and people have manifestly been of *one* mind and will; but equally obviously a class between the two, in France the nobility and clergy, in Wurtemberg the nobility and the *bourgeois* aristocracy of the writers, instead of being the link between the two, as it is meant to be, has all too often insisted on privileges and monopolies and hindered or even altogether frustrated the actualization of the principles of rational law and public welfare. [261]

Though this assumption of frequent solidarity between the monarch and the people seems rather exaggerated, it does draw one's attention to a striking change in Hegel's attitude to the monarch-controlled government as far as rational legal reform is concerned. In his first pamphlet on Wurtemberg (*Wurtemberg's Domestic Affairs*) he expects little reform from the government, which is dominated by a despotic archduke so completely that 'ultimately everything revolves round one man who *ex providentia maiorum* unites all power in himself, and guarantees neither recognition nor respect of human rights'. Also officials and administrative boards are devoid of 'all feeling for the inborn rights of men', and in the exercise of their duties are concerned only with 'historical grounds of the positive' law.[1] In that work Hegel pins his hope to the reconvening of the Provincial Diet after a long period of abeyance, and asks rhetorically, 'Whence could the Wurtembergers expect juster aid than from the Assembly of their Estates?' [151]. But in his second work on Wurtemberg (*The Wurtemberg Estates*), some twenty years later, Hegel maintains that the same monarch was now the champion of rationality in Wurtemberg, while the Estates were acting as the bulwark of positive law and traditional privileges. Contrasting the position of the Estates and the monarch at the outbreak of the Revolution in France with that in Wurtemberg some twenty-five years later, Hegel writes:

In France most of the Estates of the Realm and the popular party upheld the rights of reason and demanded their restoration, while the government was on the side of privileges; but in Wurtemberg the King brought his constitution within the ambit of rational constitutional law, while the Estates set themselves up as defenders of privileges and positive law. They even afforded the perverse spectacle of doing this in the name of the people against whose interests, far more than against the prince's, these privileges are erected. [198]

[1] Haym, op. cit., p. 67.

Here probably we find the most important cause of Hegel's tendency to exalt the role and position of the monarch in the state at the expense of the Assembly of Estates. In the monarch and his government he sees the main instrument of rationality in the contemporary world. We are not offered an explanation of this change in the character of the monarchy, but the fact that it occurred during Napoleon's hegemony over Europe is rather significant. Nor are we told what in Hegel's view has prompted a particular monarchy to become a champion of rationality. On the other hand the unsuitability of the Estates, despite their legislative power, for furthering rational legal and constitutional reform is pointed out by Hegel frequently enough. Such reform, as we have seen earlier, normally involves a sacrifice of particular rights and traditional privileges for the sake of justice or the common good. Hegel believed at one time that a representative body, under the pressure of public opinion, might be capable of such enlightened action, but in the course of years he came to take the more cynical view that men seldom give up individual or group advantages voluntarily, in response to moral motives, without a threat of force.[1] The monarch's prerogatives of legislative initiative and enactment, combined with the knowledge of academically trained civil servants, creates the possibility of reform. His independent governmental power makes its success certain by enabling him to withstand the pressure of hostile interests and to win public opinion to his side in the long run. In *The English Reform Bill* Hegel specifically attributes English backwardness in respect of the institutions of rational law primarily to the weakness of the monarchical element in the constitution (see [289–90]).

The third reason why Hegel favours a strong monarchical executive is also to be found in *The English Reform Bill*. He seems to believe that the struggle between the positive and the rational principle takes, in many countries, the form of a class struggle between the privileged and the non-privileged. In such a situation an independent government can force concessions and compromises from both sides, and achieve reforms without violence. In England

[1] Cf. e.g., the following passage in *Wurtemberg's Domestic Affairs*. 'In the following inquiry the strength of being able to rise above one's petty interest to justice is presupposed no less than the honesty to will it and not merely to pretend to will it' [152]. In *The English Reform Bill*, on the other hand, Hegel ironically implies that the fear of the July Revolution being repeated in England powerfully reinforced Parliament's sense of justice. Cf. [283–4].

the absence of a strong monarch fills Hegel with forebodings because he visualizes an impending conflict between the aristocracy and the middle class after the passing of the Reform Bill [323]. What is all the more dangerous in Hegel's view is that such a struggle can not only affect the method of furthering rationality but also seriously weaken the government itself and destroy its stability by causing within Parliament a split on fundamentals and altering the character and aim of party activity.

The lack of patriotism, the existence of powerful vested interests bent on defending the *status quo*, and the struggle between them and a middle class without privileges are factors which make government undoubtedly difficult. Hegel may have exaggerated their importance and persistence, but one can see why an active, strong, and independent monarchy should have appealed to him in such a situation. We find, however, that he is inclined to go further still and in certain circumstances to justify not merely the independence of the government from the Assembly of Estates but the suspension of the Assembly or even its complete abolition. This idea is mooted by Hegel, e.g. in *The Wurtemberg Estates*, in connexion with the opposition of the Estates to rational law, an opposition which he partly attributes to the influence of the vested interest of the 'writers'.

However indispensable the existence of an Estates Assembly is for the concept of a monarchical state, still it would be infinitely better to have none at all than to put up with the continued existence of these privileges, this oppression, deception, and suffocation of the people; better to have no Estates at all than Estates that represent the privileges of this aristocracy. [260-1]

Hegel acknowledges that a representative assembly is indispensable to a monarchical state. This does not mean, however, that any and every kind of assembly is indispensable. There are some which are so bad that, at least in the short run, the interests of the people may be better safeguarded by having no Estates at all to represent them. In other words Hegel implies that the absence of the Estates Assembly may be a *precondition* of progress towards rationality.[1] In some German states, particularly Prussia, the Estates of the Realm never met, and yet, as he points out in *The English Reform*

---

[1] Even then, however, Hegel stresses the enormous educational value of the Assembly of Estates participating in the programme of legal reform. Cf. [266-7].

Bill, that country has gone further along the path of reform than England with her Parliament. If such denial of political liberty is the price that has to be temporarily paid for the rationalization of laws and institutions, then Hegel is prepared to accept in some instances.

In *The Wurtemberg Estates* Hegel visualizes two other situations in which the Assembly of Estates may be justifiably dispensed with for a period of time. The first one is when a country is fighting for its independence. In Wurtemberg the Old Provincial Diet was abolished by the Duke in 1806 and during the subsequent ten years the country was ruled despotically. Hegel appears to approve of this temporary despotism, as a result of which Wurtemberg emerged as a new sovereign state:

> The original period of its rise occurred in circumstances in which everything for its establishment and maintenance in foreign eyes had to be raised autocratically, and therefore in internal affairs the means had to be collected by a powerful ministerial government and kept ready in firm hands for use. [160]

Here a 'ministerial government' accountable only to the Duke, legislation by decree, and the imposition of taxes without consent are justified as necessary for the establishment of a sovereign state. The other situation which, in his view, justifies the temporary abolition of the Estates is a struggle for governmental power between them and the monarch. Hegel is led to discuss the point in connexion with the demand of the Wurtemberg Diet for its ancient right of administering the funds voted and collected by it. He points out the abuses and corruption to which it can easily lead, and emphasizes its danger to the state of having in effect another sovereign power.

> If such older provisions survived, the state would cease to be a state and would come to ruin through having in it the two sovereign powers that would be there. Or, it would be truer to say, unity would be restored either because the so-called Estates, as we have seen in recent history, would upset the former government and usurp its powers, or because, as we have also seen, governments would send such Estates packing and thereby save state and people. The greatest guarantee and security of the Estates is just this, that they shall not possess a power which contradicts the nature of the thing; the greatest folly, on the other hand, is to try to find in such a power a protection for themselves

and the people: because such a power makes it right, and sooner or later necessary, to abolish such Estates. [196]

Hegel realizes that the differentiation of the supreme public authority into two bodies carries some risks. Unless both the Estates and the monarch are mutually accommodating, periodical constitutional conflicts may arise between them and undermine not only the government but also the state as a whole. The unity of the state is guaranteed by vesting sovereignty in the monarch, but if the Estates possess effective means of opposing the government and pursuing a foreign policy of their own, a formal guarantee is not of much value. The Estates' control over their own treasury, with its possibility of sending envoys to foreign powers or even hiring troops, seems to Hegel incompatible with the unity of the country and the welfare of the people. Hence in such circumstances it is right and necessary for the monarch to govern without the Estates.

At the beginning of this chapter attention was drawn to the divergent interpretations of the government's character in Hegel's writings. Much of the divergence can now be seen to be due to a wrong or at least one-sided way of looking at his political thought, the result of a static conception of the state while he himself often conceives it dynamically. The rational state and existing states do not in his view coincide as closely as is sometimes assumed, and one of the tasks of the government, over and above the ordinary ones of defence and security, is to effect the transformation from the positive to the rational. In this task of reform and revision the government faces obstacles such as the strength of vested interests, the 'positive' attitude to law, and the absence of patriotism or 'state consciousness'. It must therefore be organized appropriately and must possess the necessary power and independence from both the privileged few and the ignorant many. At times, indeed, the government may be obliged and must be able to set aside the constitution, abolish the Estates and arbitrarily restrict the autonomy of local and other authorities, deprive whole classes of individuals of privileges, and impose financial burdens and sacrifices of liberty on the nation. This, after all, is nothing but a logical conclusion from the fundamental law of reason that nothing positive, no prescriptive right, has any absolute validity. Once, however, the state's independence, unity, and rationality are no longer at stake, the powers of the government can be drastically curtailed and the government can act in a wholly different manner and spirit. The difference between a limited and an unlimited government, between a constitutional and an authoritarian monarchy, is the difference between ruling within a rational framework and striving to establish it first.[1]

Nothing in the minor works illustrates the distinction better than the conclusion of *The German Constitution*. After outlining the conditions for the reunification of Germany and sketching the organization of an effective public authority which the Empire needs, Hegel has to admit that persuasion and reasoning cannot bring about the desired effect.

> . . . Particularism has prerogative and precedence in Germany and it is something so intimately personal that thinking and an insight into necessity are far too weak in themselves to become effective in action. Thought and judgement carry with them so much self-mistrust that they have to be validated by force, and only then does man submit to them. [136]

Hence in Germany not arguments or publications but the force of a conqueror, a modern Theseus, will be the deciding factor.

Here Hegel draws sharp distinction between an individual with a particular historical mission to accomplish, and the same man after his task has been done. To unite Germany he must conquer all the many separate political authorities and abolish their independence, he must use force to overcome their vested interest in the *status quo*; he cannot wait for the consent of the people or their Estates because the latter 'know nothing at all of anything but the division of the German people' and their union 'is something totally alien' to them [135]. Once, however, unity was achieved, the despot would have to become a constitutional ruler and limit his own absolute power by granting the people a share in the public authority through a representative body. The answer to the question 'What kind of a ruler is best for Germany?' thus depended

---

[1] A traditional government, concerned with the preservation of the *status quo* which everybody accepts, obviously need not be very powerful; nor need a government in a thoroughly rationalized state. But governments operating in a transitional situation must be armed with wide and peremptory powers. Oddly enough, Locke reached a similar conclusion in the *Second Treatise of Civil Government*. In paragraphs 157 and 158 he justifies an arbitrary use of the royal prerogative to abolish rotten boroughs on the ground of rationality and concludes that 'whatsoever cannot but be acknowledged to be of advantage to the society and people in general upon just and lasting measures, will always, when done, justify itself'.

on circumstances, and would have been different before and after unification. In an analogous way a monarch, exercising absolutely the sovereignty vested in him, in order to defend the integrity of the state or to introduce rationality, will have to act quite differently when the country enjoys peace, social harmony, and good institutions. The maxim *salus populi suprema lex* will cease to apply and the Rule of Law will become the fixed and operative principle of government.

VIII

HEGEL THE POLITICAL PHILOSOPHER

> The truth about Right, Ethics, and the State is as old
> as its public recognition and formulation in the law of
> the land, in the morality of everyday life, and in reli-
> gion. What more does this truth require—since the
> thinking mind is not content to possess it in this ready
> fashion? It requires to be grasped in thought as well;
> the content which is already rational in principle must
> win the *form* of rationality and so appear well-founded
> to untrammelled thinking.
>
> HEGEL, Philosophy of Right.

IT is outside the scope of this essay to make any thorough and
systematic comparison of Hegel's minor and major political
works. Even a brief glance at the *Philosophy of Right* and the
Philosophy of History, however, reveals a vast common ground
between them and the political writings. The basic themes of the
political writings recur in the philosophical works, sometimes in
different form, sometimes almost verbatim, and greatly reinforce
the outline of Hegel's political thought developed in the preceding
chapters.

A. PHILOSOPHY OF RIGHT

1. *Political Rationality*

'*What is rational is actual and what is actual is rational.* On this
conviction the plain man like the philosopher takes his stand' [10].[1]
By this remark Hegel intended to differentiate his political philosophy from the traditional *a priori* approach of his immediate and
more remote predecessors like Fichte, Kant, Wolff, Puffendorf,
and others, as well as from any kind of Utopian theory. As he
makes clear in the Introduction, the true function of philosophy
for him was not to open up new, glorious vistas before mankind—
to show them the Promised Land—but to make men understand
the ethical world to which they belonged and which was their

---

[1] The references in brackets are to Hegel's *Philosophy of Right*, translated by
T. M. Knox (Oxford, 1942).

inescapable destiny. (It was only possible for individuals or small minorities, but not for whole societies and nations, to turn their back on the moral heritage of their civilization.) By 'actuality' (*Wirklichkeit*) in the ethical context, then, Hegel meant the whole complex of beliefs and ideals embodied in conventional religion and morality, social customs and institutions, as well as civil laws and political arrangements. Since most ordinary men do not question, indeed cannot question, the whole foundation of their moral life, philosophers should not cut themselves off from that life either, but should help others to apprehend it by reason.

Hegel's concept of reason (*Vernunft*) is highly complex, difficult, and technical, but there is little doubt about one of its senses. He means by it a special and distinct mental faculty, different from that of analytical reflection or 'understanding' (*Verstand*). Although both 'reason' and 'understanding' employ concepts, the latter differ profoundly. The concepts of reason are 'concrete' in the sense that they contain features derived from the knowledge of actual conduct or institution; the rational concept of 'monarchy' means the form of government typical of early nineteenth-century Western Europe, i.e. constitutional monarchy with representative institutions, local autonomy, civil equality, &c. The concepts of the understanding are 'abstract' since they are independent of any empirical features and are based on general categories; 'monarchy', for the understanding, means simply 'the rule of one man' where the character of the rule is left unspecified. It can be seen that political philosophy based on rational concepts presupposes the knowledge of political actuality, e.g. the manifold forms which monarchical government has taken in modern Europe. In Hegel's own terms 'the shapes which the concept assumes in the course of its actualization are indispensable for the knowledge of the concept itself' [14]. We can see then that there is a profound connexion between Hegel the political writer and Hegel the political philosopher; or, in other words, between Hegel's passionate interest in the politics of the German Empire, the Kingdom of Wurtemberg, or Great Britain, and the apparently speculative theory of the state which he elaborated in the *Philosophy of Right*. Hegel would not be true to his own idea of philosophy unless he had steeped himself in actuality and studied concepts, so to speak, in the raw.

However, while the philosopher must try and grasp concepts which are 'actualized', 'operative', or 'living', one must not assume that concepts are rational simply because they possess this character. This is where the 'plain man' and the philosopher often part company. If serfdom, slavery, and 'the subjection of women', have been accepted in a society for centuries, the ordinary folk tend to see nothing wrong in them. The philosopher, on the other hand, may more easily perceive that they are basically incompatible with the ideals of equality or freedom which the society professes and which pervade all the other aspects of ethical life. The actual of the *Philosophy of Right* is clearly not the positive of the political writings.

In the Introduction to the *Philosophy of Right* Hegel clearly distinguishes philosophical actuality and historical reality. He starts by paying tribute to Montesquieu for holding a position which was historically and philosophically true, 'namely that legislation both in general and in its particular provisions is to be treated not as something isolated and abstract but rather as a subordinate moment in a whole, interconnected with all the other features which make up the character of a nation and an epoch' [16]. Nevertheless, Hegel goes on to say, historical explanation and philosophical justification should not in any way be confused. 'A particular law may be shown wholly grounded in and consistent with the circumstances and with existing legally established institutions, and yet it may be irrational in its essential character . . .' [17]. Indeed, history is a very shaky ground on which to justify old institutions, since nothing is easier than to show that circumstances have changed in some respect. Contemporary utility is not a good ground either, because of its arbitrariness. 'Utility to whom?' or 'utility in whose eyes?' one can ask, and no answer will be satisfactory unless utility is stretched to mean that of the whole community sharing a certain ethical life, which brings one back to the concepts of rationality and actuality.

Also in the Introduction, Hegel defines what he means by positive right or law. *Formally* what makes law positive is its validity in a particular state or authority within a legal system. Law becomes positive in content or *materially* when it acquires determinate provisions (*a*) 'through the particular national character of a people, its state of historical development, and the whole complex of relations connected with the necessity of nature', (*b*) through 'the application of the universal concept to "particular" externally given, characterstics of objects and cases' (which is the work of the

Understanding), and (*c*) through the judges' verdict in courts [16]. Hegel thus portrays law (*Recht*) as a system of increasingly specific rules the 'core' of which consists of rational, universally valid principles of justice (*Gerechtigkeit*). Purely formal analysis of a given legal system or any causal historical explanation cannot of course penetrate to the core of the system. Though Hegel does not say so explicitly, the 'positive' attitude to law which he criticizes so strongly and so often in his political writings amounts to a refusal to go beyond such legalistic or historical justification or to raise questions of the ultimate validity of law.

Hegel's views about the form which positive law ought to have are very explicit in the *Philosophy of Right*. A primitive nation can do with a purely customary law, but when it acquires even a little culture the law must be written down and collected together. Such a collection is a sort of crude legal code but it lacks form, precision, and completeness. Hegel talks of the 'monstrous confusion' [135] prevailing in the English law and rejects flatly the view that customary law is superior because it is 'living'; laws do not cease to be customs by being written and codified. He disagrees with contemporary German jurists like Savigny who held that their age was not ripe for codification, and calls this an 'insult' to a civilized people and its lawyers.

Law must be known by thought, it must be a system in itself, and only as such can it be recognized in a civilized country. . . . It is just systematization, i.e. elevation to the universal, which our time is pressing for without any limit. [271–2]

Rulers who have bequeathed well-arranged and clearly formulated legal codes have been 'the greatest benefactors of their people' and 'their work was at the same time a great act of justice' [138]. 'The right of giving recognition only to what my insight sees as rational is the highest right of the subject . . .' [87]. To let law remain so confused, obscure, or technical that the mass of the people are effectively debarred from its knowledge clearly violates that right and is unjust. Besides, the reforming of positive law brings to light outdated privileges, legal discriminations, and other irrationalities and leads to greater fairness. All these points are made in the political writings.

The arguments used by Hegel to justify the rationalization of law are sufficiently general to include public or constitutional law in their scope. However, the *Philosophy of Right* is rather reticent about the formal side of a rational constitution and concentrates heavily on the material aspect, i.e. the contents of rational constitutional law. One or two references to the formal side are nevertheless to be found. First, Hegel contrasts the modern state with a primitive condition, where in default of an objective organization, the form of the state is determined by the sentiment of the ruler or privileged groups in the population. '. . . In more mature social conditions and when the powers of particularity have developed and become free, a form of rational law other than the form of sentiment is required' [177]. This form of rational law could still be an immature form consisting of customs, conventions, and traditions, with their usual characteristics of ambiguity, vagueness, and lack of clear-cut principles. However, such a form of the constitution would not be very consistent with the basic characteristic of the state as that type of human organization which employs to the highest possible degree men's thinking faculties and calls predominantly for conscious decision and action.

> The state . . . knows what it wills and knows it in its universality, i.e. as something thought. Hence it works and acts by reference to consciously adopted ends, known principles, and laws which are not merely implicit but are actually present to consciousness. . . . [165]

It would seem to follow that the constitution, which comprises the activity of the government, the representative assembly, and all other individuals and bodies concerned with the furtherance of the universal interest of the state, ought itself to possess that rational from which Hegel unambiguously demands from the law regulating the relations among private individuals.

Nevertheless Hegel's main emphasis is on the substance of the organization, and on the most important feature of that organization, namely the differentiation of the public authority into branches, organs, or powers. 'The constitution is rational in so far as the state inwardly differentiates and determines its activities in accordance with the nature of the concept' [174]. The fundamental division of powers into three—the Crown, the Executive, and the Legislature—is fairly traditional[1] but its justification is not. Hegel

---

[1] It corresponds to a large extent to Locke's distinction between federative, executive, and legislative power. Cf. *The Second Treatise of Civil Government*, Chapter XII.

rejects the adequacy of any historical or utilitarian grounds as unworthy of philosophy and deduces the necessity of the three powers from the nature of the fully developed concept. Thus the Crown stands for the 'moment' of individuality, the Executive—particularity, and the Legislative—universality, although the separation is only relative and each 'moment' participates in the other two. Hegel insists that the separation is relative also because the same 'life' or 'ideality' or sovereignty permeates them all, i.e. the powers are distinct branches of one and the same supreme public authority of the state.

Rationality in the material sense, i.e. the differentiation of state powers according to the concept, has a very important corollary. It does not depend on the subjective will and insight of anybody but is determined by objective conditions—a whole complex of deeply rooted ideals, social conditions, and established institutions. Only when these conditions are 'ripe' can a constitution be framed as a system of rational laws.

A constitution is not just something manufactured; it is the work of centuries, it is the Idea, the consciousness of rationality so far as that consciousness is developed in a particular nation. No constitution, therefore, is just the creation of its subjects. What Napoleon gave to the Spaniards was more rational than what they had before, and yet they recoiled from it as something alien, because they were not yet educated up to its level. [286–7][1]

The very question 'Who is to frame a constitution?', adds Hegel, is meaningless since it presupposes that the constitution can be invented by anybody with superior wisdom. It is also dangerous since it undermines the respect for the constitution which should 'be treated rather as something simply existent in and by itself, as divine therefore, and constant, and so as exalted above the sphere of things that are made' [178].

One feels, however, that Hegel has avoided the issue. It may be granted that the constitution in the material sense is a work of centuries and is determined by various objective conditions, but to 'frame' it may mean nothing more than to collect in one docu-

---

[1] Hegel goes on to say: 'Isolated individuals may often feel the need and the longing for a better constitution, but it is quite another thing, and one that does not arise till later, for the mass of the people to be animated by such an idea.' This conclusion might well have been drawn from his own experience of suggesting a more rational constitution for the German Empire in the last years of the eighteenth century.

ment and systematically arrange all the rules and provisions governing the organization of the public authority—to do, in other words,
what the Royal Constitutional Charter in Wurtemberg attempted
to do. Such a formulation of public law, far from detracting from
its rationality, would in fact enhance it just as codification en-
hances the rationality of customary private law. Perhaps a clue to
the curious gap in Hegel's argument lies in § 258 of the *Philosophy
of Right*. He castigates Rousseau, Fichte, and others for their
mistake in postulating as the basis of the state identical individual
wills rather than the substantial rational will which underlies them
and is the substance of the ethical life of the community. Such
theories perverted what in Hegel's view was the correct idea
(namely that the state is founded on the will of its members) into
an abstract, one-sided, and therefore false view that it is founded
on the voluntary contractual agreement of a number of individuals.

When these abstract conclusions came into power, they afforded for
the first time in human history the prodigious spectacle of the overthrow
of the constitution of a great actual state and its complete reconstruction
ab initio on the basis of pure thought alone, after the destruction of all
existing and given material. The will of its re-founders was to give it
what they alleged was a purely rational basis, but it was only abstractions
that were being used; the Idea was lacking; and the experiment ended
in the maximum of frightfulness and terror. [157]

Perhaps Hegel was afraid to stress the formal aspect of rationality
in constitutional law because those abstract political ideas were
still so prevalent and so dangerous. Perhaps he feared that to tamper
with established institutions would open the flood-gates once more
—at least when constitutional revision was undertaken by a popular
representative or constitutional assembly and not quietly prepared
by government experts and decreed by the monarch. Finally, perhaps the question of any such revision was still rather an academic
question, considering how many European states lacked some of
the essential features of material rationality. Hence clearly their
constitutions were not yet ripe for formulation in a written
document.

2. *Civil Society*

Civil society is not a concept which Hegel treats explicitly and in
a detailed manner in the minor works; in the *Philosophy of Right*,
however, it does receive systematic treatment and forms an essential

part of his political philosophy. Basically, what Hegel means by it is an aspect of the modern state[1] which secures its citizens an area of independent activity, enables them to pursue subjective ends and seek happiness as they see it, and gives them the opportunity of the ethical, intellectual, and practical training which they need in order to be members of the state *sensu stricto*.

In the course of the actual attainment of selfish ends . . . there is formed a system of complete interdependence, wherein the livelihood, happiness, and legal status of one man is interwoven with the livelihood, happiness, and rights of all. On this system, individual happiness, &c., depend, and only in this connected system are they actualized and secured. This system may be prima facie regarded as the external state, the state based on need, the state as the Understanding envisages it. [123]

The means used by the state to protect the individual are certain public authorities or specialized branches of public authority different and distinct from the three universal powers mentioned above (i.e. the Crown, the Executive, and the Legislative) precisely because their aim is the interest of specific individuals or their groups and not the general or universal interest of the community as a whole. Hegel distinguishes two such authorities: the courts of law and the police, but the latter is used in a special, now archaic, sense meaning all sorts of controlling, regulating, and administrative public bodies, including police in the narrow contemporary sense.[2] Hegel lists the following functions as fully within the scope of the 'police': security of life and property, the oversight of 'activities and organizations of general utility' [147], the reconciliation of consumers' and producers' interests, public instruction, the relief of poverty and other distress, including unemployment, and the protection of commerce. He devotes special attention to the difficulties created by the rise of 'a rabble of paupers' [150] in modern industrial societies, especially England. As far as economic regula-

[1] 'The creation of the civil society is the achievement of the modern world' ([266]; cf. also [123-4]).

[2] Cf. Adam Smith's *Lectures on Justice, Police, Revenue, and Arms*, ed. E. Cannan (Oxford, 1896), where this is the sense in which the word 'police' is used. See also N. Gash, *Mr. Secretary Peel* (London, 1961): 'P. Colquhoun['s] . . . conception of "police" was the wide contemporary definition which embraced the whole system of public regulations and agencies for the preservation of the morals, order and comfort of civil society: and his classic *Treatise on the Police of the Metropolis* (1795) had virtually nothing to say on the technical problem of creating a full-time professional body of police in the modern derivative sense' (pp. 311-12).

tion and free trade are concerned the middle course seems to him the prudent one to steer.

The individual must have a right to work for his bread as he pleases, but the public also has a right to insist that essential tasks shall be properly done. Both points of view must be satisfied and freedom of trade should not be such as to jeopardize the general good. [276]

In the *Philosophy of Right* as well as in *The German Constitution* Hegel maintains that no hard and fast principles can be laid down concerning the amount of public control. 'Spirit of the constitution', needs of the hour, accident, subjective opinions, personal arbitrariness, and so on all play a role in fixing the limit of interference: the thing can be explained historically, but not justified on rational grounds.

When reflective thinking is very highly developed, the public authority may tend to draw into its orbit everything it possibly can, for in everything some factor may be found which might make it dangerous in one of its bearings. In such circumstances, the public authority may set to work very pedantically and embarrass the day-to-day life of people. But however great this annoyance, no objective line can be drawn here either. [276]

Hegel sees one remedy against it, 'by giving authority to spheres of particular interest, which are relatively independent, [so that officials'] personal arbitrariness is broken against such authorized bodies' [291].

This brings us to the third fundamental institution of civil society, the corporation. Like 'police', this has a special meaning for Hegel and covers all sorts of trade, professional, religious, and local or municipal organizations. They have rights (*a*) to look after their own interests, (*b*) to co-opt members, (*c*) to educate them for membership, (*d*) to protect themselves against contingencies (cf. [152-3]). From one point of view they are simply an extension of the right of civil society's members to provide for the best satisfaction of their needs, but incidentally they fulfil most valuable ethical and political functions.

Under modern political conditions, the citizens have only a restricted share in the public business of the state, yet it is essential to provide men—ethical entities—with work of a public character over and above their private business. This work of a public character, which the modern state does not always provide, is found in the corporation. [278]

The membership of a corporation in Hegel's view transforms men from self-seeking individuals into co-operating members of an association with a general purpose. Moreover it gives them experience, social prestige, and certain privileges, and thus creates a group capable of leading the rest of society and standing up to the civil service (cf. [153]). Since corporations perform their educative task only when they are self-governing, Hegel insists that they must have a wide measure of autonomy. But since they have a public character and their working affects the state as a whole, they must be subject to some form of oversight by the government.

The corporation is the preserve of the *bourgeoisie* (or burghers) —one of the three classes (or Estates, *Stände*) into which civil society is differentiated according to Hegel. The other two are the landowning and the 'universal' class which consists mainly of civil servants. The basis of the class division is the method of satisfying needs and gaining livelihood. The burghers depend on the work, skill, and intelligence applied in their business, the landowners on the yields of their estates, and the civil service on the work for the universal, i.e. the state. The different types of work give rise to different attitudes, group ethos, &c., and they also stand in different relations to the public authority. In the name of 'subjective freedom' Hegel insists that each member of civil society must have the right to choose his class, profession, or occupation for himself.

The question of the particular class to which an individual is to belong is one on which natural capacity, birth, and other circumstances have their influence, though the essential and final determining factors are subjective opinion and the individual's arbitrary will, which win in this sphere their right, their merit, and their dignity. [132]

Outside these classes lie the sections of the population without any substantial property, trade, profession, or education whom Hegel leaves out of account because their contribution to civic or political life seems to him insignificant.

3. *Representation*

In the *Philosophy of Right* the nation's right of participating in the public authority, realized through a representative system, is given a fundamental philosophical justification which contrasts sharply with the pragmatic and historical approach of the minor works. The basic concept of the state itself implies some form of popular participation since 'the state is the actuality of concrete freedom'.

But concrete freedom consists in this, that personal individuality and its particular interests not only achieve their complete development and gain explicit recognition for their right (as they do in the sphere of the family and civil society) but, for one thing, they also pass over of their own accord into the interest of the universal, and, for another thing, they know and will the universal; they even recognize it as their own substantive mind; they take it as their end and aim and are active in its pursuit. [160]

Translated into plainer language this means that the ends of the state (or public interest) must be something that the nation can grasp, identify themselves with, and actively pursue. Membership of the state involves duties, but duties should not be enforced whatever the individual feels about them; on the contrary, he must be given a chance to see the ground of obligation and to will it freely. 'Out of his position in the state, a right must accrue to him whereby public affairs shall be his own particular affairs' [162]. In other words, the individual must have political rights as well as duties, over and above the rights that belong to him as a member of a family and civil society.

The organ of the state which unites the universal and the particular interests is the popular element in the legislature, the Estates.

The specific function which the concept assigns to the Estates is to be sought in the fact that in them the subjective moment in universal freedom—the private judgement and private will of the sphere called 'civil society' in this book—comes into existence integrally related to the state. [196–7]

The composition of the Estates here envisaged is somewhat different from that adumbrated in the political writings. The two non-official classes of civil society are represented through two separate chambers: the landowners through an Upper House based on hereditary peerage, primogeniture, and entailed estates, and the burghers through a Lower House consisting of deputies or representatives of the various bodies within civil society. Hegel condemns the individualistic principle of numerically equal constituencies as strongly in the *Philosophy of Right* as elsewhere.

... In making the appointment [to the Estates], society is not dispersed into atomic units, collected to perform only a single and temporary act and kept together for a moment and no longer. On the contrary, it makes the appointment as a society, articulated into associations, communities, and corporations, which although constituted already for other purposes, acquire in this way a connexion with politics. [200]

In a familiar way he condemns universal suffrage also on the ground that it puts 'the democratic element without any rational form into the organism of the state' (ibid.), and leaves the representation of 'the essential spheres of society and its large-scale interests' [202] entirely to chance.

The reasons why in the *Philosophy of Right* Hegel regards a two-chamber legislature assembly as more rational than a single-chamber one ought to be mentioned. One reason is that the two classes have different characters and thus contribute something different to the work of deliberation. A more important reason is that the Upper Chamber is in a position to 'mediate' between the government and the Lower House and to prevent excessive hostility between the two. But the Estates, as a whole, are also 'a mediating organ' since they stand between the government and the nation. 'Their function requires them to possess a political and administrative sense and temper, no less than a sense for the interests of individuals and particular groups' [197]. Hegel believes that the participation of Ministers in the work of the Estates fosters the right mentality and quotes with approval the example of England where it has brought about unity between the legislative and the executive powers [292], and led to the willingness of Parliament to vote higher taxes than anywhere else [293].

From the point of view of the public authority, the Estates, as part of the legislature, are concerned with (*a*) 'the laws as such' in so far as they require fresh and extended determination (this includes the elaboration of the constitution as well as laws dealing with private rights, rights of communities, corporations, and so on), and (*b*) 'the exaction of services' from individuals which in modern times means monetary taxation [194–5]. From the narrow point of view of private individuals the primary end of legislation and taxation is the safeguarding of, and the provision for, their well-being and happiness, but a truer concept of the Estates' function is to regard them as something educative. On the one hand, they bring the grievances, wishes, and opinions of individuals to the notice of the government and thus are a source of the government's deeper insight into the needs of civil society. On the other hand, they give the members of the Estates, and through them the country as a whole, the opportunity of learning the state's requirements.

Estates Assemblies, open to the public, are a great spectacle and an excellent education for the citizens, and it is from them that the people learns best how to recognize the true character of its interests. . . . A nation which has such public sittings is far more vitally related to the state than one which has no Estates Assembly or one which meets in private. [294]

Because of the necessity for give and take and the possibility of changing one's mind as a result of a debate, Hegel insists that representatives should be free agents and not delegates bound by specific instructions [201]. He omits, however, all mention of party organization.

An important corollary of the work of the Estates is the publicity of their proceedings. Without it representatives cannot educate and influence the mass of the citizenry. But the Estates are a two-way channel since representatives are supposed to reflect the views of the population and to bring them to bear on the government. Hence the necessity of free public communication through the press and the spoken word without which the process of mediation cannot take place [205]. Hegel's attitude towards public opinion is far more critical in the *Philosophy of Right* than in the political writings, and he expressly calls it a hotchpotch of truth and falsehood, sound judgements and half-baked fads, rational insight and blind prejudice, &c. But he recognizes its necessity as an expression of 'the formal subjective freedom of individuals' [204] to air views about politics. And this necessity is reinforced by the fact that the state's authority nowadays depends primarily on men's own insight, which public opinion helps to further.

. . . At all times public opinion has been a great power and it is particularly so in our day when the principle of subjective freedom has such importance and significance. What is to be authoritative nowadays derives its authority not at all from force, only to a small extent from habit and custom, really from insight and argument. [294]

Though Hegel does not draw the conclusion in the *Philosophy of Right*, one can see that the work of writers and commentators—or 'publicists'—in explaining and clarifying political issues is a vital aspect of public opinion, while political philosophers perform a similar task *vis-à-vis* a much smaller but more sophisticated and intellectual public.

4. *The Monarch and the Executive*

Hegel defines the executive's task as 'subsuming the particular under the universal' [188–9]. In its broadest sense it includes the activities of the police and the judiciary, but since these bear more directly on the affairs of civil society, they are included within it. The state executive *sensu stricto* is organized hierarchically and comprises (*a*) ordinary civil servants at the bottom, (*b*) higher advisory officials above them, and (*c*) supreme heads of departments 'who are in direct contact with the monarch' [189]. Hegel repeats here that the civil service must fulfil certain objective criteria of ability and knowledge, that it must be open to all qualified citizens, and that it must have security of tenure. He sees the guarantee against the abuse of its powers partly in the hierarchical control of the executive itself, partly in the power of corporations, and partly in the *esprit de corps* and ethical conduct which their work for the universal engenders.

At the top of the hierarchy the position is different. Hegel postulates a cabinet or supreme advisory council whose members are freely chosen and dismissed by the monarch. They are responsible for policy decisions by the monarch himself and for all acts of government. These presumably include foreign affairs, which Hegel regards as the special business of the head of state. Though this section of the *Philosophy of Right* is not very detailed, it gives one more insight into Hegel's views on the Ministry than any of the political writings.

The monarch is not only the chief executive but he also has a share in the legislative power, since promulgation by him is the final step in law-making. Hegel attaches the greatest importance to the monarch's 'I will', even if it is a pure formality, because 'he is bound by the concrete decision of his councillors, and if the constitution is stable, he has often no more to do than sign his name' [288]. Only in undeveloped states is there any scope for the monarch's character and personality in legislation. 'In a well-organized monarchy, the objective aspect belongs to law alone, and the monarch's part is merely to set to the law the subjective "I will"' [298]. The monarch's personal act of will differentiates the modern from the ancient world where laws were thought to be beyond human control and it expresses the modern man's determination to be the master of his political fate.

Hegel's concept of sovereignty is connected with this aspect of the monarchy. He defines it as 'the moment of ultimate decision, as the *self-determination* to which everything else reverts and from which everything else derives the beginning of its actuality' [179]. This means that the monarch is the ultimate point of reference in the legal and constitutional system of a given state, and it is because of the existence of such a point within it that the state is externally sovereign. In order that sovereignty may be grounded in something simpler and more solid than the will of an electoral college or a populace voting in a referendum, Hegel believes that the monarch should acquire his office by hereditary succession; this belief is confirmed by philosophy which demands that the individuality of the state should find concrete embodiment in an individual brought to his position in an immediate, i.e. natural way, through birth.

While in one sense the monarchy and sovereignty are identical, in another they are distinct. In this second sense sovereignty means 'the ideality of all particular authorities within it' [180]. Hegel compares this sovereignty to life which pervades an organism and makes its parts members of the organism. In this sense sovereignty resides in the state as a whole, its constitution, of which the monarchy, the executive, the Estates, and so on, are only branches or 'moments'. Sovereignty is thus closely bound up with material rationality in the state since differentiation into parts is a sign of a rational constitution. Hegel rejects the concept of the sovereignty of the people on the ground that it ignores this aspect of the matter.

... Opposed to the sovereignty of the monarch, the sovereignty of the people is one of the confused notions based on the wild idea of the 'people'. Taken without its monarch and the articulation of the whole which is the indispensable and direct concomitant of monarchy, the people is a formless mass and no longer a state. [182–3]

If the 'people' is represented ... as an inwardly developed, genuinely organic, totality, then sovereignty is there as the personality of the whole, and this personality is there, in the real existence adequate to its concept, as the person of the monarch. [183]

Thus the two aspects of sovereignty, though distinct, are ultimately interconnected although philosophy alone can prove the connexion to be necessary and rational.

B. THE PHILOSOPHY OF HISTORY

In the *Philosophy of History*[1] Hegel divides the whole course of world history (since civilized, politically organized societies first made an appearance) into four periods called Oriental, Greek, Roman, and German. In each of them a whole complex of values, customs, institutions, and laws comes into being and reaches a certain height of development, sometimes within the frontiers of a single political unit, but usually within a system of separate and antagonistic units. In the Introduction Hegel insists that the different features of each complex form an organic system, i.e. mutually interact and influence each other; and that the fundamental principles of each period are basically different from those of the others.

It follows that the political institutions of a country cannot be understood in isolation from the rest of its national culture or 'spirit', and also that political institutions characteristic of one civilization cannot be grafted on to another.

The constitutions under which world-historical peoples have reached their culmination are peculiar to them, and therefore do not present a generally applicable political basis. . . . Nothing is so absurd as to look to Greeks, Romans, or Orientals for models for the political arrangements of our time. [47]

Oriental paternalism or Greek democracy cannot therefore be valid political models for nineteenth-century Western Europe, a point which Hegel makes early in *The Wurtemberg Estates*.

The constitution which is peculiar to the modern, Germanic world Hegel calls Monarchy and he differentiates it sharply from Despotism (which is the 'principle' of the Oriental epoch). What basically distinguishes them is that particular and separate interests, which are suppressed under despotism, find a legitimate expression in the monarchical constitution, which at the same time ensures strong government by vesting ultimate control over it in one man. Hegel rejects democracy or republic as equally out of place in the nineteenth century, and his chief ground is that modern nations are too large, heterogeneous, and individualistic to guarantee the sort of spontaneous self-identification of the citizen with the state which existed in ancient Greece and republican

---

[1] Page references are to the translation by J. Sibree published by Willey Book Co. (New York, 1944). (Spelling and punctuation have been modernized.)

Rome (cf. [250], [251]). Nevertheless Hegel admits that the ancients and the contemporary Europeans share a common belief that a free constitution requires popular participation in the government, now of course no longer directly but through representatives.

The so-called representative constitution is that form of government with which we connect the idea of a free constitution and this notion has become a rooted prejudice. [48]

It is interesting to notice that at the end of his life Hegel still regarded representation as a condition of freedom and as part and parcel of the monarchical state, a view first clearly expressed in *The German Constitution*.

Hegel discusses the concept of the 'world historical individual' at length in the Introduction. Although politically organized nations seem to him the chief actors in the drama of world history, there are also outstanding individuals who make a visible mark on it, for example Alexander the Great, Julius Caesar, and Napoleon. These political giants intuitively apprehend the drift of events and by their forceful activity speed up the downfall of the old or the rise of the new at times of transition. The concept of the 'world historical individual' is clearly a development of Hegel's early views on 'political genius' expressed in *The German Constitution*.

After traversing the Oriental and Greco-Roman world, Hegel comes to analyse the fourth main epoch of world history, which he calls the 'German World', in the IVth Part of the *Philosophy of History*. The word 'German' is used by him rather vaguely to extend to the whole of Western and Central Europe which at one time or another was conquered and settled by the primitive Germanic tribes. Although a large part of that area had been under the Roman Empire and received its culture from it, it was the spirit of the Germanic people which in Hegel's view contained a new and higher principle of development and ultimately produced modern Western civilization. He defines that principle abstractly as 'the free spirit, [i.e. one] which reposes on itself—the absolute self-determination of subjectivity' [343]. When he becomes more concrete, he describes the condition of the early Germans in terms almost identical with those of *The German Constitution*.

Our first acquaintance with the Germans finds each individual enjoying an independent freedom; and yet there is a certain community of feeling and interest, though not yet matured to a political condition. [347]

The German love of independence gave rise to a kind of primitive democracy of freemen who attached themselves voluntarily to leaders and were bound to them through the fidelity of promise, and yet retained a right to decide on common affairs such as war. The peculiarity of the German political evolution was that those subjective attitudes did not immediately harden into objective laws and institutions, but developed into a mass of particular privileges. 'Thus the state was a patchwork of private rights, and a rational political life was the tardy issue of wearisome struggles and convulsions' [354]. This was the second period of the modern world, the period of medieval feudalism, which reached the nadir of political disintegration and moral corruption in the Holy Roman Empire and in Italy.

The overcoming of disintegration, which succeeded in France, England, and Spain, Hegel calls 'the transition from feudalism to monarchy' and devotes a whole chapter to it. He sees the essence of monarchy in the existence of a supreme authority over everybody in the state and the absence of individuals with constitutional power to defend their caprice. Thus monarchy implies the equal subjection of all to the law. 'In monarchy . . . there is one lord and no serf, for servitude is abrogated by it and in it right and law are recognized; it is the source of real freedom' [399]. Another aspect of monarchy is that private political power becomes converted into public power: 'Vassals become officers of the state, whose duty is to execute the laws by which the state is regulated' (ibid.). Finally, some features of the feudal system become incorporated into the constitutional monarchy.

Individuals quit their isolated capacity and become members of estates and corporations. . . . Thus the authority of the sovereign inevitably ceases to be mere arbitrary sway. The consent of the Estates and corporations is essential to its maintenance, and if the prince wishes to have that consent, he must wish what is just and reasonable. [399–400]

Hegel points out that the process of unification and centralization has sometimes taken on a violent and arbitrary form, but its intrinsic rightness is not thereby impaired. In this connexion he repeats his defence of 'Machiavelli's celebrated work *The Prince*' [403] in terms similar to *The German Constitution*. Altogether the parallelism of *The German Constitution* and this part of the *Philosophy of History* is very striking, and shows how little his views on the origin of the modern state changed during the intervening thirty years.

Although it was the French Revolution of 1789 which in Hegel's view opened a new and final period in world history, he traces the source of its principles to the Reformation. By making individual conscience the ultimate point of reference in matters of faith, the Reformation abolished the distinction between priests and laymen, dispensed with the hierarchically organized Church, and freed the human mind from the bondage of dogma and tradition. Thus it laid the foundation of freedom and equality on which the modern state rests.

In the proclamation of these principles is unfurled the new, the latest standard round which the peoples rally—the banner of free spirit, independent thought finding its life in the truth, and enjoying independence only in it. This is the banner under which we serve, and which we bear. Time, since that epoch, has had no other work to do than the formal imbuing of the world with this principle, in bringing the reconciliation implicit [in Christianity] into objective and explicit existence. . . . Consequently law, property, social morality, government, constitutions, &c., must be conformed to general principles in order that they must accord with the idea of free will and be rational. [416–17]

The immediate political effect of the Reformation, however, was different from that. It strengthened the power of the monarchs over their territories, and it consolidated sovereignty, which, during the subsequent period, in fact changed its character from private property to public authority. The establishment of supreme authority was facilitated by the rise of standing armies and the suppression of territorial magnates; here Hegel again stresses the role of Richelieu in France, and points out that the curtailment of the right of the feudal nobility was in the interest both of the king and the people. Nevertheless, Hegel recognizes that even in his own time the aristocracy form a vital link between the sovereign and the people.

. . . The aristocracy have a position assigned them, as the support of the throne, as occupied and active on behalf of the state, and the common weal, and at the same time as maintaining the freedom of the citizens. [430]

Hegel also traces the influence of the Reformation on the German Empire, and repeats all that he wrote on the subject in *The German Constitution*.

From the Reformation, the path to the French Revolution in
the intellectual realm leads through the Enlightenment. The denial
of miracles and other divine interventions in the course of nature
led to the secularization of Natural Law also in the ethical universe.

Right and [social] morality came to be looked upon as having their
foundation in the actual present will of man, whereas formerly it was
referred to the commands of God enjoined *ab extra*, . . . or appearing
in the form of particular right . . . in old parchments, as *privilegia*, or
in international compacts. [440]

Thus human will and reason came to be regarded as the criterion
of what is to be obeyed or believed. Hegel asks himself why it was
in France that the new attitude to the state first expressed itself
in political action. He answers in terms of the particularly irrational
state of affairs there ('the political condition of France at that time
presents nothing but a confused mass of privileges altogether con-
travening thought and reason' [446]) coupled with the reactionary
influence of the Church and the fact that the task of reform was not
undertaken in time by the government itself, and had to be brought
about by violence from outside. This first constitution, consciously
willed and formulated, receives tremendous praise from Hegel.

Never since the sun had stood in the firmament and the planets
revolved around him had it been perceived that man's existence centres
in his head, i.e. in thought, inspired by which he builds up the world of
reality. . . . This was accordingly a glorious mental dawn. All thinking
beings shared in the jubilation of this epoch. Emotions of a lofty character stirred men's minds at that time; a spiritual enthusiasm thrilled
through the world, as if the reconciliation between the divine and the
secular was now first accomplished. [447]

The idea, also expressed in *The Wurtemberg Estates*, that the French
Revolution inaugurated a new era in world history by giving
political arrangements a spiritual basis in universal, rational principles could not have been more forcefully expressed.

Hegel then traces the course of the Revolution in France and
its impact on the rest of Europe. He praises the freedoms of person
and property it established; then points out the unresolved problem of combining the will of all, which liberty demands, with the
ultimate decision of the monarch, which makes for strength in
the government; finally he mentions the necessity of the right kind
of disposition towards the state, 'the sense of the state' or 'political

consciousness' of the political writings, which he equates with a basic political consensus.

There may be various opinions and views respecting laws, constitution, and government, but there must be a disposition on the part of the citizens to regard all these opinions as subordinate to the substantial interests of the state; and to insist upon them no further than that interest will allow. [449]

While the one-sided search for liberty in the will of all led to the Terror and the tyranny of the National Convention, a reactionary religious and national disposition brought about the fall of Napoleon.[1] Hegel sees the source of instability in France after 1815 in the sway of atomistic concepts of freedom which are incompatible with a firm institutional order and a strong government. How to combine the will of the many with political stability is the 'problem . . . with which history is now occupied, and whose solution it has to work out in the future' [452].

Finally, Hegel considers the effect of the Revolution on Germany and the two other great European powers, Austria and Britain.

The fiction of an Empire [in Germany] has utterly vanished. It is broken up into sovereign states. Feudal obligations are abolished, for freedom of property and of person have been recognized as fundamental principles. Offices of state are open to every citizen, talent and adaptation being of course the necessary conditions. The government rests with the official world, and the personal decision of the monarch constitutes its apex. . . . Yet with firmly established laws, and a settled organization of the state, what is left to the sole arbitrament of the monarch is, in point of substance, no great matter. [456]

Hegel adds that in Germany participation in government depends on knowledge and experience, and that Protestantism supplies the disposition favourable to rational political life in general. With regard to Britain, Hegel asks whether its stability throughout the

---

[1] Hegel's comment on Napoleon well illustrates his own double concern with strong government and civil liberty of which it is a precondition. '. . . He knew how to rule, and soon settled the internal affairs of France. The *avocats*, ideologues, and abstract-principle men who ventured to show themselves he sent "to the right about", and the sway of mistrust was exchanged for that of respect and fear. He then, with the vast might of his character, turned his attention to foreign relations, subjected all Europe, and diffused his liberal institutions in every quarter' [451]. Later he makes this comment: 'Material superiority in power can achieve no enduring results: Napoleon could not coerce Spain into freedom any more than Philip II could force Holland into slavery' [453].

long period of convulsions following the French Revolution was due to the backwardness of the English nation in apprehending general principles or to the fact that they had already been realized and hence no longer excited popular interest and passion. Implicitly he denies the latter and inclines towards the former. 'The constitution of England is a complex of mere *particular* rights and particular privileges . . . and of institutions characterized by real freedom there are nowhere fewer than in England . . .' [454]. But Hegel also praises the freedom of civil society in England and the strength of the government, while condemning the moral and political corruption which makes the latter possible. The general tenor, as well as many specific comments of the concluding pages of the *Philosophy of History*, is almost identical with those of *The English Reform Bill*.[1]

C. CONCLUSION

Hegel's political thought has sometimes struck students as something apart from the main stream of Western European political theory. That stream has been thought to favour constitutionalism, democracy, and progress while Hegel seems to have championed absolutism, autocracy, and reaction. This study of his political writings, along with a glance at his two major philosophical works on politics, has shown how little substance there is in any such interpretation.

[1] Hegel delivered the *Lectures on the Philosophy of History* for the last time in the winter of 1830–1, so they and *The English Reform Bill* are virtually contemporary.

If one disregards the metaphysical assumptions of the *Lectures*, the theory of the modern state put forward by Hegel in that work and anticipated in *The German Constitution* bears striking resemblance to that of Max Weber. Cf. the following summary of Weber's views in Reinhard Bendix, *Max Weber: an Intellectual Portrait* (London, 1960), p. 380: 'Weber was very much concerned with the distinctively rational characteristics of the state, which emerged from the patrimonial and feudal struggle for power and which can be found only in Western civilization. . . . [The] preconditions upon which the modern Western state is based . . . are (1) monopolization of the means of domination and administration based on: (*a*) the creation of a centrally directed and permanent system of taxation; (*b*) the creation of a centrally directed and permanent military force in the hands of a central, governmental authority; (2) monopolization of legal enactments and the legitimate use of force by the central authority; and (3) the organization of a rationally oriented officialdom, whose exercise of administrative functions is dependent upon the central authority.' All those features of the modern state were clearly recognized and explicitly stated by Hegel.

What is equally obvious from this and the preceding chapters is that Hegel's reputation for esoteric jargon, extreme obscurity, and mysticism is not altogether justified. Implicit in the minor works, and explicit in the major ones, is a certain theory of the modern state, and that theory is not radically different in approach, method of argument, and level of theorizing from the political theory of Hobbes, Locke, Montesquieu, or Rousseau. Like them, Hegel describes or prescribes, explains or justifies, discusses origins, functions, interconnexions, and elaborates a 'model' or 'pure type' of the state which is internally consistent, pragmatically sound, largely 'actualized' in fact, and which in his opinion fits better than any other 'model' the basic social, cultural, and moral realities of nineteenth-century Western Europe. One can dispute the merits of Hegel's theory, point out its weaknesses or contradictions, question assumptions, and so on, but such treatment would not be different from that normally meted out to other thinkers.

The reason why Hegel is generally not discussed in these terms, and why he seems to stand apart from other 'classical' political theorists, is that his political thought has so to speak another dimension, the metaphysical. This metaphysics has so fascinated or repelled students that the more ordinary aspects of Hegel's thought have tended to remain in the shadow and to receive little systematic attention. 'The march of God in the world, that is what the state is.'[1] After encountering this sentence in the *Philosophy of Right* one might well lose interest in taking up questions such as why Hegel believed in a strong executive or wanted the representative assembly to be elected by organs of self-government or championed the rationalization of the legal system.

Moreover, once the metaphysical element becomes dominant, as it does in some sections of the *Philosophy of Right* and the *Philosophy of History*, the character of political theory changes. The teaching, or the insight, it provides ceases to have any practical significance. If things are as they are because God has ordained them; if ethical life is the embodiment of an all-powerful transcendent Spirit; if the individual's thoughts are mere accidents of metaphysical substances, man can but contemplate and venerate[2] but

[1] This translation has been challenged by W. Kaufmann, who suggests instead: 'It is the way of God with the world that the state *is*' (*From Shakespeare to Existentialism* (Boston, 1959), p. 91).

[2] Cf. the following passage of the *Philosophy of Right*. 'As high as mind stands above nature, so high does the state stand above physical life. Man must

not act, or influence events, or shape reality. A metaphysician is like a man at the top of the Eiffel Tower. He commands an incomparable view of the life down below, he perceives unity where others see chaos, he discovers new kinds of order and symmetry, and so on. But his very loftiness isolates him from the world of practical affairs and his splendid vision may bring comfort or aesthetic pleasure, but not the kind of guidance men need in political life.

Hegel could have kept his political theory quite distinct from his general philosophy, and in his minor works he does achieve such separation. But in the two *Philosophies* the theory of the state becomes incorporated into, on the one hand, a general theory of ethical life and, on the other, a theory of progress and historical change, both heavily speculative and the former an integral part of a whole philosophical system. Apparently Hegel thought that only by transposing politics to the metaphysical plane and giving his concepts a speculative underpinning could he establish their validity. It is this quest for absolute proof, this passion for certain knowledge in politics, which constitutes one of the distinctive features of Hegel's political thought. It is, incidentally, what sometimes gives his works an air of intellectual arrogance and intolerance, and makes him dismiss contemptuously concepts that have not been speculatively treated.

Professional philosophers, especially in England, have shared a strong antipathy to metaphysics for fifty years or so. Yet fashions change also in philosophy, and in a new intellectual climate Hegel's speculative daring may be counted as more of a virtue than a vice. There is, however, no need for students of political theory to wait for a renaissance of metaphysical philosophy. Hegel's political thought can be read, understood, and appreciated without having to come to terms with his metaphysics.[1] Some of his assertions may

therefore venerate the state as a secular deity, and observe that if it is difficult to comprehend nature, it is infinitely harder to understand the state' [285]. However, 'the state' in this context does not mean the institutional framework or the system of authorities but the ethos which pervades them. Cf. T. M. Knox's comment on the distinction between 'the strictly political state' and 'the state proper' in his edition of the *Philosophy of Right*, pp. 364, 365.

[1] Perhaps there is a parallel with Hobbes here. He seemed to think that the most original and important part of his political philosophy was the treatment of politics as a science of bodies in motion and the use of a geometric mode of demonstration. Today we tend to ignore Hobbe's atomistic philosophy, while his specifically political ideas continue to be studied with great interest.

seem less well grounded than they might otherwise have been; some of his statements and beliefs may puzzle one; some intellectual curiosity may be unsatisfied when metaphysics is left out; a solid volume of political theory and political thinking will still remain.

Reduced to its simplest terms, Hegel's political thought consists of four fundamental propositions: (1) the modern state is a constitutional monarchy with a strong, bureaucratic executive balanced by popular participation in government and areas of individual, social, and local autonomy; (2) the legal and institutional structure of this state is in process of transformation by the thoughtful application of theoretical principles to the traditional framework. These are the ideas which chiefly permeate the non-philosophical writings. The philosophical ones add two more: (3) political life in any epoch is shaped and determined by the dominant spiritual and material forces of that epoch, its total culture and civilization; and (4) the ultimate explanation of the character of each epoch and the transition from one to another is to be sought in the nature of a metaphysical entity called Spirit, Mind, or Reason. This study has been an attempt to throw light on the first and second of those ideas. May one hope at least that a sociologist will soon consider the third. Whether or not a philosopher takes a fresh look at the fourth?

PART II

TRANSLATIONS

T. M. KNOX

PREFACE

THESE translations have been made, by kind permission of Dr. Felix Meiner, from Hegel's *Schriften zur Politik und Rechtsphilosophie, hrsg. von* Georg Lasson, second edition, Leipzig, 1923. Page references to this edition are printed throughout the translations in square brackets. One advantage of this is that Dr. Pelczynski has been able, in giving page references to Lasson, to give references to this translation also. So far as the translator is aware, none of these essays has been translated before into any language. Divisions into chapters or sections are Lasson's. Hegel's long paragraphs have occasionally been subdivided. Hegel's italics have normally been ignored and most of his page references to the published *Proceedings of the Wurtemberg Estates* have been suppressed.

There is scope for a Ph.D. thesis on Hegel as a stylist. The essays on the Wurtemberg Estates and the English Reform Bill are political journalism; they occasionally show how well Hegel could write if he chose, but they are at times diffuse and clumsy: their style resembles that of the *Phenomenology* and they do not display the terseness, the clarity, and the concentrated energy of expression characteristic of the numbered paragraphs in the *Encyclopaedia* or the *Philosophie des Rechts*. The essay on the German constitution is similar in style to that of some of the early theological writings, and, like them, it poses problems to a translator which this translator cannot claim always to have resolved. It was never published, and the difficult manuscript, never revised by its author for publication, may not always have been correctly deciphered. The translator has tried to write English, but his task is to translate and not to paraphrase, and since German writers constantly complain about the obscurity of Hegel's style a translator may perhaps be allowed to ask for indulgence if his version is not invariably perspicuous. If in places the translation is not easy to follow the translator makes bold to claim that the German is no less so. Even in writing political journalism, Hegel occasionally allowed himself incursions into theoretical abstraction.

It is a pity that the essay on the *Proceedings of the Wurtemberg Estates* has not been translated in its entirety, but many of its sections are of such purely antiquarian interest that their appearance here did not seem justifiable, because the *raison d'être* of the translations is to illustrate and support Dr. Pelczynski's essay. The translator has supplied a short summary of the sections omitted.

Footnotes initialed H. are either Hegel's or else, in *The German Constitution*, are drawn from his marginal comments or rejected drafts. Those initialed L. are Lasson's. The remainder are the translator's. He has mainly confined himself to an attempt at elucidation, or, more frequently, at supplying information which a late twentieth-century schoolboy can no longer be supposed to have at his command.

In making the translation, the translator has occasionally been helped by reference to an earlier text of *The German Constitution* published by G. Mollat in 1893 and to two texts of *The English Reform Bill*, one edited by L. Boumann in vol. xvii of the original edition of Hegel's collected works (vol. xx in Glockner's edition) and the other edited by J. Hoffmeister in *Hegels Berliner Schriften* (Hamburg, 1956). These texts are referred to in footnotes as 'Mollat', Boumann', and 'Hoffmeister' respectively.

The translator has received substantial help from his colleagues Professor C. T. Carr (in the translation of *The German Constitution*) and N. Gash (in the terminology of *The English Reform Bill* and in footnotes to that essay) and also from Professor W. Witte of the University of Aberdeen. All his translations have been read by Dr. Pelczynski, who has made many helpful suggestions. To these scholars who have given so generously of their time and trouble the translator records his gratitude. But it is necessary for him to add that for the errors and infelicities that remain the entire responsibility is his own.

T. M. KNOX

St. Andrews, November 1962

WHEN I wrote the first paragraph of this Preface, I was unaware that, in 1953, Professor C. J. Friedrich had published, with Random House, New York, a translation of the fragment on the *Recent Domestic Affairs of Wurtemberg* and of selected passages in *The German Constitution* and the *English Reform Bill*.

I have taken the opportunity of this reprint to correct mistakes on pages 145 and 184.

T. M. K.

Crieff, August 1968

I

THE GERMAN CONSTITUTION

[INTRODUCTION]

[3][1] GERMANY is a state no longer. The older professors of constitutional law had the idea of a science before their minds when they were handling German constitutional law, and consequently they did set out to establish a concept of the German constitution. But they could not become of one mind about this concept before the modern professors[2] gave up trying to find it. They now no longer treat constitutional law as a science but only as a description of what exists empirically and not conformably with a rational idea, and they believe that they can ascribe to the German state no more than the *name* of an empire or a body politic.

There is no longer any disputing about which concept the German constitution falls under.[3] What can no longer be brought under a concept exists no longer. Had Germany been supposed to be a state, we could only follow a foreign political scientist[4] and call the present dissolution of the state 'anarchy', if the parts had not made themselves into states again, to which a show of union is still left, not indeed by a bond which exists now but by the memory of an old one; just as fallen fruit is recognized as having belonged to its tree by the fact that it lies under the tree top, but neither its position below the tree nor the tree's shadow which falls on it can save [4] it from rotting or from the power of the elements to which it now belongs.

The health of a state is generally revealed not so much in the

---

[1] Numbers 3 to 323 so placed in square brackets are page references to Lasson's edition. Four-figure numbers in square brackets are dates inserted by the translator.

[2] Rosenzweig, *Hegel und der Staat* (Munich and Berlin, 1920, vol. i, p. 239), says that the reference is to writers such as J. J. Moser and to Majer, *Teutsche Staats Konstitution* (1800). See also [49–50].

[3] i.e. under which of Aristotle's types of constitution it falls. H. [4–5 fn.].

[4] Voltaire. H. [5 fn.]. Bryce, *Holy Roman Empire* (London, 1910), remarks that the Emperor Charles IV (1347–78) 'legalized anarchy and called it a constitution' (p. 246).

calm of peace as in the stir of war.[1] Peace is the state of enjoyment and activity in seclusion, when government is a prudent paternalism, making only ordinary demands on its subjects. But in war the power of the association of all with the whole is in evidence; this association has adjusted the amount which it can demand from individuals, as well as the worth of what they may do for it of their own impulse and their own heart.

Thus it was in the war with the French Republic that Germany found by its own experience that it was no longer a state: it became conscious of its political situation quite as much in the war itself as in the peace that closed it. The tangible results of the peace are: the loss of some of the finest German territories with some millions of their inhabitants; a burden of debt (more severe in the south than in the north) which prolongs the misery of war far into the peace; and the fact that, apart from those states which have come under the dominion of the conquerors and so under foreign laws and customs, many others will lose what is their greatest good, namely their existence as independent states.

The peace makes it appropriate to consider carefully what are the inner causes, the spirit, of these results, and in what way the results are only the external and necessary appearances of that spirit. So too this consideration in itself befits anyone who does not surrender to what happens but recognizes the event and its necessity. By such recognition he differentiates himself from those who see only arbitrariness and chance, because their own folly convinces them that they would have managed everything more wisely and more fortunately. Such recognition is of importance for most people, [5] not so that they can learn from experience how to act better on a future occasion, but only because they [derive satisfaction] from it and from the intelligent judgements on the individual events which it entails. Those who so act in the midst of these great affairs that they could themselves direct them are very few; but the others have to wait on events with understanding and insight into their necessity. However, from that experience of mistakes which are[2] an outburst of inner weakness and unwisdom, those who have made the mistakes are less likely to learn than others—indeed they only strengthen their habit of making mistakes.

---

[1] Cf. Hegel, *Werke*[1], vol. i, p. 373; and *Philosophie des Rechts*, § 324 *Anm.* (cited below as *Ph.d.R.*)

[2] Reading *sind* for *ist*.

Others can recognize the mistakes, and this insight of theirs puts them in a position to derive advantage accordingly. If they are at all capable of doing this, and if in addition they are materially in a position to do it, they thereby on both counts possess an insight which the thinking of the man not in public life may lack.

The thoughts contained in this essay can have no other aim[1] or effect, when published, save that of promoting the understanding of what is, and therefore a calmer outlook and a moderate endurance of it alike in words and in actual contact [with affairs]. For it is not what is that makes us irascible and resentful, but the fact that it is not as it ought to be. But if we recognize that it is as it must be, i.e. that it is not arbitrariness and chance that make it what it is, then we also recognize that it is as it ought to be.[2] Yet it is hard for the ordinary run of men to rise to the habit of trying to recognize necessity and to think it. Between events and the free interpretation of them they insert a mass of concepts and aims and require what happens to correspond with them. And when doubtless the case is nearly always otherwise, they excuse their concepts on the plea that while what dominated them was necessity what dominated the event was chance. Their concepts are just as restricted as their insight into things, which indeed they interpret as mere isolated events, not as a system of events ruled by a single spirit. Besides, whether they suffer under events or merely find them contradicting their concepts [6], they find in their assertion of their concepts the right to complain bitterly about what has happened.

Recent times above all have saddled the Germans with this vice. In the constant contradiction between what they demand and what happens contrary to their demand, they seem not merely fault-finding, but, when they talk of their concepts alone, false and dishonest, because they ascribe necessity to their concepts of law and duties, while nothing happens in accordance with this necessity. Thus they become accustomed either to a constant contradiction between their words and the facts or else to an attempt to make events different from what they really are and to twist their explanation of them to suit certain concepts.

---

[1] Rosenzweig (op. cit., vol. i, p. 129) infers that Hegel is not writing a *Prince* addressed to a possible saviour of his country. But Hegel does make a sort of appeal to a Theseus before his essay ends.

[2] Cf. Preface to *Ph.d.R.*

But anyone would be gravely in error who tried from the concepts of what ought to happen, i.e. from the laws of the land, to get to know what does generally happen in Germany; the dissolution of the state is recognizable above all when everything happens contrary to law. He would err similarly if he supposed that the real ground and cause of this dissolution is the colour[1] assumed by the laws. It is precisely because of their concepts that the Germans seem so dishonest as neither to acknowledge anything as it is, nor to accept it as pretty much what it is in its own actual inherent strength. They remain true to their concepts, to right, and the laws; but events are wont not to correspond with these, and thus the people who have an interest in so doing struggle to accommodate theory and practice to one another by words with the force of concepts.[2] But the concept which includes all others in itself is the concept that Germany as such is still a state because it was a state once, and the forms are still there from which their living soul has flown.

[7] The organization of this body called the German constitution was built up in a life totally different from the life it had later and has now. The justice and power, the wisdom and courage of times past; the honour and blood, the well-being and distress of generations long dead; and the relationships and manners which have perished with them; all these are expressed in the forms of this body. But the course of time and of the civilization that has been meanwhile developing has sundered the fate of that past from the life of the present. The building in which that fate dwelt is no longer supported by the fate of the present generation. It stands without being necessary or useful to the interests of this generation, and what it does is isolated from the spirit of the world. While these laws have lost their former life, the vitality of the present day has not known how to concentrate itself in laws. Every centre of life has gone its own way and established itself on its own; the whole has fallen apart. The state exists no longer.

This form of German constitutional law is deeply grounded in what has been the chief fame of the Germans, namely their

---

[1] Reading *Farbe* with Rosenkranz, *Hegels Leben* (Berlin, 1844), p. 241, and Mollat. Lasson reads *Form*. In either event it seems necessary to read *angenommen* for *genommen*.

[2] See below, [15], where instances are given of 'words with the force of concepts' which are useful when political theorists are hard put to it to reconcile their theory with the actual political situation.

drive for freedom.¹ This drive it is which never allowed the Germans to become a people subjecting itself to a common public authority (*Staatsgewalt*),² even after every other European people had become subject to the dominion of a state of its own making. The stubbornness [8] of the German character has held out against being subdued to the point where the individual parts [of Germany] would have sacrificed their particular [interests] to society, united themselves together into a universal whole, and found freedom in a common, free subjection to a supreme public authority.

The quite peculiar principle of German constitutional law stands in undivided connexion with the state of Europe at the time³ when the nations participated in the supreme power directly, and not through the mediation of the laws. Amongst the peoples of Europe the supreme state-power was a universal authority in which each individual had a sort of free and personal share. This free and personal share, dependent on an arbitrary will, the Germans have not wished to transform into a free share independent of an arbitrary will, a share consisting in the universality and force of laws. On the contrary they have constructed their own latest situation⁴ on the old foundation of an arbitrary will which is not opposed to law but rather knows no law.

The later situation arises immediately from the earlier, in which the nation was a people without being a state, i.e. from the period of the old German freedom. In this period the individual stood on his own feet in his life and activity. He had his dignity and his fate not in connexion with a class but in dependence on himself. Equipped with his own brains and brawn, he either moulded the world to his own pleasure or else was shattered by it. He belonged to the whole in virtue of manners, religion, an invisible living spirit, and some few large interests. Otherwise, in his industry and activity,

¹ The reference is to the old German freedom described in the pages of Tacitus, *Germania*. Cf. Montesquieu, *Esprit des Lois* xi. viii. This harking back to the remote past was a commonplace of political writers in Hegel's day (see Rosenzweig, op. cit., vol. i, p. 239). Cf. Gibbon (ed. Bury, London, 1925), vol. i, pp. 254–5.

² There is no satisfactory translation of this word. What Hegel means by it is made clear on [13], [26–27] below. He also uses the word *Staatsmacht*, though it is not clear whether he attaches to it a different sense. 'Public authority' and 'state-power' are consistently used in this translation as renderings of these two words.

³ During the early development of the feudal system.

⁴ Presumably the age of the 'enlightened despots'.

he refused to be restricted by the whole; [9] his limitations he imposed on himself without doubt or fear. But what lay within his sphere was so much, so entirely, himself that we could not even call it his property; on the contrary, for what belonged in his eyes to his sphere, i.e. for what we would call a part only and for which therefore we would risk only a part of ourselves, he risked life and limb, soul and salvation. He knew nothing of the division and calculation on which our [criminal] law depends, so that a stolen cow is not worth the trouble of risking one's head or setting one's individuality openly against a power, like the state's, ten times or infinitely superior to one's own; he was completely and entirely involved in anything his own. (In French *entier* means both 'entire' and 'self-willed'.)

Out of this arbitrary activity, which alone was called freedom, spheres of power over others were built by chance and character, without regard to a universal and with little control by what is called the public authority, since this authority scarcely existed at all in opposition to individuals.

These spheres of power became fixed as time passed. The branches of the state's universal power became a multiform exclusive property, independent of the state and distributed without rule or principle. This multiform property does not constitute a *system* of [10] rights, but a *collection* [of rights] without principle, whose illogicality and confusion needed the keenest insight, when a collision [between rights] occurred, to rescue it as far as possible from its contradictions; still more was compulsion and a superior power needed to reconcile rights with one another; though in relation to the whole state the need was for a most special divine providence[1] to maintain the state at all.

Political powers and rights [in the Empire] are not offices of state devised in accordance with an organization of the whole. The burdens and duties of individuals are not determined by the needs of the whole. On the contrary, each individual member of the political hierarchy, [i.e.] each princely house, each estate,[2] each

---

[1] This sarcasm is directed against J. S. Pütter, *Historische Entwickelung der heutigen Staatsverfassung des teutschen Reichs* (Gottingen, 1786), Eng. tr. (London, 1790), vol. iii, p. 308. Hegel draws continually on this book.

[2] *Stand*. The word means profession, or class, or estate (i.e. the nobility or the clergy, the Estates of the Realm), but more often Hegel uses it in this essay to mean city-state or principality or even, occasionally, the Estates Assembly. In these translations the word is usually translated 'estate' or 'estates', but where

city, guild, &c., anything which has rights or duties in relation to
the state, has won them for itself, and in this sort of restriction of
its power the state has no other function but to acknowledge the
loss of its power. The result is that if the state loses all authority
while yet the individual's ownership rests on the power of the
state [11], the ownership of those who have no support but the
state's power—which is equally null—must necessarily be very
shaky.

The principles of German public law are therefore not to be
derived from the concept of a state in general or from the concept
of a specific constitution such as monarchy, &c.; and German constitutional law is not a science derived from principles but a register
of the most varied constitutional rights acquired in the manner of
private rights.[1] Legislative, judicial, spiritual, and military powers
are confused, divided, and conjoined in the most irregular way and
into the most disparate portions just as multiplex as the property
of private individuals.

it means Estates Assembly the translation is 'Estates', with a capital letter. For
Hegel's meaning here, cf. Bryce, op. cit., pp. 400–1 footnote: 'One day's journey
in Germany might take a traveller through the territories of a free city, a
sovereign abbot, a village belonging to an imperial knight, and the dominions
of a landgrave, a Duke, a prince and a king, so small, so numerous, and so
diverse were the principalities.' The Empire was a *systema civitatum*, a *regnum
divisum in plures respublicas*, and the *civitates* or *respublicae* were as diverse in
character as Bryce's note indicates. 'The medieval "nation" was a conglomera-
tion of families; its members did not think of themselves as members of one
family comprehending the whole nation' (H. Arendt, *The Human Condition*
(Chicago, 1959), p. 29, fn.). The German estates or city-states had progressed
some distance beyond this medieval idea, but not far, and, in Hegel's view, not
nearly far enough.

[1] The following passage from another draft, taken with all that follows,
clarifies Hegel's meaning: 'Possession came before the law: it did not arise from
law but was simply acquired first and then made a legal right afterwards. Thus
fundamentally and originally German constitutional law [or the right of the
German state] is strictly private law [or a private right], and political rights are
a legal possession, a property. Just as individual *A* has acquired or inherited or
bought or been presented with a house, and *B* a garden, so Estates member *A*
owns 6 peasants and *B* 600. Just as individual *C* has cornfields and vineyards,
estate *C* has higher and lower jurisdiction over 5 houses and tithes over 100
villages, while official position *D* has part of the controlling power over 2,000
citizens and a right to vote on the war or peace of all Germany, though the
holder of another position has part of the power of control over a million people
and no vote at all on the war and peace of all Germany. Legislative, judicial, &c.,
powers are divided up between holders of office in the most manifold ways—
just as manifold as the ways in which private property is divided and distributed
between individuals. . . . But the legal basis is the same in both cases' [11–
12 fn.].

By decrees of the Diet[1] (*Reichstag*), peace treaties, Compacts of Election,[2] family settlements, decisions of the Imperial court, &c., the political property of each individual member of the German body politic is most carefully defined. The [12] care taken in this connexion has been extended to anything and everything with the most punctilious scrupulosity. Age-long efforts have been devoted to apparently insignificant things like modes of address, protocol in processions and seating, the colour of numerous furnishings,[3] &c. It is to the German state that we must ascribe the best organization for settling with the greatest precision everything which has a bearing on rights, no matter how trivial it may be. The German Empire is a kingdom, like the kingdom of nature in its productions, unfathomable as a whole and inexhaustible in detail, and this is the aspect which fills those initiated into the infinite minutiae of the laws with such amazement at the venerability of the German body politic and such admiration for this system of justice carried out down to the last detail.

[13] This system of justice, which consists in the maintenance of each part in separation from the state, stands in violent contradiction to the necessary claims of the state on its every individual member. The state requires a universal centre, a monarch, and Estates, wherein the various powers,[4] foreign affairs, the armed forces, finances relevant thereto, &c., would be united, a centre which would not merely direct but would have in addition the power necessary for asserting itself and its decrees, and for keeping the individual parts dependent on itself. By law, on the other hand, independence, almost or even wholly complete, is guaranteeed to the individual Estates. If there are aspects of independence which are not expressly and formally fixed in Compacts of Election, decrees of the Diet, &c., they are still none the less sanctioned in practice—a more important and more comprehensive legal title than all the others. The German political edifice is nothing [14]

---

[1] The Assembly of the Estates at Ratisbon. A sort of Parliament.

[2] *Wahl-kapitulationen*—engagements entered into by the person elected as a condition of his election, e.g. as Emperor or to the throne of Poland. Cf. *Ph.d.R.*, § 281.

[3] 'The solemn triflings of the Diet . . . have probably never been equalled elsewhere. Questions of precedence and title, questions whether the envoys of the princes should have chairs of red cloth like those of the electors or only of the less honourable green. . . . These and such as these it was their chief employment not to settle but to discuss' (Bryce, op. cit., pp. 400–1).

[4] i.e. judicial, military, &c.

but the sum of rights which the individual parts have wrested from the whole, and this [system of] justice, which carefully watches to see that no power is left over to the state, is the essence of the constitution.

Now let the unhappy provinces, which come to ruin with the helplessness of the state to which they belong, complain about its political position; let the head of the Empire and the patriotic estates which were the first to be hard pressed call in vain on the others for common co-operation; let Germany be pillaged and disgraced: the constitutional lawyer will still know how to show that all this is entirely in accordance with law and practice, and that all these misfortunes are trivialities in comparison with the application of this [system of] justice. If the unsuccessful way in which the war has been waged depends on the behaviour of individual estates, one of which sent no contingent at all and very many of which sent not soldiers but raw recruits, while another paid no Roman Months,[1] while another again withdrew its contingent at the time of greatest danger; if many estates concluded peace treaties and compacts of neutrality; if nearly all of them, each in its own way, nullified the defence of Germany: nevertheless constitutional law proves that they had the right to behave in this way, the right to bring the whole into the greatest danger, harm, and misfortune. Because there are rights, the individual estates and the whole must most strictly preserve and protect rights of this kind, the right to total destruction. For this legal edifice of the German state there is perhaps no more appropriate superscription than

Fiat justitia, pereat Germania!

---

[1] *Römermonate.* Payments made to the Emperor in medieval times to finance the few months during which he journeyed to Rome and back for his coronation by the Pope. In 1521, at the Diet of Worms, a certain number of infantry and cavalry were voted to the Emperor for a contemplated expedition to Rome which did not take place, but a list (*Matrikel*) was then prepared of the exact quota to be supplied by each of the Estates. In 1541 three 'Roman Months' were granted to the Emperor for defence against the Turks, each Month being computed at 12 florins for a cavalryman and four for an infantryman. Hence arose a sort of national impost which continued down to Hegel's time. As often as the Diet thought fit, a certain number of Roman Months were granted to the Emperor for military purposes, so that every Estate had to pay so many times 12 or 4 florins per Roman Month as the number of cavalry or infantry entered against it in the quota list of 1521. The Roman Months, unlike the *Kammerzieler* (see below, p. 170, fn. 1), were not a perpetual tax because they could never be levied without a special vote of the Diet (Pütter, op. cit., vol. i, pp. 506 ff.).

In the German character one feature, if not a rational one, at least to some extent a noble one, is that it regards law as such, whatever its basis or consequences, as something sacrosanct. If Germany is perishing as a separate and independent state, as it to all appearance is, and if the German nation is finally perishing altogether as a people, it is ever a pleasing spectacle to see [15] in the vanguard, amidst the spirits of destruction, the fear of the law.

Such a spectacle the political situation and the constitutional law of Germany would afford if Germany were to be regarded as a state. Its political situation would have to be treated as legal anarchy, its constitutional law as a legal system opposed to the state. But everything harmonizes with the view that Germany is no longer to be regarded as a unified political whole but only as a mass of independent and essentially sovereign states. Yet, it is said, Germany is an 'empire', 'a body politic', it stands under 'a common imperial head' in an 'imperial union'. To these expressions as legal titles no disrespect is to be paid; but an essay concerned with concepts can make nothing of titles of this sort; though from the definition of the concepts it may make clear what meaning such titles may possess. Of course expressions like 'Empire', 'Imperial Head' are often taken for concepts, and they must be makeshifts in emergency.

The constitutional lawyer who cannot call Germany a state any longer, because otherwise he would have to grant many inferences which follow from the concept of a state, and which he yet may not grant, has recourse, since Germany is still not to count as a 'non-state', to taking the title of 'Empire' as a concept. Or, since Germany is neither a democracy nor an aristocracy but has been supposed to be essentially a monarchy, while the Emperor on the other hand is not to be regarded as a monarch, his title of 'Imperial Head' is used as a makeshift even in a system where not titles but defined concepts are supposed to rule.

By the use of the quite general concept of 'Imperial Head', the Emperor is consigned to a category along with the one-time Doge of Venice and the Sultan of Turkey. These equally are heads of states, but the former was the most restricted head of an aristocracy, while the latter is the most unrestricted head of a despotism. And since the concept of a 'Head' covers all sorts of variations in the scope of the supreme authority of the state, it is completely

vague and [16] therefore valueless. It professes to express something and at bottom has expressed nothing.

In the scientific and historical field we must fight shy of such
meaningless expressions, even if in actual life the German genius
uses them as expedients. Grant the stubbornness of the German
character in continually resting on its own will in civil life; grant
separate and irreconcilable state interests in the political field;
but suppose that for other important reasons a unity is none the
less to be established in civil life or in politics: then there is no
better means to the end than to find some general expression which
satisfies both sides and which yet leaves both sides at home with
their own will. The result is that the difference remains as it
was before, or, if in fact one side must give in, then at least the
acknowledgement of giving in is evaded by the use of this general
expression.

With such general expressions the Germans have kept alive for
centuries a show of union in which in fact no member has yielded
one jot of its claims to independence. Reflection on this phenomenon, at any rate if it is to be scientific, must cling to concepts,
and, in judging whether a country is a state, must not dally with
general expressions but must bring into consideration the range
of power left to what is to be called a state. Since closer examination reveals that what is called in general terms 'constitutional law'
[or rights of the state] consists in rights *against* the state, the question would arise whether in spite of all this a *power* still accrues to
the state in virtue of which it really is a state. If what is necessary
to this end is examined more closely and compared with the condition of Germany in respect of the state's power, it will appear
that Germany cannot in strictness be called a state any longer. We
proceed to go through the various chief powers which must be
found in a state.

[§ 1. CONCEPT OF THE STATE]

[17] A multitude of human beings can only call itself a state if
it be united for the common defence of the entirety of its property.
What is self-explanatory in this proposition must none the less be
stated, namely that this union has not merely the intention of
defending itself; the point is that it defends itself by actual arms,
be its power and its success what they may. There will be no one

to deny that Germany is united in law and in words for its common defence; but in this matter we may not distinguish between laws and words on the one hand, and facts and actuality on the other, nor may we say that Germany [18] is armed in common, not of course in fact and actuality, but still by law and in words. Property and its defence by a political union are things which refer wholly and entirely to reality; whatever their ideal existence may be, it cannot be a state.[1]

Plans and theories claim reality in so far as they *can* be carried out, but their value is the same whether they be actualized or not. A theory of the state, however, signifies state and constitution only in so far as it is actual. If Germany were to profess to be a state and a constitution, although its constitutional forms were without life, and the theory of them without actuality, it would be speaking an untruth. But if it were to promise in words to afford common defence in actuality, we would have to ascribe to it the weakness of age, which still wills though it can no longer do, or the dishonesty which does not abide by its promises.

If a multitude is to form a state, then it must form a common military and public authority. The manner, however, in which the consequential particular operations and the aspects of union are present, or the particular type of constitution [adopted] is immaterial for the formation of a multitude into an authority. [19] These particular details may in general be present in an extreme multiplicity of ways, and, even in some specific state, complete irregularity and heterogeneity may obtain in these matters. In dealing with this topic we must keep two things distinct: first, what is necessary if a multitude is to be a state and a common authority, and, secondly, what is only a particular modification of this authority and what belongs not to the sphere of the necessary but, as regards theory, to the sphere of the greater or lesser good, and, as regards actuality, to the sphere of chance and caprice.

This distinction has an aspect very important for the peace of states, the security of governments, and the freedom of peoples. If the general public authority demands from the individual only what is necessary for itself, and if it restricts accordingly the arrangements for ensuring the performance of this minimum, then beyond this point it can permit the living freedom and the individual will of the citizens, and even leave considerable scope to

---

[1] Reading, with Mollat, *ein Staat ist.*

the latter. Similarly the public authority, concentrated necessarily at the centre, in the government, is regarded by the individuals at the periphery with a less jaundiced eye when it demands what it regards as necessary and what everyone can see *is* indispensable for the whole. This would avoid a danger: for if both the necessary and the more arbitrary are alike in the power of the centre of the public authority, and if they are both demanded with the same strictness, as by the government, the citizens may confuse both things together, become as impatient with the one as with the other, and bring the state, as regards its necessary claims, into jeopardy.

In that part of a state's actual existence which belongs to chance, we must include the actual manner in which the whole public authority may exist in a supreme point of union. [20] Whether the holders of authority be one or many, whether the one or the many are born to this distinction or elected to it, is immaterial for the one thing necessary, i.e. the formation of a multitude into a state, just as immaterial as the uniformity or lack of uniformity of civil rights between the individuals who are subjects of the general public authority. Similarly beside the point is the inequality of nature, talent, and mental energy, which makes a more powerful difference than inequality of civil relationships. The fact that a state counts amongst its subjects villeins, burghers, free noblemen, and princes with subjects of their own in turn,[1] and the fact that the relationships of these particular classes as particular members of the state do not exist in a pure form but in infinite modifications, is as little a hindrance to the formation of a multitude into a state as the fact that the particular geographical members of the state constitute provinces variously related to the internal constitutional law.

So far as strictly civil laws and the administration of justice are concerned, a similarity of laws and legal procedures would no more make Europe a state than a similarity of weights, measures, and money; [21] nor does a difference in these things cancel the unity of a state. If it did not lie in the concept of the state that the more detailed determination of legal relationships affecting the property of one individual against another's did not concern the state as

---

[1] 'The Czar of Russia has villeins amongst his subjects, burghers of towns which have municipal constitutions, free noblemen, and princes who themselves in turn have subjects, people so uncivilized, still in the state of nature, that they hardly know even the name of law and government. So too in every other European state the relation of the citizens to the supreme political power is the reverse of uniform' (H. in another draft [20 fn.]).

a public authority (since the latter has to determine only the relationship between the state and property as such), the example of almost all European states could teach us this, since the more powerful of the genuine states amongst them have laws that are through and through the reverse of uniform. Before the Revolution, France had such a multiplicity of laws that, apart from Roman Law, which prevailed in several provinces, Burgundian Law, Breton Law, &c., ruled elsewhere, and almost every province, indeed almost every city, had its own customary law. A French writer said truthfully that a traveller in France changed laws as often as he changed post-horses.

Equally outside the concept of the state is the question to which particular power legislation belongs or how far and in what proportion the various estates or the [22] citizens in general are to participate in it. Equally irrelevant is the character of the courts, i.e. whether in the various instances the members of the court are to be hereditary or appointed by the supreme authority or freely entrusted with responsibility by the burghers or commissioned by the courts themselves. What scope a specific jurisdiction should have, whether that jurisdiction should be fixed by chance, whether there is a common court of the last instance for the whole state, &c. —these questions too are irrelevant.

Equally independent of the [concept of the] state is the form of administration in general, and it may thus be multiform, like the arrangements for magistracies, the rights of cities and estates, &c. All these things are only relatively important for the state, and for its true essence the form of their organization is immaterial.

Inequality of taxes on the different classes in accordance with their *material* resources is to be found in all European states and so, to a greater extent, is inequality on the *ideal* side, i.e. inequality in fiscal *rights* and *duties* and in the origin of these. The fact that through the inequality of wealth there arises an inequality in the contributions made to state expenditure is so little a hindrance to the state that on the contrary modern states [23] are based on it. The state is just as little affected by the unequal basis on which payments are made by the different estates of the nobility, the clergy, the burghers, and the peasantry;[1] and, apart from everything

---

[1] 'Apart from differences between estates, the enormous difference between provinces in France is well known. . . . In some provinces salt was under 6 sous per lb. and in others it was over 12 sous' (H. in another draft [23 fn.]).

called privilege, the difference between the estates provides the reason for their contributing in different proportions, because the proportion can be determined only in regard to what is produced and not by the fundamental element in what is taxed, i.e. not by labour, which cannot be computed and is inherently unequal.[1]

Whether the different geographical parts of a state are differently taxed, what changes and subordinate systems[2] taxation passes through, whether in respect of one and the same field a city has the land tax, a private individual the ground rent, an abbey the tithes, the nobleman the hunting rights, the commune the grazing rights, &c., and whether different estates and bodies of all kinds become individually circumstanced in relation to tax paying; all these matters and others like them are accidentalities remaining outside the concept of the public authority, for which, as the centre, only the fixed quantum is essential, while the disproportionate convergence of the revenue is immaterial so far as its origin goes. Thus in general the whole arrangement of the revenue may lie outside the state itself; yet the state may none the less be very powerful whether (i), as under the old feudal system, the vassal's personal exertions in times of emergency [24] provide at the same time everything he needs in the [course of the] service he gives to the state, while for everything else the state has the source of its revenues in the crown lands, or whether (ii), as is also conceivable, overall expenditure is defrayed in this latter manner, in which event the state would not, even as a money power, as it must be in modern times, be a centre to which taxes were paid. On the contrary, what the state receives as taxes, in accordance with the exact arrangements governing most of them, is on the same footing of particular rights as [the revenues of] others who in relation to the state are private individuals.[3]

[1] Hegel is maintaining that the fundamental difference between the Estates of the Realm (or, here, social classes) is a difference in wealth; that the essential thing in wealth is the labour which produces it; but only something quantified can be taxed, and therefore taxes must be on wealth and not on labour, which differs qualitatively from person to person and is not in itself quantifiable. Cf. *Ph.d.R.*, § 299 *Anm.*

[2] This phrase, which occurs again below [27], refers to different levels in the German constitutional hierarchy, e.g., city, village, commune.

[3] The meaning, especially of the last clause, is obscure, and the entire sentence is suppressed altogether by Mollat. 'Under the feudal system what now has the form of a general impost for defraying state expenditure had the form rather of

In our day the tie between members of a state in respect of manners, education, language may be rather loose or even non-existent. Identity in these matters, once the foundation of a people's union, is now to be reckoned amongst the accidents whose character does not hinder a mass from constituting a public authority. Rome or Athens, like any small modern state, could not have subsisted if the numerous languages current in the Russian Empire had been spoken within their borders, [25] or if amongst their citizens manners had been as different as they are in Russia or, for that matter, as manners and education are now in every big city in a large country. Difference in language and dialect (the latter exacerbates separation even more than complete unintelligibility does), and difference in manners and education in the separate estates, which makes men known to one another in hardly anything but outward appearance—such heterogeneous and at the same time most powerful factors the preponderating weight of the Roman Empire's power (once it had become great) was able to overcome and hold together, just as in modern states the same result is produced by the spirit and art of political institutions. Thus dissimilarity in culture and manners is a necessary product as well as a necessary condition of the stability of modern states.

Religion is that wherein men's innermost being is expressed, and, even if all other external and separated things may be insignificant, men yet recognize themselves in religion as a fixed centre; only thereby could they have been able to transcend the variety and mutability of their other relationships and situations and so to win confidence in one another and become sure of one another. Here in religion at least an identity might have been thought necessary, but this identity too is something which modern states have found that they can do without.

In northern Europe, religious unity has hitherto always been

the private property and right of the feudal overlord who defrayed from his domains the expense of suzerainty, administration, justice, embassies, &c. . . . Expenditure for war had to be defrayed by each vassal himself' (H. in another draft [40 fn.]). Under the alternative which Hegel visualizes, state expenditure would be met from the crown lands, and any other revenue which the state received it would receive only from some particular property which was burdened in some particular way, i.e. it would receive it as a private property right. Hence the state would in this respect be on the same footing with the nobleman, city, abbey, &c., mentioned earlier in the paragraph. The whole passage depends on distinguishing between a constitutional right to the proceeds of taxation and a private property right to income from, e.g., land.

the fundamental condition of a state. Nothing else was known, and without this original oneness no other oneness or trust has been found possible. Occasionally this very bond has become so potent that [26] more than once it has suddenly transformed into one state peoples which were otherwise strange to one another and national enemies. The state so produced has not been merely a holy community of Christians, nor yet a coalition uniting their interests and their activity in pursuit of these. On the contrary, as a single worldly power, as a state too and as one people and army, it has conquered the fatherland of its eternal and temporal life in a war against the East.[1]

Before this time, and also later when Christendom was divided into nations, similarity of religion has no more prevented wars or united peoples into a state than dissimilarity of religion has in our day rent the state asunder. The state's authority, as purely and simply the state's right, has known how to separate itself from the religious authority and its right, how to maintain stability enough on its own account, and how so to organize itself as to have no need of the Church, to separate the Church again from the state, and to put it once more into the position which in its beginnings it occupied in relation to the Roman state.

Of course on the political theories of our day, partly propounded by would-be philosophers and teachers of the rights of man and partly realized in tremendous political experiments,[2] everything we have excluded from the necessary concept of public authority (except what is most important of all, language, education, manners, and religion) is subjected to the immediate activity of the supreme public authority and in such a way that it is settled by that authority itself and driven by it down to the last detail.

It is to be taken for granted that the highest public authority must carry the supreme oversight of these afore-mentioned aspects of the domestic relationships of a people and their organization (which has been settled by chance and ancient arbitrary decisions); equally obvious is it that these aspects may not hinder the chief activity of the state, since on the contrary this activity must secure itself before all else, and to this end it is not to spare the

[1] This reference to the Crusades may be compared with Hegel's treatment of the same subject in his *Philosophy of History*.

[2] The reference is to Fichte's police state described in his *Naturrecht* (1796) (cf. Hegel, *Werke*[1], vol. i, pp. 234–43, and *Ph.d.R.*, Preface) and to the French Revolution.

subordinate systems of rights and privileges. Nevertheless, it is one great virtue of the old states in Europe that while the public authority is secure so far as its needs and its progress are concerned, it leaves free scope to the citizens' own activity in details of the administration, judicial and others, partly in the nomination [27] of the necessary officials, partly in the management of current affairs and the administration of law and customary usages.[1]

The size of modern states makes it quite impossible to realize the ideal of giving every free individual a share in debating and deciding political affairs of universal concern. The public authority must be concentrated in one centre for deciding these matters and, as government, for executing these decisions. If this centre is secure on its own account in virtue of the awe of the masses, and is immutably sacrosanct in the person of a monarch appointed in accordance with a natural law and by birth, then a public authority may without fear or jealousy freely hand over to subordinate systems and bodies a great part of the relationships arising in society and their maintenance according to the laws. Each estate, city, town, commune, &c., can itself enjoy freedom to do and to execute what lies within its area.

Just as laws on these matters have gradually proceeded as a hallowed tradition directly from custom itself, so the constitution, the organization of the lower jurisdiction, the rights of the citizens therein—i.e. rights of municipal management, collection of taxes, whether national or those necessary for the municipalities themselves, and the legal application of the latter—all these things and those connected with them have been set up by native impulse. They have grown up of themselves, and since ever they saw the light they have maintained themselves similarly.

The organization of the ecclesiastical establishments, which is so far-reaching, has just as little been created by the supreme public authority, and the whole ecclesiastical estate maintains and perpetuates itself more or less internally. The huge sums paid annually in a large state for the poor, and the consequential and wide-ranging arrangements which pervade all parts of a country, are not defrayed by levies which the state would have to adjust, nor is it at the state's [28] command that the whole system is maintained and carried on. The mass of the relevant property and contributions depends on foundations and gifts by individuals, and so does

---

[1] This presages *Ph.d.R.*, § 260, and Hegel's conception of 'civil society'.

the whole system and its administration and realization, without any dependence on the highest public authority. Most of the internal social arrangements for each special sphere of need have been made by the free action of the citizens, and their continuation and life has been maintained by just this freedom, which has been undisturbed by any jealousy or anxiety on the part of the supreme public authority, except that of course the government sometimes supports them and sometimes checks the over-abundant growth of one provision of this sort which might otherwise suppress other necessary provisions.[1]

However, in recent theories, carried partly into effect, the fundamental presupposition is that a state is a machine with a single spring which imparts movement to all the rest of the infinite wheel-work, and that all institutions implicit in the nature of a society should proceed from the supreme public authority and be regulated, commanded, overseen, and conducted by it.

The pedantic craving to determine every detail, the illiberal jealousy of [any arrangement whereby] an estate, a corporation, &c., adjusts and manages its own affairs, this mean carping at any independent action by the citizens which would only have some general bearing and not a bearing on the public authority, is clothed in the garb of rational principles. On these principles not a shilling of the public expenditure on poor relief in a country of 20 or 30 million inhabitants may be incurred unless it has first been not merely allowed but actually ordered, controlled, and audited by the supreme government. The appointment of every village school-master, the expenditure of every penny for a pane of glass in a village school or a village hall, the appointment of every toll-clerk or court officer or local justice of the peace, is to be an immediate emanation and effect of the highest authority. In the whole state every mouthful of food is brought from the ground that produces it to the mouth that eats it along a line examined, computed, adjusted, and directed by state, law, and government.

[29] This is no place to argue at length that the centre, as the public authority, i.e. the government, must leave to the freedom of the citizens whatever is not necessary for its appointed function of organizing and maintaining authority and thus for its security at home and abroad. Nothing should be so sacrosanct to the

---

[1] This passage appears to bear the stamp of Hegel's study of English newspaper reports of parliamentary debates.

government as facilitating and protecting the free activity of the citizens in matters other than this. This is true regardless of utility, because the freedom of the citizens is inherently sacrosanct.

But, as regards utility, if we are to reckon what advantage is produced by the citizens' management of their affairs through special bodies, their courts, their appointments to the offices entailed in these, &c., then the reckoning is threefold. The first calculation concerns something tangible, namely the money which flows on this system into the hands of the supreme public authority; the second concerns intelligence and the excellence with which everything happens in a machine at a uniform pace in accordance with the shrewdest calculation and the wisest ends; but the third concerns the vitality, the contented mind, and free and self-respecting self-awareness which arises when the individual will participates in public affairs so far as their ramifications are matters of indifference to the supreme public authority.

On the first reckoning, the tangible one, the state whose principle is universal mechanism fancies, without hesitation, that it has the advantage over the state which leaves detail in great part to the rights and individual action of its citizens. But it must be noticed in general that the machine state cannot possibly have the advantage unless it imposes heavier taxes on everyone. Since it takes over all branches of government, the administration of justice, &c., it must be burdened at the same time with the expense of all this, and if the whole machine is organized as a universal hierarchy, then this expense must be covered by systematic taxation. On the other hand, (i) if the state hands over to the individual bodies interested the making of arrangements requisite for such purely contingent and individual matters as the administration of justice, educational expenses, [30] contributions in support of the poor, &c., and also for providing the cost of these, then it sees these costs defrayed otherwise than in the form of taxes. The man who requires a judge or an attorney or a teacher, or who cares for the poor of his own volition, pays and pays then only; there is no question of a tax; no one pays for a court, an attorney, a teacher, a priest unless he needs one. (ii) If, for the lower official appointments in the court or the management of municipal or corporation affairs, one of the members of one of these bodies is chosen, then he is paid by the honour which thereby accrues to him, while if he is supposed to be the servant of the state, then he has to demand pay from the state because here this inner honour is lacking. These two points, (i) and (ii), even if, as is not to be expected, more money might have to be contributed by the people under (i), produce the following effects: the first produces the difference that no one pays out money for something he does not need, for something which is not a universal requirement of the state; while the second produces an actual saving for everybody. The net result is that the people feel themselves treated under (i) with reason and by necessity and under (ii) with trust and freedom: (ii) constitutes the prime difference revealed by the second and third modes or reckoning.

A mechanical hierarchy, highly intellectual and devoted to noble ends, evinces no confidence whatever in its citizens and can thus expect nothing from them. It has no assurance in any action not ordered, carried out, and arranged by itself; thus it bans free-will gifts and sacrifices; it displays to its subjects its conviction of their lack of intellect, its contempt for their capacity to assess and do what is compatible with their private interests, and its belief in general profligacy. Thus it cannot hope for any vital action, any support from its subjects' self-respect.

There is a difference here so great as to be beyond the grasp of the statesman who allows for nothing which cannot be reckoned in hard cash. It shows itself primarily in the ease and welfare, the honesty and contentment of the inhabitants in one state, as compared with the dullness, the baseness (continually lapsing into [31] shamelessness), and the poverty [of those] in another. Where, in things of the greatest moment, it is only the contingent aspect of the event that lies on the surface, a state of the latter kind determines this contingency and makes it necessary.

It makes an infinite difference whether the public authority is so organized that everything on which it can count is in its own hands while for this very reason it can count on nothing else, or whether apart from what is in its own hands it can count also on the free devotion, the self-respect, and the individual effort of the people—on an all-powerful invincible spirit which the hierarchical system has renounced and which has its life only where the supreme public authority leaves as much as possible to the personal charge of the citizens. How dull and spiritless a life is engendered in a modern state where everything is regulated from the top downwards, where nothing with any general implications is left to the management and execution of interested parties of the people—in a state like what the French Republic has made itself—is to be experienced only in the future, if indeed this pitch of pedantry in domination can persist. But what life and what sterility reigns in another equally regulated state, in the Prussian, strikes anyone who sets foot in the first town there or sees its complete lack of scientific or artistic genius, or assesses its strength otherwise than by the ephemeral energy which a single genius[1] has been able to generate in it for a time by pressure.

Thus we do not merely distinguish in a state, on the one hand, the necessary element which must lie in the hands of the public authority and be directly determined by it, and, on the other, the element which is necessary indeed simply for the social unification of a people but which for the public authority is in itself contingent. We also regard that people as fortunate to which the state gives a free hand in subordinate general activities, just as we regard a public authority as infinitely strong if it can be supported by the free and unregimented spirit of its people.

In Germany there is no fulfilment of the illiberal demand that laws, administration of justice, imposition and collection [32] of taxes, &c., language, customs, education, and religion be regulated and governed by one centre of power: on the contrary there is the most disparate multiplicity in the ordering of these matters. But this would not hinder Germany from being a state if in other respects it were organized as a public authority.[2] . . .

[§ 2. MILITARY POWER]

. . . The propagation of this martial talent proves in itself that these hosts of armed men are not useless. For centuries past there has been no important war between the European powers in which German courage has not won honour at least, if not laurels, in which rivers of German blood have not flowed.

Despite the abundance of its inhabitants, their martial talents, the readiness of its men to shed their blood, and despite its wealth of the requisites, inanimate and animate alike, for war, no country is so defenceless as Germany, less capable of self-defence, let alone conquest. Merely to aspire to self-defence, not to speak of attempting it, is still significantly honourable.

---

[1] i.e. Frederick the Great.
[2] At this point there is a gap in the manuscript. In Lasson's view, however, the missing part cannot have been considerable.

Military power consists of course in the soldiery of the greater and smaller estates. As for the latter, these armies, forces, corps, or whatever they may be called, may generally be no more than soldiers on parade or police duty, not warriors who know nothing higher than the fame of their regiment and their service. The military spirit which uplifts the heart of every warrior in a great regiment when he hears the words 'our army', this pride in his profession and service, the soul of a regiment, cannot flourish in the watchmen of an Imperial city or the bodyguard of an abbot. The sort of reverence for a still unknown individual which the sight of him in the uniform of a great regiment arouses cannot accrue to the uniform of an Imperial city. 'I have been twenty, thirty years in this service' on the lips [33] of the bravest soldier in a small estate of the Empire creates quite a different impression and effect from what the words produce when uttered by an officer in a great regiment. The self-respect of the man and the reverence that others have for him grows with the size of the whole to which he belongs. He shares in the fame accumulated for it by centuries.

The insignificance of the separate small military corps owing to their trifling numbers is bad enough without its being intensified by the clumsiness and other inconveniences in the arrangements they entail. There must be very great disadvantages if, on the outbreak of war, the smaller estates then enlist their soldiers for the first time, often do not appoint their officers till then, and so send untrained men into the field; if one estate has to supply the drummer and another the drums, &c.; if, owing to the number of estates which amalgamate their contingents, there is a dissimilarity in weapons, drill, &c., and the levies are unacquainted with their officers; and if each estate has the right itself to look after the victualling of its own forces, with the result that apart from the unnecessary expense, what has prevailed is the greatest disorder in the service and an embarrassing surfeit of civil personnel and camp followers. In theory there legally belong to a detachment of twenty men drafted from different estates precisely twenty forage clerks, bakers, &c., from the same estates. The Imperial quota[1] is some centuries old so that it no longer corresponds to the present

---

[1] *Matrikel.* See above, p. 151 n. Each estate was required to provide its own contingent with supplies, even on active service. One regiment might be made up of contingents drawn from a number of estates and each contingent required to have its own baggage wagons, bakers, hospital, &c. There was no general commissariat (Pütter, op. cit., vol. iii, pp. 99 ff.).

proportionate size and power of the estates and thus gives rise to discontent, complaints, and perpetually outstanding liabilities; and districts occur in it whose geographical position can no longer be ascertained. These things and a hundred others of the kind are too well known for their mention not to be wearisome.

Now if the insignificance of the military forces of the smaller estates disappears when they are amalgamated and mustered into an Imperial Army, still the aforementioned disadvantages, and countless others, put the utility of this army in war below that of all the armies in the rest of Europe, even the Turkish not excepted, and the very name 'Imperial Army' has been on other grounds especially ill-starred. While the name of other armies, even foreign ones, rouses thoughts of bravery and formidability, the name of the Imperial Army, mentioned in a company of Germans [34], used to brighten every face and give rise to every sort and kind of witticism. Everyone drew from his stock of anecdotes to find one to entertain the company. When the German nation is held to be serious and incapable of comedy, what is forgotten is the farces of the Imperial wars which were outwardly conducted with all possible gravity, but inwardly were simply laughable.

While the organization of the Imperial forces with all its consequences has not been improved in any respect, the general craving to make jokes about it has been diminished by a sense of the misfortune it has produced and by the disgrace of Germany. The Imperial troops have been able to be of some use only because in the last war many aspects of this organization, e.g. the commissariat, have been handled illegally and unconstitutionally.

Still more disadvantageous than all these features in the character of the Imperial Army is the fact that, strictly speaking, no such army has ever been mustered at all. And in this fact there is most clearly shown the dissolution of Germany into independent states.

On the theory of the constitution, the Imperial forces could be a formidable army, but practice, this powerful principle of German constitutional law, reveals something quite different. If only too often we see an enormous number of German soldiers in the field, it is a matter of course that [35] they are there not as an Imperial Army for the defence of Germany but for lacerating its vitals and tearing its flesh from its bones.[1] What is called the German

[1] As is clear from another draft, Hegel is thinking of the Thirty Years War and the Seven Years War ([34–35] fn.).

constitution not only cannot avert wars of this kind; it makes them right and legal.

The German army is all the more inconsiderable when it is summoned to the protection of Germany. Although the quintuple contingents from Hanover, [or] Brandenburg, [or] Saxony, [or] Bavaria, [or] Hesse constitute armies on their own account and [when all] united are a formidable force, and although they would overcome the clumsiness of the smaller contingents that were united with them, still they are then dependent on something other than the laws of Germany, and their co-operation for its defence is just as unreliable and accidental as the co-operation of some foreign power.

The Austrian contingent the Emperor, as ruler of other kingdoms, is compelled to raise far beyond his official (*ständischen*) obligations, as a result of the weakness and unreliability of the army which it is incumbent [on the estates] to enrol. [36] He is thus compelled to let Germany have the benefit of the exertions and the scope of his power from other sources. But so far as the other large contingents are concerned, the Empire can count neither on their legal strength nor even on their dispatch. It cannot be sure that the estate which has indeed dispatched its contingent will not, in the midst of war and at moments of the greatest danger, enter on its own account into treaties of neutrality or peace with the enemy of the Empire, and surrender fellow estates, which are under attack, to their own weakness and the devastating ascendancy of the enemy.

Although the right of the estates in constitutional law to conclude alliances with foreign powers and to make their choice between enemies and Germany is restricted by the clause 'in so far as such alliances do not conflict with duty to the Emperor and the Empire', this clause as a legal principle is made ambiguous in practice or rather is eliminated altogether. It is not just a matter of fact, but [37] it may also accord with votes by the estates in the Diet, that the other obligations of the estates do not permit them to participate in raising a contingent for the Imperial forces or in paying contributions for the war.

When the more important estates thus cry off from any share in the general defence, this puts others in a position of helplessness which compels them to evade distress and danger to themselves, and therefore at the same time their duties to the whole. It would be wholly unnatural to demand that they should reckon on and contribute to a protection which notoriously protects nothing and which is in default legally and constitutionally as a result of the right [of the individual estates] to conclude treaties. Thus it is inevitable for the weaker to put themselves under the protection of the more powerful of their fellow estates who are friendly to the enemy and to weaken thereby the general mass of the common authority. In this way then, the more powerful estates gain not only by saving themselves strain but also by winning credit from the enemy for their inactivity. They gain too because [38], while they weaken the general mass through the contribution made to them by those compelled to come under their protection, they profit from the latter in return for the protection afforded.

But even if several large contingents are actually mustered, their common effectiveness is disrupted by the instability of their relationships and the precariousness of their association. These levies are not at the free disposition necessary for assuring the execution of a military design, and what is required for carrying out the plan not only of a campaign but of single operations is not orders but negotiations. Moreover it is impossible to avoid calculating whether the contingent of one estate is used overmuch while others are spared and whether the equality of rights is infringed, just as in other political conditions there used once to be a dispute about the place of greatest danger, and dissatisfaction arose about not using some troops at all.

The jealousy of the different corps which regard themselves as different nations, and the possibility of their withdrawing at the most critical moments, are circumstances which necessarily prevent an Imperial Army from producing an effect proportionate to its respectable numbers and military worth.

If the military weakness of Germany is not a result of cowardice or military incompetence or ignorance of those skills [39] which in modern times are as indispensable as courage is for victory, and if at every opportunity the Imperial contingents afford the strongest proof of their courage and military sacrifice and show themselves worthy of their ancestors and the ancient martial fame of the Germans, then it is the arrangement of the whole and the loosening of all its bonds which lets the exertions and sacrifices of single individuals and corps go for nothing, lays on them a curse which nullifies and sterilizes their efforts, strive as they will, and puts them on a level with a peasant who sowed the sea or proposed to plough the mountain tops.

[§ 3. FINANCE]

The same situation in which the German public authority finds itself in military matters prevails in finance, and, now that the European states have more or less departed from the feudal system, [40] finance has become a more essential part of the power which lies directly in the hands of the supreme public authority.

In the organization of finance there are two extremes. On the first, every outlay required either for a public office, down to the meanest justice of the peace or policeman and even farther down the scale, or for some sort of public requirement which yet is restricted to one village alone, as well as every sort of revenue, flows in the first instance as tax into the coffers of the supreme government and then is distributed again by the state to the smallest branches of public activity through all the media of laws, account settlements, and officialdom, no group of officials being an appeal of the last resort in relation to anything. The other extreme is the German absence of financial system.

Germany is not harassed by cares arising from the great political questions and problems about the sort of taxes, state debts, and credits which will be fairest, least extravagant, and not bearing more hardly on one estate than another, or about other things which in other states demand the exercise of the greatest talent and in which any mistake has the direst consequences. In Germany there is no superfluous [41] meddling by the state in every public expenditure; on the contrary, a village, a city, a city guild, &c., itself looks after financial matters which are its concern alone, under the general oversight but not at the command of the state. Nor in Germany is there any financial organization which would concern the public authority itself.

The ordinary finances of Germany are definitely restricted solely to the *Kammersteuer* paid by the estates for the maintenance of the *Kammergericht*. They are therefore very simple and no Pitt is required for their management.

The regular expenses of the other supreme Imperial court are borne beyond that by the Emperor. In recent times a beginning has been made towards establishing a fund for them by auctioning reversions of Imperial fiefs.

Even in regard to that one financial arrangement just mentioned, the *Kammerzieler*, numerous complaints have arisen about failures to make payments.[1] What is remarkable, if you want to grasp the character of the [42] German constitution, is the reason why Brandenburg is not paying the additional amount decreed many years ago, namely that it is doubtful whether in such matters as general contributions to the state's needs a majority decision is binding on individuals. If this be doubtful, then what alone constitutes a state is missing, i.e. national solidarity in relation to the public authority.

On the fundamental principle of the feudal system, the contingents are paid by the estates themselves and supplied with all necessaries. It has been recalled above[2] that in the last war pressing needs induced several estates to give up exercising their right of supply and to arrange with the Emperor the beneficial expedient of a private agreement for a common commissariat. So, too, smaller estates on this occasion made no use of their right to send their own troops into the field themselves, and they came to terms with larger estates whereby the latter would arrange to raise the contingent due from the smaller ones. Here is [43] the dawning of a transformation: instead of arranging to send their own contingents and to supply their needs, the estates make money contributions to a common centre which then takes over this duty and organizes its discharge. This is the start of a transition from separate and almost personal services into a genuine state organization of war and finance and its transfer to the supreme head, whereby alone the concept of a state is realized in fact. Even if all this be so, however, it is clear that this whole new relationship has affected only unimportant estates and has been a matter of passing chance.

As for the expenses which are to be contributed jointly under the

---

[1] The two supreme courts were (*a*) the *Kammergericht* (translated below as 'Supreme Court') at Wetzlar and (*b*) the *Reichshofrath* (translated as *Supreme Aulic Council*) at Vienna. The *Kammersteuer* or *Kammerzieler* was an Imperial tax levied on the estates from 1548 onwards for defraying the expenses of the Supreme Court. The delays at Wetzlar had made the Supreme Court a laughing-stock in Hegel's day, but the Aulic Council was held in greater respect. There were many disputes about the scope of the jurisdiction of the two bodies; in general the Aulic Council had jurisdiction in all suits affecting whole principalities, while the Supreme Court dealt with suits between individuals; but this distinction was not hard and fast, and the Aulic Council did sometimes deal with suits of the latter kind. In certain circumstances a litigant could choose which of the two courts to proceed in (see [54]).

[2] Not in terms but by implication on [34].

name of Roman Months to meet the requirements of modern war-
fare over and above the mustering of troops, the case is exactly the
same as it is with the dispatch of contingents. On reckoning these
cash balances available to the German Empire for war operations
it has been shown that about one-half of what was decreed has in
fact accrued. In the final months of the war before the opening of
the Congress of Rastatt,[1] published statistics of the net cash
balances revealed a total of 300 guilders in one month and 400 in
another. While in other states the balance in the supreme war-
chest, especially if so small as this, is not published at all, the
publication of this [44] in the German Empire has no particular
influence on the enemies' war and peace operations against the
Empire's.

The principles prevailing here, that the decisions of the majority
have no binding force on the minority, that in virtue of its other
obligations the minority cannot subscribe to the imposition of
Roman Months decreed by the majority, are the same as those that
prevail in connexion with the duties of the estates in the matter of
the Imperial Army.[2]

If formerly there was a sort of central financial power in the
Imperial customs, dues by Imperial cities, and the like, still those
times were so far removed from the idea of a state and the concept
of a general authority that these revenues were regarded as wholly
the private property of the Emperor. The Emperor could sell
them, and, though this is beyond all comprehension, the estates
could buy them or mortgage them and ultimately could mortgage
them irredeemably. In the same way even the state's direct
authority [45] was bought or mortgaged. No clearer sign of the
barbarity of a people that forms a state could be met with.

Still there is no denying that the need to produce finances for
Germany has been felt from time to time and that proposals have
been made for setting up pecuniary resources for the Empire as
a state. But as the estates could not be minded to establish this
financial power by laws regulating contributions, since that would
be to bring about something like the arrangement governing taxes

---

[1] 1799, between France and the Empire.
[2] 'It accords with Imperial law that in the matter of Imperial taxes the minority,
provided it be Protestant, is not bound by a majority vote. But Brandenburg's
reason for not paying the increased *Kammerzieler* rests not on this proviso but
on the claim that it is altogether undecided whether a majority vote has binding
force' (H. in another draft [44 fn.]).

in a state, two things had to be reconciled: (*a*) the devising of a permanent fund for the state, and (*b*) means to avoid placing burdens on the estates or obliging them in any way. The latter was the most conspicuous requirement and thus the whole was not taken seriously but was only a pious wish. With wishes of this kind an attitude and mien which professes to be quite specially patriotic conceals a real inner indifference to the object wished for and at least the firm determination not to let the object cost one anything. Thus if the Empire gave its serious attention to a financial organization, someone, envisaging the best interests of the German Empire, might express the wish that a mountain of gold would grow up in Germany and that every ducat minted out of it and, once issued, not spent for the Empire [46], should run away at once like water. In that event there is no doubt that such a well-wisher would be regarded by a group of honourable citizens as the greatest German patriot that ever lived, because the idea that they would not have to pay anything would strike them at once before ever they realized that a wish of this kind would not bring a penny into the Imperial treasury. And if they did actually realize this they would discover that despite their professions it was only wishes of their own that they had expressed.

All this apart, former Diets have met the need of such a fund by earmarking for defraying Imperial expenditure not any ideal or imaginary resources of this kind but, without requiring any estate to sacrifice something of its own, actually existing territories and real estate, just as the huntsmen in the story set aside a real and not an imaginary bear for the payment of their score.[1]

For centuries past there has been a law earmarking for the foundation of an Imperial fund all those territories which were in the hands of foreign powers—*when* the German Empire recovers them again. In those very wars in which the Empire had the opportunity of recovering them again, the Empire has managed always so to arrange matters as to lose more territory and so to increase the Imperial fund. Consequently the loss of the left bank of the Rhine has its more comforting aspect: it is a route to the possibility of founding an Imperial exchequer.

[47] We can be sure that, if even now a German professor of constitutional law were told about the fatal lack of finance, he

---

[1] But in the story the bear was never caught; the score was never paid, and the earmarked resources never accrued to the Empire either.

would defend on these lines the perfection of even this aspect of the German constitution. Even if reflections of this sort, profound in their own day, were capable of sustaining the hopes placed in them in the present political situation of Europe and Germany by the German character, so sanguine in hopes of this kind, still they cannot come into the reckoning at all in considering whether Germany has the sort of power which in our day belongs to the essence of a state, or has in fact a financial power at the present time in which I am writing.

If an estate incurred expenses on behalf of the state in a war (not a foreign one but one against another estate which was in rebellion and under the Imperial ban), there was once a special way of bearing this national expenditure and compensating the estate concerned, namely that if the execution of bans and other decisions of the Supreme Courts were actually set on foot, as is not always the case, the expenses fell on the party defeated not merely in law but in war as well. (In the Seven Years War the Imperial army of execution got no compensation for its trouble.[1]) That [48] method of securing payment for the costs of execution was formerly a powerful spur at times to the actual execution of a ban, since the territories of the party on whom the decree was executed were retained by the executor without the need for any other legal title or further calculation. For example, the Swiss came into possession of most of the old Hapsburg hereditary estates[2] and the Bavarians of Donauwörth,[3] &c.

A mass of people which, owing to this dissolution of military power and this lack of finances, has not been able to erect a public authority of its own is incapable of defending its independence against foreign enemies. It must of necessity see its independence disappearing, if not at once then gradually. In war it must be exposed to plunder and devastation of every kind, and most of its cost it must bear for both friend and foe. It must lose provinces to foreign powers. Since the authority of the state over its individual members has been destroyed and its suzerainty over its vassals has been lost, it must comprise only sovereign states which, as sovereign, are related to one another by force and cunning;[4] the stronger of

---

[1] The Emperor claimed, and exercised, the right to use *the army* to execute the judgements of the Supreme Court—in this instance to execute the decree which put Frederick the Great under the ban of the Empire.

[2] i.e. south of Lake Constance, *c.* 1463.

[3] *c.* 1586 (Pütter, op. cit., vol. ii, p. 26).   [4] Cf. *Ph.d.R.*, §§ 333 and 340.

them expand; the weaker are engulfed; and even the more considerable of them are impotent against a great power.

[§ 4. THE EMPIRE'S TERRITORY]

[49] The territories which the German Empire has lost in the course of several centuries are items in a long and melancholy inventory. Since in general the laws of the constitution and the organization of the public authority have been extinguished and can settle little or nothing to speak of, the constitutional lawyers must restrict themselves to the description of the empty and now meaningless symbols or insignia of the past and its claims, while those claims carry with them the comforting feeling with which an impoverished nobleman preserves the relics of his departed ancestors—a consolation which has the advantage of remaining secure and undisturbed. These portraits [50] cannot make caveats against the present owners of these baronial estates, and equally the constitutional claims of the German Empire have not aroused in any Minister any anxiety on the score of his opposition to them. Both the nobleman and the lawyer may give themselves over in peace to their harmless and innocent rejoicings.

If the constitutional lawyers still amuse themselves with expounding the claims of the Holy Roman (and German) Empire to Hungary, Poland, Prussia, Naples, &c., still the political insignificance of such rights prompts the remark that they concern not the German Empire as such so much as the Roman Imperial dominion, the Head of Christendom, and Master of the World, and that 'the Roman Emperor and the King of the Germans', as his title has put it, were essentially different.[1] The German Empire could have neither the interest nor the will nor latterly the power to assert what could be comprised in 'the supremacy of the Emperor'. It could not maintain such an unnatural union of territories separated by both geographical situation [51] and national individuality, especially since it neither would nor could support those territories which really are integral parts of itself.

Traces have been preserved down to quite recent times of the connexion with the kingdom of Lombardy, but that kingdom cannot

---

[1] Rosenzweig (op. cit., vol. i, pp. 106, 238) says that legal textbooks, such as those of Häberlin (1794) and Leist (1805), still expounded the claims of the Empire to Burgundy and dilated on the Emperor's position as above all the rulers of Christendom.

be regarded as an essential part of the German kingdom proper, especially because it was itself an independent kingdom, and the character of being an estate of the Empire, which some of its states had enjoyed, had already long lost its force.

But almost every Imperial war has ended with the loss of some of those territories which were essential parts of the German Empire and which actually possessed and exercised privileges as estates thereof.

This loss is strictly of two different kinds: there is the actual subjection of German territory to a foreign power and its emancipation from all Imperial rights and duties; but we must also regard it as a loss to the state that so many territories, though remaining in all their former legal and ostensible relationship to Emperor and Empire, have retained monarchs who, while being or having become members of the Empire, are simultaneously rulers of independent states. [52] This is apparently no loss; apparently things are left as they were; but actually it has undermined the foundations on which the cohesion of the state rests, because it has made these territories independent of the authority of the state.

Without going farther back, we give now only a short review of how, from the Peace of Westphalia onwards, the impotence of Germany and the inevitable German fate have been revealed in relation to foreign powers. Of course we deal only with its loss of territory in the peace treaties, because the mischief of war is immeasurable on any reckoning.

By the Peace of Westphalia [1648] the German Empire lost all connexion not only with the United Netherlands but also with Switzerland whose independence had already been long[1] an established fact in practice but was now formally recognized. This was a loss not of a possession but of claims, and so a loss insignificant in itself but important to the German Empire, which has often shown that it places more value on chimerical claims and rights utterly devoid of reality than on actual possession.

[53] So too Germany now formally ceded to France the bishoprics of Metz, Toul, and Verdun which it had already lost a century or more earlier. But an actual loss for the Empire was the cession [to France] of the Landgravate of Alsace (in so far as it had been Austrian) and the cession of the Imperial city of Besançon to Spain.

[1] Since 1499.

These territories lost all connexion with Germany; but while a greater number than these remained in their legal and theoretical dependence, the fact that they had foreign monarchs as rulers laid the foundation of their actual separation in practice.[1] For example, Sweden gained Upper Pomerania, part of Lower Pomerania, the archbishopric of Bremen, the bishopric of Verden, and the city of Wismar. The Margrave of Brandenburg, Duke and later King of Prussia, received the archbishopric of Magdeburg, and the bishoprics of Halberstadt, Minden, and Kammin.

Even if the ruler of Brandenburg had not become a sovereign at the same time, this diminution in the number of German estates and their fusion in one whole would have produced an effect little different from building a powerful state which could now refuse to be subject to the authority of the German Empire and could resist it, as it could not have done had it been divided between several estates.

[54] Apart from this diminution which has been mentioned, several other separate estates, such as Schwerin, Ratzeburg,[2] &c., succumbed.

Another fact was equally destructive of the German state. Foreign powers, by force as much as by invitation, interfered in German affairs, devastated the country from one end to another, and more or less dictated the peace terms. By this peace treaty the German Empire ceded to these powers the guaranteeing of its own constitution and internal relations, and thus recognized its inability to maintain its constitution and its being as a state, while at the same time it put its internal affairs at the mercy of the interest of foreigners.

Other internal weaknesses were (a) granting appeal exemptions[3] to several territories, (b) also, to some extent, letting a defendant choose which Imperial court to appear before (by delaying his choice a defendant could equally delay the legal process against him), (c) more serious than all this, the confirmation of the right

---

[1] The acquisitions of France were handed over to her in full sovereignty; but Sweden became a member of the German Diet for what she received (Bryce, op. cit., p. 389).

[2] Mecklenburg received them both in compensation for ceding Wismar to Sweden.

[3] It was granted at this Peace that in future there would be no appeal whatever to the Imperial courts of judicature from the German territories ceded to Sweden (Pütter, op. cit., vol. ii, p. 64). For a list of all the exemptions granted to other princes, see ibid., vol. ii, pp. 236–7.

whereby not only in religious questions (nor even only in those purely mundane or external ones bound up with a religious position) but also in other matters affecting the whole Empire, a majority of votes in the Diet was not to be binding, and (*d*) the proviso that the German [55] Empire might no longer redeem its sovereign prerogatives which had been mortaged to the Imperial cities.[1]

In the next peace treaty, that of Nimwegen [1678–9], which was concluded without any representatives from the Empire, though the Empire ratified it, including the clause that no objection was to be taken to it on the part of the Empire,[2] the Empire's supremacy over the Dukedom of Burgundy was abandoned; some stretches of territory in northern Germany changed their overlord, and in the south the French garrison rights in German fortresses were altered.[3]

But apart from its losses in peace treaties the German Empire displays phenomena peculiar to itself which have seldom arisen in other states. When peace was at its most profound, i.e. after the Treaty of Nimwegen, ten Imperial cities in Alsace as well as other territories were lost to France.[4]

The Peace of Ryswick [1697] was concluded when an Imperial delegation[5] was there, but there only in such a way that it was not admitted to the discussions along with the envoys of other powers; it received information only at the pleasure of the Emperor's envoy and was called in only to support his vote. This treaty confirmed the French possession of those territories and secured for the Empire in exchange an Imperial fortress, Kehl; but it contained [56] the famous clause about the religious situation in the conquered territories surrendered by France,[6] which gave the Protestant estates so much to do and helped to bring so much trouble in connexion with the Palatinate.

---

[1] Details in Pütter, op. cit., vol. ii, pp. 92–93.

[2] The translation here assumes that after the words *vom Reiche* in Lasson's text the following words which were in Hegel's earlier draft have dropped out: *ratificiert wurde, und damit auch die Klausel desselben, dass.* . . .

[3] Details in Pütter, op. cit., vol. ii, pp. 305–9.

[4] Some details in Pütter, op. cit., vol. ii, pp. 310–11.

[5] i.e. a delegation from the Estates as distinct from the Emperor, whose representative was there separately.

[6] i.e. all French possessions on the right bank of the Rhine. The French insisted that the 1,922 places concerned should remain Catholic despite the fact that under the Peace of Westphalia they ought to have become Protestant again (Pütter, op. cit., vol. ii, pp. 318–24). See below, p. 194.

In the negotiations for the Baden peace treaty [1714] no Imperial delegation had any part and the treaty concluded produced no immediate change for the German Empire. Austria regained Breisach and Freiburg.

This is really the last peace which the German Empire has concluded.[1] If in a tabular conspectus of German history from the Peace of Baden to the Seven Years War you find neither declarations of war nor treaties of peace, you would have to believe that in this long period Germany enjoyed the profoundest peace, whereas its soil was as much as ever the scene of battles and devastations.

The peace treaties which Sweden made with Hanover, Prussia, Denmark, and Russia after Charles XII's death[2] not only deprived it of the place its valiant king had won for it amongst the European powers by force, but lost it its power in Germany. Thereby, however, the power of the German state gained nothing, because the territories which Sweden lost came to German princes who succeeded to Sweden's fear of German unity.

[57] At the Peace of Vienna [1738] Germany lost nothing except its tie with Lorraine, which was slight anyway. The Empire did not accede to the ratification of this treaty.[3]

In the war of the Austrian Succession, Germany was the theatre of protracted devastations. Its greatest princes were involved in it. Armies of foreign monarchs came to blows on German soil and yet the German Empire was most profoundly at peace. The power which had taken Sweden's place, Prussia, grew during this war.

Much more devastating still, especially for northern Germany, was the Seven Years War. This time the German Empire was indeed at war, at war to execute an Imperial ban;[4] but its enemies did not even do it the honour of recognizing that it was at war or of making peace with it.

Finally, the Peace of Lunéville [1801] has not only deprived Germany of many rights of suzerainty in Italy, but has wrested

[1] Hegel had second thoughts and wrote in the margin: 'N.B. see next page, Peace of Vienna.'
[2] Treaties of Stockholm 1719, 1730; Peace of Nystad 1721.
[3] The Diet did give powers to the Emperor to conclude peace on the terms agreed. But the formal treaty prepared thereafter was not ratified by the Empire, for the Emperor Charles VI died and events took a different turn (Pütter, op. cit., vol. ii, pp. 481–2).
[4] On Frederick the Great.

from it the whole left bank of the Rhine. Moreover it has diminished the number of German princes and laid a foundation for further reducing considerably the number of the German estates and making the single parts of the whole all the more formidable to the whole and to the smaller estates.

If in war-time one-half of a country is a theatre of civil war or if it gives up the general defence and by neutrality puts the other half at the mercy of the enemy, then it must inevitably be lacerated in war and dismembered at its end. The strength of a country consists not in the number of its inhabitants and troops, nor in its fertility, nor in its size, but solely in the manner whereby all these things can be used for the great end of common defence as a result of the rational association of its parts in a single public authority.

[§ 5. CONSTITUTIONAL LAW[1]]

[58] In its army and its finances Germany does not form any public authority of its own, and therefore it must be regarded not as a state but as a congeries of independent states. The greater of these act independently even in foreign affairs, but the smaller must follow some single general course. The associations which from time to time come into existence for some specific end called the 'German Empire' are always partial and are concluded in accordance with the personal favour of their members, and so they lack every advantage which the coalitions of other powers may have. Even if these latter coalitions are of no long duration and even if in certain cases, e.g. in war, they do not work with the success and vigour which the same power would have if it were concentrated entirely under one government, still the expedients and measures appropriate to the end and aim of the coalition are taken intelligently and everything is organized with a view to that end. But the coalitions of the German states are bound by such formalities and restrictions and by such endless provisions (framed to produce just this result) that the whole effectiveness of the coalition is paralysed, and the end originally envisaged is in advance made impossible of attainment.

What the German Empire does as such is never an act of the whole but only of an association with a greater or lesser scope. But the means of achieving what the members of this association

---

[1] Mollat suggests as a title of this section 'Imperial Legislation and Justice'; Lasson suggests 'Legal Organization'.

ordain are not taken to this end. On the contrary, the first and only concern is to maintain those circumstances of the members which determine their separateness and ensure that they shall not be associated.

Associations of this sort are like a heap of round stones which are piled together to form a pyramid. But they are perfectly round and have to remain so without any dovetailing, and so, as soon as the pyramid begins to move towards the end for which it has been built, [59] it rolls apart or at least can offer no resistance [to dissolution]. As a result of such an arrangement, these states are deprived not only of the infinite advantage of a political union but also of the advantage of independence, the advantage of being able to join with others for single common ends; against such an eventuality they have put themselves in chains in advance, and thereby every unification is destroyed or even nullified at its start.

Now despite the fact that the German estates have thus cancelled their unification and deprived themselves of the possibility of uniting intelligently for transient and immediate ends as the need of the hour or the exigency of the situation may dictate, the demand is still there that Germany shall be a state. A contradiction is set up: the relations of the estates are to be so fixed that no German state is possible or actual, and yet Germany is to count simply as a state: it is to be regarded simply as one single body. For centuries this mentality has plunged Germany into a series of illogicalities between its will to make a state impossible and its will to be a state. Between the estates' jealousy of every kind of subjection to the whole and the impossibility of existence without this subjection, Germany has been made miserable.

The solution of the problem of how it is possible for Germany both to be and not to be a state offers itself very easily, namely that Germany is a state in theory and not in reality; formality and reality differ; empty formality belongs to the state, reality, however, to the non-existence of the state.

The system of the theoretical state [*Gedankenstaat*] is the organization of a constitution which is powerless in what belongs to the essence of the state. The obligations of each individual estate to the Emperor and the Empire, to the supreme government which consists in the Imperial head in conjunction with the Estates, are determined down to the last detail by an infinity of solemn and constitutional Acts. These duties and rights make up a system of laws in accordance with which the constitutional position of every single estate and the obligatoriness of its service [60] are settled in detail; and the contribution of each individual estate to the general [good] is supposed to be made only in accordance with these legal enactments. But the nature of this legal arrangement consists in this, that an estate's constitutional position and its obligations are not fixed by universal laws proper; on the contrary, on the analogy of civil rights, the relation of each estate to the whole is something particular in the form of a property. This has an essential effect on the nature of the public authority.

An Act issued by the public authority is a general Act and in virtue of its genuine generality it carries in itself the rule for its application. The matter it affects is general, homogeneous. The Act of the public authority carries in itself a free and general determinacy and its execution is at the same time its application. So too, since there is nothing separately distinguishable in the matter to which the Act is applied, its application must be determined in the Act itself and no unmalleable or heterogeneous material hinders its application.

If an Act is issued by the public authority that every hundredth man of a given age is to enlist as a soldier, or that a certain percentage of wealth or a specific tax on every acre of land is to be paid, the Act is quite general, affecting either men of a given age, or wealth, or land, and no distinction is drawn between man and man, this wealth or that, this land or that; the specifying [of the amount of the tax] which applies to homogeneous areas can be settled entirely by the public authority. The *hundredth* man, the *five* per cent., &c., are quite general specifications which require no special conditions in their application to a material which is homogeneous; for no lines are laid down which would first have to be obliterated or to which the specifications would have to be adapted, like, for example, the straight line on a tree-trunk along which it is to be sawn.

If, however, the field to which a law is to be applied is multiplex in character for this law itself, then the law cannot completely carry in itself the rule for its application. On the contrary, a special application is required in respect of each particular part of the field, and between [61] the law and its execution there enters a special act of application, and this act is a matter for the judiciary.

It follows that an Imperial law cannot provide a general rule for drawing lines and divisions *on a blank sheet* nor can it carry into effect the actual arrangement [of lines and divisions] in accordance with one such single rule. On the contrary, the field with which an Imperial law is concerned confronts it with definite characteristics of its own, determined long ago, and before the law can be carried into effect it is first necessary to find out how far the special line and form borne by each part of the field can be accommodated to that prescribed by the law, or how much binding force the general law has for each part. This is what a judicial authority has to find out if and when contradictions arise. In regard to these judicial findings, it turns out in fact that (i) findings are of course supposed to be reached but the court is so organized from the start that it is impossible for it to find much, (ii) what is found in theory is not realized in fact, it remains a finding in thoughts only, and (iii) finally the whole business of reaching findings is made little less than impossible, because the special character which the field has stands in the same relation to a general law as a straight line does to a curve, and thus right from the start there is an irreconcilability between a law issuing from the public authority and this special character of the general field confronting that authority. On this analogy the theoretical state with its system of constitutional and public law is the straight line, while the figure in which the theoretical state is to be realized has the form of a curve, and any schoolboy knows that the two lines are incommensurable. The curved formation is not exactly made irreconcilable with the straight line *de facto*; the figure does not assume the form of power, illegality, and arbitrariness: on the contrary, the fact that it is this incommensurable line is elevated likewise into the form of *law*; it acts *rightly* in disagreeing with constitutional law, legally in disagreeing with public law.

Thus if the problem of how Germany is at once a state and no state at all is to be solved, it must, if it is to be a state, exist purely as a theoretical state, while it is its non-existence [62] that must have reality. Now if the theoretical state is to be a state explicitly, the judicial authority which was to annul the contradiction, apply to actuality what was only theoretical, and thus realize it and make actuality correspondent with it, must be so constituted that even its work of application remains theoretical. Consequently the general orders which make a country a state would be paralysed in their transition into reality. The transition would indeed be settled and organized, for these orders are meaningless unless their purpose is that they shall be carried into effect, but the act of transition would also be turned into an *ens rationis*.

The paralysis of this transition may occur at each one of its stages. A general regulation is made; it is now to be carried into effect and in case of resistance legal procedure is necessary. If the resistance offered is not made by legal process, the execution of the regulation remains dormant; but if it is legally made, a decision can be hindered; if a decision issues, no consequences may follow. But this *ens rationis* of a judgement is meant to be executed and a penalty should accompany [non-compliance]; therefore an order issues to compel the full execution of the judgement. This order in turn is not carried out, so a judgement follows against those who have failed to execute it, requiring them to do so. Once again no consequences follow, and therefore it must be deemed that punishment shall be executed in full on those who fail to execute it on anyone who does not execute it on, &c., &c. This is the barren history of how one step after another which is to make a law work is made an *ens rationis*.

[63] If, then, it is for the judicial authority to find how the particular rights of individuals are to be placed in comparison with their general obligations to the Empire and how far a contradiction between these is actually a matter for the court, it depends on the organization of the court in its business of pronouncing judgement (not to speak at present of the question of the execution of the judgement) whether that business is not made more difficult for it from the start and whether, since the judgement, if not executed, is just an abstraction, the organization is not such that the question of reaching this abstraction does not arise at all but remains just an *ens rationis*.[1]

The organization of the judicial authority in relation to the mere pronouncement of judgement is such that great hindrances lie in the way of its essential feature which is here discussed, namely its task of making the general [64] ordinances of the state as such prevail against individual citizens. In the Imperial judiciary the administration of constitutional rights is intermingled with that of civil rights. Both classes of rights are subject to the same tribunals.

---

[1] Hegel has a double abstraction in mind; the first is a judgement that remains unexecuted; the second is the idea of a judgement which is never actually propounded.

The Imperial Courts are the supreme courts of appeal for civil rights and constitutional rights. The scope of their judicial authority in constitutional matters is restricted in any case, because the most important questions of this sort belong to the Diet, and also because many matters hitherto belonging to the Supreme Courts are settled by arbitration procedures;[1] but, in addition, it is exposed even in the mere pronouncement of judgement to endless difficulties and is made dependent on a mass of accidents which become necessities precluding its effectiveness.

The conjunction of civil and constitutional proceedings has the general result of increasing the mass of business before the present Imperial Courts to such an extent that they cannot dispatch it. It is recognized by the Emperor, the Empire, and the Supreme Court that the Supreme Court, not to speak of the Aulic Council, has not grown enough for the mass of its business.

No evil seems simpler to handle or more capable of easy relief. Even if several separate courts were not to be instituted, the number of judges in the existing courts could be increased and the dispatch of business thereby immediately accelerated; or one existing court could be subdivided, and by this means several courts could be established appropriate to the matter in hand. But such a simple expedient cannot be carried into effect in Germany. Of course it has been resolved upon, and the number of the members of the Supreme Court has been raised to fifty,[2] [65] but the German Empire could not raise the money for their salaries. In the course of time the number of judges sank to twelve, or even less, but has now at last reached twenty-five.

Official statistics reveal that the number of pleas annually pending far exceeds the number of those it is possible to decide, even though the statement of a single matter at issue lasts only several months instead of years, as used to happen. It follows of necessity, and published figures show, that many thousand suits are lying undecided, and the sollicitation [for a hearing], even if its worst abuses are gone and Jews no longer establish a trade in this line, is a necessary evil still. When it is impossible for all pending pleas to be decided, the parties must make every effort to see that their case takes precedence on the list for judgement.

[1] *Austrägalinstanzen*—a procedure for settling a dispute between two princes by the arbitration of a third prince (Pütter, op. cit., vol. i, p. 361; vol. iii, pp. 176 ff.).
[2] By the Peace of Westphalia in 1648. The number reached 25 in 1782.

A thousand other disputes about the presentation to assessor-ships and the *itio in partes* have often reduced the Supreme Court to impotence for several years,[1] and they hinder the course of justice on their own account quite apart from the fact that the Supreme Court has dawdled deliberately, on the principle of making the great feel its power.

In the Aulic Council, whose members are appointed by the Emperor, a lot of these evils do not occur, and no case e.g. of *itio in partes* has arisen, despite the right to it; and many forms are calculated to promote justice directly instead of [66] clogging it with the delays of pure formalities. Thus it is natural that in recent years justice has been sought to an increasing extent in the Aulic Council.

The need for an improvement in judicial arrangements has always been too clamant for people not to have given thought to it. But the result of the last attempt of Joseph II to arrange for a Visitation of the Supreme Court[2] (a Visitation legal indeed but in abeyance for two centuries), and the reason why unsettled business has just dissolved, are in general the same as those governing Im-perial justice as a whole, namely: the estates do associate for the administration of justice but in this union they will not give up any of their existence in relation to one another and that existence rests on separation and the negation of common action. They join together, but without the will for any common end.

Thus, pronouncing judgement is itself hindered, apart from any question of its execution. But we all know how it stands with the execution of the decisions of the Supreme Courts if they are to have any bearing on constitutional law and important matters. Besides, the more important business of this kind belongs to the Diet and not to the Supreme Courts and consequently it is thrown at once out of the legal into the political sphere. When the supreme public authority speaks, it is not applying laws but making one.

[1] Disputes about appointment of the members of the Supreme Court were usually on the question whether for this turn a Protestant or a Roman Catholic should be appointed. *Itio in partes*—the right of deciding matters affecting religion by negotiation and not by majority vote (see [78]). This was part of the religious settlement at the Peace of Westphalia.

[2] A Visitation with a view to revising the Statutes of the Court and accelerat-ing its business was decreed by Joseph II in 1767. Disputes about who the visitors were to be and about their powers lasted until 1776 when such visitors as were in office disbanded without having achieved anything at all (Pütter, op. cit., vol. iii, pp. 136 ff.).

Apart from all this, things of greater importance, such as the possession of territories, &c., are withdrawn from the formal procedure of the Diet [67]. By the Compact of Election and other fundamental laws it is settled that such matters are to be decided not by the Supreme Courts and the supreme judicial power, but by amicable arrangement between the contending estates; and when amicable arrangement is impossible, the matter is settled of necessity by war.

The succession question in Jülich-Berg[1] was so far from being settled legally that it [68] gave rise to a Thirty Years War. So too in the Bavarian succession problem[2] in recent times it was not the Supreme Courts but cannon and politics that spoke. Even in matters concerning less powerful estates it is not Imperial justice which gives the decisive verdict. It is well known that, in the disputed succession to the Houses of Saxony, 206 decisions[3] were issued by the Aulic Council in relation to the lands of the extinct lines of Coburg-Eisenberg and Römhild, and yet the most important points in dispute were settled by agreement. Similarly we know that, in the Liége affair, not only did the Supreme Court pronounce judgement, intimate it for execution, and call on several estates to execute it, but these estates fulfilled their obligation; but no sooner was a start made on the task than the most powerful estate among the executors did not content itself with being a mere executor of the Supreme Court's judgement but set to work with good intentions of its own, and, when an arrangement which was to have been settled otherwise than by legal process could not be carried through, it gave up the role of executor altogether.[4]

---

[1] This is a slip for Jülich-Cleve. Hegel gets it right below [101]. The Jülich-Berg question belongs to the eighteenth century.

[2] 1777. On the death of Maximilian Joseph, Elector of Bavaria, the Empire made an agreement with the collateral heir, the Elector Palatine, for the cession to Austria of part of the Bavarian territories. But the Bavarians called for aid from Prussia, and war ensued between Prussia and the Empire.

[3] Between 1680 and 1735 (Pütter, op. cit., vol. ii, p. 354).

[4] In 1780 the Bishop of Liége appealed to the Supreme Court against his subjects. The court upheld him and remitted the execution of its judgement to Prussia, the Elector of Cologne, and the Elector Palatine. Prussia, instead of complying, tried mediation, which failed. It sent troops which occupied Liége without resistance, promises having been given for indemnifying the Liégeois. The Bishop appealed again to the Supreme Court, which upheld him once more and instructed the other two Executors to implement its decision. Prussia withdrew altogether and the Bishop triumphed (Bühler, *Deutsche Geschichte*, Berlin, 1954, vol. v, pp. 44–45).

In such a delicate situation when there is a misunderstanding between prince and subject, a mediation between them may be desirable. On the other hand, however, if, once legal judgements have been pronounced, [69] their execution is to give place to another mediation, the whole situation at the point to which the thing has developed is topsy-turvy. By something apparently good at the moment the essential principle of the constitution is deranged. It would be truer to say 'that occasions like this make it obvious that this principle was deranged long, long ago.

It seems that a distinction must be made here. It is too obvious that the mutual relations of the powerful estates are settled by *politics*. But the smaller ones seem to have to thank their *legal* bond with the Empire for their existence. No Imperial city has thought itself capable on its own account of resisting its great neighbours, fellow estates of the Empire. A knight of the Empire is equally aware that he cannot defend his direct dependence on the Emperor against a prince either by his own effort or even by association with the rest of the body of knights. The thing speaks for itself, and it is needless to quote the fate of knights in France. An attempt (still less a successful attempt) like that of Francis of Sickingen to conquer an Electoral Princedom[1] is no longer among the possibilities of the present time, just as associations of Imperial cities or abbots cannot achieve now what they could once.

[70] Since it is not the power of the individual estates, or the power of their association if they conjoin, which maintains them, they have nothing to thank for their existence as direct fiefs of the Empire, and as relatively independent states, except the bond with the Empire and the legal constitution established by the Imperial peace.[2] But now there is the question of the means of maintaining this so-called legal tie and therewith the existence of knights, abbeys, Imperial cities, courts, &c. Obviously the means cannot be their individual power—since power, as states, they have none; the means must again be political. If politics is not at once seen to

---

[1] As leader of the knights of Swabia and the Rhineland, Francis (1481–1523) took arms in 1522 against the Elector Prince of Trèves in order to acquire the Princedom for himself. He was defeated by the united forces of Trèves, the Palatinate, and Hessen.

[2] *Landfriede*. In 1495 Maximilian I promulgated this perpetual peace of the Empire which finally made illegal the old *Fehderecht*, the right to pursue private feuds, and feuds between principalities, &c., by force of arms. It was a substitution of the rule of law for the rule of force within the Empire.

be the basis of the existence of the less powerful estates, this is only because we stick to ratiocination about the Imperial bond which constitutes membership of the Empire and forget the means whereby this bond is upheld.

[71] States like Lucca, Genoa, &c., maintained themselves for centuries without any Imperial tie until they suffered the fate of Pisa, Siena, Arezzo, Verona, Bologna, Vicenza, &c.—in short we could enumerate the entire geography of Italian cities, princedoms, dukedoms, &c. The apparently more powerful Republic which had previously swallowed so many independent cities was brought to an end by the advent of an adjutant who delivered the peremptory command of the general of a foreign power.[1] While hundreds of Italian sovereign countries drew blanks in the lottery of fate, some of them won the small prize of a somewhat more prolonged independence; but they subsisted only because of the jealous politics of neighbouring greater states against whose power they had been able to embark on a struggle in earlier centuries, though in comparison with them they were now, without any foreign loss, most disproportionately weak. But in the equal share of booty, in the equality of growth or decay, the jealousy of politics was equally satisfied, and, in the resulting combinations of interests, states like Venice and Poland were lost.

The change from the mailed fist to politics is not to be regarded as a change from anarchy to constitutionalism. There is no real alteration in principle but only on the surface. In the days before the Imperial peace, the aggressed [72] or those eager for conquest went at one another at once without preliminaries. In politics, on the other hand, men calculate before they come to blows and they do not risk great interests for the sake of small gain: but when they think themselves secure they shirk nothing.

Since the mass of the German states do not constitute a power, the independence of their individual units can be respected only so long as the advantage of other powers requires and so long as higher interests or rights of indemnification are not at risk. So far as interest goes, when the French armies had occupied half of Germany, France annulled the independent states and direct Diet members in the Netherlands and in the territories on the left bank

---

[1] Venice. Napoleon sent Junot, his A.D.C., with an angry message to the Venetian Senate and took an early excuse to declare war. His troops occupied Venice within a few months in 1797.

of the Rhine which were ceded to her later by the peace treaty. She could as easily have also annulled the constitutions of the territories on the right bank, and even if this destruction of the independence of so many principalities, dukedoms, bishoprics, abbacies, Imperial cities, and baronies could have had no legal validity, she could still by this means have hurled these territories into still greater misfortune, if politics, i.e. respect for Prussia and fear of harsher peace terms, had not averted this. It was averted too by [consideration of] the advantage derived from an old fixed ordinance for the payment of contributions which, according to the French official press, were raised in these territories *in small measure*.

This transition from naked to calculated power has of course not been made all at once; on the contrary, it has come about through [73] a legal constitution. Of course Germany could be regarded as more of a state at the Imperial peace than it is today. Under the feudal constitution the state's power was split into numerous parts, but the parts were so many that none of them was powerful enough to withstand the whole. But, as if fate had not destined Germany to such a situation at all, it soon overcame disgust with the absence of rights, and the quest of a firmer bond through the Imperial peace, by means of the deeper interest of religion which divided the peoples for ever.

[§ 6. RELIGION]

Amidst all the storms of the lawless situation in the days before the Imperial peace there still persisted, in respect of the relation of the estates to one another and to the general interest, a certain togetherness of the whole. Although the fulfilment of obligations seemed to depend not merely on the free will of the estates in general but on the will of individual estates, and although their legal connexion seemed very weak, still an inner connexion of dispositions prevailed. When religion was uniform, and when the still embryo *bourgeoisie* had not introduced a great heterogeneity into the whole, princes, dukes, and lords could regard one another more easily as a whole and accordingly could act as a whole. There was no state power opposed to individuals and independent of them as there is in modern states. The state's power and the power and free will of individuals were one and the same; but these individuals always had the will to let themselves and their power coexist in a state.

But when, through the growth of the Imperial cities, the *bourgeois* sense, which cares only for an individual and not self-subsistent end and has no regard for the whole, began to become a power [74], this individualization of dispositions would have demanded a more general and more positive bond. When, through the advance of culture and industry, Germany was now pushed into the dilemma of deciding whether to obey a universal power or break the tie [between the estates] for ever, the original German character swung it preponderantly towards insistence on the free will of the individual and on resistance to subjection to a universal, and it thus determined Germany's fate in accordance with its old nature.

In the course of time a number of great states have been built up along with the dominance of trade and commercial wealth. The unruliness of the German character could not directly encourage the development of independent states, while the old free strength of the nobility could not withstand the rising masses. Above all, the *bourgeois* spirit that was gaining countenance and political importance needed a kind of inner and outer legitimation. The German character betook itself to man's inmost heart, to his religion and conscience, and based dispersal on that foundation, so that separation in externals, i.e. into states, appeared as a mere consequence of this.

The original unruly character of the German nation determined the iron necessity of its fate. Within the sphere settled by this fate, politics, religion, want, virtue, power, reason, cunning, and all the forces that move the human race played out their mighty and apparently disorderly game on the wide battlefield permitted to them. Each behaves as an absolutely free and independent power, unconscious of the fact that they are all tools in the hands of primordial fate and of time that conquers all things, i.e. of higher powers that laugh at their boasted freedom and independence. Even want, that mighty creature, has not mastered the German character and its fate. The universal distress of the wars of religion, and especially the Thirty Years War, has rather developed and strengthened that fate, and the result of these wars has been a greater and more consolidated separation and dispersal.

[75] Instead of severing itself from the state as a result of its own inner division, religion has dragged this division into the state

and made the greatest contribution to annulling the state. It has so interwoven itself with what is called the constitution that it has become a basis of political rights.

In the individual states of which Germany consists, even civil rights are linked with religion. Both religions have an equal share in this intolerance, and there is nothing to choose between them. Despite the intolerance which is legal in the Empire, the princes of Austria and Brandenburg put a higher value on freedom of conscience in religion than on the barbarity of legal rights.

The débâcle of the religious disruption was exceptionally serious in Germany because the political bond was not so loose in any other country. The dominant religion must have been all the bitterer against apostates because, with the loss of the religious tie, it was not only the inmost link between men that was snapped, but almost the only link, whereas in other states a number of other connexions still remained firm. Partnership in religion is a deeper partnership, while partnership in physical needs, in property, and in gain is a humbler one; and the demand for separation is inherently more unnatural than the demand for an enduring union. Thus the Catholic Church showed itself as the more fanatical, because its demand looked in general to union and to the most sacred element in this union; it was prepared to hear of grace and toleration but never of right, i.e. of that permanence of separation for which Protestantism pressed. Finally both these opponents united to exclude one another from civil rights and to gird and establish this exclusion with every kind of legal pedantry.

[76] On the surface things are the same: in Catholic territories civil rights are denied to Protestants, in Protestant territories to Catholics. But the ground seems different. The Catholics were in the position of oppressors, Protestants of the oppressed. The Catholics denied to Protestants, on the ground that they were criminals, the free exercise of their religion in a Catholic territory. When the Protestants were dominant, this ground disappeared along with the fear of being oppressed. The ground of Protestant intolerance could only be either the right of retaliation for the hatred and intolerance of the Catholics—which would have been too unchristian a motive—or a lack of confidence in the power and truth of their own faith, and a fear of being easily corrupted by the splendour of the Catholic worship and the enthusiasm of its adherents, &c.

In the last century especially, there was dominant this eternal fear that the Protestant faith might be outwitted and overcome by stealth, this zealous belief in its own impotence, this fear for the cunning of the enemy, and the inducement to fortify God's grace by innumerable security measures and legal bastions.

This legal position is maintained with the greatest acrimony when it is regarded by some of the opposite party as a matter of grace. Of course from one point of view grace is lower than law, since law is definite, and what is legal is made for both parties something not subject to caprice, while grace is in the eyes of the law caprice only. But by this clinging to mere law as such the higher significance of grace has been obscured, so that for long past neither party has risen above law or allowed grace to take precedence of law. What Frederick II did in relation to the Catholics and Joseph [II] to the Protestants was grace contrary to the law as laid down in the Treaties of Westphalia and Prague. It accords [however] with the higher natural rights [77] of freedom of conscience and the non-dependence of civil rights on faith. But these higher rights are not only not recognized but actually excluded by the Peace of Westphalia and the religious peace, and their exclusion has been most solemnly guaranteed by both Protestants and Catholics alike. From this point of view these guaranteed rights are so little a subject for boasting that the grace which is spurned is infinitely superior.

Religion is a still more important fundamental determinant of the relation of individual parts of Germany to the whole; of course it has made the greatest contribution to the rupture of political union and to the legalization of this rupture. The times in which religion was split were too inapt for the separation of Church from state and for maintaining the state despite the division of faith. The princes could find no better ally than the conscience of their subjects in their endeavour to withdraw from the supremacy of the Empire.

As a result of the Imperial laws which have been gradually developed accordingly, the religion of every country, of every Imperial city, is legally established, either as exclusively Catholic, or as exclusively Protestant, or as a parity between the two. But what happens if a country now so far infringes the Westphalian treaty as to transfer from pure Catholicism to pure Protestantism or vice versa, or from parity to either of these?

No less fixed is the religion of the votes in the Diet, the Supreme Court, the Aulic Council, the individual offices and services, &c. The most important of these constitutional matters which are dependent on religion is the so [78] famous *itio in partes*, the right of this or that religious party not to submit to a majority vote. If this right were restricted to religious affairs, its justice and necessity would need no defence. The separation [of the minority] would do no direct damage to the state because it would concern only those matters which in the last resort have nothing to do with the state. But on the strength of the *itio in partes* the separation of the minority from the majority is legitimated in any political question even though it has nothing to do with religion. On war and peace, on the dispatch of an Imperial army, on taxes, or in short on all these few matters which ancient times have still left standing as the shadow of a whole, the majority of votes is not legally decisive. Without recourse to political activity, the minority, if made up of a religious party, can block the functioning of the state.

It is to go too far to maintain, as some do, that this right is on the same footing with the sacrosanct right of insurrection contained in the numerous French constitutions constructed in the last decade. [79] We must regard Germany as a state already dissolved, and its parts, which do not submit to the majority of the whole, as independent and self-subsistent states. If their division cannot bring them to a common decision, it also has neither the dissolution of all social bonds nor unending civil wars as its inevitable consequence.

But while religion has completely rent the state asunder, it has yet afforded an inkling in a remarkable way of certain principles on which a state can rest. Since the split in religion has torn men apart in their innermost being, and since none the less a bond was supposed to remain, the bond had to be an external one in relation to external things such as making war: and this bond is the principle of modern states. Precisely because the most important parts of constitutional law were interwoven with the religious disruption, two religions were interwoven with the state and then all political rights were made dependent on two, or, in strictness, three[1] religions. This is apparently contrary to the principle of the independence of state and Church, and to the possibility of there being a state despite differences in religion, but in fact the principle is

[1] i.e. Protestantism, Roman Catholicism, and parity between the two.

really recognized because there *are* different religions and Germany *is* supposed to be a state.

[80] More important is another division produced likewise by religion and still more closely connected with the possibility of the state. Originally votes in Imperial debates and on Imperial decrees rested entirely on the personality of the princes. They had votes only when they appeared in person, and the ruler of different, even separated, countries had only one vote. His person and his territory, his personality and his capacity as representing his territory, were to all appearance not distinct. The religious disruption introduced a difference here. On which side was his vote to be cast if a prince and his country were of a different religion and if a vote had legally to be counted only to one or other of the religious parties?

As a political power, he certainly ought not to have been on either side, but the times were not ripe for this. Indeed, originally, reflections like this were not made at all. The Count Palatine of Neuburg, a Protestant country, who became Catholic in the seventeenth century,[1] was reckoned amongst the Catholic votes in the Diet and the Supreme Court; on the other hand [81], the vote of the Elector of Saxony who changed his religion at the end of the same century [1697] was still reckoned as Protestant, as happened later too after the Dukes of Hesse and Wurtemberg had changed their faith [1749; 1721].

Although previously it was only princes with a territory and a people to rule who had a seat and a vote in the Diet, so that a country was inseparable from the notion of having a place in the Diet, this distinction between the person of a prince and his representation of his country, even in respect to the universal German state, became clearer and all the easier to make when, within his country itself, this separation between the person of the prince and his subjects became established through that country's Estates Assembly. The Palatinate, which had no such Assembly, went over to the Catholic side without resistance, and the struggle of its people against its Catholic princes as a result of religious grievances has lasted down to our own day. On the other hand, in Hesse and Wurtemberg this distinction had already become legal as a result of [the existence of] Estates Assemblies. The country's religion

[1] He became Catholic in 1614 and his vote was reckoned as Catholic in 1654 when the scheme for settling the religious affiliation of the voters was drawn up.

was given the upper hand so far as relations with the German Empire were concerned, and given prominence over the personality of the prince, who appeared in the Diet not as an individual but as a representative.

[82] Attention to this distinction which religion has occasioned has now been extended to other differences: countries which have come under one prince have preserved their individual votes for him. Here too what has been made a principle is the prince's capacity as a representative, not the singularity of the individual, or his personality, as it used to be in former times, when the ruler of different princedoms had only one vote, and when, if one princedom was divided between different princes, each of them had a vote of his own.

But just as what nourishes a healthy body would only corrupt a sick one still further if it were given it, so this true and genuine principle that it is a territory which confers the power and right of a vote has contributed all the more to the dissolution of the German Empire now that it has been introduced into it.

[§ 7. THE POWER OF THE ESTATES]

In the course of time, changes in manners, in religion, and especially in the comparative wealth of the estates had the effect of severing their inner bond of connexion which had depended on their common character and general interests. Thus external legal bonds were necessary if Germany was to be united in a state after its inhabitants had ceased to be one people and become just a mass.

[83] One thoeory of such unifying ties is what constitutes a part of German constitutional law. The old feudal system could turn into a state on the modern model, on which all the European states that have not experienced a revolution in recent times are more or less organized, provided that no one of the vassals was or could become paramount. Of course even a mass of weaker vassals could become a power by organizing themselves into a firm body against the state, as happened in Poland;[1] and the lustre of the Imperial Crown could not itself have furnished the Emperor with power sufficient to meet it. But even if the minority in Germany is not

[1] The reference is to the body of Polish nobles who from the second half of the fourteenth century managed to extort more and more privileges for themselves and so paved the way for a disastrous weakening of the royal power in the seventeenth and eighteenth centuries.

subject to the decrees of the majority, still this right, grounded on the *itio in partes*, is always limited to some extent; moreover, what can paralyse the activity of the whole is not an individual vote but only a religious party; and even if one individual estate regards itself as in general not subject to the majority—e.g. when Prussia refused to pay the increased *Kammerzieler* it alleged the principle that it was still undecided whether the majority vote on a tax question was binding without qualification—and even if each estate makes peace and concludes treaties of neutrality on its own account, still all these rights and circumstances came later. It was conceivable that, had the Emperor acquired an adequate force on the strength of the territories of his own house, and had individual vassals been unable to grow to an overwhelming size, the feudal system in Germany could have upheld the state. It is not the principle of the feudal system which has cut away Germany's potentiality of becoming a state: on the contrary, it is the disproportionate aggrandisement of single estates which has annulled the very principle of the feudal system and the stability of Germany as a state.

[84] The power of these individual states has inhibited the growth of a state-power in Germany, and their aggrandisement has made such a power ever more impossible. The German character's stubborn insistence on independence has reduced to a pure formality everything that might serve towards the erection of a state-power and the union of society in a state; and to this formalism it has clung just as obstinately. This obstinate adherence to formalities is only to be interpreted as resistance to the *reality* of union, a reality averted by the maintenance of this formal temper; and this immutability of form is passed off as immutability of the thing.

When the Roman Emperors terminated the anarchy of the Roman Republic and brought the Empire together into a state again, they preserved all the external forms of the Republic [85] intact. But to achieve the opposite aim in Germany, every sign of the German political union has been conscientiously preserved for centuries, while the thing itself, the state, disappeared long ago; it has disintegrated, not indeed into downright anarchy, but into numerous separate states. In the millennium that has elapsed since Charlemagne, the constitution appears to have undergone no change at all, since the newly elected Emperor even now has at his

coronation Charlemagne's crown, sceptre, and orb, and even his
shoe, his coat, and his jewels. An Emperor today is thus presented
as the very same Emperor that Charlemagne was because he even
wears Charlemagne's own clothes. Although the Margrave of
Brandenburg now maintains 200,000 troops, his relationship to
the German Empire seems [86] to be still the same as it was when
he had not 2,000 regulars in his standing army, because the
Brandenburg envoy now, as then, presents the Emperor with oats
at his coronation.

This German superstitious adherence [87] to purely external
formalities and ceremonial, so laughable to other nations, is very
well aware of itself. What it displays is the primordial German
character which cleaves with unbroken tenacity to self-willed independence. In the maintenance of these forms the German forces
himself to descry the maintenance of his constitution. Manifestoes,
public documents, tell exactly the same tale.

Mention was made above[1] of the loss suffered by Germany at
the hands of foreign powers. What is to be reckoned as still more
of a loss to Germany as a state, however, is the fact that, by
becoming owners of German Imperial territories, foreign princes
have become members of the German Empire. Every aggrandisement of any such ruling house is a corresponding loss for the
constitution of Germany. This constitution has been able to persist only because the House of Austria, which may be called the
Imperial House, though not made strong enough by the German
Empire to resist to some extent the principle of complete dissolution, has been put in a position to resist it by the power of its
territories outside Germany. The German constitution has even
no guarantee against several German territories becoming unified
in the hands of a single House, with complete legality, through
inheritance. On the contrary, since the state's authority is treated
throughout in the legal form of private property, there can be no
question of any resistance to a unification of this kind which
normally is more important in politics than familial and private
rights are. Naples and Sicily were separated from Spain and the
right of this [Imperial] family to them was recognized; so, separated
too, Tuscany was kept by the Imperial House.[2]

---

[1] [4] and § 4.
[2] After the Medici line failed, Francis Stephen of Lorraine became Duke,
and at his death in 1765 it became an hereditary possession of the second son of

Just as the old Roman Empire was destroyed by Nordic bar-
barians, so too [88] it was from the north that the principle
of destruction entered the Roman-German Empire. Denmark,
Sweden, England, and, above all, Prussia are the foreign powers
whose standing as estates of the Empire has given them at one
and the same time a centre separate from the German Empire and
a constitutionally proper influence on its affairs.

In this regard Denmark played only a transient and short-lived
role in the early years of the Thirty Years War.

The Treaty of Westphalia consolidated generally the principle
of what was then called German freedom, namely the dissolution of
the Empire into independent states; it diminished the number
of these states as well as the only chance then available of the
whole's dominating the parts; it strengthened separation by fusing
independent states into larger ones. Moreover, it conceded to
foreign powers a legal interference in German internal affairs,
partly by ceding some Imperial territories to them, partly by
making them guarantors of the constitution. In all ages, if one
party in a civil war calls on a foreign power for aid, that has been
regarded as the height of malevolence, and, if there could still be
any question of punishment when the state was in its death throes,
as the worst of crimes. When the very vitals of a state are being
mauled by civil war, in the midst of this most horrible of all evils,
there still prevails in the mutual hatred of the hostile parties (and
this is the greatest of all hatreds) the principle that all together
should still have formed one state; and even if this union had been
supposed to be brought about by tyranny itself, nevertheless what
is most sacrosanct in man, the demand for union, did still remain.
But the party which calls foreign powers to its aid abandons this
principle. By its very act it has simply annulled the state's unity,
even if its deliberate and genuine intention were just to find protection in foreign aid against the oppression which it was incapable
of warding off by its own power.

After Denmark's attempt, in the Thirty Years War, to become
the saving genius of Germany had miscarried [89] and when,
without resisting or opposing Ferdinand's[1] armies, what is called
German constitutional law and all laws of every kind were dumb,

the Hapsburgs. It had been a fief of the Empire in the twelfth century and early
in the eighteenth century the Emperor had tried to reassert his ancient claims.
  [1] Ferdinand of Styria, later Emperor Ferdinand II, the Jesuit.

the illustrious Gustavus Adolphus came on the scene with well-nigh the antipathy of the German estates. His heroic death on the battlefield prevented him from fulfilling his role as saviour of political and religious freedom in Germany. This intention of his Gustavus declared in advance; he entered into the most specific treaties with the German princes on matters affecting the whole nation and put himself at their head in a free, noble, and magnanimous spirit; he broke the armies of oppression and freed the countries not only from this burden but from the still more pressing burden of the deprivation of religious rights. His headquarters were a church; he and his men went into battle intoning the most fervent hymns. His victories restored religion along with the rights of which the German princes had been deprived. He did not return to the Count Palatine his reconquered hereditary possessions; he held other countries in his sway and had other plans in his head which his death prevented him from bringing to fruition, and which the further course of war let his Chancellor fulfil only to the extent that at the peace[1] the foreign power [Sweden] kept a part of Lower Pomerania, the archbishopric of Bremen, the bishopric of Verden, and the city of Wismar. On the theory of the German Empire these [estates] remained its dependants, but in practice they were divorced from it and its interest, so that apart from its political influence as a power and over and above its influence in law as a guarantor [of the German constitution], Sweden itself acquired a lasting influence by right as a member of the Empire.

Men are foolish enough not to look beyond the idealism of those who unselfishly go to the rescue of freedom in politics and religion; foolish enough to overlook, in the inner warmth of enthusiasm, the truth which lies in power, and so to suppose that a human work of justice and dreams fulfilled is secure against the higher justice of nature and truth. This latter justice avails itself of necessity to compel men under its power, be conviction, theory, and inner enthusiasm what they may. This justice, which provides that a foreign power admitted by a weaker state to a share in its internal affairs acquires possession therein, was expressed in [90] the Treaty of Westphalia in the case of the Dukedom, later the Kingdom, of Prussia. This Duke had kept the archbishopric of Magdeburg and the bishoprics of Halberstadt, Kammin, and Minden.[1] Even though the House of Brandenburg, unlike the House which then

[1] See above [53].

succeeded to the ducal dignity of Pomerania, &c., was not at the
same time an external foreign power, the diminution of the number
of German estates and their concentration in one power, though
a purely native one, would none the less have had the effect of
diminishing the power of the Empire as a whole, because the
previously smaller parts now constituted a power capable of with-
standing the power of the whole.

By the peace treaties which it was compelled to make after the
death of Charles XII with Hanover, Prussia, Denmark, and Russia,
Sweden lost the place won so meteorically for it amongst the
European powers by its courageous king, and therewith its power
in Germany. But the power of the German state gained nothing
thereby, because another centre of resistance [Prussia] to it had
already been building itself up more and more. The territories
which Sweden lost did not pass directly either to the German
Empire to serve as capital for the Imperial exchequer or to their
own princes, but to princes who already were fellow members of
the Empire and who now were in a position to threaten the unity
of the state.

In the profound peace claimed by the German Empire at a time
when it was filled with war everywhere, Hanover, which then had
a ruler in common with England, played a part which, however,
had no further outcome; it was not upholding any principle to
which Germany's interest was directly attached. There was no
question of defending political or religious freedom, and, in general,
Hanover has not risen in the sequel to that degree of influence in
Germany which Sweden and, later, Prussia sustained. England's
constitution and its too remote interests prevented any amalgama-
tion between Hanover's German tie and England's political ties
[91] like that effected, as a result of his own natural adherence to
his German ties, by the first Duke of Brunswick who ascended the
English throne.[1] The cleavage of interests between England and
the Electorate of Brunswick was at its clearest in the Seven Years
War when France was so pleased with the project of conquering
America and India in Hanover[2] but then experienced in the event
how little the devastation of Hanover contributed to the miseries

---

[1] George I, Elector of Hanover and Duke of Brunswick.

[2] The elder Pitt had a similar idea. He 'assured his countrymen that they
should be no losers [by advancing subsidies for the defence of Hanover] and
that he would conquer America for them in Germany' (Macaulay, *Essays*, Works,
Edinburgh edition, London 1897, vol. vi, p. 72).

of the English people. Amid this separation [of interests] and thus in this diminished influence on Germany, the King of England has remained an estate of the German Empire.

In the same war Germany did not lose Silesia, but the power [Prussia] whose size is the chief obstacle to the unity of the German state became greater still by absorbing it, and it maintained its possession of it in the Seven Years War which arose later from this conquest. In this war the German Empire did declare war against one of its members [Prussia], but that member did not do the Empire the honour of recognizing it. It happens of course that a state against which war is actually being waged is not recognized; but in reality it *is* recognized by the very fact that war is waged against it, and it gains full recognition when peace is made with it. But the enemy of the German Empire scarcely did it the honour of recognizing that it was at war with it, and its war was not recognized in a peace, because with the German Empire no peace has been concluded.

This war had in common with older wars the character of being a civil war between German estates. One group of estates let its troops join the Imperial Army of Execution[1] in accordance with the decrees of the Diet; another group withdrew altogether from this obligation to the German Empire and as sovereign estates, allied themselves with Prussia. No general interest counted any longer. An old Protestant jealousy of Austria brought religion into play to some extent; this was fostered by the Empress's known enthusiasm for the Catholic faith, which had exposed her otherwise maternal heart to intrigues resulting in the oppression of Protestants in her states, and by other circumstances, such as the Pope's blessing on the Austrian supreme commander's sword. [92] But the element of animosity which arose on this side was present on both sides only as a public feeling: the war itself affected no such more general interest; all that was at stake[2] was the private interest of the belligerent powers.

Since then the Prussian power has mounted in Poland. The number of the German estates has diminished again by three, Bavaria, Anspach, and Bayreuth. In this connexion the results of the war with France have not yet blossomed to the full.

Thus, first, by religion and the advance of culture; secondly, by the fact that the Germans have been united not so much by the

---

[1] See above p. 173, footnote 1. [2] Reading *es galt* for L.'s *er galt*.

might of an external political tie as by the might of their inner character; and, thirdly, by the lack of any political principle for obstructing the supremacy of single estates, the German state has been dissolved, because no state-power has been left to it. The old forms have remained, but the times have changed, and with them manners, religion, wealth, the situation of all political and civil estates, and the whole condition of the world and Germany. This true condition the old forms do not express; they are divorced from it, they contradict it, and there is no true correspondence between form and fact.

Germany arose contemporaneously with almost all the European states and out of the same situation. France, Spain, England, Denmark, Sweden, Holland, and Hungary grew each into a single state and have so remained, though Poland has perished. Italy is partitioned and Germany is collapsing into a mass of independent states.

Most of the European states were founded by Germanic peoples, and out of the spirit of these peoples their constitution has been developed. Amongst the Germanic peoples every free man's arm was counted on and his will had its share in his nation's deeds. Princes were chosen by the people, and so were war and peace and all acts of the whole. Anyone who wished participated in council; anyone who did not so wish forbore of his own will and he relied on a similarity of interest with the others.

With the change in manners and way of life each individual was more preoccupied with his own necessities and his own private affairs. [93] By far the greater number of free men, i.e. the strictly *bourgeois* class, must have had to look exclusively to their own necessities and their own living. As states became larger, those people who must have had to concern themselves exclusively with their own affairs formed a class of their own. There was an increase in the mass of things needed by the free man and the noble, who had to maintain themselves in their social position respectively by industry or by work for the state. The foreign relations involved in the greater complexity of national affairs became stranger to every individual. As a result of all these changes the management of national affairs became more and more closely concentrated in a centre consisting of the monarch and of the Estates, i.e. of one part of the nation consisting of (*a*) the nobility and the clergy speaking personally in dicussion on their own account and (*b*) the third estate, [speaking] as representative of the rest of the people. The monarch manages national affairs, especially in so far as they concern foreign relations with other states; he is the centre of the state's power; from him everything issues which requires legal compulsion. The legal power is thus in his hands; the Estates participate in legislation and they pass the budget which supports the state's power.

The system of representation is the system of all modern European states. It did not exist in the forests of Germany, but it did arise from them; it marks an epoch in world-history. The continuity of world-culture has led the human race beyond oriental despotisms, through a republic's world-dominion, and then out of the fall of Rome into a middle term between these extremes. And the Germans are the people from whom this third universal form of the world-spirit was born.[1]

This system did not exist in the forests of Germany, because each nation must on its own account have run through its own proper course of development before it encroaches on the universal course of world-history. The principle which elevates it to universal dominion first arises when its own peculiar principle is applied to the rest of the unstable cosmos. Thus the freedom of the German peoples necessarily became a *feudal system* when in their conquests they deluged the rest of the world.

[94] The fief-holders remained among themselves, in relation to one another and to the whole, what they were before, namely free people; but they became subjects, and they entered at once into a relation of obligation to the man they had followed or whom they had freely, without any obligation, placed at their head. The contradictory characteristics of a free man and a vassal were reconciled, in that fiefs were fiefs of the Empire, not of the prince as a person. The connexion of the individual with the whole people now acquires the form of duty, and his possession of a fief and a power is not dependent on the prince's whim; on the contrary, it is legal and proprietorial and thus heritable. If in despotisms there may be a sort of heritability in the title of Hospodar, it is still a sort which itself depends on [a despot's] whim; or if such a heritable power goes with a separate and more independent state, such as Tunis, the state pays tribute and, unlike the fief-holder,

[1] Here in germ is Hegel's *Philosophy of History* as expounded in his lectures in Berlin twenty or more years later.

has no share in deliberations on matters of common concern.[1] In these deliberations the vassal's personal and representative capacities are not distinguished; as a representative he portrays his territory; he is its man; it occupies the pinnacle of his interest; he is personally one with it. Besides, in many states, the vassal's own men, apart from being subjects, are also burghers; or individual free men, who have not become barons,[2] have united into burghs; and this *bourgeois* class has acquired representation on its own account.

In Germany, that part of the *bourgeoisie* which has representation of its own in the universal state [i.e. the Empire] is not at the same time a subject. Subjects have no separate representation in the Empire, but they have it through their princes, and they have it again, in relation to their prince, within the confines of the particular state which they constitute.

In England, ownership of estates no longer provides a measure of the higher and lesser nobility's character as representative of one part of the nation, but this has not made that class's significance in the state merely personal. The peer who has a seat and a vote in Parliament is, in virtue of primogeniture, a representative of his great family; [95] but the Chancellor of the Exchequer, the younger son of the Earl of Chatham, is *Mr*. Pitt. A member of a noble family who is not the eldest encounters the general obstacles to a career by which every *bourgeois* is confronted. Advancement to the highest honours is open as readily to the *bourgeois* as to the son of a duke; both have to rise above these obstacles by talent, character, and education. So also in the Austrian monarchy it is in tune with social etiquette to address every decently dressed man as *Herr von*; for every such person the way is open to the highest military and political positions; the man who attains them is raised to the nobility and made equal to them except in respect of those circumstances which, as in England, qualify for [Parliamentary] representation.

[1] In the eighteenth century Moldavia and Wallachia were under Turkish rule. The title of Hospodar or governor was sold by the Sultan to the highest bidder, but it could be inherited, though the Sultan could transfer it at will from one family to another. Tunis was conquered by Turkey in 1574, but the office of Bey was hereditary in one family till the beginning of the eighteenth century and in another for the next hundred years; Tunis had more independence from Turkey than Moldavia, &c., had, and of course had no voice in the Turkish government.

[2] i.e. (as in Scotland) owners of freehold estates, who were frequently commoners.

France's misfortune must be sought entirely in the complete disintegration of the feudal system and the loss of France's true character. As a result of the decline of the States General, the higher and lower nobility no longer appeared in the character of representative, the character on which its chief influence in the political organization depended. On the other hand, their personality was intensified in the highest degree and to a shocking extent. At the same time, effect is no longer given to the representation of the Third Estate, and in the new *États généraux* no gradual transition had been made from the previous harsh arrangement to one more satisfactory.

From youth upwards the nobility are exempt through their capital from the taint of business and the pains of earning a livelihood. Consequently they have preserved a freedom of disposition as a result of a temper hereditary, carefree, and unruffled by affairs. They are thus the better adapted for the martial courage which sacrifices all possessions, all cherished property and habits, to self-restraint and self-adaptation to the whole existing order; better adapted too for a more liberal handling of affairs of state and for a certain freedom in dealing with them which is less dependent on rules and which, according to circumstances, situation, and need, can be more self-confident and can vitalize the administrative machine into something freer. Thus if the nobleman in his personal capacity has a pre-eminence in all states, a single nobleman, just because his pre-eminence is personal, must find himself freer, i.e. in any possible rivalry, [96] because, this apart, the organization of our states, which is elaborate, multi-departmental, and exigent of toil beyond words, also necessitates the hard labour and hard-won skills and attainments of the *bourgeois*. With the earlier rise and now the recently full-grown importance of this class[1] the way must stand open to the skills and attainments which are raising the character of this class above itself.

This process whereby the difference [between nobility and *bourgeois*] is being diminished by nature and in most modern states (e.g. in Prussia, to some extent, in civil affairs; in England, Austria, and other states in military affairs also) has been intensified to the extreme in France. There judicial positions and a military career are closed to birth, and the person as such is made into a principle.[2]

---

[1] Reading, with Mollat, *Stands den über*.
[2] Hegel refers to the *carrière ouverte aux talents*.

Representation is so deeply interwoven with the essence of the feudal constitution in its development along with the rise of the *bourgeois* that we may call it the silliest of notions to suppose it an invention of the most recent times. By the transformation of free men into masters, the feudal constitution, i.e. in modern countries, a state, has been developed[1] in which each individual no longer has a direct voice himself in any national affair; on the contrary all obey a whole founded by themselves, i.e. a state, and its branches and particularizations (the laws), an abiding fixed centre to which each individual has a mediate relation derived from representation. All modern states subsist by representation, and its degeneration alone, i.e. the loss of its true essence, has destroyed France's constitution, though not France as a state. It came out of Germany; but there is a higher law that the people from which the world is given a new universal impulse perishes in the end before all the others, while its principle, though not itself, persists.

[§ 8. THE INDEPENDENCE OF THE ESTATES]

[97] The principle which Germany has given to the world it has not developed for itself, nor has it known how to find in it a support for itself. It has not organized itself in accordance with this principle; on the contrary, it has become disorganized by failing to develop its feudal constitution into a state-power and by wishing instead to remain everywhere true to its original character, i.e. to the independence of the individual on the universal, on the state. It has collapsed into a multitude of states whose mode of subsistence depends on solemn engagements amongst themselves and is guaranteed by great powers. But this mode of subsistence does not rest on their own power and force; it is dependent on the politics of the great powers.

What real guarantee remains for the existence of the individual states?

Since they lack a real state-power, this guarantee could rest only on the absolute venerability of the rights which have been raised to such a pitch by the lapse of centuries and by innumerable solemn peace treaties that they cannot possibly be infringed. It is generally fashionable everywhere to make into a *moral* power the

---

[1] 'The admission of money into the Highlands will soon put an end to the feudal modes of life, by making those men landlords who were not chiefs' (S. Johnson, *Letters* (Oxford, 1952), vol. ii, p. 184).

mode of political existence which the individual states possess, and so to implant its sacrosanctity in men's hearts as to make it something no less fixed and inviolable than the generally accepted morals and religion of a nation.

But often, especially in France recently, we have seen even morals and religion most bitterly assailed by command and by authority. Even if such extremely dangerous experiments turn out to the ruin of their authors or at least produce only a very ambiguous result, still religion and morals are themselves exposed to the influences of the age and to an imperceptible alteration.

Apart from this, however, morals and religion are not at all on the same footing with constitutional rights. Even if it be said that there can be nothing more sacrosanct than right, still in respect of private rights grace is higher, for it can forgo its right. The right of the state is higher too, because if it is to exist the state cannot possibly [98] allow private rights in their whole range and implications: taxes, which the state must exact, are already a negation of the right of property. If political rights are supposed to have the force of private rights, then they carry in themselves a sort of contradiction: for they would presuppose that those who had firm political rights of this kind against one another stood in a legal relation under a suzerain with authority and power in his hands; but in that event the reciprocal rights of both parties would no longer be political rights but only private rights, i.e. property rights.

Such a legal relation is supposed to have a ground in the constitution of the German Empire. But, for one thing, there is always a downright contradiction in supposing that relationships bearing directly on the state, and not property only, are to have the form of private rights, while, on the other hand, since no state-power exists any longer in Germany, the treatment of political rights as private rights, and their equal security and stability with private rights, disappears, and private rights enter the general class of political rights.

We all know what absolute venerability these political rights have. Every peace treaty—and peace treaties are precisely the contracts on which the political rights of the powers are grounded in relation to one another—contains the fundamental article that friendship is to exist between the contracting powers. Apart from this article, the treaty contains the settlement of their other relations, particularly those that had previously been the *casus belli*. The fundamental article expresses the maintenance of a friendly understanding in such general terms that it is clear at once that it is not to be taken *au pied de la lettre*.

The Turkish Empire seems almost to maintain its relations with foreign powers on the footing of being at peace with all of them until it is itself attacked, and only occasionally have the politics of the rest of Europe succeeded in plunging Turkey into a political war. Elsewhere, however, the relation of states to one another is so many-sided, and every single matter settled in a peace treaty has in turn so many facets, that despite all their precise determination there still remain innumerable facets of the matter about which dispute is possible. No power attacks a stipulated right directly and immediately; [99] in some undetermined facet of the thing differences arise which upset the peace in some way, and which, as a result of the state of war, loosen the foundation of the other determinate rights.

This annulment of mutual political rights is in the first place a consequence of the state of war. Treaties and the matters determined in them might well subsist; they may not be directly infringed or openly attacked with naked force; treaties are not trifled with. But if dissension arises otherwise over points and circumstances not clearly settled, everything else which had previously held treaties firm is overturned.

Wars, be they called wars of aggression or defence—a matter on which the parties never agree—would be called unjust only if the peace treaty had stipulated an *unconditional* peace on both sides. And even if the phrase 'perpetual peace' and 'perpetual friendship between the powers' is so turned, it must in the very nature of things be understood as carrying the proviso: until one party is attacked or treated like an enemy.[1] No state can bind itself to let itself be attacked or treated as an enemy and yet not to arm itself but to keep the peace.

But the potential modes of enmity are so infinite that there is no determining them by the human intelligence, and the more determinations there are, i.e. the more the rights that are established, the more readily does a contradiction between such rights arise. If one party insists, up to the limit of the concession, on a right

---

[1] This is Hegel's first criticism of Kant's essay *On Perpetual Peace* (1795). Cf. *Ph.d.R.*, § 324 and notes *ad loc.* in Eng. tr. (Oxford, 1942).

conceded to him, he comes up against some other right conceded to the other party. Look at the manifestoes and public documents which, on the occasion of a dispute between two states, contain on both sides an accusation against the behaviour of the other power and a justification of its own!

Each party grounds its behaviour on rights and accuses the other of an infringement of a right. The right of one [100] state *A* is infringed by state *B* in a right *a* which accrues to *A*, but state *B* avers that it has upheld its right *b* and that this is not to be taken as an infringement of the right of *A*. The public takes sides; each party claims to have right on its side; and both parties are right. It is just the rights themselves which come into contradiction with one another.

There are philanthropists and moralists who decry politics as a struggle and a device for seeking one's own advantage at the expense of the right, as a system and work of injustice. The ranting, indifferent public, i.e. a mass without interests or motherland of their own, whose ideal of virtue is the peace of a tavern, accuse politics of dubious fidelity and unrighteous instability; or at least if they do take sides, they are on that account mistrustful of the form of law in which the interests of their state appear. If these interests are their own too, they will also uphold the legal form; but it is not this but the private interests which are their true inner driving force.

If the philanthropic friends of right and morality had an interest, they could understand that interests, and rights with them, could themselves collide with one another, and that it is silly to set up an opposition between right and the interest of the state or, to use the expression which is still more hateful to morality, the 'advantage' of the state.

Right is the advantage of one state, acknowledged and settled by treaties. Since in treaties generally the varying interests of the states are settled, though as rights these interests are so infinitely many-sided, they must come into contradiction, and so must the rights themselves. It depends entirely on circumstances, on the combinations of power, i.e. on the *judgement* of politics, whether the interest and right which is coming into jeopardy is to be defended by the power with its whole strength. If it is, then the other party can of course allege a right of its own, since it too has just the opposite interest which collides with the first, and therefore

a right too. Thus war, or the like, has now to decide, not which
of the rights [101] alleged by the two parties is the genuine right—
since both parties have a genuine right—but which of the two
rights is to give way. War, or whatever it may be, has to decide
this, precisely because both contradictory rights were equally
genuine; thus a third thing, i.e. war, must make them unequal so
that they can be unified, and this happens when one gives way to
the other.

The venerability and moral power of rights may stand fast and
remain, but how should it be put in a position to uphold them?
As a result of the indeterminacy of rights, conflict *may* sometimes
arise, and at other times contradiction *must* arise from their determinacy, and in this discord the right must maintain itself by its
power.

It is senseless that what is called 'the rights of the German
estates' should be supposed to subsist on the strength of its inner
venerability and as a moral power, while—since the afore-mentioned
contradiction occurs in fact—no power can be or is available to
maintain it in the whole range of its multiplex character. Inevitably
a situation would have arisen in which what prevailed was a real
anarchy, not merely passive but active, namely the old mere right
of the mailed fist[1] which, in the eternal discord over such ill-defined
ownership, gave possession to the arm which was stronger at the
moment, and maintained it in possession until the arm of its
opponent had become the stronger.

This situation, however, the *Landfriede* has directly rectified,
and it has produced for the smaller states a situation of security
which is upheld by their impotence in comparison with the greater
ones. So far as the more powerful states are concerned, it has been
said already[2] that the possession of the Jülich-Cleve inheritance
was the occasion for the Thirty Years War, and as little in this
instance as in others, e.g. the Bavarian succession, did judicial
proceedings settle the matter. Apart from this, however, the number of disputed cases which have occasioned a war would seem
trifling in comparison with the infinity of disputed cases which
must have arisen from the infinite complexity of rights and which
yet of course are, shall I say 'laid aside'?—no, 'left in peace'. It is

---

[1] *Faustrecht = Fehderecht*, the right which led to private wars between magnates until these were ended by the *Landfriede* [70].
[2] See above [67].

common knowledge that the German nobility is entangled in endless and innumerable law-suits; that law-suits instituted a century
or centuries ago [102] still remain lying; and, moreover, that an
infinite number of claims, i.e. rights that have not come to realization, lie at rest in the grave of the archives of every prince, duke,
nobleman, and Imperial city. Could all these rights once find
a voice, what a confused and unending pandemonium there
would be!

Claims are undecided rights. Quiescence is imposed on them not
by judicial decisions, for they have not been decided, but by the
fear of the law (for a claim is always better than an adverse judgement, a possible suit better than one lost), and by the fear of the
stronger who, when an open feud breaks out in their neighbour-
hood, must, on the basis of the relatively new and more general
legal claim, take up the cudgels for the security of their territory
and its boundaries, and in this situation those without power would
find no advantage for themselves, whether these operations were
against them or were intended to benefit them. Thus feuds have
ceased; the *Landfriede* has restored quiet, i.e. it has silenced but
not decided the contradiction of rights. The party already in possession is left in the enjoyment of the thing legally at issue—*beati
possidentes*; no *right* of possession has been determined. Thus it is
not a situation wherein possession depends on right—the situation
of a state—which preserves a measure of quiet in Germany. On
the contrary, amidst the amazing differences between the power of
the estates, the guarantee of the estates is fear and politics, not the
venerability of the rights themselves on which they depend, not
an inner might proper to the estates themselves.

A state-power then, as has been shown, is lacking [in Germany]
and lacking necessarily because the objective of such a power,
namely the immutable maintenance of rights, would be impossible.
In this situation, even if no legalized harmony [between the estates]
is to be expected, one might yet come about by free negotiation.
It is conceivable that the mass of isolated estates, being in the old
position of co-operating for a common end when and in so far as
[103] each individual one willed, might revert to their old behaviour: i.e. even if no permanent and standing bond existed
between them, they might associate freely at a time of distress or
danger. Thus they might construct out of their separate powers
a state and a state-power to meet the crisis; and they might do this

as much in internal affairs, if their rights were attacked, as in external affairs, if they were attacked either *en masse* or in one of their individual members.

One such specific case is [united resistance to] the former attacks on the Protestant religion. Here the objective arose not from the ambition [of the princes] which was quite indifferent to their subjects, but out of the inmost interests of the populace. No objective but this could have united the princes and their peoples so single-mindedly, so freely and so enthusiastically, so utterly to the oblivion of their rivalry in other respects. Any other objective touches the peoples themselves less; in face of any other objective, other disputed interests may come to mind and prevail.

However, we know to what a shameful end the Smalkaldic League came.[1] The whole League was full of the petty strivings of vanity; it was so sunk in the enjoyment of pluming itself on itself and its noble work, and so satisfied in advance of doing anything, that it was scattered at the first onset. Yet even here some members of the League bore themselves bravely and actually ventured on battle, but the Protestant union of the following century [1608] already announced its utter nullity by the nullities surrounding its origin, and this was completely revealed as soon as it set to work.

We can but also regard as an inner bond of this kind the so-called Princes' League[2] set up in opposition to Joseph II whose attitude appeared dangerous to many estates. The idea of the Princes' League made a brilliant appearance as much because of the prince who headed it as because of the one against whom it was directed, and also because it engrossed public opinion owing to numerous pamphleteers, talented and other, on both sides. [104] The public voice seemed to have some sort of meaning; if the splendour of his deeds encircled Frederick II, they had been done in the past, and their result—Silesia in Prussian hands, state-administration, religious and civil laws in the Prussian territories—had already been achieved; from these nothing more was to be expected for the rest of Germany, and indeed nothing accrued; thus what was of greater interest was a hope in the dawn of an all-embracing new

---

[1] 1521. A League of Protestant states. Hegel is punning on *schmählich* (shameful) and *schmalkaldisch*.

[2] 1785. Formed by Prussia with Saxony, Hanover, Brunswick, Mainz, *et al.*, to oppose Joseph II's renewed designs on Bavaria.

German century. But of the League of German Princes there is nothing to report beyond the exercise of public opinion and the stimulation of numerous hopes and fears. It never came to action or expression, so there is equally nothing to say about its essentiality. Brandenburg's independence of the German Empire had its origin long before, and whether it would have grown or diminished if the League of Princes had been set to work is an open question on which there is nothing to say.

As for free alliances against foreign powers, these would simply have had the status of Imperial wars if Germany had not lacerated itself internally instead of arming itself against a foreign enemy (Müller, p. 70; League with William of Orange against Louis XIV; League of Augsburg, 1688).[1] What the princes and estates did was far more the free will of individual circles of association than the legal and universally binding resolve of a body politic. Brandenburg appears still associated with the Empire, not, however, on account of its obligations to it. It worked independently, with the Prussian crown as its chief end.

The wars of this [seventeenth] century were civil wars.

In the course of the last war against France, in the period when danger threatened for Germany, a more general will for the defence of Germany did seem to be developing. Almost all the German states did participate in it, but we cannot find any moment at which all of them co-operated simultaneously. Even in those who did participate there was no true unity. On the contrary, for most of the war [105] the most powerful states stood aloof.

In the Peace of Westphalia the old independence of the parts of Germany was firmly settled—though in entirely altered circumstances—and therefore Germany was prevented from becoming a modern state and having a state-power. Experience since then has taught us that the spirit of the subsequent age has completely changed, since each individual estate has acted for the whole only by its own free will and agreement. Even in the most pressing emergencies, when interests most urgently affecting all parts are at stake, no common and united co-operation is to be expected.

[1] The reference is to J. G. Müller, *Darstellung des Fürstenbundes* (1787). See, in the only edition accessible to the translator (Tübingen, 1811), Book II, Chapter 16, p. 84. William of Orange was the soul of resistance to France and was one of those chiefly instrumental in forming, as the League of Augsburg, a coalition of the Emperor and the Empire, Holland and Spain, Savoy, England, and Sweden. But parts of the Empire were already under French dominion.

In the Peace of Westphalia this statelessness of Germany was organized. Writers like Hippolytus à Lapide[1] have given precise expression to the inner character and tendency of the nation. In the Peace of Westphalia Germany renounced establishing itself as a secure state-power and surrendered to the good will of its members.

This confidence that the general welfare of Germany rested on the free will of its parts may be regarded, if you like, as the effect of a spirit of integrity on which the German nation prides itself so much. It sounds fine if, on the one hand, the state-power is dissipated and put into the hands of the individual [estates], while, on the other hand, there is a demand, and with the demand an expectation, that these individuals shall freely co-operate. The German estates which concluded the Peace of Westphalia would have thought themselves injured by mistrust if there had been any mention of the possibility that, given such a separation, they could and would avert their eyes from the best interests of the whole and that each could and would act for its own interest even if, so far from corresponding with the general interest, it was in contradiction to it. The general unity, the obligations of the individual [estates] to the whole, the best interests of the whole, were most solemnly recognized and guaranteed, and at every difference on these matters, even when it issued in the most frightful wars, each of the two parties justified itself, so far as law went, by wellfounded manifestoes and arguments.

[106] Consequently the thing is played out of the sphere of will and private interest into the sphere of judgement; and, given the general will to act in the best interests of the whole, it would be intelligence which would have to devise the mode of action most compatible with the general good; and if this is determined by the majority, the minority would inevitably have had to adhere to the majority decision. But this neither is nor can be the case, not only because there is no state-power but also because the individual [estate] has the right to make alliances, conclude peace, &c., in accordance with its own judgement of what the general good is. If, when disunity and war occur, someone—a private individual of course, for a Minister cannot take this ground—were actually honestly to think that the war had its origin only in the lack of

[1] i.e. B. P. Chemnitz, *De ratione status in Imperio nostro Romano-Germanico* (Stettin, 1640).

a general judgement of whether something accorded with the good of Germany, and conceived the hope of producing unanimity by working on this conviction, he would achieve nothing except to make himself a laughing-stock by his good nature. He should rather have tried to generate the view that a mode of action which should have been general was in conformity with the private interest of each individual [estate].

It is everywhere a recognized and familiar principle that this private interest is the most important consideration. This interest cannot be regarded as standing in contradiction to rights, duties, or morality; on the contrary, each individual estate, as a particular state, *must* decline to sacrifice itself to a universal from which it can expect no aid, and the prince of any province, the magistrate of an Imperial city, has laid on him the sacred duty of looking after his territory and his subjects.

[§ 9. THE GROWTH OF STATES IN THE REST OF EUROPE]

It is the Peace of Westphalia which has consolidated the independent situation of the parts [of Germany]. In themselves they would have been incapable of independence; their alliance crumbled and they and their territories, without being able themselves to offer any resistance, [107] fell into the hands of Ferdinand, a political and religious despot.[1]

The expedition of Gustavus Adolphus, so far as his nation was concerned (though not so far as he was concerned himself, since he died at the height of his fortunes), would be put in exactly the same class as the expeditions of his successor, Charles XII.[2] In both instances the Swedish power had succumbed in Germany if Richelieu's politics, carried out on the same lines by Mazarin, had not adopted and maintained its cause.

To Richelieu's lot there has fallen the rare good fortune of being regarded as its greatest benefactor both by the state of whose greatness he laid the true foundation and also by the state at whose expense this happened.

[1] Ferdinand the Jesuit, King of Bohemia 1617–37, Emperor Ferdinand II 1619–37. The alliance of 1608 crumbled eleven years later at the outbreak of the Thirty Years War, i.e. at Ferdinand's attack on Protestant privilege in Bohemia.

[2] Sweden was unable to retain all the conquests of Gustavus, and Charles XII came to grief at Poltava (1709).

France as a state and Germany as a state had both of them the same two inherent principles of dissolution. In the one Richelieu completely annulled these principles and thus raised it to be one of the most powerful states; in the other he gave these principles full play and thus cancelled its existence as a state. In both countries he brought completely to maturity the principle on which they were intimately grounded: in France the principle of monarchy, in Germany the principle of developing a multitude of individual states. Both principles had still to struggle against their opposite. Richelieu succeeded in bringing both countries to their fixed and mutually opposed systems.

The two principles which hindered France from becoming one state in the form of monarchy were the nobles and the Huguenots. Both made war with the Crown.

The nobility, including members of the royal family, intrigued with armies against the Minister. Of course sovereignty in the monarch had long been sacrosanct and elevated above all claims, and the nobility brought armies into the field, not to claim sovereignty for themselves, but to make themselves the immediate subjects of the monarchy as Ministers, governors of provinces, &c. Richelieu's merit in having subjected the nobility to the ministry, the immediate emanation of the public authority, has at a superficial glance the appearance of ambition. Whatever his enemies were, they do seem to have fallen as a sacrifice to his ambition; in their revolts and conspiracies they protested, with the greatest truth indeed, their innocence and their dutiful [108] attachment to their sovereign, and they regarded their armed resistance to individual Ministers as neither a civil nor a political crime. But they gave way not to Richelieu as a man but to his genius, which linked his person with the necessary principle of the unity of the state and made the public officials dependent on the state. And herein lies political genius, in the identification of an individual with a principle.[1] Given this linkage, the individual must carry off the victory. The merit of a Minister who does what Richelieu did, i.e. give unity to the executive power of the state, is infinitely higher than the merit of adding a province to a country's territory or rescuing it in some other way from distress.

The other principle threatening a dissolution of the state was the Huguenots whom Richelieu suppressed as a political party.

[1] Cf. *Ph.d.R.*, § 318, *Zusatz.*

His procedure against them is not at all to be regarded as a suppression of freedom of conscience. They had their own armies, fortified towns, treaties with foreign powers, &c., and thus formed a sort of sovereign state. Consequently the nobility had formed in opposition to them the League which had brought the French state to the brink of the abyss. Both the opposed parties were an armed fanaticism elevated above the power of the state. In destroying the Huguenot state Richelieu destroyed at the same time the right of a League and he made short work of its unrighteous and unprincipled legacy, i.e. the insubordination of the nobility. Though he annihilated the Huguenot *state*, he left them freedom of conscience, churches, worship, civil and political rights, on a parity with the Catholics. By his statesmanlike logic he discovered and exercised the toleration which was made to prevail more than a century later as the product of a more civilized generation and as the most brilliant fruit of philosophy and the softening of manners. It was not ignorance and fanaticism in the French when, in the war and in the Peace of Westphalia, they did not think of the separation of Church and state in Germany, when they made religion a basis for a difference of political and civil rights, and when they made prevail in Germany a principle[1] which they had renounced in their own country.

[109] Thus France, England, Spain, and the other European countries have succeeded in pacifying and uniting the elements which fermented within the state and threatened to wreck it. Through the freedom of the feudal system, displayed to them in Germany, they have succeeded in attaining a centre in which all power is concentrated and which is freely established according to law—it does not matter in this connexion whether this centre has a strictly monarchical or a modern republican form, since the latter also falls under the principle of a limited monarchy, i.e. one bound by law. From this epoch of the development of countries into states there dates the period of the power and the wealth of the state and the free and lawful prosperity of individuals.

Italy, on the other hand, has had the same course of fate as Germany, except that Italy, since development had gone further there at an earlier period, brought its fate earlier to the complete fulfilment which Germany is now at last encountering.

The Roman-German Emperors long claimed over Italy a

---

[1] i.e. *cuius regio eius religio.*

supremacy which, as in Germany, usually had only so much power, and later any power, in so far as it was upheld by the personal might of the Emperor. The Emperors' aim of keeping both countries under their rule has destroyed their power in both.

In Italy every place acquired sovereignty for itself. Italy ceased to be one state and became a throng of independent states—monarchies, aristocracies, democracies, as chance decreed; and the degeneration of these constitutions into tyranny, oligarchy, and ochlocracy soon became obvious. Italy's situation cannot be called anarchy, because the multitude of opposed parties were organized states. Despite the lack of a strict constitutional link, a majority of them continually united in common resistance to the Imperial overlord, while the remainder united to make common cause with him. The Guelphs and Ghibellines, which once embraced Germany as well as Italy, appeared [110] in Germany in the eighteenth century as the German and the Austrian party—with modifications arising from altered circumstances.

The individual parts of Italy had not long dissolved the earlier state and risen to independence before they aroused the lust of conquest in greater powers and became the theatre of wars between foreign powers. The small states, which set themselves up as a power against a power a thousand times and more greater than they, underwent a necessary fate in their downfall, and alongside a lament for this there stands the sense of the necessity and the guilt which pygmies bring on themselves when they are downtrodden by measuring themselves with giants. Even the larger Italian states which had grown by swallowing up a lot of smaller states went on leading a vegetable existence without power or real independence, as a pawn in the games of foreign powers. They maintained themselves a little longer by their cleverness in submitting skilfully and at the right time, and in avoiding complete subjection by continually going half-way to subjection: but complete subjection did not fail to come in the end.

What ultimately happened to the mass of independent states—to Pisa, Siena, Arezzo, Ferrara, Milan, and hundreds of others, each a city-state on its own, to the families of many sovereign dukes, counts, &c., to the princely houses of Bentivoglia, Sforza, Gonzaga, Pico, Urbino, &c., and to the innumerable lesser nobility? The independent states were swallowed by greater ones and they by greater ones still, and so on. One of the greatest, Venice, received its *coup de grâce* in our own day by a letter from a French general, delivered by an aide-de-camp. The most brilliant princely houses now have neither sovereignty nor any political or representative significance. The most noble families have become courtiers.

In the period of misfortune when Italy plunged into its distress and became a battlefield for the wars which foreign princes waged on its soil, it provided the resources for wars and at one and the same time was their victim. It entrusted its own defence to assassination, poison, and treachery or to the swarms of a foreign rabble which with their mercenaries were always expensive and destructive and, more often than not, fearsome and dangerous, with some of their [111] leaders rising to become princes. Germans, Spaniards, Frenchmen, and Swiss plundered the country, and foreign cabinets decided the fate of the Italian nation. Profoundly moved by this situation of general distress, hatred, disorder, and blindness, an Italian statesman grasped with cool circumspection the necessary idea of the salvation of Italy through its unification in one state. With strict logic he pointed out the way necessitated more by this salvation than by the corruption and blind folly of the time. Machiavelli addresses himself to Lorenzo de' Medici and speaks of the present as a favourable moment for the conquest of Italy, but he is dominated by the deep feeling that this is the only way to end Italy's misfortune. In the following words he summoned his Prince to adopt the lofty role of a saviour of Italy and acquire the fame of making an end of its misfortune:

'And if, as I have said, it was necessary in order to display the greatness of Moses that the people of Israel should be slaves in Egypt, and to perceive the magnanimity of Cyrus that the Persians should be oppressed by the Medes, and to illustrate the excellence of Theseus that the Athenians should be scattered, so at this hour, in order that the greatness of an Italian genius might be recognized, it was necessary that Italy should be reduced to its present condition, and so to be more enslaved than the Hebrews, more oppressed than the Persians, and more scattered than the Athenians; without a head, without order, beaten, despoiled, lacerated, and overrun, and the victim of ruin of every kind.

'And although before now there has been a gleam of hope that this man or that might have been appointed by God for her redemption, yet at the highest course of his career he was cast aside by fortune, so that now, almost lifeless, she awaits one who may heal her wounds and put a stop to the devastation and plunder [112] of Lombardy, to malversation and extortion in the kingdom of Naples and in Tuscany, and cure her of those sores which have long been festering. . . . Here is perfect justice: "justum enim est bellum quibus necessarium, et pia arma ubi nulla nisi in armis spes est" [Livy, ix. 1]. . . . Everything has worked together for your greatness, the rest must be done by you. God will not do everything, for he will not deprive us of free will and the share of glory that falls to our lot. . . .

'I cannot express the love with which [the liberator of Italy] would be received in all those provinces which have suffered under these foreign invasions, with what thirst for vengeance, with what steadfast faith, with what piety, with what tears. What doors would be closed against him? What towns would refuse him obedience? What envy would oppose him? What Italian but would give him homage?'[1]

We can assume that a man who speaks with such genuine sincerity had neither baseness of heart nor frivolity of mind. As for the former charge, the name of Machiavelli carries with it the seal of disapproval in public opinion, and Machiavellian principles have been made synonymous with detestable ones. The idea of a state which a people is to constitute has for so long failed to get a hearing owing to the foolish vociferousness of what is termed 'freedom' that perhaps the complete misery of Germany in the Seven Years War and the recent French war, the advance of reason, and the experience of French libertarian madness are all together insufficient to lift into the belief of nations or into a principle of political science the truth that freedom is possible only when a people is united into a state by legal bonds.

Machiavelli's fundamental aim of erecting Italy into a state was misunderstood from the start by the blind who took his work as nothing but a foundation of tyranny or a golden mirror for an ambitious oppressor. [113] But even if his aim were accepted, it was said that the means were detestable, and thus moralizing had further room for displaying its platitudes, such as that the end does not justify the means. In this instance, however, there can be no question of any choice of means. Gangrenous limbs cannot

[1] This quotation from the last chapter of Machiavelli's *Prince* was cited by Hegel from a French translation which Lasson has translated into German. It is translated here from the Italian text.

be cured with lavender water. A situation in which poison and assassination are common weapons demands remedies of no gentle kind. When life is on the brink of decay it can be reorganized only by a procedure involving the maximum of force.

It is utterly senseless to treat the execution of an idea directly created out of an insight into the Italian situation as a compendium of moral and political principles applicable indifferently to any and every situation, i.e. to none. You must come to the reading of the *Prince* immediately after being impressed by the history of the centuries before Machiavelli and the history of his own times. Then indeed it will appear as not merely justified but as an extremely great and true conception produced by a genuinely political head endowed with an intellect of the highest and noblest kind.

It would not be out of place to say something, generally over-looked, of the other genuinely idealistic demands which Machiavelli makes on an excellent prince and which since his day have never been fulfilled by any prince, not even by the one who attacked him.[1] But what are called the detestable means which Machiavelli advised must be looked at from another point of view. Italy was to become a state: this counted as a valid principle even at the time when the Emperor still counted as the supreme feudal over-lord. This is the general maxim which Machiavelli presupposes; this he demands, this is his principle in the face of the misery of his country. This puts a totally new complexion on the procedure of the prince. What would be detestable if done by individual to individual, or by one state to another, or by state to individual, now appears as just punishment. To engineer anarchy is the supreme or perhaps the only crime against a state, [114] because all crimes of which the state has to take account are concentrated in this. Those who assail the state directly, and not indirectly as other criminals do, are the greatest criminals, and the state has no higher duty than to maintain itself and crush the power of those criminals in the surest way it can. The state's execution of this supreme duty is not a means; it is punishment; or if punishment were itself a means, then every infliction of punishment on any and every criminal would have to be called detestable and every state would be in the position of using detestable means, death or long imprisonment, for the sake of its own maintenance.

[1] i.e. Frederick the Great in his *Antimachiavel*.

The Roman, Cato the Younger, has the distinction of being cited by everyone who raises the cry of 'freedom'. He was the greatest supporter of entrusting sole dominion[1] to Pompey, not because he loved Pompey but because in his eyes anarchy was the greater evil. He killed himself [46 B.C.] not because what the Romans then still called freedom, i.e. anarchy, had been suppressed but because his stubbornness of character would not submit to his despised and hated foe [Caesar]. Pompey's party, to which he belonged, was only one party against another's, i.e. Caesar's. His death was a party matter.

The man on whom Machiavelli had pinned his hopes for the salvation of Italy was in all probability the Duke of Valentinois, a prince[2] who, with the help of his uncle and by bravery and deceit of every kind, had constructed a single state out of the princedoms of the Dukes of Ursino, Colonna, Urbino, &c., and the territories of the Roman barons. Even if all the deeds that he and his uncle have been saddled with by no more than mere rumour or the hatred of their foes are set aside, still their memory as men is stigmatized by posterity if posterity may venture to judge men morally; and the Duke and his uncle have perished, but not their work. It is they who have acquired a state for the papal throne; its existence Julius II[3] knew very well how to exploit and make formidable, and it persists to this day.

[115] Machiavelli ascribes[4] the fall of Caesar Borgia not only to political mistakes but also to the accident that just at the most critical moment, at Alexander's death, he was himself on a sick bed. Nevertheless we must rather descry in his fall a higher necessity which did not allow him to enjoy the fruits of his deeds or to exploit them to greater effectiveness, because nature, as appears in his vices, seems to have intended him rather for ephemeral splendour and for being merely an instrument for the founding of a state. Moreover the greater part of the power to which he soared rested on no internal or external natural right; it was only grafted on the alien shoot of his uncle's spiritual dignity.

Machiavelli's work remains a great testimony to his age and to

---

[1] i.e. consulship without a colleague in 52 B.C.

[2] i.e. Caesar Borgia (1476–1507), son of Pope Alexander VI. 'Uncle' is a euphemism for 'father'.

[3] Pope 1503–13, in succession to Pius III who reigned only one month after the death of Alexander VI in 1503.

[4] *Prince*, Chapter VII.

his own belief that the fate of a people which hastens to its political downfall can be averted by genius. In connexion with the misunderstanding and hatred which his *Prince* has encountered, and in considering its peculiar fate, it is noticeable that a modern monarch [Frederick the Great], whose whole life and actions have expressed most clearly the dissolution of the German state into independent states, made this Machiavelli the subject of his academic exercise. He raised against him moral cries whose emptiness he has himself shown not merely in his conduct but expressly in his literary works. For example, in the Preface to his History of the First Silesian War he denies that treaties between states are binding when they no longer accord with the best interest of a state.[1]

Apart from this, however, the more wily public could not fail to observe the genius of Machiavelli's works while yet it thought too morally to approve of his principles. With good intentions it wished to rescue him and so it resolved the contradiction honourably and ingeniously enough by holding that he was not serious in what he said. The whole thing was ingenious persiflage and irony. [116] The public which scents irony here must be complimented on its ingenuity.

Machiavelli's voice has died away without effect.[2]

[§ 10. THE TWO GREAT GERMAN POWERS]

For centuries past Germany has shared the fate which once was Italy's, the fate of being the theatre of civil wars. (How long is it since an Imperial war was waged with the general co-operation of the members of the Empire?) But Germany has also shared, in common with Italy, though much later, the fate of being the theatre of wars between foreign powers. By foreigners[3] she has been pillaged, robbed, cursed, and despised; and when peace has come they have usually reduced her territories. Sweden was strictly the first foreign power to gnaw at her vitals to any extent and to help to shatter the pre-existent but tottering system of confederation.

[1] i.e. the Preface to the first volume of his *Histoire de mon temps* (*Œuvres historiques de Frédéric le Grand* (Berlin, 1846), vol. ii, pp. xvi ff.).

[2] With this appreciation of Machiavelli compare Hegel, *Werke*, vol. ix, pp. 407–8 (1st edn.), p. 487 (2nd edn.).

[3] Reading *Fremden*, with Mollat. L. reads *Freunden*, but if Hegel wrote that, it must have been a *lapsus calami*.

Since then it has been foreign powers that have divided Germany's lot, though even earlier she had ceased to be formidable abroad. Since then she has ceased to manage her internal affairs independently and on her own account or to decide her own fate. She has renounced her own fortunes.

Germany's fate, however, is essentially distinct from Italy's in this, (a) that the states into which Italy was split were able, thanks to the general European situation, to maintain themselves for a long while against many greater powers, and (b) that their disproportionate size did not make their power equally disproportionate. Just as Greece was able not only to resist the Persians but to conquer them, so a city like Milan was once able to defy Frederick's[1] power and hold out against it, and later on Venice held out against the League of Cambrai.[2] But the resistance of small states to great has now ceased altogether to be possible; and the sovereignty of the German states has on the whole developed [117] at a period when this possibility no longer existed. Thus the German states have not passed from association into complete separation but directly into associations of another kind. The mass of Germany has not broken up into numerous pieces and then remained for a long time split into them; on the contrary, in the whole mass new kernels were formed round which the parts torn from the whole collected into new masses.

Religion and political independence were of old the central interests round which the German estates grouped themselves: both these central points were formative of their political system. But these centres have vanished. Religion[3] has not only been upheld; the spirit of the age has put it out of all danger; similarly, the estates too have been put in possession of independence. But alongside the Austrian power which used to arouse apprehensions on the score of its being called a universal monarchy, there has been developed the Prussian monarchy which, strong enough in itself, maintained itself in the Seven Years War against the power not only of the Austrian monarchy but of several others, and since then has grown still further in Polish and French territory.

---

[1] i.e. Frederick I (Barbarossa), 1152–89.

[2] 1508, between France, Spain, the Papacy, and the Empire. Venice succeeded in dividing her enemies, but Venice was never again the formidable power that she had been before the League (H. M. Vernon, *Italy 1494–1790* (Cambridge, 1909), p. 26).

[3] i.e. in general, freedom of religious practice, but, in particular, Protestantism.

As a result of this accession of power, Prussia has outstepped the sphere of the common interest in maintaining independence and is therefore no longer to be regarded as the natural centre for maintaining the independence of the estates. It may wish to ally itself with other estates; in such an alliance it is not dependent on the support of the German princes; it can look after itself. Thus the bond between it and the German estates is unequal, for it needs the bond less than they do, and the advantage must be likewise unequal. Prussia may itself arouse apprehensions.

In the last war four[1] political systems have appeared in Germany, first, the Austrian, second, the Emperor's, third, the neutral one, and fourth, the Prussian.

[118] [i] Austria has had no direct supporter, except perhaps some unimportant princes like the Bishop of Brixen[2] who was in the middle of the Austrian states. As the Imperial House it asked the German estates for support and common co-operation. [ii] To the Imperial system there belonged all the less powerful estates, especially those of southern Germany, above all the spiritual estates and the Imperial cities which could maintain some sort of independence only if a German Empire subsisted somehow.

[iii] The third system is principally the system of Bavaria, Baden, and Saxony which have acted, without any political connexion with Austria or Prussia or the Empire, in accordance with their own special interest as regards war or peace or neutrality.

[iv] The fourth system comprises the estates of northern Germany. Through Prussia's mediation they concluded a neutrality pact with France and went under the protection of Prussia which has undertaken to guarantee the peace of northern Germany.[3]

After Prussia had made peace with France, several northern states adhered to this peace treaty, and, terrified by the French military success in the 1794 campaign, more than half Germany bound itself to this neutrality. When the French pressed forward into Bavaria in 1796, the city of Nuremberg decided not only to

---

[1] In Hegel's original draft he wrote 'three'. The neutral one was added as an afterthought and this has brought what follows into disorder (L.). The 'disorder' is clear in the following few pages, where the argument flows uneasily and there are awkward repetitions.

[2] i.e. Bressanone, about fifty miles south of Innsbruck. The bishopric was a direct fief of the Empire.

[3] This is something new in Germany and it deserves notice (H., but he deleted this sentence).

join this neutrality but to make itself entirely a Prussian municipality. It was occupied by Prussian troops, after Prussia, a few
years previously, had asserted its ownership of part of its territory
on the strength of old claims, and taken it into its power, just as it
had cancelled the immediate dependence on the Empire of numerous knights in French territory. Thus from the German Empire
neither Nuremberg nor the knights could get any aid.

The estates of northern Germany have not even acquired the
guarantee of their neutrality in the form of the once [119] usual
circles of association. Prussia is not just one of the participants in
this bond but its head and guarantor, and the estates contribute
to the expenses of the Demarcation Commission.[1] But there is no
league council in permanent assembly; it has assembled only at
certain dates for discussing and deciding the regulation and continuation of these measures and the contributions to their cost.

But the real political situation of the estates came clearly to light
when, early in 1800, the estates which were not assembled were
minded to hold a new assembly. Prussia forbade this assembly and
debate, on the ground that, as guarantor of the peace of the north,
it had to decide the measures to be taken to this end.

When the northern coalition against England's claims over
neutral shipping seemed to be drifting into war with England,
Hanover—one of the chief members of the league—whose
neutrality had been guaranteed, was occupied, along with other
Imperial cities, by Prussia and so could expect no support from
Germany. It was required to disband its own troops and to take
over the maintenance of the Prussian detachment. The peace was
ratified by the Estates of the German Empire, but Prussia had its
own ratification of the peace officially and directly announced in
Paris independently.

The entire history of the war, the cleavage of northern Germany
from southern, the separate treaties of neutrality and peace concluded by the north, while the south languished in the grimmest
misery and so saw itself utterly forsaken by the north, make it clear
not only that Germany is split into independent states but also
that their interest is utterly divided. The political bond is as loose
as it was in the Middle Ages and no free unification is to be
expected. When Germany was deprived of its territories on the

[1] i.e. the Commission which determined the boundaries of French and
Prussian influence. Cf. below [121].

left bank of the Rhine and when half of it was overwhelmed and sacked by the enemy, the most powerful of all interests [i.e. Prussia] gave no help either voluntarily or conformably with its tie with the Empire. The other estates had cut themselves aloof [120] from all co-operation; some of them because, having accepted a guarantee of neutrality from another prince, a foreign one at that, they had *ipso facto* renounced both the right of co-operation, i.e. that of joining again in co-operation with all the other estates, and also the power of consulting thereon with their fellow estates.

When war broke out again, Sweden did indeed offer to send its contingent. But it was rumoured that Prussia had refused to allow it free passage through the neutral zone. Brandenburg, not only in this war, had severed its interest entirely from the interest of the German Empire and it caused other estates to sever their interest likewise. Thus it put them in the position of remaining thus severed and, as guarantor, it could legally and by force compel them to remain in that position. Further, it deprived the Frankish knights of their immediate dependence on the Empire, and the Imperial city of Nuremberg of a part of its territory; in an hour of crisis it handed over the whole of the magistrates' powers in that city to the occupying forces. Moreover, it occupied Hanover, with which it was allied for the sake of the peace and security of northern Germany, disarmed it, and imposed on it a requisition for the commissariat. All these actions made it clear, what had long been an accomplished fact, that Prussia is not to be regarded as a German Imperial princedom on an equal footing with the other estates, but as an individual, sovereign, and powerful state, not as an estate capable of assuming equal obligations along with other estates in a league.

It is the last war above all that has brought more truth into the relations of states. States stand to one another in a relation of might; illusions on this matter have vanished; this relation has been universally revealed and made to prevail. The weaker states have been brought to realize that they cannot equalize themselves with the stronger. If a republic like Geneva behaved as a sovereign state and boasted, εὔχετο, of being the first to send an ambassador to the French Republic and to give it formal recognition, still the relation of Geneva to France, as soon as it was taken seriously, was speedily determined differently.[1] [121] On the other hand,

---

[1] It was excluded from the Helvetian Republic and annexed by France.

Bonaparte made the Republic of San Marino a present of a few cannon, because there was there no relationship of which anything serious was to be made beyond an occasion for exaggerated talk about reverence for republics.

The republic of Geneva has vanished. But the independence, the peace, and, if you like, the neutrality of the republics[1] of Batavia, Helvetia, Cisalpinia, and Liguria are guaranteed by a strong garrison.

This then is the sort of relation which links mightier with weaker states in accordance with the actual difference of their strength.

The relations between Austria and Germany are spelt out from ancient times till now, and they would have had to have fallen out differently if Austria had renounced the Imperial crown and then, now simply a great sovereign power, had made with its neighbours treaties of protection and guarantee, especially if it had made them at times of extremity. In comparison with Brandenburg, Austria is here at a serious disadvantage. Austria's ties are old, but in peace-time Brandenburg, in contrast, does not need to enter any fixed ties, while in war it can make terms with those who are in extremity, weak, and its suppliants. Today everything is to be reckoned in figures, so the terms can be made ten per cent. lower than what is feared from the enemy; or, since the enemy is in general so incalculable that *everything* is to be feared from him, *any* definite terms are less formidable than the enemy's indeterminate conditions. In these circumstances at least the extent of one's loss is known, and this is itself a great consolation.

Moreover, there was a popular opinion in the Rhineland that if one part of a state was within the line of demarcation while the other was outside it and liable to the public and private levies of the French, and if the estates of both parts were supposed to make common cause for the mutual adjustment of taxes, then the part under French rule declined to agree to parity and equal shares because it expected to be the loser thereby. This popular opinion may be ungrounded. But it makes the people's judgement on the matter obvious to everyone.

[122] Brandenburg had also the advantage of having the greater powers as its friends or, since, apart from these friendships, it had

---

[1] In 1801 the German Emperor was forced to recognize these four client republics which began as outposts of revolutionary influence but were kept firmly in subjection by Napoleon.

no other alliances or protective relationships, of treating them as enemies. Even a guarantee treaty it can renounce at once, because, like any political treaty, it is something specific and isolated, and the essence of political treaties implies that its cancellation is not perfidy, as this war above all has taught us, when so many treaties were broken, concluded again, and broken once more. Austria's ties with the estates, on the other hand, do not appear to rank as political treaties of the usual kind. When it has put itself into the usual relationship against one estate of the Empire, as Prussia can, all the estates feel themselves attacked at once. But when Prussia does this it seems quite natural, just as it does in the case of France, &c.

On the strength of its power and the manifestation thereof in the ways mentioned above, Prussia has risen above a level of equality with the other estates. A pure interest in their political independence they can find only in themselves and this is what makes conceivable an association of them, a true estates-confederacy. But conceivable only, because some of the estates are so disproportionate in power in comparison with one another that they are incapable of any true equal association.

An abbey, an Imperial city, a nobleman directly [a vassal of the Empire], may be far less frightened of becoming an object of the Austrian monarchy's than of a lesser power's lust for aggrandisement. Although it is a great monarchy, Prussia as a power stands, in respect of this capacity of perturbing small states and using small advantages, rather on the level of moderately sized states because (i) its political skill, like that of the French, is always a calculating skill; its military power was disproportionate to its size, and therefore it had to seek the sum of small advantages, just as the French Republic always acted on general principles, followed them with its forces into the smallest details, and brought under them all special rights and ties. Further, because (ii), one might say, Prussia's modern politics have not proceeded from the principle of royalty or majesty, but from the *bourgeoisie*, and [123] now, e.g. in contrast to the Austrian power, are in the position of a *bourgeois* who has built up his resources toilsomely penny by penny through his labour in contrast to the free nobleman who has inherited wealth and whose possession rests on his estate and remains the same even if in small things he gives a free hand to his servants or his neighbours. His wealth is not a sum (a sum, it is to be noted, is diminished by the removal of a single part) but something permanent and unalterable.

The small estates which must have the gravest anxieties about their independence can join themselves confidently only with a power whose political position and magnanimity has alike the capacity and the inclination to guarantee it. We have seen the princes of the Church, abbeys, and Imperial cities continually joining with the Emperor and most faithfully observing their obligations to him and the German Empire.

Even if the more powerful estates of the Empire had been willing to make mutual treaties and had found a way of ensuring that their coalition would evade the fate of all coalitions, even if the unification of their forces had formed a power capable of resisting one great power, they still would not be in the position of having their anxieties limited to one power only, because this one power must necessarily have feared the association of other powers against itself, and against the union of several powers a coalition would achieve nothing, partly because of its inferior army and partly because of the geographical separation of its members. Its geographical position has been formed in much the same way as the area of great empires. From the military point of view it is in itself thoroughly weak, and because the coalition was something new, its member states would also not be rich enough to gird themselves with a series of fortresses.

Its politics must associate such a coalition with this or that greater power according to circumstances, and its fate must be the common fate of a weaker ally or a weak enemy.

The fate of the German estates stands directly between the politics of two great powers. Now both of these are alike in this that their relation to Germany [124] is primarily a political one. This is truer of Prussia's relation than of Austria's because the latter carries the throne of the Emperor and therefore has been controlled from ancient times till now by the weight of infinitely numerous rights.

The other interests in which the powers differed have been ironed out. It was through the difference in these interests that Prussia became great, because it joined hands with the interests opposed to the House of Austria or set itself at their head. But time itself has cancelled the cleft between the Austrian interest and that of a great part of Germany, while Prussia's interest has been cleft apart from that of the German estates.

One chief interest, in the defence of which Prussia appeared as leader, was *religion*.

The German estates themselves (particularly Saxony and Hesse in the early days) and foreign powers (Sweden and France) had formerly championed this interest against the Emperor, and at that time Prussia played no part or, as Brandenburg, only a subordinate part. In the Seven Years War this interest came to the front not so much on the part of the opposing powers as in popular opinion, and it was not without its effect. A sort of mistrust always remained, and if the Protestants did not see themselves attacked as Protestants, still they constantly feared the possibility. The will [to persecute], the height of bigotry, an influence of the new compliant Pope, they ascribed to the Jesuits, to priests generally, and always to the House of Austria which, [they thought, would persecute] as soon as it was in a position to do so. They descried in Prussia the guarantor and, if it came to an actual crisis, the saviour of their freedom of faith and conscience.

The petty and fanatically aimed politics of the Jesuits has long ago ceased to be the politics of the court. At least since Joseph II's day the Protestants' anxiety on this score has disappeared. Joseph II's policy was not just the whim of a single monarch which [125] can die away again with his death (like the Edict of Nantes, Richelieu's policy, and what Matthias[1] did for the Protestants of his country). On the contrary, his successors have abided by these same principles, which indeed have now passed over into the firm universal structure of civilization and the basis of politics.

Later on, one object of interest to the Protestant party amongst the Imperial princes was the plight of Protestants in the Palatinate, the one remaining relic in contradiction to the principles of our time; but even this has now gone. The spirit of the age and the practice of governments, now fixed and pursued on principle, has diminished to an amazing extent the importance of the *corpus evangelicorum* and with it that of its chief leader.

The mania of the Catholic states for securing the dominance of the Catholic religion has subsided and with it the crooked means

---

[1] The reference is probably to the Emperor (1612–19) who acquired Bohemia from his brother (Rudolf II) in 1611 and who gave the Protestants certain privileges there. His intransigent successor, Ferdinand the Jesuit, overturned this conciliatory policy.

which were formerly used to induce the German Imperial princes to adopt Catholicism and which aroused such an amazing amount of fear and anxiety in the Protestants. The Catholic party no longer places any value on them because the state has already learnt on its own account to separate itself from the Church, and experience has shown in addition that means of this sort have produced the bad effect of mistrust and enhanced obstinacy rather than any actual benefit. In a short time the person of the prince has become distinct, so far as religion is concerned, from his country. (*a*) Even if the prince became Catholic, the relation of his country to the Diet remained Protestant. Thus a prince converted to Catholicism lost power in his Protestant country not only because his conversion made him generally mistrusted but also because he was deprived by *Reversalien*,[1] &c., of the influence which a Protestant prince has over the Church of his country. Thus he is put in the position of the Catholic prince of a Catholic country where the Church is entirely independent of the temporal power in respect of its property and its possession of abbeys, as well as in respect of other arrangements, while on the other hand the Protestant prince of a Protestant country is Bishop and head of the Church. [126] (*b*) Moreover, princely houses that were Catholic have become Protestant in recent times.

Means of the kind described have been abandoned by the Catholics; the Jesuit order has been suppressed; even in Catholic countries toleration has been introduced and, contrary to the illiberal provisions of the Peace of Westphalia, civil rights have been conceded to Protestants. The result is that the long lists, prepared by constitutional lawyers, of princely conversions to Catholicism, the exposition of Jesuit perfidies, the recital of the oppression and tribulation of Protestants in Catholic countries, have become matters of history concerned with things long past and are no longer bugbears for the present.

By the power of foreign support the Protestants have for long been freed from the fear of seeing their faith suppressed by force, though they have never been much athirst for a martyr's crown. The fact that proselytism is no longer court policy has freed them to some extent also from their former fear of Hell, their fear that this faith of theirs might be taken from them by cunning and that

---

[1] Solemn engagements by princes to protect the rights, privileges, and freedom of their subjects.

their conscience might secretly be spirited away. Passage of time has given them more confidence and assurance that they are in possession of the truth. For long past we have heard nothing about a Catholic confessor's being regarded by the Diet as a power and therefore influencing the Emperor through the Diet.

Berlin journalists have tried to reawaken this fear of Hell in the Protestants by making the frightful din of those who smell Jesuits everywhere, but this is now no longer a cabinet matter, no subject for discussions in the Diet; it looks more like tomfoolery or possibly an outburst of an extremely restricted interest, of some disagreement between branches of the order of Freemasons.

Another interest was the salvation of what used to be called German freedom from what was called [127] 'universal monarchy', or, later, even an 'oriental system'.

For ten years past the whole of Europe has fixed its attention on the frightful struggle of a people to gain freedom; and for that reason the whole of Europe has been in general motion. Inevitably, therefore, concepts of freedom have suffered alteration and have been purged of their former emptiness and vagueness. Hitherto German freedom has meant only the non-dependence of the estates on the Emperor; their dilemma was 'either slavery and despotism or else the breaking of the political bond'; older times knew no third possibility.

Since Charles V's day, the Spanish and the Austrian monarchy have not been combined; and for the last century the two of them have been possessed by quite different families. Austria has lost great provinces; France and England have raised themselves to a parity of power with her; Prussia and Russia have developed; for long past Austria has ceased to be the monarchy without an equal in Europe. A *system of the balance of power in Europe* has been formed, i.e. a system whereby all European powers normally take one side [or the other] in a war, and each power is prevented from reaping the fruits of even the most fortunate war either by itself or even in connexion with its advantageous gains. Wars have so altered in their inherent nature that the conquest of a few islands or of a province costs many years of effort and gigantic sums.

The idea of a universal monarchy has always been an empty word. The fact that when it was planned it never was actualized shows the impossibility of its actualization and also the emptiness of this concept; but in modern times there cannot any longer be even any question of it.

Nevertheless, Austria remains supreme in Germany, i.e. more powerful than any single German estate, more powerful than many of them taken together. But at the same time Prussia has advanced to this position too. As a danger to the German estates, Austria and Prussia stand on the same footing. What used to be called German freedom would have to be on its guard against both.

[§ 11. FREEDOM OF CITIZENS AND ESTATES]

[128] By laying hold of one of two principles—the danger to the Protestant religion and the fear of universal monarchy—it has been possible for a state to acquire great influence in Germany. The first of these exists no longer. In respect of the second, lust for aggrandisement at the expense of the German estates, Austria and Prussia stand on much the same ground, if Austria is not still in the van.

It is clear, however, that, as a result of ten years of war and the misery of a large part of Europe, so much has been learnt, at least in theory, to make us more inaccessible to a blind clamour for freedom. In this bloody game the cloud of freedom has evaporated; in trying to embrace the cloud, the nations have flung themselves into an abyss of misery, and definite concepts and forms of thought have become embodied in public opinion. Clamour for freedom will be of no effect; anarchy has become distinguished from freedom; the notion that a firm government is indispensable for freedom has become deeply engraved on men's minds; but no less deeply engraved is the notion that the people must share in the making of laws and the management of the most important affairs of state. The guarantee that the government will proceed in accordance with law, and the co-operation of the general will in the most important affairs of state which affect everyone, the people finds in the organization of a body representative of the people. This body has to sanction payment to the monarch of a part of the national taxes, but especially the payment of extraordinary taxes. Just as in former days the most important matter, i.e. personal services, depended on free agreement, so nowadays money, which comprises influence of every other kind, is equally so dependent.

Without such a representative body, freedom is no longer thinkable. Once freedom is so defined, all vague ideas vanish, along with all the emptiness of the clamour for freedom. This notion of freedom is not something, like a scientific concept, which individuals come to know by learning; on the contrary, it is a fundamental principle [129] in public opinion; it has become part of sound common sense. Most German states have representation of this kind. The Estates Assemblies in Austria, Bohemia, and Hungary have freely granted to their monarchs extraordinary contributions for the war against France.

The interest of this German freedom naturally seeks protection from a state which itself rests on this system of freedom. The interests formerly dominant in Germany have to some extent disappeared. Thus Prussia can no longer be linked with them; no Prussian war can now count in public opinion from the start as a war for German freedom. The true, abiding, and, in these days, keenest interest [of the German estates] cannot now find any protection in Prussia. The estates of the Prussian provinces have lost their significance owing to the power of the King's authority. A new and artful tax-system has been introduced into the Prussian territories, and it has been made to prevail also in the newly acquired territories which had privileges and taxes [determined] in accordance with ancient rights and customs.

Against this burden of taxes in the Prussian state, against the suppression of privileges, Prussia's German subjects can expect aid neither from the Emperor nor from the Imperial courts of judicature.

Simply because the Imperial hereditary lands are on their own account a state which is grounded on representation and in which the people has rights, and more especially because of the legal aid available in the Imperial Aulic Council, the estates of the German territories (apart from the less powerful estates like the Imperial cities, &c.) have a natural interest in looking to the Imperial palace and expecting to find support there for what the world now understands by German freedom.

This sort of freedom must naturally always have to suffer the more the other sort of German freedom has grown and the more the power of the state over its individual members has diminished.[1]

[1] The two sorts of freedom are: (i) freedom 'under an overlord for the conduct of national business with the co-operation of the people through its representatives' (see below [131]); or (ii) freedom of the estates in complete independence of any overlord, but with all their internal business settled by magistrates or other officials responsible solely to the prince.

By the Peace of Westphalia the sovereignty, or at least the supremacy, of the Emperor over Imperial cities [130], which was ceded to him and which in the course of time was mortgaged to the Imperial cities, i.e. to their city councillors, was declared to be irredeemable. The sheriff (or whatever title he had in other cities) appointed by the Emperor must always have been treated with a certain respect by the city councillors. They were always in a way under the supervision or under the eye of a person independent of themselves who was bound to be influential on the strength of his connexion with the Imperial overlord. From the time when the freedom of the Imperial cities was in a way completely assured because the state-power mortgaged to them was made irredeemable by the Peace of Westphalia, the other sort of freedom has suffered all the more. It is well known how so many Imperial cities were sunk under the load of taxes, neglect of judicial proceedings, burdens of debt, and, in general, inner corruption. In them the citizenry had no supervision of the management and bestowal of public offices, no voice in the fixing of taxes; imposts and their expenditure, and nominations to office, have come entirely into the power and the whim of city councillors. By the Emperor's help some cities have succeeded in freeing themselves from this German freedom of the city councillors; before the last war others found their finances plunged into great difficulty and confusion as a result of this system, and the war has no little intensified this confusion.

In the princes' states since the Peace of Westphalia the *Kammer-zieler* and the expenses of military contingents and envoys to the Diet have devolved on the Estates Assemblies.

In 1672, twenty-four years after the achievement of German freedom in the Peace of Westphalia, the Council of Princes sent to the Emperor a decision of the Diet whereby the previous method of making a contribution to the national expenses in accordance with agreements was cancelled, and the princes were given a remit to assess what [131] they would consider necessary for the needs of their country.[1] This extension of princely power whereby the then princes had annulled the whole principle on which modern states rest and had prepared—what consequences?—for their successors, this extension of German freedom, if you like to call it so, was hindered by the Emperor Leopold [1658–1705]. He did not

[1] Pütter, [op. cit.], ii, pp. 271–3 ff. (H.) Eng. tr., vol. ii, pp. 288–94.

ratify the Diet's decision which would have justified him in his German territories, in Bohemia, and in Austria, in cancelling their rights. If the connexion, ever persisting in a fashion, between the Burgundian circle and the Empire had otherwise been upheld, the Emperor would have been justified by the Diet in cancelling there the rights of the estates which had deteriorated into a despotic aristocracy, and in carrying out the project which wrecked Joseph II more than a century later.[1]

From the point of view of the interest of this German freedom the relation of the Emperor to Germany appears in a different light, and his relation is very different from that of Prussia. The might of the age has caused the great popular interest to revert to its source as a need, which, however, has not yet found satisfaction in a corresponding political organization.

The principle of the original German state, a principle spread from Germany over the whole of Europe, was the principle of monarchy, a political power under an overlord for the conduct of national business with the co-operation of the people through its representatives. The form of this principle survives in what is called the Diet; but the thing itself has vanished.

In Europe's long oscillation between barbarism and civilization, the German state has not completely made the transition to the latter; it has succumbed to the convulsions of this transition; its members have torn themselves apart to complete independence; the state has been dissolved. The Germans have failed to find a middle way between subjection, despotism, what they called universal monarchy, on the one hand, and complete disintegration on the other.

[132] 'Fight for German freedom' had the negative meaning of 'striving against universal monarchy', while positively it became an endeavour after the complete independence of the members. In this endeavour the countries stood by their princes and were at one with them, but they were bound to find that in the sovereignty of the princes German freedom was not achieved—on the contrary.

At the same time, however, the bent of the estates is primarily

---

[1] (a) Joseph II tried and failed to enforce feudal rights. (b) In 1784 he suggested giving the Elector of Bavaria the Austrian Netherlands, with the title of King of Burgundy in exchange for the Bavarian dominions. This project was foiled by Frederick the Great (Bryce, op. cit., pp. 400, 527).

towards their own country; they have lost all bearing on the whole [Empire]. Formerly the princes often summoned an Estates Assembly before going to the Imperial Diet and they deliberated in common with their country. The Estates Assemblies are usually against Imperial wars and against contributing to their cost, and yet at the same time they owe their existence to the Empire: this contradiction, this disunion of Germany, has made its home everywhere in the popular mind. Bavaria, Hesse, &c., regard themselves as foreign countries; this disengagement they express above all in their Estates Assemblies which stand directly connected with the people, and they look on everything which their prince does in virtue of his [Imperial] ties as alien to themselves and not their concern. Their will is precisely to remain on their own, as the Swiss do in their neutrality. But the whole constellation of circumstances is opposed to this remaining on one's own. There is no longer any neutrality for a weak state if it is near or in between powerful belligerent states—or it can be neutral if it likes in the sense of letting itself be plundered and mishandled by both.

While in theory the interest of the provinces and their Diets is bound up with the existence of a political power in Germany, in practice this interest in Germany has become alien to the provinces —in Germany who cares anything for Germany, whence could patriotic feeling for Germany come? What passive benefit the individual provinces and their Diets derive from Germany they enjoy; they recognize it but do nothing whatever for it; for it lies deep in human nature to interest oneself only in something for which one acts, something with which one can co-operate in resolve and deed, something into which one can put one's will. Some method whereby the provinces could co-operate for a universal end would have to be created.

[§ 12. THE UNIFICATION OF GERMANY]

[133] The fate of Italy has been to come for the most part under the dominion of foreign powers. Most of its estates have gradually become entirely dependent politically on these great powers. Gradually they have entirely succumbed, beginning with the smaller and the ecclesiastical estates, while a few, two or three or so, have maintained themselves somewhat longer in existence as states of the size of a district or a few districts. If Germany after several wars were not to suffer this same fate it would have to

organize itself anew into a state. What essentially constitutes a state, namely a state-power directed by an overlord with the co-operation of the parts, would need to be constructed. Everything inessential—the dependence of the administration of justice, the management of revenues, religion—all this must be excluded from the state's *necessary* character.

Persistence of the German Empire would be possible in one way only, namely by organizing a state-power and bringing the German people once again into connexion with Emperor and Empire.

The first requisite would be achieved if the whole military force of Germany were concentrated together into one army. In such an army every more important prince would be a general by birth; he would command a regiment of his own in it and would have the appointment of its officers, or he would have his own body-guard, or garrison for his capital, detailed from it. To the smaller estates, companies or smaller detachments would be detailed. Of course the Emperor would have the supreme command of this army. The expenses of the army, met now for the most part by the Estates Assemblies and not, as formerly, by the prince from his crown lands, would thus be borne by the provinces. These ex-penses the Estates Assemblies would have to authorize annually, and for this purpose they would have to unite together into one body from all the provinces. This of course could not be managed by deputing some members of the existing Estates Assemblies to this end, because, for one thing, many of the provinces have no Estates Assembly, and, for another, the expense would be too high for the very small estates. But if, for the purpose of raising the army, it were already necessary to have subdivided Germany for military purposes, [134] each district being divided into smaller districts quite independently of the other jurisdictions and suze-rainties which would have had nothing to do with the military subdivision, then from the lower subdivisions delegates could be chosen in accordance with the number of inhabitants, and these delegates would have to authorize the burdens necessary for up-holding the state's power.

For this purpose these delegates would form a group with the Cities Bench in the Imperial Diet. In any case this Bench[1] has

---

[1] The Diet was divided into three Benches or Colleges: (i) Electors, (ii) Princes (including prelates), (iii) Cities (Pütter, op. cit., vol. iii, pp. 256 ff.).

suffered a diminution owing to the loss of several cities, and it is a question whether it may not suffer still further diminutions, to the advantage of many of the smaller cities in the matter of compensation.[1] Hamburg would also have to be called on to send its delegates. The smallest Imperial cities of a thousand or a few thousand citizens have a voice in the Diet and a whole province like Bohemia or Saxony has none. Such small Imperial cities as still survive would have to allow their surrounding territories to share in their entitlement to send a delegate.

Apart from all this, there is no knowing what significance the Cities Bench possesses. There are three Colleges in the Diet, but a majority vote decides nothing. If the College of Electors and the College of Princes do not agree, then the matter rests undecided and the College of Cities cannot turn the scales.

The complete revolution would be that the provinces should now pay directly to Emperor and Empire the money which they pay directly to their prince and only indirectly to Emperor and Empire.

The Emperor would be placed again at the head of the German Empire.

It would be open to question whether the cantons[2] of the knights would send their delegates to the Council of Princes or to the College of the Cities. They would authorize their charitable subsidies[3] along with the other subventions, and as absolute landowners they would have to be affiliated to the College of Princes.

Another question would be whether the princes would resolve to make from their crown lands and other territorial incomes a contribution in common, or whether each would meet the cost of his own regiment or bodyguard in part from these sources. In general, each prince would be left free [135] to contribute as much as he liked from his own resources for embellishments to his own regiment over and above the general contribution which would be made for it by the whole state. If the princes granted and contributed sums from their crown lands to a common centre, then the knights

---

[1] Compensation was required for failure to fulfil Imperial obligations, but no such compensation could be exacted from a city lost to the Empire.

[2] The division of Germany into cantons ceased about A.D. 1100 and the name 'canton' was retained only to distinguish a few divisions of the territories of the knights, i.e. of the free nobility of the Empire (Pütter, op. cit., vol. i, p. 187).

[3] The immediate nobility of the Empire were not included in the *Matrikel* of 1521 (see above, p. 151, footnote), but Charles V introduced the custom of their making a voluntary payment to the Imperial chest. This voluntary payment was called a charitable subsidy (Pütter, op. cit., vol. i, p. 509).

would have to be associated with them. In any case, the true nobility, i.e. owners of territories of knights who were direct vassals of the Empire, belong originally entirely to the category of the princes and in their origin were not different from them.

Still another question would be whether the princes, if they did not wish to appear in person in the College of Electors or the College of Princes, should be allowed to be represented by nobles of their own line or at least by their most eminent vassals. In an assembly so constituted the sort of procedure which depends on dictating prepared statements for minuting[1] would not be applicable; debate and vote would be by word of mouth, and, if the representatives were drawn solely from princely families and the highest nobility, their talents and distinction would confer an exalted position and appearance on such a princely assembly.

If all parts of Germany were to succeed by these means in making Germany into one state, an event of that sort has never been the fruit of deliberation, but only of force. This has been true even when the event has accorded with the general culture of the day and when the need for it has been deeply and distinctly felt. The common people in Germany, together with their Estates Assemblies, who know nothing at all of anything but the division of the German people, and to whom a national union is something totally alien, would have to be collected together into one mass by the power of a conqueror; they would have to be compelled to treat themselves as belonging to Germany.

This Theseus would have to have the magnanimity to grant to the people he would have had to fashion out of dispersed units a share in matters that affected everyone. Since a democratic constitution like the one Theseus gave to his own people is self-contradictory in modern times and in large states, this share would have to be some form of organization. Moreover, even if the direction of the state's power which he had in his hands could insure him against being repaid, as Theseus was, with ingratitude, still he would have to have character enough [136] to be ready to endure the hatred with which Richelieu and other great men who wrecked men's private and particular interests were saddled.[2]

---

[1] *Protokoll-diktieren.* See [207].
[2] Dilthey suggested that Hegel had Napoleon in mind as his 'Theseus', but Rosenzweig argues more plausibly that Hegel was thinking of Archduke Charles of Austria (op. cit., vol. i, pp. 125–7).

Once man's social instincts are distorted and he is compelled to throw himself into interests peculiarly his own, his nature becomes so deeply perverted that it now spends its strength on variance from others, and in the course of maintaining its separation it sinks into madness, for madness is simply the complete separation of the individual from his kind. The German people may be incapable of intensifying its obstinate adherence to particularism to that point of madness reached by the Jewish people—a people incapable of uniting in a common social life with any other.[1] The German people may not be able to carry separatism to such a pitch of frenzy as to murder and be murdered until the state is wiped out. Nevertheless, particularism has prerogative and precedence in Germany and it is something so intimately personal that thinking and an insight into necessity are far too weak in themselves to become effective in action. Thought and judgement carry with them so much self-mistrust that they have to be validated by force, and only then does man submit to them.

[1] Hegel is thinking of the first chapter of his own contemporary essay, 'The Spirit of Christianity' (see Hegel's *Early Theological Writings*, tr. Knox, Chicago, 1948, pp. 182–205).

II

ON THE RECENT DOMESTIC AFFAIRS OF WURTEMBERG, ESPECIALLY ON THE INADEQUACY OF THE MUNICIPAL CONSTITUTION[1]

[150] IT seems high time for the people of Wurtemberg to give up wobbling between fear and hope, and oscillating between expectancy and being deceived in their expectancy. I will not say that, when things were changing or when the past was being preserved, it was also time for anyone who was concerned only with his own narrow advantage or the advantage of his class, and who consulted only his own vanity, to abandon these meagre wishes, to let these petty cares slide, and to enjoin himself to care for the universal instead. But for men of nobler wishes and purer enthusiasm it may above all be time to focus their will, so far lacking a definite object, on those parts of the constitution which are based on injustice, and to direct their energies to the necessary alteration of these parts.

Calm satisfaction with the present, hopelessness, patient acquiescence in a fate that is all too great and powerful have changed into hope, expectation, and a resolution for something different. The picture of better and juster times has become lively in the souls of men, and a longing, a sighing for purer and freer conditions, has moved all hearts and set them at variance with the actuality [of the present]. The urge to break through paltry barriers [151] has pinned its hopes to every event, to every glimmer [of change], and even to violent actions. Whence could the Wurtembergers expect juster aid than from the Assembly of their Estates? The passage of time and the postponement of the satisfaction of these hopes can do no more than purify the longing and separate out its genuine and false elements; yet time can but strengthen the urge towards what satisfies a genuine need; the longing will

---

[1] The original title was "Town Councillors ought to be elected by the people' and 'people' was subsequently altered to 'citizens'.

penetrate all the more deeply into men's hearts as a result of the delay; it is no casual dizziness which passes off. Call it a fit of fever if you like, but it is a fit that ends only in death or after the diseased matter has been sweated out. It is the still healthy force's effort to expel the disease.

General and deep is the feeling that the fabric of the state in its present condition is untenable. There is general anxiety that it may collapse and hurt everyone in its fall. Given this heartfelt conviction [about the state], is this fear to become so powerful that men will leave it to good luck to decide what is to be jettisoned and what retained, what is to stand and what to fall? Should men not wish to abandon the untenable fabric themselves and examine with a calm eye what really is untenable in it? For judging that matter, justice is the sole criterion. The courage to do justice is the one power which can completely, honourably, and peaceably remove the tottering edifice and produce something safe in its place.

How blind they are who may hope that institutions, constitutions, laws which no longer correspond to human manners, needs, and opinions, from which the spirit has flown, can subsist any longer; or that forms in which intellect and feeling now take no interest are powerful enough to be any longer the bond of a nation!

When features and sections of a constitution are no longer believed in, all attempts to manufacture confidence again by boastful bungling or to whiten the sepulchre with fine words can only cover their ingenious inventors with shame and then pave the way for a much more frightful outburst, in which the need for reform joins hands with revenge, and the mob, ever deceived [152] and oppressed, visits dishonesty with punishment. It is not only dishonourable but contrary to all sense, when things are felt to be tottering, to do nothing but wait confidently and blindly for the collapse of the old building, which is everywhere decaying and has its foundations undermined, and to submit to being crushed by the falling beams.

If a change is to happen, then something must be changed. So obvious a truth needs to be stated, because fear, which suffers, is distinguished from courage, which wills, by the fact that men driven by fear do feel and grant the necessity of a change, but, when a start is to be made, exhibit the weakness of wanting to retain everything they have, just as a spendthrift who is under the necessity of limiting his expenditure finds indispensable every article of his previous needs which he has been told to curtail, and so refuses to give up anything until at last he is deprived of indispensable and dispensable alike. An example of such weakness a nation, or at least the Germans, may not afford. In the cool conviction that a change is necessary they should not now be afraid to examine everything in detail. What they find to be unjust, the sufferer of injustice must demand shall be removed and its unjust possessor must freely and willingly sacrifice.

This strength of being able to rise above one's petty interest to justice is presupposed in the following inquiry, as well as the honesty to will it and not merely pretend to will it. Only too often some reservation lies behind wishes and enthusiasm for the general good, the reservation: 'so far as this accords with our own interest'. Such a readiness to give an affirmative answer to all reforms is startled and grows pale as soon as it is called upon to be ready.

At a far remove from this hypocrisy, let every individual, every class, start of its own accord to weigh its position and its rights before beginning to make demands on others and before trying to find the cause of the ill outside itself, and if it finds itself possessed [153] of inequitable rights, let it strive to redress the balance in favour of others. Anyone who likes may regard this demand to begin at home as blind and ineffective, and he may set aside hopes of this kind as wrong. . . .

III

PROCEEDINGS OF THE ESTATES ASSEMBLY IN THE KINGDOM OF WURTEMBERG
1815–1816

[157] THE task begun two and a half years ago[1] of introducing a representative constitution and so completing a German monarchy which we have seen arising in our own day[2] has aroused from its start such a universal interest among the German public that nothing could please it more than the publication of the *Proceedings of the Assembly of the Wurtemberg Estates*. The hopes accompanying the start and the progress of these proceedings must now give place to their outcome and to judgement thereon. The thirty-three volumes, with which alone this essay is concerned, do not contain the completion of what the King[3] had chiefly in view, but they do form an historical whole in that (i) they display the issue up to the death of the King who founded the monarchy and started on the second step, that of giving it a free internal constitution. This step, being the proper development of the monarchy in its main characteristics, could be regarded as attaching to his government. (ii) On the other hand, the work appears, so far as the Estates are concerned, as something completed, in that a committee appointed by them to draft a constitution had fulfilled its task. This draft likewise has appeared in print.

Further, these *Proceedings* display in the main only one side of the labours connected with this undertaking, namely the labours appearing publicly in the proceedings of the Diet. The inner history

---

[1] i.e. in March 1815; see below [162].

[2] Wurtemberg, formerly a duchy, became a kingdom in 1806, when the old constitution was abrogated [236]. On this abrogation Napoleon grimly remarked to the Wurtemberg Minister: 'I have made your master a sovereign, not a despot.' Hegel recounts this in a letter of 28 Aug. 1807 and adds: 'The great teacher of constitutional law sits in Paris. . . . The German princes have not yet grasped the concept of free monarchy, nor attempted to realize it. Napoleon will have to organize all this' (*Briefe*, ed. J. Hoffmeister, vol. i, p. 185).

[3] Frederick II, previously Duke, King from 1806, d. 1816.

of the labours of the Cabinet and the Ministry is hidden away here along with what went on amongst the populace outside the Assembly, e.g. the probably external aims and activities of the members of the Diet and whatever else is usually reckoned as belonging to the secret connexion of events and actions. [158] But, naturally, the public interest has been particularly attentive to the published part of the *Proceedings*, which in any case has eminently the character of affording dignified materials for history. The so-called secret motives and intentions of single individuals, as well as anecdotes and subjective impressions, have been regarded as the most important thing in the psychological view of history which was still in vogue not so long ago. But this view has now been discredited, and history strives once more, in accordance with its dignity, to set forth the nature and the march of the thing in its substantial being, and to afford an understanding of men of action from what they do. The conviction has now become general that from accidentalities neither the thing itself, nor characters in their genuineness, either issue or are to be understood.

The historical events confronting us here have the special attraction of not containing such a considerable proportion of what is past and gone as a history of more distant times does: the great ends and interests, like the lesser personal and extrinsic aims, are present still. The concepts concerning the matter at issue, which we must bring with us to this event, we may not cull from any more remote age, especially not from the civilized age of Greece and Rome: they are peculiar to our own day. Thus these ideas on a political constitution, and especially on the inclusion of a part whereby the people is conceded an influence on it and a public life, are not seen here as the thoughts of one essayist, compared, e.g., with the thoughts of another; on the contrary what we see is a German government and a German people engaged in an intellectual labour on these matters, and thoughts employed in the rebirth of an existent reality.

[§ I. THE KING'S CONSTITUTION]

[159] The age had produced a new task for Wurtemberg and the demand for its discharge, the task of erecting the provinces of Wurtemberg into a state. After the nonsensical arrangement called the German Empire (described most aptly by an historian,[1] who

---

[1] Voltaire. See above [3].

was at least intelligent, as 'anarchy made into a constitution') had reached the end it deserved, an ignominious end suited to it even in externals, the Wurtemberg of that time acquired an enlargement of territory up to more than double its previous size.[1] But, into the bargain, this whole, whose parts had previously been fiefs of the German Empire (the part constituting the Duchy having also been a Bohemian sub-fief), threw off this subordination and, with its prince's acquisition of the dignity of King, crossed the frontier into sovereignty, into the position of a state, i.e. into that of one of the actual German realms which are taking the place of the nonentity which had borne only the empty name of an 'Empire'.

Epochs like this are extremely rare, and equally rare are the individuals to whom fate has assigned the founding of states as their distinctive lot. The history of these few generally disappears into the mists of antiquity or into an age of savage or at least primitive manners, when, to be sure, a state visible from without had come into being, though its *inner* construction lay in the simple customs of the people and the character of its head. The historical rise of articulated constitutions has extended through a long series of centuries; the few fundamental traits underlying this process were developed and supplemented from time to time at some single point by the need of the hour, by necessity and force of circumstances. The point of view on which the closer [160] study of this formative process turns is fairly simple: on the one hand, there were the struggles of the government to master the might and the pretensions of the aristocratic middle term[2] and to acquire for the state its rights against it, while on the other hand there were the struggles of the third estate, often simply called 'the people', against the same middle power, and sometimes even against the government itself, to wring civil rights for itself and maintain an attitude of defiance. Thus on a general view a constitution is seen to have arisen as an aggregate: development has not proceeded uniformly; single parts have been retarded, others have swollen to disturbing proportions. Hence such a constitution resembles an old house whose simple original form has been changed by a long series of owners, as families have grown and as the need of the hour required, into a collection of nooks and corners which have

---

[1] The Empire was dissolved by Napoleon in 1806. The kingdom of Wurtemberg was largely his creation in 1805–6. Further territory was acquired in 1810.

[2] The Crown and the masses are the other two.

their own suitability but which in sum make up a formless and unintelligent whole.

The intellectual development of the age has afforded the *idea* of a state and therewith of its essential unity. Twenty-five years of past and mostly terrible history[1] have given us a sight of the numerous attempts to grasp this idea and a costly comprehensive *experience* [of their outcome]. Propitious circumstances finally granted to the ruler of Wurtemberg [favourable] *external conditions* as well as the exceptional advantage of not meeting with the aristocratic middle term as a hindrance fixed in advance, i.e. as a privileged landed nobility, but as an element which now seemed for the first time capable of being incorporated [into a representative constitution]. The King thus seemed to be placed in a unique historical position, that of being able to give a constitution that was all of one piece.[2]

Of the sovereignty acquired [by Wurtemberg] one side was completely achieved when the state existed and was recognized as such in *foreign* eyes. The original period of its rise occurred in circumstances in which everything for its establishment and maintenance in foreign eyes had to be raised autocratically, and therefore in internal affairs the means had to be collected by a powerful ministerial government and kept ready in firm hands for use. The time had now come when not only the might of the state but its *will* could come to life. The fortune and the struggles [161] of the European governments and their peoples had brought things to the point at which the sovereignty of the German kingdoms could be freed from the fetters under which they had lain till then, and

---

[1] i.e. since 1789.

[2] For Hegel the only genuine unity is not an aggregate but a syllogism, i.e. a unity of differences, or of extremes united by the mediation of a middle term. A constitution becomes a rational unity, in his view, only if the Crown on the one hand and its subjects on the other are united by the Estates Assembly as a mediating organ (*Ph.d.R.*, § 302) between the two. The principle of representation brings the people into the constitution as one of its organs. The King was fortunate in not finding in Wurtemberg a privileged nobility as a hindrance to his constitutional liberalism, because in Wurtemberg the nobility had always enjoyed fewer irrational privileges than they had elsewhere. What the King of Wurtemberg possessed was not only a knowledge of other attempts to give reality to the *idea* of an organic state or a knowledge of their *outcome*, but favourable *external conditions*, i.e. the recognition of Wurtemberg as an independent kingdom. The stage was thus set for a constitutional experiment which might have some chance of success. What foiled the King's plans was the preference of the Estates Assembly for old bottles; they forgot the changed and enlarged Wurtemberg and the new wine which the King saw it had produced.

had thereby introduced the possibility of at least *promising* free constitutions to the peoples. But a necessity higher than that lying in the positive bond of a promise lies in the nature of the concepts which have risen to become a universal conviction and which attach to monarchy, as essential chracteristics, the formation of a representative constitution, the rule of law, and popular influence on legislation. Frederick II [of Wurtemberg] now took this second step as well, the step of fashioning the monarchical state *internally*.

It was possible to fulfil the promise [to give a constitution] in a way which could be regarded as the wisest, and could even be given out as the justest, but which would have been the most perfidious counsel that Ministers could ever have given. If the princes of the new states had desired the total betrayal of their peoples and wished to acquire honour before God and man, they would simply have given back to their peoples what are called the 'old' constitutions; 'honour' in Heaven and on earth because, on the evidence of so many public pronouncements, and also, and especially, of recent history, we could infer that the peoples would have flocked into the churches and sung loud *Te Deums*. The princes would have won for themselves, in the eyes of Machiavelli's shade, the fame of the subtle politics of men like Augustus and Tiberius who likewise allowed the forms of the preceding constitution (a republic in that instance) to subsist while the thing itself existed no longer and could not possibly be brought back—a situation and betrayal which the Romans accepted and which made impossible the erection of a rational and monarchical constitution, the concept of which the Romans had not yet discovered.

This political manœuvre might have suggested itself to our princes the more readily if, on the basis of the experience of the last twenty-five years, they had compared together (*a*) the perils and terrors associated with the construction of new constitutions and with a real situation,[1] produced on the basis of theories, and on the other hand (*b*) the secure calm and nullity into which the institutions of the former Estates constitutions have sunk; and [162] then if with [reflection on] this already existing nullity they had linked reflection on how these institutions, like those Roman ones which Augustus and Tiberius had allowed to survive, had altogether lost, in the totally different conditions that had

---

[1] i.e. in France.

supervened, the little significance and consequence that they might seem to have retained in a fief of the German Empire.

King Frederick has shown himself superior to the temptation of this deception. On 15 March 1815 he called together the heads of princely and ducal houses in his kingdom, a selection of the rest of the nobility, and a number of representatives of the people, chosen by the citizens. The history of these *Proceedings* opened with the ever-impressive scene of the King's addressing this full Assembly of the Estates of his realm for the first time from his throne.

He began by explaining what had already been done: his subjects and the parts of his country, previously so diverse, had been united in an indissoluble whole; so far as civil rights were concerned, distinctions of class and religious confession had disappeared; the public imposts had been made proportionately equal for all; and by this means everyone had been made into *a citizen of a state*.

Next he avowed to his people their loyalty and obedience, to the army its courage and the honour it had brought to the name of Wurtemberg, to the public servants the support given him in all his efforts, and to his subjects in all classes their willing submission to the hard burdens incidental to the age and to the hard struggles of every kind whereby preservation and security had been won.

Then he declared that he was laying the coping-stone of the fabric of the state by giving his people a constitution.

Next he made a closing appeal to the sitting members, as being those through whom the nation was called to unite with the head of the state in exercising the most important rights of government: 'Let us unite together to confirm with mutual trust the sacred bond between me and my subjects [163] in order to further the national affairs, as this Assembly is called upon to do by the constitution.'

Finally he invited the Minister of the Interior to announce the Articles of the Constitution. After they had been read, the King bound himself to abide by them and transmitted them by his own hand to the President of the Assembly.

There surely cannot be a greater secular spectacle on earth than that of a monarch's adding to the public authority, which *ab initio* is entirely in his hands, another foundation, indeed *the* foundation, by bringing his people into it as an essentially effective ingredient.

Elsewhere the great working of a political constitution, and indeed most other acts of government, are seen happening, uncomprehended and without publicity, only in a series of scattered actions and accidents, and the public appearance of their Royal Highnesses and their Majesties has been gradually restricted to birthday festivals and the solemnization of marriages. This may have tempted us to prolong our glance at this scene (where the appearance of His Majesty corresponds to the inner worth of his action) as at the sight of something beneficent, sublime, and authoritative. But it would at once occur to us to think that we ought to apologize for prolonging our glance like this. This is because the endeavours in which we have been accustomed to see representatives of the princes engaged, the vanity and ineffectiveness of the former national Assembly (the German Diet), have made into an all-pervasive mood such surliness in face of acts like the King's, such moral and splenetic self-satisfaction in face of the public interest and the appearance of His Majesty, that the mention of these things and, it may be, the view of regarding such an appearance as capable of rousing generous feelings, has been open to the risk of being taken as not serious at all and as scarcely even good-natured, or of being judged as the folly of a court and as an intentional deluding of slaves. Our political deadness is incapable of joy at scenes of this kind, and profound thinkers turn away from them, as mere externalities, to the substance of the thing and to reflections thereon of their own. So here is the place to mention briefly the substance [164] of the thing, namely the contents of the Articles of the Constitution which the King gave.

They are contained in sixty-six paragraphs, divided into two parts. Part I (§§ 1–46) is entitled 'The Constitution of the Estates', Part II (§§ 47–66) 'General Provisions in Relation to the Constitution of the Kingdom and the Rights and Duties of His Majesty's Subjects'. Thus Part I is the more comprehensive and Part II the less developed.

By Part I the King granted a representative Estates [Assembly] with the following principal provisions: It is to consist of (*a*) *ex officio* members and (*b*) elected members, both in one Chamber. Eligibility for (*b*) is not limited to any one estate; Crown officials, non-commissioned officers and privates, the clergy, physicians, and surgeons are barred; the only other qualification is an age of at least 30 years and membership of one of the three Christian

Churches;[1] possession of a specific amount of property is not made a condition. A voter is required to have a net income of 200 guilders [*Gulden*] from real estate and to be at least 25 years old. The Estates assemble only when summoned by the King and must be summoned every three years. After this period elapses, one-half of the elected representatives retire, but they are eligible for re-election, and new elections are held to fill the vacancies. The Assembly does not last for more than six weeks and is prorogued or adjourned or altogether dissolved by the King. The elected deputies, as well as the Chancellor of the University, the General Superintendent of the Evangelical Church, and the Catholic Dean have their travelling expenses and subsistence (5 florins 30 crowns per day) paid. Ministers may be present during any period when the Assembly sits. In the years when no Estates Assembly is summoned, a committee of twelve members, elected by the Assembly from amongst its own number, meets for the discharge of pressing business, but an increase in taxation or a change in legislation is not within its power.

[165] For introducing new imposts and either direct or indirect taxes, and for increasing these, the consent of the Estates is necessary. Existing taxes remain as the [financial] basis of the King's government during his life. The computation of the incomings, and the expenditure of the taxes, are laid before the Estates every year. The fixing of a civil list for the King is the subject of further debates.

The Estates have a similar share in legislation; without their concurrence no new general law can be promulgated if it affects personal freedom or property or the constitution. In this matter the Crown has the initiative; but the Estates may submit to the Crown legislative proposals as their wishes, and in the event of a negative reply may repeat them thrice in future Assemblies. If the final answer is negative, reasons must be given for it, and in the light of these reasons the Estates may propound new suggestions.

Further, the Estates are permitted to lay before the King general wishes, ideas, and complaints, and the King promises to give a decision on every approach from the Estates. He also promises to take up complaints made to them by individual subjects of his, if the government authorities have manifestly refused to take them up.

Finally, the Estates may demand the appointment of an inquiry

[1] Roman Catholic, Lutheran, Calvinist.

into [the actions of] the state officials. When the King consents, as he must, then judgement is to be given by the Estates tribunal in cases of treason and concussion,[1] and by ordinary process of law in other cases.

[§ II. THE ESTATES]

[166] The infinite importance and liberality of the rights here conceded to the Estates, and likewise the simplicity and straight-forwardness of these provisions, examined impartially and without regard to anything except their content, undoubtedly do the greatest honour to the prince who gave them and to the age in which constitutional law has been purged of privileges and matured into [a set of] principles. A deed of this kind acquires more merit still when it is compared with the formlessness, illiberality, and obscurity in which, under constitutions both at home and abroad, especially under the old constitution of Wurtemberg, the people's rights are often overlaid by privileges and particularisms, stunted, restricted, and made ambiguous, and frequently even reduced to an empty show. Are the provisions quoted above not just those constitutional foundations which must be recognized and adopted with nothing less than the highest approval? What might be missing in them cannot be something opposed to them but only [some] supplements and more developed provisions which yet would accord with these universal truths of constitutionalism. What still survives [in the King's constitution] from *positive* constitutional law is in the main only the privilege of the aristocratic establishment [to have seats in the Diet]. Apart, however, from the fact that *rational* constitutional law has recoiled from the democratic abstractions which have discarded the institution of aristocracy out of hand, the privilege of what is in any case an existent actuality has been placed by further provisions at a very far remove from [what it was under] the old feudal law.

In this matter it is only this above all that needs remark, that in the Royal constitutional Charter this [aristocratic] element, united with the elected representatives in one Chamber, is granted only fifty votes, while these others have seventy-three votes, and therefore an important preponderance. This proportion of political power diverges considerably from that which comes on the scene

---

[1] i.e. extortion by threats or violence: a term drawn from Roman law.

in a bicameral system and already has important authority on the strength of its antiquity and its having been introduced more generally. The contrast between this voting proportion and that adopted in the provisional Estates Assembly [167] in the Kingdom of Hanover, where the knights are given one more vote than the *bourgeois* element, may be mentioned in passing, since the Wurtemberg Estates have frequently referred, in the *Proceedings* that follow, to the liberal expressions of the Hanoverian embassy to the Vienna Congress in the matter of German constitutional affairs.

[1. *Restrictions on Electoral Rights*]

What might seem still more unexpected is the further extension of, and the almost complete freedom granted to, the democratic principle as a result of the manner of electing representatives, so that the democratic element enters the organization of the state in a very nearly unrestricted form. The few tempering conditions visible here, apart from the fact that the *ex officio* members do not constitute a separate Chamber of their own, may be found in the provisions that the electoral assemblies have as presidents the chief Crown officials and, in fair-sized cities, the provincial governors, and that persons, such as the returning officer and his deputy, called in for election business, are not eligible for election in the districts where they discharge this duty, though they are so eligible in other districts.

The qualification for election as a representative is, as has been said, limited by very few conditions. In the first place all state officials, the clergy, physicians, and surgeons are debarred. The obvious reason for excluding the last two classes may also be taken to apply to the first, namely that their official duties do not allow them (*a*) to be absent for any longish period or (*b*) to undertake business of other kinds. (*b*) loses some of its force in relation to the *ex officio* members who hold Crown offices, in that they might, as has indeed not been prescribed, be allowed substitutes on every occasion, and (*a*) likewise loses some of its force in relation to civil servants working in the place where the Estates assemble, usually, of course, the capital. Even if this be disregarded, however, these considerations are not in themselves significant enough to justify an arrangement so extremely important for the primary object at issue. [168] In the draft of the fundamentals of the new Estates constitution, at which the King worked himself, and which he transmitted (in a speech to the Council of State convened on 11 January 1815) for consideration by a special commission of counsillors and senior officials, there still appears the provision that civil servants, so far as their duties allow, shall be eligible for election.

This matter is of great importance and the reviewer will expatiate on it further. In the first place we must not overlook the bearing of the fact that in large states such as France, for example, and England to a greater degree still, the whole social system at home, and the far-reaching foreign ties, give individuals in relation to wealth, culture, and the habit of living and acting in more general interests a position which is quite different from what it is in a country more restricted in size, social system, and wealth. In such smaller countries the large majority of those who acquire an academic or any more general culture find themselves obliged to seek their living and their social ties in some public service. Hence, public servants apart, disproportionately fewer people are to be found who could bring to an Estates Assembly a significant judgement or experience of public affairs, and still fewer who could be called 'statesmen'. Part of the nobility are out of account from the start as being *ex officio* members [of the Estates]; while another part is in the service of the Crown. Thus the nobility cannot in general be counted on to fill the ranks of eligible deputies—on the contrary. The class of advocates, which of the remaining classes is the one that may demand first consideration in this connexion, is tied in its concepts and activities primarily to the principles of private and *positive* law; these principles are opposed to those of constitutional law, i.e. of the rational public law which alone is relevant to discussion of a rational constitution. Thus the genius of an all too famous statesman[1] hit the mark exactly here when he declared advocates [169] to be the people most unfitted to advise on and transact public business. What the mentality of advocates has effected in the history of the Estates Assembly of Wurtemberg will appear in the sequel [197 ff.].

The legal exclusion of this class might well be contested from the point of view of abstract right, but not more so than the exclusion of physicians and surgeons; the organization of a state rests, however, on a concrete wisdom totally different from a formalism derived from private rights. A really peculiar product of the old

---

[1] Napoleon. See *Philosophy of History*, *Werke*[2], vol. ix, p. 540.

Wurtemberg situation, i.e. the class of writers, which is of the first importance for Wurtemberg's Estates constitution, you will learn about in due course.[1] The contribution which may be made to an Estates Assembly by the class of merchants, craftsmen, and other proprietors, important as it is, cannot rise here to the numerical proportion which it has in England, for example, nor can it replace what is lost by the exclusion of public officials.

Now, however important this exclusion may be by reason of its diminishing the stock from which capable deputies can be drawn, it is much more important still in connexion with the [political] attitude, that element which must preponderate if an Estates Assembly is not to grow into the most dangerous evil that can arise in a state. This fundamental property may be called in general terms a 'political consciousness'. It is something more than abstract insight or mere honesty and a mentality favourable to the welfare of the whole and the best interests of individuals. Not only landowners but also craftsmen and all other individuals possessed of property or skill have an interest in maintaining a civil order, but their *primary* aim here is the *private* aspect of their own possessions. If deputies to the Estates bring there a sense for private interests and private rights as their primary aim on which everything else is supposed to be dependent and consequential, then they proceed to beat down the state's demands so far as possible; of necessity they find the state superfluous, not indispensable for their own ends, even if not inappropriate for other purposes. In short, they approach their work with the will [170] to give and do as little as possible for the general [weal]. It is not here in question what mentality deputies *may* have, from whatever class or condition they are drawn; in political institutions, as in any rational organization, *chance* is not to be reckoned on; the only question is: what does the nature of the thing (of the Estates, in this instance) entail?

A political consciousness is principally acquired, however, in habitual preoccupation with public affairs. By this means not only is the infinite intrinsic worth of the general [weal] felt and recognized, but experience is gained of the resistance, hostility, and dishonesty of private interest, and the battle with it, especially with the stubbornness which results from its having been established in the form of law, is fought to the end. Since the Deputies

[1] In Section VI of Hegel's essay. See below [245–61].

are *elected*, an important consideration is that the electors should in the main come from a background in which a political consciousness is present and in which it develops. The former French Minister of the Interior, Vaublanc,[1] in his draft of a law regulating elections to the Chamber of Deputies, frankly included the stipulation that Crown officials of every kind, alone with the clergy, should constitute the majority of voters in the Departments. Everyone agrees that the English constitution is upheld solely by what are called its *abuses*, i.e. by the utterly unequal and therefore the unjust and even the sometimes altogether absurd privileges in respect of electoral rights; and it is on account of these alone that it is possible for the government to count generally on a majority of votes.

It is a mark of the uneducated to regard the English opposition as a party against the government or against the Ministry *as such*; even if the opposition does not limit its attack to individual ministerial measures only (as happens with the independent members, though otherwise they vote as a rule with the Ministry) but fights the Ministry at any and every point, still the fight is only against *this* single Ministry, not against [171] any and every Ministry or against government as such. What it is often charged with, as if with something bad, namely that all it wants is to form a Ministry itself, is in fact its greatest justification. This is the exact opposite of the tendency that we often see praised in the Germans and their Estates as the intrepidity of freedom and the defence of the citizens and their rights, the tendency to get the better of the state and to wrest it so far as possible of its powers.

German history must be left to show how far the appearance in the Diet of what was formerly called the third estate had its origin in the relation which the heads of the cities, as officials of the prince, bore to the Ministry; how far by their later entry the town council members have also acquired a share in membership of the Diet in their country; and also how far the original officials participated in council to start with and only in the course of time came to have their votes decisive.

In the Compact of Tübingen (1514), which is regarded as the fundamental article in the constitution of the old Duchy of Wurtemberg, the Duke's officials are expressly named along with one from the city law-court and one from the city council as those who were to be the Deputies of the Province to the Diet. But, on appeal

---

[1] Minister 1815–16 in the Duc de Richelieu's administration.

to the Imperial Commissioners, the Estates succeeded, only six years later, in 1520, in getting the officials eliminated again. This was a bad example which the Estates gave of the immutability of compacts solemnly concluded so recently.

There is ready to hand the objection against the eligibility of officials to be deputies that, being in the service of the Crown, they will *naturally* speak and act in its interest, and this may occasion the idea that the prince's interest is opposed to the interest of the people and the state. But service to the *person* of the prince (in household appointments) is something different from service given to government and state, and the view that what is done in the interest of government and state is *against* the interest of the people distinguishes the mob from the citizens.[1]

[172] The great events of recent history, the fight for Germany's independence, have imbued the youth in our universities with a higher interest than mere concentration on future bread-winning and making an income. Some of them have shed their blood together that the German provinces might acquire free constitutions. They have brought back from the field of battle the hope of working some day or other towards that end and of participating in the political life of the state. Their academic education has equipped them for this purpose and destined them in the main for the public service. Are they, along with the whole class of academically educated people, who generally expect the same destiny, to lose the capacity to become members of the Estates, representatives of the people?

In this connexion we must take note of the important fact that the altered situation of the former service of the Crown is a significant element in Germany's transition from its earlier barbarity and disorganization to the rational system of a political life. On this matter something may be cited from the Appendix to Part 25 of the *Proceedings*: there it is mentioned that in the thirteenth and following centuries the official positions in connexion with the Chamber were usually given in the first place only to persons drawn from the nobility with a certified considerable income from real estate and with prestations[2] of vassals; but they found an excuse for giving up exercising the official duties which had become

---

[1] i.e. the interest of the government may be against that of the mob, but not against that of citizens who participate in government.

[2] A medieval legal term meaning dues of various kinds payable by vassals.

irksome in their eyes and letting them be discharged by a surrogate from the citizenry, with directions to him not to be too industrious. Later on these offices, like those of magistrate, judge, &c., were simply handed over to private individuals drawn from the citizenry who looked on this, not, as happened subsequently, as a favour, but as a great burden which they had to assume. This annoyance was not imposed on any one for too long a period; complete exemption from these official duties counted as a special favour, and numerous examples of this are quoted in the passage mentioned above.

In the position of these ministerial officers, even if it implied in other respects a vassalage and even [173] something of serfdom, there was no longer any question of supposing that they were only *for* the interest of the prince *against* the people in the sense in which the prince's servants were later taken to be almost his dependants and a class excluded from the people as a whole. This latter position they had in virtue of the fact that both the revenues which they had to raise and assess, and also the judicial and magisterial power which they had to exercise in the name of the prince, counted rather as the rights of the private property and private authority of a third party against the citizens than as state revenues and state duties. But as the domanial possesions of the family trusts of the princely families have continually approximated to the character of state property, while the rights of sheriffs and others over vassals and serfs have begun to acquire the character of public duty and public power, the prince's servants have risen beyond the dependence of their salaries on the prince's whim to a position in which they hold their office by right and acquire the dignity of servants of the state. This transition from the administration of private property to the administration of state rights is one of the most important that has come about through time. It has rescued the officials from the situation they were in during the period of the old Wurtemberg constitution. This is one of the changes confirmed and consummated by the general transition of a non-sovereign princedom into a state.

Since positive constitutional law, which the Estates Assembly has made the principal basis of its claims, has history as its basis, the general remark may be added here that it is precisely history which teaches us to recognize the circumstances in which a constitutional provision was rational, and, in this instance, for example, affords the conclusion that, if the exclusion of Crown officials from the Estates was rational once, it is so no longer under altered conditions.

The fact that the Estates Assembly has forgotten both the old situation of the ministerial group and the explicit arrangements in the Compact of Tübingen and also [174] the difference between the former *Crown* servants and *public* servants is intelligible enough. But what is more surprising is that the Ministry seems to have instigated the exclusion of civil servants.

Another closely related circle of public activity, the councils and courts of the cities, was specified in the constitution of the old Duchy as one from which the deputies to the Diet were to be drawn. Of course to be a city councillor is no bad preparatory school for functioning in the Estates. City councillors,[1] like civil servants, spend their lives in the daily activity of helping to administer the civil order. They know by experience how laws and institutions work and what counter effects of evil passions they have to fight and withstand. Further, they are themselves drawn from the citizenry, they share its more limited interests, and may enjoy its closer confidence. Only from one end of Germany to the other there has been such a loud complaint about the incompetence, laziness, and indifference of local administrations, if not about their deeper corruption and iniquity, that their organization seems first to need a rebirth before men could be trained in them and drawn from them possessed of capacity and reliability for a greater sphere of action. The right of the councillors themselves to appoint to vacancies in their number will certainly have been a principal reason for their having sunk so far. What otherwise might be called despotism, i.e. the fact that many governments have deprived city councillors and other local officials of the administration of the locality's property and the other foundations and institutions concerned with churches, schools, and the poor, may not only find its justification in this incapacity but may even have appeared as an inescapable duty. It is on this same ground of incompetence that often nothing but a pure formality has been left to town councillors, as magistrates, of the share they were supposed to have in the administration of justice. The proceedings and the decision thereon have been put into the hands of the Crown judges and senior officials, or there has had to be recourse

---

[1] These, of course, were also the magistrates.

to the opinions [175] of counsel and solicitors. Governments thus found themselves induced to take out of the hand of town councillors their former share in the administration of justice.

Now even if the organization and character of town councillors hitherto can arouse few hopes of their providing worthy deputies to the Diet, still this article [of the old constitution] would have deserved to be not entirely forgotten. Only, of course, extensive modifications would have been required to remove the exaggeratedness and one-sidedness of this barrier [against their service as deputies].

[2. *Electoral Rights*]

But the other equally far-reaching extreme in the king's constitution is to be found in the fact that (i) the eligibility of deputies is almost as good as unrestricted, and (ii) voting qualifications are equally insignificant: apart from being twenty-five years old, voters are required only to have an income of 200 guilders from real estate.

To impose conditions of this latter sort on voting qualifications has hitherto been foreign to German institutions, and only in recent times has the idea become current; we propose to comment on it further. The most striking thing about it is that, according to such dry abstract provisions as both of those cited, the electors appear otherwise in no bond or connexion with the civil order and the organization of the state as a whole. The citizens come on the scene as isolated atoms, and the electoral assemblies as unordered inorganic aggregates; the people as a whole is dissolved into a heap. This is a form in which the community should never have appeared at all in undertaking any enterprise; it is a form most unworthy of the community and most in contradiction with its concept as a spiritual order. Age and property are qualities affecting only the individual himself, not characteristics constituting his worth in the civil order. [176] Such worth he has only on the strength of his office, his position, his skill in craftsmanship which, recognized by his fellow citizens, entitles him accordingly to be described as master of his craft, &c. Popular ideas are so familiar with worth of this sort that we say of someone that 'he is something' only when he has obtained an office, become master of his craft, or has in some other way been accepted into a specific sphere of civil activity. On the other hand, of one who is only twenty-five years old and the owner of real estate that brings him in 200 or more guilders a year, we say 'he is nothing'. If a constitution nevertheless makes him something, a voter, it grants him a lofty political right without any tie with the other civic bodies and introduces in one of the most important matters a situation which has more in common with the democratic, even anarchical, principle of separatism than with that of an organic order.

The great beginnings of internal legal relationships in Germany which presaged the formal construction of the state are to be found in that passage of history where, after the decline of the old royal executive power in the Middle Ages and the dissolution of the whole into atoms, the knights, freemen, monasteries, nobility, merchants, and tradesmen formed themselves into societies and corporations to counteract this state of disorganization. These groups then rubbed up against one another for a while until at last they found a tolerable *modus vivendi* as neighbours. Since the supreme public authority whose impotence was the direct cause of the need for these corporations was something so loose, these sectional communities forged their bonds of connexion all the more tightly, strictly, even painfully, until they came to constitute a cramping formalism and the spirit of a guild which, because of its aristocratic nature, was a hindrance and a danger to the development of the public authority. After the development of the supreme powers of the state had been completed in recent times, these subordinate communities and guilds were dissolved or at least deprived of their political role and their relation to internal constitutional law. Now, however, it would surely be time, after concentrating hitherto mainly on introducing organization into the circles of higher state authority, [177] to bring the lower spheres back again into respect and political significance, and, purged of privileges and wrongs, to incorporate them as an organic structure in the state. A living interrelationship exists only in an articulated whole whose parts themselves form particular subordinate spheres. But, if this is to be achieved, the French abstractions of mere numbers and quanta of property must be finally discarded, or at any rate must no longer be made the dominant qualification or, all over again, the sole condition for exercising one of the most important political functions. Atomistic principles of that sort spell, in science as in politics, death to every rational concept, organization, and life.

Furthermore, it is as well to remember that the exercise of a wholly occasional calling, like that of being a voter, easily ceases to be of interest in a short time and in any case depends on an accidental attitude and a momentary preference. This calling is exhausted by a single action, an action occurring only once in a few years; when the number of voters is large, the individual may regard as very unimportant the influence of his own vote, all the more because the deputy whom he helps to elect is himself in turn only one member of a numerous assembly where only a small number can ever give evidence of being of much importance, and where in any case the contribution made by *one* vote out of many is unimpressive. On psychological grounds it is to be expected that the interest of the citizens would drive them to seek the franchise most eagerly and to regard it as important and as a distinction; one would expect them to push to exercise this right, and actually to cast their votes with great circumspection and without any ulterior motive. But experience has shown that the excessive gap between the importance of the effect which is supposed to ensue, and the extremely small influence which the individual seems to himself to have, soon produces the result that the enfranchised become indifferent to this right of theirs. While the laws were originally concerned with excluding many citizens from the franchise, [178] legal arrangements soon became necessary to induce those entitled to votes to put in an appearance at the polling-booth. The example of England, so often used superficially, where there is such a serious agitation about parliamentary elections, is not here in point. In this part of the English constitution the most influential feature is just the privileges and inequalities of voting rights, while the very reverse is the case in the atomistic system.

However, it is obvious that these criticisms of the abstract principles of number, quantum of property, age are not meant to go the length of depriving these factors of their importance and influence. On the contrary, if the legal qualification for voting in elections and eligibility for election are themselves linked with the other political institutions, then these factors exercise their influence automatically. When this influence is settled by law and when a certain age, quantum of real estate, &c., is required, e.g. as a qualification for membership of a town council, magistrates' court, office in and membership of a corporation, guild, and the like, this is far more appropriate than bluntly and directly imposing such dry and purely external conditions on the high interest of Estates membership.

The object of such conditions is to provide a guarantee of the fitness of electors and elected. In any event this guarantee is partly negative in character and partly a mere presumption. There is, however, a totally different and a positive guarantee in the trust placed by the government in public officials or by communities and fellow citizens in the community officials, in their election to official positions and their admission to corporations. There is further trust on the ground that, in virtue of actual activity and participation in the organic life of the state and the nation, they have acquired the necessary skill and a sense of governing and obeying and giving the electors an opportunity to assess and test the attitudes and competence of the elected.

Provisions of the kind which presuppose a nation as a mass rather than a state and divide it generally by numbers into particular masses and by age and a specified property qualification into two classes [179] cannot possibly be called *political* institutions. They do not suffice to strip the people's share in national affairs of its democratic formlessness or to attain the end of not leaving to chance the acquisition of fit deputies for a National Assembly. A political institution cannot be content with the mere demand that something ought to happen, with the hope that it will happen, with barring certain factors which might impede its happening. It deserves its name only when it is so organized that what ought to happen does happen.

[3. *The Right of Making Taxes Dependent on Consent*]

Since the reviewer has expatiated at such length on these other matters, his remarks on the rest must be shorter.

The Estates have been granted the prerogative that without their consent no new taxes may be levied and that the existing ones are not to be increased. Wurtemberg may indeed have been the first German country where the Estates came so early into possession of this right in such a public and specific way. The Estates which we have seen arising or reviving elsewhere either contain very restricting elements drawn from the feudal constitution, or else their development and the determination of their activity appears in such a provisional and troubled light that it could not be compared with the free, candid, and clear form which the King of Wurtemberg wished to give to his own Estates.

The bloody struggle of the Tyrolese[1] against constitutional forms which they regarded as running counter to their old ancestral rights has aroused universal interest. When in the end the old constitution was successfully introduced, the monarch reserved to himself the fixation of the amount of the national revenues and allowed to the Estates only their distribution. Now there may be a dispute whether the old Wurtemberg Estates already possessed the right granted to them under the King's constitution, or [180] not, and whether their right was not formerly much more comprehensive—a dispute without practical interest, all the more because it is therefore so apt to serve as a proper *querelle d'Allemand*.[2] We may well say that, by the provision that the existing taxes were to continue and that it was only their elevation which was to require consent, the Wurtemberg Estates were formally placed once more in the position occupied by the Wurtemberg deputies of old. The direct and indirect taxes which flowed into the prince's exchequer, as they still do, and which depend on ground-rents, dues, tithes, doing work, &c., are seigneurial rents and a property (in the sense that 'property' has in *private* law) of the ruler or the state: they have an *existing* system as their basis and therefore need no approval from the Estates. The rest of the taxes proper, direct and indirect, i.e. the revenues raised in accordance with *constitutional* law, were fixed by concordat (reached through the influence of the supreme court and ratification by the Crown officials) both in respect of their amount and also their application to the ends of the state, i.e. to payment of the national debt and the remuneration of the armed forces of both the district and the royal household; thus here too the Estates were tied to an existing system as to a law. Now from all the stipulations and special provisions under which the old Estates exercised the right of consenting to taxation generally and not merely to a rise in payments, it might be possible to justify a more general outlook and infer the proposition that the old Estates possessed this right of consent in a more comprehensive sense; but this right then acquires an entirely new position

---

[1] The reference is to the revolt of 1809, led by Andreas Hofer.

[2] The French phrase for a quarrel about nothing, or for hair-splitting, originated in the later part of the sixteenth century. The translator owes this note to Professor I. D. McFarlane.

and an incomparably greater scope and importance as a result of the new position of Wurtemberg now that it has become an independent state instead of a fief of the Empire. While it was a fief, war and peace were not made by any one estate of the Empire, but by Emperor and Empire; the sacrifices demanded by war were fixed, in part, once for all in a quota-list.[1] We pass over the fact that the formalistic obstinacy of the German estates in doing nothing whatever which could be evaded, legally or otherwise, [181] resulted in making imposed exertions all the greater—the cost thereof falling just as inescapably on their province.

Against the resistance of the Estates the prince found general support and aid in the Imperial courts. But after Wurtemberg became an independent state, the right of the Estates to consent to taxation acquired a similar independence and thus an entirely new meaning which makes it quite inappropriate to call attention to the preceding state of affairs. In the new circumstances, the state needed entirely new guarantees against selfish attitudes and against the presumption of the Estates, because the old guarantees which the government had in Emperor and Empire were no longer available. A totally new element had arisen, the political one, into which the Estates were transplanted and of which hitherto they had been deprived.

The particular history of Germany affords examples enough of the urge of the old estates towards passive neutrality while they were politically null. They liked best to refrain from any intervention in world affairs; they preferred to endure with shame whatever happened rather than rise to independent decision, to action, and to honour. With this urge to dishonour and inactivity in foreign affairs there goes a tendency to turn activity rather against the government than against external enemies. Only too often the Estates have seen in times of crisis nothing but a favourable opportunity to put the government in a difficulty, or to prescribe conditions for making the efforts it demanded for the sake of its own and its people's honour and welfare, and to acquire privileged rights against it. Only too often have they succeeded in bringing on their country misfortune and disgrace for the moment, and, for the future, a cramping and weakening of the power of the government, and therefore a lasting foundation of inner and outer disruption. From the political nullity to which the German people

[1] *Matrikel.* See above, footnotes on pp. 151, 165.

was reduced by its constitution, from the inability of the numerous tiny bodies which made up the greater part of the Imperial estates to have any will and decision of their own [182], there arose inevitably a spirit of immersion in private interests, of indifference and even hostility to the thought of having a national honour and making sacrifices to retain it.

In the English people, for example, the sense of national honour has permeated the different social classes more generally. Hence parliament's right to sanction taxation annually has a meaning totally different from what it would have in a people brought up to a sense of merely private concerns and, being remote from any political standpoint, gripped by the spirit of narrow-mindedness and private self-seeking. Against such a spirit governments required a new guarantee aimed at the state's preservation, because they had lost the old guarantee, insufficient in any case, afforded by Emperor and Empire. The right of participating in fixing public taxation, whatever its form in the past, is now, when the Estates have no superior except the government of their state, which they confront on equal terms, inherently an infinitely higher and more independent sphere of authority than it was before. It has given them a connexion with and an influence on war and peace, on foreign politics generally, and on political life at home.

Owing to the fact that the King's constitution provided that the existing taxes were to be taken as basic for the lifetime of the reigning monarch, a limitation, in form at least, was placed on the right of assessing taxes. As a matter of fact this right is restricted in any case by the *necessary* requirements of the state. This necessity should nowadays be perfectly obvious, having regard to the magnitude of taxation: in all states, and most of all in the richest of them, like England, the needs of recent years have pushed taxation to heights undreamt of hitherto, and France, Austria, and other countries have aided themselves in their financial difficulties only by arbitrary and dictatorial action. Now, not to speak of need, the existence of which has never been disproved, and not to speak of the impossibility of basing a financial system on any other principles, the Wurtemberg Estates could [183] have put up with this Article out of gratitude to the prince who was the first, and now after two and a half years has been the only, one to give his country such an explicit and liberal constitution. 'All classes in the country, all the provinces of the Empire', as the Count von Waldek said at the start of the first speech by a member of the Estates Assembly at the opening of its sittings, 'vied with one another in expressing feelings of gratitude to this prince for his decision to introduce a constitution', the prince whom Count von Waldek proceeded to praise on the ground that

(*a*) he had led Wurtemberg during all the storms of the last decade with unusual strength ('unusual' qualities, he went on to say, 'have always characterized the rulers of Wurtemberg': a broader historical conspectus provides for this ambiguous word 'unusual' the more precise meaning, except in the case of Duke Christopher,[1] of arbitrary dictatorialness or weakness of character);

(*b*) he had given to Wurtemberg a considerable extension of its boundaries (i.e. through the so-called mediatization of the German estates that hitherto were immediate fiefs of the Empire[2]—an extension which Waldek characterizes as a contra-legal state of affairs, as an encroachment on the rights of the mediatized princes and the vassals entrusted to them by God, an extension from which those whose incorporation had brought it about could not withdraw, but only because their power must thereby have been weakened);

(*c*) he now loses no opportunity to cancel that result of events in 1806 which was opposed to his will, namely the cancellation of the constitution founded for all time by his illustrious ancestors. (The whole course of the *Proceedings* shows that the opposition of the Estates turned on the one point that by the King's constitution the old constitution was *not* restored, and that the result referred to was *not* cancelled.)

[184] In any case, as everyone knows, the demand of the Estates that, even in the King's lifetime, their consent should extend to the taxes already existing had no success on account of the King's early death. It is equally well known that, by their failure to accept the King's constitution under which debates on taxes would have been conceded to them at a change in government, they have deprived themselves of such debates.

[1] Duke 1550–68. He introduced a system of ecclesiastical and educational organization.

[2] Immediate vassals became mediate vassals by being brought under princes, like the ruler of Wurtemberg, who were themselves immediate vassals. These 'mediatized' princes generally kept their titles and many of their powers, but these were exercised as an *imperium in imperio*.

[4. *The Fundamentals of the Constitution*]

In order to complete the historical epitome of the chief features in the Constitutional Charter, its second half would need to be cited, the 'General provisions relative to the constitution of the kingdom and the rights and duties of the King's subjects'. These, however, permit of neither summary nor criticism; they are simple organic provisions which speak for themselves and make up the rational basis of constitutionalism. For example (§ 52): 'All subjects are equal in the eyes of the law; they are eligible for all official positions; from these they are excluded neither by birth nor by membership of any of the three Christian denominations.' § 53: 'The laws require that all shall make proportionately equal contributions to the public charges and taxes.' § 55: 'Every subject has the right to emigrate if he is exempt from military service or has completed it.' § 56: 'Every subject is at liberty to choose his profession and occupation according to his free inclination, and to educate himself for it.' And so on.

These principles allow of this comment only, that it would never have occurred to the Imperial Estates to cast them aside, and only a cross-grained perversity, or obduracy, or what you will, could have induced an Estates Assembly not to mention them and to give no credit to the ruler [185] who was making them in express terms the fundamental determinants of the rights and duties of his subjects. Whatever connexion the older constitutions may have had with such principles, in those constitutions they were linked to particular and external conditions, entangled in them, even obscured by them. The presence of rights in those constitutions was not a matter of principle, i.e. of rationality and absolute right. On the contrary, they appear there as single acquisitions, due to the favour of special circumstances and restricted to this or that conjuncture of events, as if they could equally well be lost in circumstances of misfortune. It is an infinitely more important step forward when intelligence has made headway up to a knowledge of the simple bases of political institutions and discovered how to comprise these bases in simple sentences like an elementary catechism. If the Estates Assembly had caused the twenty paragraphs containing these general provisions to be hung on placards in the churches, impressed on young people as they were growing up, and made a permanent feature of school and church instruction, then we would have been less amazed than [we have been] by an Estates Assembly that ignores them and has not appreciated the value of their public recognition by the government and their being universally known.

But because of their generality these principles constitute no more than an outline of legislation that is still to be drafted, like the Mosaic law or the famous *Droits de l'homme et du citoyen* of more recent times. For legislation already·in force, or for a government and administration which already exists, they are the permanent regulators which must underlie any revision or extension of what already exists, whenever revision or extension be necessary. The King's Constitutional Charter stops short at these general fundamentals. It does not contain their further development, nor does it take in more specific provisions which might already be present as political institutions. Organic constitutional provisions and laws proper approximate very closely to one another in any case, and the further task of developing them and subsuming already existing institutions under them could [186] have provided the Estates Assembly with the principal subject for its activity.

[§ III. THE ATTITUDE OF THE DIET]

These then are the chief features of the manner in which the King had intended to enlarge the previous constitutions of his kingdom by adding the important limb of popular representation and by recognizing and proclaiming the universal principles of justice in political life. The grafting of this limb on the constitution, and thereby the introduction of the basis for developing and applying legal principles further, he thought he had arranged and completed by actually summoning the Estates in accordance with the provisions of the Constitutional Charter, by binding himself publicly to abide by the Charter, by solemnly transmitting it to the Estates, and by promulgating it as the instrument which gave them their authority. Now one might have expected the further course of history to show how this new creation, the Estates, operated within the sphere granted to it and how there worked in it this important vital element grafted on to the organism of the state. But it is not the history of such an assimilating and vitally active operation that unfolds before our eyes. On the contrary, the members summoned to the Assembly decline to allow themselves to be incorporated into the state as one of its limbs; they declare themselves indeed to be Estates, but Estates of another world, of a time long past, and demand that the present be changed into the past and reality into unreality.

[1. *Refusal to Accept the New Legal Position*]

At the very same sitting, on 15 March, when the King hoped to have completed the internal constitution of his realm, the first thing was that both the previously privileged classes and also those summoned to constitute the Estates declared with one voice [187] that they stood outside the new legal constitution of the state and declined to participate in the new constitution given by the King.

To begin with, the agnates of the royal house declared that they wished explicitly to reserve the rights of the old arrangement for themselves and for all future agnates, heirs, and heirs of heirs of the royal house.

Next, a number of the mediatized princes declared that they awaited from the congress of monarchs at Vienna the definition of their rights and privileges, and for this reason they could not commit themselves in advance to a particular Estates constitution; therefore they declined to take any part in the proceedings.

There was intercalated into the first address of the Estates (though on whose authorization is not obvious) a general declaration that the other princes and counts and the entire nobility could participate only with a reservation of their rights and subject to the decision of the congress.

To these reserved rights a strikingly wider meaning was given above all in a petition submitted to the Estates by Count von Waldek on behalf of the house of the Counts of Limpurg.[1] It is stated therein that 'this noble house has never accepted the abdication of the Roman Emperor' (an abdication accepted by all other potentates in Europe) and 'after the dissolution of the Confederation of the Rhine[2] it has come again into the *legal* possession of all its former rights; the *actual* possession of these is lacking up to the present, but only contrary to law'. In other words, incorporation into the state of Wurtemberg, and subjection to it, was here being formally renounced, with the addition that the Count was ready, as soon as constitutionalism had been established in Wurtemberg,

[1] Limpurg was a county in Hall, a duchy incorporated into Wurtemberg in 1803.

[2] Established by Napoleon in 1806 and dissolved in 1813 at the start of the war of liberation from France.

to specify the conditions on which the county of Limpurg would be ready to become subject to Wurtemberg by treaty.

The attitude of the King's Ministers to such pretensions on the part of the mediatized princes, pressed as they were *ad absurdum* [188], even to the non-recognition of the Roman Emperor's abdication, does not matter; but it may seem incomprehensible that an Estates Assembly should concede a share in its deliberations, and a vote on its decisions, to members who formally declare that they do not legally belong to the Kingdom of Wurtemberg at all; that of course they will take part in making decisions which are binding on the people of Wurtemberg, but that these decisions are not to be binding on those who have thus helped to make them; and that only after constitutionalism has been established with their aid will they declare on what conditions they will be pleased to join it.

Even if the phenomenon of people presumptuous enough to make laws for others, while asserting that they are not to be subject to them themselves, is common enough elsewhere, it may be more difficult to find examples of such a degree of flabbiness in Estates that they acquiesce in this sort of thing and grant participation in debates and decisions to those who insist on a condition which is so high-handed and contrary to royal authority.

Still another estate, the prelates, took after a few days the meaningless step of proposing in an address, though only as a wish, that, as a separate estate, they should be represented in the Estates Assembly and that their former rights might be conceded to them. (In the Assembly of the former Duchy of Wurtemberg all fourteen prelates had a seat and a vote; they were therefore not *represented* there but appeared as *ex officio* members, as peers.)

Of the two prelates who were already members of the Assembly, the one who was summoned as Chancellor of the University of Tübingen declared that he did not know whether he represented the university, or the Church, or the learned professions; the other, summoned as the General Superintendent of the Evangelical Church, made the naïve remark that a good friend had advised him not to sign the petition of the other prelates, so that he could appear impartial and so be able to support their cause all the more.

[189] The entire Assembly thus takes up a position directly opposed to the actual world situation. It spurns the constitution given by the Crown along with, therefore, the instrument on the strength of which it was called together. It takes a line of its own

and decides on the rejection of the constitution in a way opposed to the general constitution of Europe and Germany as recently settled by all the European powers.

The Assembly did not reject the King's constitution on the ground that it was contrary to the rights that subjects could claim in a political consitution on the strength of the eternal rights of reason. One might have expected that, before rejecting it, the Assembly would have first analysed the Charter, as it never did, and that it must at least have recognized its general principles. On the contrary, it rejected it on the ground that it was not the old constitution of Wurtemberg—not merely in so far as it differed therefrom (in this matter too it did not preface its rejection with any analysis) but flatly and explicitly because it was simply not this old constitution, because the act whereby the Estates were brought on the scene was not simply the restoration and revivification of the old constitution.

The dead, however, cannot be revived. The demand made by the Assembly proved that it had not only no conception but not even any inkling of the problem that had to be solved. It showed that it treated the necessity of the problem as merely the pleasure or whim of the King or his ministers and thought it had to do with something accidental and not with the nature of the thing itself. It granted indeed that some circumstances were new and that they necessitated the introduction of modifications. For these new circumstances there counted in its eyes only a few externalities (which scarcely affect the substance of the difference between the old and the new situation), namely (i) the arrival of a class of the nobility which, as has been said above ([187–8]), took the view that, in law, and therefore in relation to the constitution in respect to which alone legal standing was relevant, they were not a section of the subjects at all, and indeed they refused to let the state, with the concurrence of the Estates, assign to them a constitutional and civil status within the [190] realm. (ii) Secondly, the adoption of subjects belonging to another Christian denomination into the civil rights enjoyed by the Lutherans. This was something which in any case did not affect the nature of the constitution, just as the first point should not have been a matter affecting it either. A further ground for modifications was thought to be the expansion of the country by more than half its previous size. In actual fact this could have provided a very important reason against the mechanical introduction of the old constitution of Wurtemberg. But the Assembly tried to prove, by legal arguments drawn from bygone cases, by the old positive constitutional law, and by the formal concept of incorporation, that the newly introduced part of the kingdom had a right to the constitutional benefits of the other part. At bottom, however, this whole attitude, and especially the legal argument, was revealed, in comparison with the thing of real importance, as something frivolous and, into the bargain, as a *querelle d'Allemand*. For even if Wurtemberg had not expanded and had remained entirely within the territory which had enjoyed the old constitution, the change in the situation in that territory, i.e. the need and necessity of a new constitution, would have remained the same.

[2. *The 'Good Old Law'*]

As a clearer illustration of this necessity we may now develop several aspects of the unfavourable results which would have accrued from reintroducing the old constitution of Wurtemberg in circumstances quite different from those that have just been mentioned. The culture of the age demanded at least the scrutiny and sifting of the political constructions and constitutions which had ended in a formless edifice like the constitution of the German Empire. Our[1] ecclesiastical Counsellor, Dr. Paulus, has prepared an invaluable collection of the chief charters of the original Wurtemberg constitution; you have only to consult it to see that constitutional bases of such a character [191] are an inexhaustible armoury of arguments for lawyers and advocates; they are, too, a framework whereby the people is deprived of knowledge of the constitution and, more or less, of even the thing itself, a framework with which the age can no longer be satisfied. The fact that under this formalism something must have been achieved and that an activity apparently concerned with forms alone must also have had an influence on the matter too will be discussed below.[2]

With the 'unfavourable results', however, we may contrast those called beneficial, but especially the law which is supposed to be made regardless of results; the latter contrast is just the one the Estates have drawn *ad libitum* and *ad nauseam*.

[1] i.e. in Heidelberg.
[2] In passages not translated, [225 ff.] and [275–6]. H. refers to a special committee set up by the Estates to revise the old constitution and to the worth of its labours in respect of the *form* of constitutional law.

Such a comparison gives rise to the usual endless argumentation, because there can be no final decision on such reasonings and counter-reasonings if no Praetor is available to provide it. What alone matters is the nature of the thing, and in the present instance this is quite simple. The change, prepared for centuries and now late enough completed, is the afore-mentioned transition of the more important German countries from the status of Imperial fiefs to the status of sovereignty, i.e. of states. Under the former status the prince on the one hand and the country and his people on the other (despite the fact that the people were subjects, often down to the level of villeinage) confronted one another with an independence which on both sides might approximate almost to rights of sovereignty. Between the two stood the Emperor and Empire as an external bond which kept both in this [mutual] independence and also provided the link they needed—their relation resembled that between two private individuals who are each independent persons. The ties they made with one another were based on subjective needs and preferences; but simply because they are also in a state and are subject to the authorities and the courts, these ties become contracts; making contracts acquires its full and actual meaning and the independence and ties of the individuals are upheld. But the more impotent this mediating and supreme authority [192] is shown to be, the more ill-off both parties must have been in their [mutual] conflicts, because they could not separate, being tied together as government and subjects even in their very independence of one another.

A situation like this in which prince and people were linked by an external power led to the result that political rights proper were found on the side of the subjects. Amongst rights of this kind there were most of those arising from the feudal system; but it would be superfluous to touch on these here because in old Wurtemberg there was only an insignificant nobility, and its rights in any case were of no great importance in politics. Special mention, however, is due to the right of the former Wurtemberg Estates to keep the exchequer in their hands. Tied up with this right of theirs was the right not only to enjoy allowances themselves but also to appoint officials, advisers, and above all a Committee, and to fix salaries for all of these out of the exchequer. The Committee itself had the administration of the chest from which it drew the remuneration fixed in total by the Estates; but over and above this, so far-reaching was its right of administration, it decreed additional stipends and allowances to itself, and decreed and paid out to its members and other individuals salaries and pensions for real or imaginary services. This expenditure of public moneys for personal ends, for oneself, an expenditure which honour will spurn to keep secret, was exempt from all control.

The inner collapse and moral quagmire implicit in such private plunder, and the whole situation that makes it possible, is very closely related to a downright collapse of the state, in that the Estates, with the exchequer in their hands, may for the sake of their own ends enter into relations with foreign powers as a sort of sovereign power themselves. From their possession of the exchequer it was an easy step to the maintenance of their own forces, and it would be simply absurd to make laws forbidding the Estates to do the latter while putting the former into their hands and so giving them the power and the means to do it. When the aforementioned supreme and mediating authority of the Emperor and [193] Empire was still available, such a result could be prevented on single occasions, i.e. when that authority was effective and when on occasion it chose to act; but it remained a matter of chance whether such a result was to be prevented or not. In the German Empire, however, there has been no lack of examples of estates being authorized to raise their own forces, e.g. the city of Emden in East Friesland. Moreover, in that same territory, which was farther removed from the effective operation of the Empire, the Estates raised troops of their own against their prince, concluded treaties with powers abroad, called their armies into their country and paid them. In this matter there can hardly be a more instructive history than von Wiarda's excellent *History of East Friesland*:[1] it provides a consistent picture of the most shameful, miserable, and destructive collapse resulting from transactions between the prince and the Estates in whose hands those rights were placed which belong to the sovereign. On a larger scale the same events occurred in the history of France and England before these countries had completely developed into states, not to mention Poland. The only difference is that these histories are relatively free from that distasteful element in Germany, namely its complete [domination by] legal and documentary formalism.

Von Wiarda had access to the archives of the East Friesland

---

[1] By T. D. von Wiarda, 10 vols., Aurich and Leer, 1792–1817.

Estates in whose service he was and who commissioned him to write his book. The Wurtemberg Estates have not instigated a similar history. Moser, a famous man,[1] who was qualified to write it and who also was their legal adviser, they exiled from their midst. However, amongst other publications, there is a remarkable brochure which casts a light, during one period at least, on one aspect of this matter, i.e. on the Estates' independent administration of the exchequer. Its title is: *The administration of the Wurtemberg exchequer by the former, but now dissolved, Committee of the Wurtemberg* [194] *Diet members, drawn from the accounts, acts, and charters of the Estates (s.l.,* 1799). The Assembly of the Diet, called together again in 1796 for the first time after about twenty-five years, investigated the accounts of the Committee it found in office;[2] this brochure supplies a part at least of the results of this investigation. The Preface summarizes it as follows: The results of these accounts comprise some tons of gold which have not only been spent illegally, but run into millions and amount to the enormous sum of 4,238,000 guilders from the last Diet in 1771 to the beginning of the present one in March 1797 when an end was made of this monstrous Committee. Think: 4,238,000 guilders of public money which the Committee had sworn, and were in duty bound, to administer and spend honestly!

This result may justify mention; but to draw from it a detailed picture of the depths to which this Estates administration has let itself sink is not in place here. It would be necessary to emphasize in particular the numerous payments which the members of the Committee drew for themselves in respect of every transaction, important or not, over and above their ordinary remuneration (e.g. the payment to a Treasury official for declaring his agreement with the Duke's decision) and lots of other things that might be called downright trickery, and in the list of them the same family names occur with peculiar frequency. Moreover the pretty examples of diplomatic experiments and embassies, and especially their remuneration, would be worth remark; in the accounts from 1778 to 1781 there appears a sum of 5,000 guilders made over to a foreign Councillor for a journey to St. Petersburg to push forward the

[1] J. J. Moser, 1701–85 [L.]. Imprisoned 1759–64 for writings against the Duke. The father of German constitutional law which he expounded in 50 volumes for the use of lawyers.

[2] It was this Assembly in 1796 which inspired Hegel to write the essay of which a surviving fragment [150–3] is translated above.

national affairs that had gone awry there (?); and 8,700 guilders for a journey to Munich on commercial business.

It does not help matters to say that these squanderings and pillaging of state funds were abuses and illegalities; if in twenty-six years the sum of public money illegally spent can amount to four millions, the laws under which [195] illegality on this scale is possible are certainly good for nothing. A good constitution is of course a good one only if illegalities are punished or rather prevented altogether.

If this happens in the green tree, we may well ask what is to happen in the dry. What *will* happen in the dry, if pillaging and squandering happened at a time when the Emperor and the Imperial courts were still superior to the Estates, when the Estates themselves had brought to a close a wearisome and extremely expensive process against their prince on the score of extortions and illegalities, and had shouldered a huge burden of debts whose discharge may not have been completed in the nearly fifty years that have elapsed to the present hour—a period that we hear lauded as the age of integrity in Germany, of dignity in the Estates, an age of happiness achieved by the constitution, in contrast to the corruption, luxury, and injustice of the modern age?

But the evil arising from the fact that the independence of the Estates made it possible for them to pillage the exchequer may remain a natural consequence of this fact, or it may be checked by laws and changes in institutions. Yet, so far as the state is concerned, there always remains the disadvantage that the independence of the Estates in disposing of a national exchequer and administering it makes it possible [for them] to hinder and indeed block the march of the state both in respect of internal affairs and also, in particular, in relation to political ties with other states—ties which in any case were further removed from the Estates and indeed were often obnoxious to them and in general were formerly no business of the German Estates at all. The idea of putting into the hands of the Estates, or of any corporation within the state, a military force and army independent of the government would generally be regarded as an expedient ruinous to the state; but there would be hardly any difference between this and allowing to any such corporation the disposal of a part or the whole of the exchequer and the power to pay salaries and pensions therefrom. It may look as if the Estates of one of the old German countries who were deprived of this former power of theirs lost a great deal of their privileges and powers. But it has already been remarked[1] that, owing to the transition [196] of a country from being an imperial fief into being a sovereign state, the Estates have gained infinitely in privilege and power, and with this new growth [of the state] their former privilege is quite irreconcilable. If such older provisions survived, the state would cease to be a state and would come to ruin through having in it the two sovereign powers that would be there. Or, it would be truer to say, unity would be restored either because the so-called Estates, as we have seen in recent history, would upset the former government and usurp its powers, or because, as we have also seen, governments would send such Estates packing and thereby save state and people. The greatest guarantee and security of the Estates is just this, that they shall not possess a power which contradicts the nature of the thing; the greatest folly, on the other hand, is to try to find in such a power a protection for themselves and the people: because such a power makes it right, and sooner or later necessary, to abolish such Estates.

It should be added that the qualitative difference between a fief and a state entails a radical alteration in the precise form of the relation between prince and vassals in the former. Since prince and country, as property-owners and possessors of special prerogatives, confronted one another as privileged *individuals* and so stood under a third party, the power of Emperor and Empire, they were subject to a Praetor, and this made it possible for them to conclude contracts with one another and have relations with one another on the footing of *private* law. Even in more recent times, when truer concepts have taken the place of the old idea, adopted thoughtlessly and irrationally, that governments and princes had a divine authority, the expression 'contract of the state' appeared to contain even yet the false thought that the concept of contract was applicable in the *state* to the relation of prince and subjects, government and people, and that the legal specifications of private rights, which flow from the nature of a contract, could and even should find their employment in this context. It takes only a little reflection to realize that the connexion of prince and subject, government and [197] people, has an original and substantial *unity* as its very basis, while in a contract almost the opposite is the case, since it

[1] The reference is to [180–2].

proceeds from the mutual independence and indifference of the two parties. An assocation which they enter in relation to some matter is a casual tie arising from the subjective need and choice of the parties. A contract of that kind is essentially distinct from a political bond which is a tie objective, necessary, and independent of choice or whim. It is an absolute duty and it is on it that rights depend; in a contract, however, the choice of the parties sets up reciprocal rights and it is only from these that duties flow.[1] When a country ceases to be an Imperial fief and makes the transition to a state, the former independence of its two sides, mediated as it was by a third power (supreme and mediatory), disappears, and with it the entire contractual relationship.

[3. *The Fundamental Error*]

The fundamental error in the position adopted by the Wurtemberg Estates lies in this, that they start from *positive* law; they looked on themselves almost entirely as still standing at this same point, and they demanded rights on the sole ground that they had been possessed of them before. They acted like a merchant who proposed to ply his trade just the same on a ship, in which his capital was sunk, even though it had gone to the bottom, and to expect others to advance the same credit to him on the strength of it as before; or like a landed proprietor whose sandy soil had been covered by fertile humus as a result of a beneficent flood and who yet proposed to plough and farm it exactly as he had done before.

What we see in the behaviour of the Estates summoned in Wurtemberg is precisely the opposite of what started twenty-five years ago in a neighbouring realm and what at the time re-echoed in all heads, namely that in a political constitution nothing should be recognized as valid unless its recognition accorded with the right of reason [198]. We might have feared that the leaven of the revolutionary principles of that period, of abstract concepts of freedom, had not yet fully fermented or been digested in Germany and that Estates Assemblies there might take the opportunity to make similar experiments and so give rise to disturbances and dangers. Wurtemberg at any rate has provided a comforting demonstration that this evil spirit does not walk there: but [it is also clear] that the portentous experience in France and outside it, in Germany

[1] With this argument, cf. *Ph.d.R.*, §§ 75, 258.

as well as there, has been lost on these Estates—the experience that at one extreme the rigid adherence to the positive constitutional law of a bygone situation and, at the other extreme, abstract theories and shallow chatter, have both alike been the bulwarks of selfishness and the source of misfortune in France and outside it.

The Wurtemberg Estates wanted to resume the standpoint of the old Estates. They have not concerned themselves with the content of the King's Constitutional Charter; they have not asked or sought to prove what rational law is or what accords with it. Instead they have simply stuck to the formalism of demanding an old positive law on the ground that it was positive and in accordance with the contract. One must regard the start of the French Revolution as the struggle of rational constitutional law against the mass of positive law and privileges by which it had been stifled. In the proceedings of the Wurtemberg Estates we see the same struggle between these principles, only the roles are reversed. In France most of the Estates of the Realm and the popular party upheld the rights of reason and demanded their restoration, while the government was on the side of privileges: but in Wurtemberg the King brought his constitution within the ambit of rational constitutional law, while the Estates set themselves up as defenders of privileges and positive law. They even afforded the perverse spectacle of doing this in the name of the people against whose interests, far more than against the prince's, these privileges are erected.

[199] One might say of the Wurtemberg Estates what has been said[1] of the returned French *émigrés*: they have forgotten nothing and learnt nothing. They seem to have slept through the last twenty-five years, possibly the richest that world history has had, and for us the most instructive, because it is to them that our world and our ideas belong. There could hardly have been a more frightful pestle for pulverizing false concepts of law and prejudices about political constitutions than the tribunal of these twenty-five years, but these Estates have emerged from it unscathed and unaltered.

'Old rights' and 'old constitution' are such fine grand words that it sounds impious [to contemplate] robbing a people of its rights. But age has nothing to do with what 'old rights' and 'constitution' mean or with whether they are good or bad. Even the abolition of

---

[1] By Talleyrand (or Dumouriez) of the courtiers who surrounded Louis XVIII in 1795 or 1796, and not therefore of returned *émigrés*.

human sacrifice, slavery, feudal despotism, and countless [other] infamies was in every case the cancellation of something that was an 'old right'. It has often been repeated that rights cannot be lost, that a century cannot make wrong into right, but we should add: 'even if this century-old wrong has been called right all the time', and further that an actual positive right a hundred years old rightly perishes if the basis conditioning its existence disappears. If you like to spin words, you can maintain that, if a husband or a wife dies, the survivor still retains his or her right in relation to the other, or that a merchant whose ship has been swallowed by the sea still has his right to it. From time immemorial the disease of the Germans has been their clinging to formalisms of this kind and their preoccupation with them. Thus almost the entire content of the activity of this Wurtemberg Estates Assembly has been confined to the barren assertion of a formal right with all the obstinacy of an advocate. Some few voices, amongst others the President of the Assembly (Prince zu Hohenlohe-Öhringen), tried in vain to lead the Estates to the thing itself, to wean them on occasion from purely formalistic proceedings. [200] But even the pestle that has pounded the age through twenty-five long years has had no effect on them.

[§ IV. THE COURSE OF THE PROCEEDINGS] [200-25]

[(1) Hegel objects to the reading of set speeches and the absence of debate and he contrasts this procedure with the admirable rules of the English Parliament. (2) Napoleon's return from Elba raised the issue of national defence. The Estates made patriotic speeches but when the King asked for money to raise and equip a larger army, the Estates proposed to make their compliance conditional on the reintroduction of the old constitution, which would have a 'magical' effect. (3) Since the Estates rejected the King's constitution the question arose of their position in constitutional law. They did not wish to recognize *de facto* the new constitution under which they had been summoned, and consequently they raised endless questions of form about the wording of their minutes and the appointment of their officials. They really had three possible courses of action: (*a*) If they hesitated to accept the King's offer they should at least have recognized an obligation to study it. (*b*) They could have accepted it while reserving the right to work over its vague elements and to produce detailed legal provisions accordingly. (*c*) They could reject the King's offer and produce a new constitution of their own for his acceptance (although it is obvious that an Estates Assembly, which presupposes an existent constitution, is ill equipped for making one, and history shows that nations have entrusted constitution-making to individuals like Solon, or have had constitutions imposed on them by individuals, like Moses, with divine authority). What the Estates actually did was to request the King to reintroduce the old constitution, although they asserted that they could not specify its content since the official records of the country were not available to them and it would take lawyers years to establish from the records what the content of the good old law was. This shows how far the Wurtemberg Estates were from understanding that a constitution must be built on rational concepts and not empirically.]

[§ V. THE FUTILITY OF THE ESTATES] [225–44]

[A committee is appointed to prepare for discussion with representatives of the King the preliminary articles of a constitution. The Crown conceded the substance of most of them, but the Estates replied that their principles and the King's attitude could not be reconciled. They begged him to restore the old constitution without further delay and they added a list of their grievances. What they still failed to do was to give any content to their principles and therefore they stuck to formalities and never really grappled with the substance of the matter at issue.]

[§ VI. THE WRITERS' INSTITUTE[1]]

[245] One amongst the mass of grievances incidentally touches on what was called the 'Writers' Nuisance'. In his not too wearisome recollections Herr von Forstner lifts this out of 'the melancholy litany of grievances' and gives it a more detailed elucidation which makes the public acquainted with an institution altogether peculiar to Wurtemberg, the Writers' Institute, and displays a state of affairs which is a moral, legal, and intellectual quagmire. It throws light on, *inter alia*, an important matter—interest in the good old law—and because of its far-reaching influence it is to be considered [here] more closely.

[1] *Schreiberei-Institut*—'Writers' is used here in the Scottish sense of, e.g. 'Writers to the Signet'.

[1. *Treatment of the Matter by the Estates*[1]]

[2. *The History of the Writers' Institute*]

[249] The exhaustive memorial of Advocate Griesinger[2] states at the very start that its author will refrain from outlining the melancholy picture of all 'the crying and wellnigh incredible facts amassed in the petitions and memoranda submitted to the Estates about the Institute, because another member has undertaken this task'—a task that has not yet seen the light of day. But Griesinger's memorial along with the few printed petitions contains quite enough to show up in detail what is in fact the 'extraordinary and almost incredible' nature of this so famous Wurtemberg institution and what its relation is to the Estates Constitution. . . . [The passage omitted is concerned with the Law Courts in Wurtemberg in the sixteenth century.]

[251] These writers now, our proper subject here, are defined by Advocate Griesinger as men practising in legal and fiscal matters, and he finds the peculiarity of the Wurtemberg writers in the fact that they practise without having been academic students at all. But the fact that this is the case too in other countries, at least to a certain extent, is both familiar and natural, because a university education at any rate is unnecessary for a great part of a writer's duties. The peculiarity of the Wurtemberg Writers' Institute is clearly seen from Griesinger's memorial, and from the petitions, to lie altogether elsewhere. It clearly emerges from these that for every office district a town or office writer is available (i.e. the greater municipalities have a town writer of their own, while the remainder of the district, which is called an 'office', has its own office writer in addition); he has the monopoly of arranging the writing of everything in the district which has to be calculated or engrossed legally and officially.

Senior officials, i.e. those concerned with justice, police, the exchequer, and forests, likewise need writers to help them; but this is necessary for their business in other countries too. The only thing about this which can be regarded as peculiar in Wurtemberg is that none of these assistants is drawn from the class of qualified

---

[1] This section merely recites the delay in dealing with proposals for reforming the Institute.

[2] This took five days to read in the Estates Assembly, and occupies 192 pages of print.

jurists, accountants, or foresters; all these helpers are trained only by their routine [duties] and they are not destined one day to occupy the office in whose business they are occupied. The forestry offices [252] have long been set aside for the nobility; the *bourgeois* clerk is therefore from the start deprived of the ability to aspire to one of them. It is not made a condition of being appointed to an office that qualified jurists, after completing their university studies, shall acquire the requisite practical skill by apprenticeship to an official for one or more years, though this preliminary training is a legal requirement in other states. Griesinger says several times that the qualified jurists fancy themselves far too superior to enter as clerks to an official.

A petition before the Estates Assembly from the town of Urach contains the complaint that the—disproportionately large—district of the senior official who formerly had his seat at Urach had been reduced in size; *inter alia* the pretty thought is expressed that previously the numerous subordinate offices had the advantage of providing to the qualified jurists, who were inexperienced in the business, a preliminary training—for what?—for the management of larger official districts! As if the difference were not simply one of the quantity of business; in quality the two posts were the same. The citizens belonging to the smaller official districts thus simply became the *animae viles* on which the inexperienced appointee was to be trained for office, and that because they belonged to a geographically smaller district. The legal practice which elsewhere the qualified jurists receive for their preliminary training under the supervision and guidance of an actual official here devolves on the writers alone. This makes clear the importance of the writers both in relation to an inexperienced appointee and also absolutely, because the qualified appointee to an office over 20,000 people or more, which comprises not only legal duties but also the police and branches of the administrative and judicial powers, has only writers as his assistants.

[3. *The Writers' Nuisance*]

But the dominating feature in the picture of the Institute or Nuisance (because 'Writers' Nuisance' appears in the speeches and petitions as a technical and recognized synonym [253] for 'Writers' Institute') is the monopoly allowed to the municipal and official writers. Further, to exercise their monopoly, they have ten (or twenty as need requires) subordinate writers, some of them kept at the centre to do their work, others sent out to villages and towns. (The details of their writing work must be read in the evidence in the *Proceedings*.)

Apart from work connected with marriages, the apportionment of taxes, the writing of tax-notices and tax receipt books, the assessment of every individual citizen's taxable property, the entry of charges resulting from the sale of houses and properties, &c., and the apportionment of communal expenditure for municipal and official damages,[1] there are two things in which the oppression and nuisance of the writers seem principally to consist.

First, they have to prepare the legal documents in matters where there is no dispute, contracts, marriage settlements, wills especially, dowry inventories (i.e. specifications of the property of a newly married couple), inventories of estates and bankruptcies, divisions of inheritances, and the like. Of the last of these we read: 'In almost all divisions of an inheritance there is not as much ready cash as the amount of the fees due to the writers; consequently the best piece of property is publicly sold in order to get ready money. Things are no better for the newly married: either the cost of the inventory consumes the money that in their position has been painfully saved, or they must begin by incurring debts or they must sell some property', &c. The consequence of such procedures is declared to be the general impoverishment of the lower classes. For example, a young bridegroom cannot himself draw up the inventory required by the existing laws or give it to whom he pleases to engross and have it legally entered. Only the monopolist writer can manage this, and it will be explained in a minute with what prolixity and at what fees he dispatches his work in general. In the petitions and other memorials there is unanimity in the complaints not only about the nature of the legal [254] dispositions themselves, which entail endless engrossing and untellable expenses, but also about the overcharging and the nuisance which multiplies twice and even tenfold what is legally allowed.

The second activity of the writers which is worth further remark is the preparation of the accounts of the mayor (i.e. of the municipality and its affairs), the poor box, the church, the charities, the

---

[1] In this terminology, the building of a new bridge, for example, or a town hall would be called a 'damage'. [H.]

hospital, the guardians, &c., in general the accounts of endowments for the church and the poor, while in addition they have the audit and revision of communal and trustee accounts. Something quite extraordinary comes in sight here, namely that the mayors and managers of municipal property, endowments for the poor, &c., do not themselves draw up the accounts of their financial administration or arrange privately for this to be done; they must arrange for the accounts to be manufactured in the writing factory of the official scribe. The expenses of this are charged to the municipality, and here indeed the name 'damages of office' under which these expenses go is appropriate enough.

As for these expenses which fall thus swollen on to the municipalities, frightful examples are quoted, e.g. the preparation of the accounts of a place in new Wurtemberg which earlier cost 1 guilder 30 crowns is now raised in cost to 50 guilders since the recent introduction of the old Wurtemberg method of writers' [monopoly]. A hamlet that earlier required no accounts because it had no revenues now has an account made for it with some ingenuity and the cost has mounted to 56 guilders 20 crowns. These and lots of other examples would be amusing to read if they did not amount to such infamous and unheard-of overcharging. One other case: the communal account books of Mögglingen were handed over by the town's writer to a series of writers, one after another, to be engrossed; to these writers together, who had not made one entry in the account, the commune had to pay 900 *fl.*— say 900 guilders—for reading the account books and examining them, one writer doing one part and another another. That was the cost of the account before a single line of it was written, and the man who at the end really drew the account had, of course, to be rightfully paid all over again for his labour, i.e. for doing the whole job.

[255] One of the most striking complaints amongst the national grievances collected by the Estates Assembly was the often considerable increase in the cost of administering communal property, endowments for the poor, &c. The Assembly ascribed the whole evil to the annulling of the old constitution. From the statements about the Writers' Institute it appears that these complaints arose especially in the recently acquired parts of the country, and the printed detailed municipal accounts show that it is precisely the introduction of this old-Wurtemberg nuisance which has caused an immense increase in administrative expenses. Plenty of examples

could be cited of unauthorized charges and the immense volume of the accounts, e.g. in the accounts of a communal poor endowment and other similar accounts, all of which have to be prepared in duplicate or triplicate, the schedule of craftsmen was inserted *in extenso*, again in duplicate or triplicate.

This practical method of impoverishing the citizens, whether legally or illegally, hangs together with the grim picture painted of the manners of this class [of writers], their ignorance, vulgarity, rudeness, arrogance, &c. 'This class has never at any time been respected in Wurtemberg. High respect was very rightly paid from time to time to individual members of this class, but this tacitly implied the general contempt of the class because excellent writers were always very scarce.' The dark colours of Griesinger's first chapter were not ground by the author himself; they were culled from writings on this Wurtemberg class by other authors old or recent, and their testimony is unanimous. Amongst them indeed are authors who themselves belonged to this class and must have known it best. Nothing harsher can be said of any class of men than what is contained in these sketches.

Yet a greater encroachment than all this is the fact that there must be paid to the principal writer (i.e. the town's writer or the office's writer) the same sum which his deputed writers earn or exact [256] for their work according to their own reckoning. This brings on the scene a new kind of circumstance. Not only has the principal the monopoly of writing in his own territory but, being supposed to be the inspector of the actions of his subordinates, he has to draw all over again, not for work of his own, but, as if he were the dynast, the very same sum acquired by his clerks for their labour, and this excessive exaction has led to grave complaint already. This payment to the official or municipal writer is over and above the seigniorial taxes imposed on such documents, and it goes into his private pocket. It is justly said [by Griesinger] that 'the [subordinate] writers are always money-makers for the official and municipal writers; the latter always gain by every illegal and excessive charge and by the prolixity of their subordinates—it is impossible to conceive anything worse than this arrangement'.

The conception of a dynastic or feudal relation in accordance with which the official or municipal writer raises funds from the citizens as if they were subjects, or writers' vassals as they might be called, appears fully developed in the following instance: a year ago a farmer who was heir to a dead brother, a Catholic priest, and who had a dispensation from producing an inventory and a division [of the inheritance], was charged 200 guilders by an official writer on the ground that owing to the dispensation he could not give an account of the share due to him. It is further specified that the heir actually paid the sum and the official writer pocketed it without giving a receipt; and it is *not* said that this extortion has had repayment and jail or some other punishment as its consequence. Obligations arising from the feudal relationship involve a right of the feudal overlord to ground and soil and a duty of his to protect his vassals. But from these conditions the revenues of the official and municipal writers are exempt. If the Wurtemberg citizens are really burdened with this subservience or vassalage to the writers, as is *de facto* the case, and the Estates cannot deny it, it would at least be more appropriate and juster to give the state the benefit of this subjection [257] and lease this monopoly in its name instead of letting these revenues fall, without being payments for work, into the hands of private persons, many of whom are thus as well off as a bishop in Austria or France.

It has been said above ([254]) that the mayors, like other municipal officials, administrators of endowments for the poor, &c., do not themselves prepare the accounts of their stewardship, because this task is allotted to the privileged writers. It is important *ab initio* [to notice] that these municipal officials and administrators of endowments are regarded as legally incompetent. But still more important than this, and even than the afore-mentioned growing expense which thus falls on municipalities and endowments, is the consequential dependence of all the municipal authorities on the municipal and official writer. Of this further encroachment on the organism of the state there is a description in a petition from Gmünd which exhibits in official documents the monstrosity of the writers' organization in its various branches. On the matter here in question it says: 'In connexion with communal accountings the writer gets hold of all the documents supporting the daybook, and the receipts of the so-called accountant, without giving a specific receipt for them. From that moment onwards the mayor is his slave; he has had his last peaceful sleep, because he is ceaselessly troubled by the thought that he has knowingly surrendered his credit, honour, and good name to an unknown stranger. Many a one now makes payments in advance forthwith and departs to another quarter [258] of the kingdom. If at last the business is begun by one of his successors, the accountant's period of misery starts; he has made improper payments, receipts are missing, a considerable deficit is evident; the accountant's future is a fortress or a penitentiary. If now, conscious of innocence, he is on the point of despair, things take a new turn after the appropriate means have been adopted: the receipts are found again, or made out, &c. The accountant in the presence of personages or documentary witnesses signs the account, which he finds totally unintelligible, and he understands as little as he did in connexion with the deficit charged against him earlier, that now at last he is to get a sum due to him.'

So in hands like these are the municipal authorities! In hands like these the people! When we hear talk of the *good* old law, well might we cry with the Prophet: 'O my people, they which lead thee betray thee.'[1] But however far we may be from taking as general this picture which has a personal reference, it none the less is certain that it is not from personalities but from institutions of the kind described that there issues the inevitable dependence of municipal authorities, of municipalities, and, taking into consideration the above-mentioned wider jurisdiction of the writers, even of individual citizens, on the municipal and official writers. The municipal authorities formerly had the sole choice of deputies to the Estates, and a majority of the members of the Estates Committee[2] were drawn from the class of writers. In Griesinger's memorial we read: 'The reform or the recasting of the Writers' Institute, despite the often-felt and indeed notorious imperfection of the Institute, must inevitably have found its greatest opponents in the representative members of the Estates, most of whom *were* writers or who at least *had been* influenced by writers, because their interest was in downright contradiction to the essential reform of the Institute.' There is nothing more to be said. But was this '*were*' and '*had been*', which looks like some past history of the Estates and its Committee long ago, not also a description and a history of this very Estates Assembly itself? Has this Assembly done anything at all to cleanse such an Augean stable? Had this abuse not raged in *its* vitals too? [259] Have the ever-repeated efforts of

---

[1] Isaiah iii. 12. Hegel quotes, as usual, from memory. A.V. and Luther say, instead of 'betray', 'cause thee to err' or 'mislead thee'.

[2] See above [192].

Herr von Forstner, who never let himself get tired by the Assembly's delays, been able to secure, after a year or more, even a reference to a committee, let alone a debate, still less a decision on the matter?

It is characteristic that the complaints and grievances have come almost entirely from new Wurtemberg, as if old Wurtemberg were so actively and passively involved in this state of affairs that it had on the one hand no consciousness of the situation or any sense of it except a resigned despair, and, on the other hand, simply a privileged conscience completely secure in the good, old, guaranteed law! It might have made its own contribution to the fact that the writers of old Wurtemberg, who had to be used above all in the new territory as men experienced in their profession, lived worse there, as in a conquered country, than at home. But these men of business[1] who had grown up, and been educated, accustomed to the old Wurtemberg law and the so highly praised old constitution, commended themselves ill to their new countrymen and equally ill did they commend to them this old law and this old constitution.

But the Ministry might be reproached for summoning an Estates Assembly, the composition of which it must have known, instead of advising the King to add at the head of the changes he had undertaken in the upper floors of the state such prior ones as would have enabled him to accomplish the regeneration of the unhappy situation of the mass of the people. So long as there existed this *bourgeois* aristocracy, peculiar to Wurtemberg, which, through writing, drew episcopal incomes as their revenues and exercised a general power over the municipalities, their officials, and their private citizens, so long as these officials and the communities themselves were not torn from the clutches of this privileged caste, so long as this element of moral and intellectual degradation which ensnared the minds and filched the purse of the masses had not been blotted out, no true concept of law, freedom, and constitution could take root, [260] and the Ministry could expect nothing but that a majority of the elected deputies would be drawn from this element.

It might be regarded as magnificent that the King was the first of the German princes to give to his people Estates so organized as to become defenders of the rights of the whole nation and not just of one class, with the result that the constitution of the Estates

---

[1] Reading *Geschäftsleute* with *Werke*, vol. xvi, p. 335.

would be lifted out of the popular indifference, hostility, even contempt, into which the earlier German Estates had fallen in the eyes of the public. Old Wurtemberg has had no significant nobility of its own, but what has been rooted in it is this less brilliant but more oppressive aristocracy [of the writers]. But so long as these chains [261] on the people were not burst, no genuine popular representation was possible. However indispensable the existence of an Estates Assembly is for the concept of a monarchical state, still it would be infinitely better to have none at all than to put up with the continued existence of these privileges, this oppression, deception, and suffocation of the people; better to have no Estate at all than Estates that represent the privileges of this aristocracy.

The Ministry could likewise discern the principles of the other aristocracy which was supposed to have only just been incorporated in Wurtemberg or, according to a section of it, was yet to be incorporated in it.[1] It must have been foreseen that this class would begin by reserving its own rights—rights which, thus unspecified, left undecided the position of this class in the state and which in their old range are incompatible with any and every political organization.

In most cases of great political upheaval prince and people have manifestly been of *one* mind and will; but equally obviously a class between the two, in France the nobility and clergy, in Wurtemberg the nobility and the *bourgeois* aristocracy of the writers, instead of being the link between the two, as it is meant to be, has all too often insisted on privileges and monopolies and hindered or even altogether frustrated the actualization of the principles of rational law and public welfare.

The general position occupied by the intermediate class, that of constituting the intelligence of a nation and directly administering its rights and its duties, makes it possible for this class, if against the nation it defends its own privileges, to deceive the nation into the idea that the nation is on the side of this its enemy. The result is the spectacle, as disgusting as it is tragic, of wrong, called right for a century, being recognized as right and reducing the nation to despair, of wrong being supported by the nation itself, deceived as it has been by the name given to wrong.

[1] See above [187–8].

[§ VII. THE CLOSE OF THE PROCEEDINGS] [262–80]

[In July 1815 the King proposed an adjournment so that his Ministers and officials could have time to examine the list of grievances advanced by the Estates. The Estates replied that this disturbed them because they were more concerned about the constitution than about the grievances. They regarded adjournment as productive of an incurable split between the King and the country.

In spite of this attitude of theirs, the King recalled the Estates in October. He explained that it would be purposeless to impose the old constitution on the additional territories which Wurtemberg had recently acquired. His constitution, which was subject to amendment, was devised for both new Wurtemberg and old, and it preserved everything useful in the old constitution.

The Estates replied as before. The King was to give solemn recognition to the old constitution as valid for the entire kingdom, subject only to such modifications as might be mutually agreed.

The Estates did appoint a committee to draft a constitution. Its work was completed by 17 September 1816. Parts of the draft were read out, but they had not even been discussed when the King died at the end of October. In the whole course of its long and expensive deliberations the Assembly failed not only to reach agreement with the King but also to come to any conclusion of its own about the content of the constitution it desired.]

IV

THE ENGLISH REFORM BILL

[283] THE prime object of the Reform Bill now [1831] lying before the English Parliament is to bring justice and fairness into the allotment of the parts played by the different classes and divisions of the people in the election of members of Parliament, and to do this by substituting a greater symmetry for the most bizarre and haphazard anomalies and inequalities which prevail at present. There are numbers, localities, private interests, which are to be ordered differently; nevertheless, it is on the nobility, the very heart and vital principle of the constitution and condition of Great Britain, that this alteration presses in fact. This is the aspect of the present Bill which deserves special notice. And the aim of this essay is to assemble here these higher aspects of the matter which have been discussed in the parliamentary debates up till now. The fact that in the House of Commons the Bill encountered opposition from so many members, and that the second reading was carried by the chance of one vote, cannot cause surprise, because it is just the powerful aristocratic interests in the Lower House that are to be attacked and reformed. If the Bill were opposed by all those who themselves or whose constituents are to lose their former prerogative and influence, there would at once be a most decided majority against the Bill. The promoters of the Bill could rely only on this, that now a sense of justice had mastered the obstinacy of privilege in those whose advantage lay in those prerogatives—a sense that acquired great strength from the anxious impression [284] produced on interested Members of Parliament by the neighbouring example of France. [Moreover] the almost universal opinion in England about the need of reform always tended to make itself felt as a motive of the first importance in Parliament. But even if public opinion in Great Britain were almost always for reform to the extent, or within the limits, proposed in the Bill, we would still have to be allowed to examine the substance of what this opinion desires, all the more so because in recent times we have not infrequently experienced that its demands have proved to be

impracticable, or, if practicable, pernicious, and that public opinion has now turned just as vigorously against what immediately before it had vigorously demanded and appeared to welcome. The ancients who had belonged to democracies from their youth onwards, and who had lived through a long series of experiences in them and applied their thoughtful reflection to these, had different views about popular opinion from those that are now current on more or less *a priori* grounds.

[285] [I. THE NECESSITY OF A REFORM OF THE FRANCHISE]

The proposed reform starts from the undisputed fact that the bases on which was determined the share held by the different counties and boroughs in England in parliamentary seats had been completely altered in the course of time, [and] that therefore the 'rights to this share' had become completely at variance with the principles of these bases and contradictory to everything that in this part of a constitution appears to the simplest common sense as obviously right and fair. One of the most important opponents of the Bill, Robert Peel, grants[1] that it may seem easy to expatiate on the anomalies and absurdity of the English constitution; and its follies are expounded at length in all their details in the parliamentary debates and in the newspapers. Therefore it may suffice here to recall the chief points, namely that the right of electing to seats in Parliament has been retained by thinly populated towns or even by their councillors (who co-opt their colleagues) alone without their fellow citizens, and thus by places reduced to only two or three residents (and leaseholders at that), while many cities that have prospered and flourished in recent years and have 100,000 inhabitants or more have no right of election; and between these extremes there is still the greatest variety of other inequalities. The first result is that the election to a large number of parliamentary seats is in the hands of a small number of individuals. It is calculated that a majority of the House is at the disposal of 150 peers. Secondly, a still more significant number of seats is purchasable—some of them [286] a recognized marketable commodity so that the possession of one of these seats is acquired by bribery or the formal payment of a specific sum to the electors or in general is reduced in numerous other ways to a matter of cash.

---

[1] The reference is probably to Peel's speech of 3 March 1831 (*Speeches*, vol. ii, p. 280).

It will be difficult to point anywhere to a similar symptom of a people's political corruption. Montesquieu[1] pronounced *virtue*, the unselfish sense of duty to the state, to be the principle of the democratic constitution. In the English constitution the democratic element has an important sphere in the people's participation in the election of members of the Lower House, of the politicians who have the most decisive role in settling public affairs. Of course it is the almost unanimous view of the pragmatic historians[2] that if in any nation private interest and a dirty monetary advantage becomes the preponderating ingredient in the election of Ministers of state, then the situation is to be regarded as the forerunner of the inevitable loss of that nation's political freedom, the ruin of its constitution and even of the state. To counter the Englishman's pride in his freedom, we Germans may well cite the fact that even if the old constitution of the German Empire had likewise become a formless aggregate[3] of particular rights, it was only the external bond of the German states, and political life within these, so far as concerned elections to their Diets[4] and the corresponding franchise, was free from the absurdity of the English system, and no less free from the [political] corruption that permeates every class of the English people. Now even if alongside the democratic element in England the aristocratic is an extremely important power; even if purely aristocratic governments like Venice, Genoa, Berne, &c., are reproached with finding their security and strength by submerging their subjects in universal sensuality and moral corruption; and even if it be reckoned as freedom to cast one's vote entirely on caprice, which motive is supposed to determine the will; [287] still it must be recognized as a good sign of the reawakening of a moral temper in the English people that one of the feelings which the need of a reform brings with it is an antipathy to the [political] depravity [to which I have referred]. Equally, however, we can see that the right way to pursue improvement is not by the moral route of using ideas, admonitions, associations of isolated individuals, in order to counteract the system of corruption and avoid being indebted to it, but by the alteration of institutions. The common prejudice of

---

[1] *Esprit des Lois*, vol. iii, p. 3, and Hegel, *Ph.d.R.*, § 273.
[2] See Hegel, *Ph.d.R.*, § 3, and note 15 thereto in Eng. tr. (Oxford, 1942).
[3] See above, *The German Constitution*, e.g. [9–10].
[4] Reading *Landständen* with Boumann.

inertia, namely to cling always to the old faith in the excellence of an institution, even if the present state of affairs derived from it is altogether corrupt, has thus at last caved in. A more thorough-going reform is all the more required in that, at the opening of every new Parliament, the opportunity presented by bribery peti-tions has given rise to proposals for improving [the system], but they have remained without any significant success. For example, the recent and most proper proposal to take away the franchise from one place where bribery has been proved and to transfer it to the city of Birmingham, and thereby to display an equitable inclination to redress the most striking inequality with extreme moderation, was manœuvred off the field by the parliamentary tactics of Ministers, especially of Peel, the Minister otherwise praised for his liberal views.[1] A great step forward at the opening session of the present Parliament has thus been reduced to for-bidding candidates to distribute any more badges to electors favourably disposed to them. Since the great majority of members of both Houses, who are the judges in bribery cases,[2] are involved in the system of corruption, while the majority of members of the Lower House owe their seats to this system, charges of bribery against an enfranchised place, and their investigation and trial, have been exposed as downright farces and even as shameless procedures, too publicly and too loudly for anything to be expected along that route now except redress in isolated instances.

[288] The other usual ground taken in Parliament against attacks on positive rights is the [appeal to the] wisdom of our ancestors, but this appeal cannot be upheld in this matter. This wisdom is to be ascribed to the distribution of the parliamentary franchise according to the *then* existing population of counties, cities, and boroughs, or according to their importance in other respects; and there is far too sharp a contrast between that and what has come to be the modern population, wealth, and importance of districts and interests. Another point not broached in discussion is the loss of capital which so many individuals [would] suffer and the loss of income of a still greater number; the monetary gain derived from direct bribery is illegal, though all classes are interested in it either

---

[1] This is not quite fair to Peel. This involved matter, i.e. proposals to transfer Penryn to Manchester and East Retford to Birmingham, is discussed in N. Gash, *Mr. Secretary Peel* (London, 1961), pp. 470–1 *et al.*

[2] Hegel is wrong here. The House of Lords had no jurisdiction in electoral cases, which were tried solely by a committee of the Commons.

as bribers or bribed. The capital value lost to the boroughs which are to be deprived of their franchise is based on the fact that, in the course of time, a political right has been transformed into a pecuniary asset. Although the acquisition [of a seat], at a price which is now getting lower, has happened just as bona fide as the purchase of slaves, and although under new laws what the English Parliament considers carefully in such a case is the maintenance of real property, and, in the event of a loss occurring, compensation accordingly, no claims of this sort have been made in the present discussions, nor has any difficulty been raised on this score.[1] But this circumstance may be an effective motive against the Bill for a number of Members of Parliament.

On the other hand another legal principle especially characteristic of England is indeed attacked by the Bill. This is the character of 'positivity' which preponderates in the institutions of English law, public and private alike. It is true that every right and its corresponding law is in *form* something positive, ordained, and instituted by the supreme power in the state, something to which obedience must be given just because it is a statute. But at no time more than the present has the general intelligence been led to distinguish between whether rights are purely positive in their material *content* or whether they are also *inherently* right and rational. In no constitution is judgement so strongly induced [289] to attend to this distinction as in the English, now that the continental nations have allowed themselves to be imposed on for so long by declamations about English freedom and by England's pride in her system of law. It is well known that the latter rests entirely on particular rights, freedoms, privileges conferred, sold, presented by or extorted from kings and Parliament on special occasions. Magna Charta and the Bill of Rights, which concern the most important foundations of the English constitution and which have received further definition in subsequent parliamentary legislation, are concessions wrung [from the Crown] by force, or else acts of grace, agreements, &c., and constitutional rights have stuck by the form of private rights, which they had at their origin, and therefore by the accident of their content. This inherently

[1] While English legislation normally provided for compensation when it encroached on private property, the Reform Bill did not propose any compensation to the owners or other interested parties in boroughs selected for disfranchisement. Hence parliamentary representation was in fact not regarded in England as a species of private property.

disconnected aggregate of positive provisions has not yet undergone the development and recasting which has been carried out
in the civilized states of the Continent, and which the German
provinces, for example, have enjoyed for a longer or shorter
period.

Hitherto England has lacked the features which constitute the
major part of these glorious and fortunate advances. Amongst these
features the chief is the scientific remodelling of law, whereby, on
the one hand, general principles have been applied to and carried
through the particular specifications [of law] and their complexities,
while on the other hand concrete and special cases have been
reduced to simpler provisions. This remodelling has made it possible for the newer continental states to produce statute books and
political institutions framed preponderantly on general principles,
a process in which, so far as concerns the contents of justice,
common sense and sound reasoning have been allowed their proper
share. Next, a still more important feature in the transformation
of law must be mentioned—the deep insight of princes in making
the guiding stars of their legislative activity, with which the
monarch's due power is linked, such principles as the state's well-
being, the happiness of their subjects, and the general welfare, as
well as and above all the sense of an absolute justice, and in doing
this with a view to making way for these principles and giving
them reality in face of merely positive privileges, traditional private
interest, and the stupidity of the masses. [290] The reason why
England is so remarkably far behind the other civilized states of
Europe in institutions derived from true rights is simply that there
the governing power lies in the hands of those possessed of so
many privileges which contradict a rational constitutional law and
true legislation.

This is the situation on which the projected reform is meant to
have an important effect. Not, however, that it has been intended
to produce this effect by enlarging the power of the monarchical
element in the constitution; on the contrary, if the Bill is not to
meet with universal disapproval immediately, jealousy of the power
of the throne, that most stubborn of English prejudices, must
remain untouched, and the proposed measure owes part of its
popularity instead to the fact that by it the Crown's influence is
seen to be further weakened. What rouses the greatest interest is the
fear in some quarters, the hope in others, that the reform of the

franchise will bring in its train other reforms of substance. The English principle of 'positivity' on which, as I have said, the whole of English law rests, does through the Bill actually suffer a shock which in England is entirely new and unheard of, and one instinctively suspects that more far-reaching changes will issue from this subversion of the formal basis of the existing order.

[2. INSTANCES OF ABUSES TO BE REMOVED]

Some expressions of these points of view have occurred in the course of parliamentary debates, though rather cursorily. The promoters and friends of the Bill may really believe that it will not lead on to anything beyond the point it reaches itself or, in order not to irritate the opposition more seriously, they may not let their hopes become more vocal, just as the opposition too may not represent their real concern as a prize of victory; because they own much, they have, of course, much to lose. But the fact that no more is said in Parliament about this more materialistic aspect of reform [291] is due in great part to the convention that, when important matters are before this assembly, the bulk of the time is taken up by members' explanations of their personal position; they give their opinions not as business men but as privileged persons and as orators. In England a broad field for reform is open, comprising the most important aims of civil and political society. The necessity for reform begins to be felt. Something of what has been indicated [above] on this subject may serve as an example of the amount of work which is over and done with elsewhere and which still waits to be done in England.

Amongst the expectations of material improvements there is above all the hope for economies in administration. But however often this theme is started by the opposition as something absolutely necessary for easing the pressure [of taxation] and the general misery of the people, every time the statement is repeated that all efforts to this end have hitherto gone for nothing, and that the hope held out to the people by Ministers, and even in the speech from the throne, has every time been deceived. These declamations have been repeated in similar words every time taxes have been reduced in the last fifteen years. For finally fulfilling the people's hopes better prospects are held out in a reformed Parliament, i.e. in the greater independence of a greater number of members on the Ministry, whose weakness and whose hard-heartedness to the people and its interests, &c., has been blamed for a continuing extravagant expenditure. But if we bring under consideration the chief heads of public expenditure in England, it appears that there is no great room for economy: first, interest payments on the enormous national debt cannot be reduced; secondly, the cost of the army and navy, pensions included, is most closely connected not only with the political situation, and especially with the interest of trade, the basis of England's existence, and the danger of internal revolts, but also with the habits of military and naval men and their demand not to fall behind other classes in good living and luxury; and thus in this field there can be no cuts without risk. The calculations made public as a result of the outcry against the so notorious sinecures [292] have shown that even their total abolition, not to be effected without great injustice, would be nothing to speak of. But there is no need to expatiate on these material matters but only to notice that the indefatigable pains that Hume[1] took to examine the finances down to the last detail have gone all along without result. This cannot be ascribed solely to the corruption of the parliamentary aristocracy and the Ministry's obsequiousness to it, needing its help as it did—that aristocracy which procures for itself and its relatives all sorts of gains through sinecures, and, in general, through lucrative posts in the administration, the army, the Church, and the court. The relatively very small number of votes which proposals for reducing expenditure usually gain points to a slender hope in the possibility of, or to a faint interest in, such lightening of the so-called general pressure [of taxation] against which Members of Parliament are of course protected by their wealth. That fraction of them which counts as independent tends to be on the side of the Ministry, and this independence sometimes shows itself inclined to go farther than would have been expected from its usual attitude and the reproaches of the opposition. This happens on occasions when the Ministry expressly displays a special interest in a financial grant. For example, some years ago an extra salary of £1,000 proposed by the Ministry with great vigour for Huskisson,[2] who was so highly

---

[1] Joseph Hume (1777–1855), who took 'the sense of the House for a saving of eighteenpence' and added 'retrenchment' to his radical party's watchword.

[2] When he became President of the Board of Trade in 1823 he resigned his agency for the Cape, a salaried office of £1,200 per annum.

regarded and who gave up a lucrative post because of his official business at the Board of Trade, was voted down by a large majority. So also the same thing has frequently happened with proposals for increasing the establishment of the royal princes which, for England, is not extravagantly assessed. In these cases affecting a personality and a sense of dignity, passion has overcome the luke-warmness usually evinced by Parliament for economies.

This much at least is clear, that no Reform Bill can directly annul the causes of high taxation in England. The example of England and France might in fact lead to the induction that countries in which the administration of the state depends on the assent of assemblies [293] chosen by the people are those most heavily burdened by taxes.[1] In France, where the aim of the English Reform Bill—extending the franchise to a more considerable num-ber of citizens—has to a large extent been achieved, the budget has been compared, in French newspapers, with a hopeful child who is to make significant progress daily. In order to hit upon radical measures for diminishing the oppressive character of the English political administration, it would have been necessary to trespass too deeply on the inner constitution of particular rights. No power is available, having regard to the enormous wealth of private in-dividuals, to make serious arrangements for diminishing the pro-digious national debt substantially. The exorbitant cost of the chaotic administration of justice (which makes the road to court open to the rich alone), the poor-rate which a ministry could not introduce in Ireland where need and justice alike demanded it, the utilization of ecclesiastical revenues (to be further mentioned below), and many other great branches of society, presuppose, for the making of any change, other changes in the power of the state than those stipulated in the Reform Bill.

Occasionally reference has been made in Parliament to the aboli-tion of *ecclesiastical tithes, manorial rights, and the game laws* which has come about in France. All this, it is said, would come about under the auspices of a patriotic king and a reformed Parliament. And the drift of the argument seems to characterize the cancellation of rights of that kind as a lamentable overthrow of the whole constitution, quite apart from the fact that it had had appalling anarchy as its conse-quence in France. We all know that in other states rights of this kind have vanished without any such consequences; not only so, but

[1] Cf. *Ph.d.R.*, *Zusatz* to § 302.

their abolition is regarded as an important basis of increased welfare and essential freedom. Therefore something more may be adduced here about them.

First, as to *tithes*, the oppressive character of this tax has been obvious in England for long past. A special hatred is generally directed against a tax of this kind, but in England [294] this hatred cannot astonish anyone, since in many districts there the clergyman has collected for him every day every tenth jug of milk from the cowherds, a tenth of the day's eggs, &c. Moreover, this tax has been cavilled at on the score of unfairness, because the more the produce of the ground is increased by industry, time, and expenditure, the higher the tax rises, with the result that the improvement of agriculture, in which large capital resources have been sunk in England, is burdened with a tax instead of being encouraged. The tithe belongs to the Church of England; in other countries, Protestant ones especially, either recently or long ago (in Prussian territory more than a century ago) tithes have been abolished, or made redeemable, unostentatiously and unobtrusively without either spoliation or injustice. The ecclesiastical revenues have been deprived of their oppressive character and they have been raised in a more appropriate and becoming manner.

But, in England, the nature of the original justification of tithe is essentially fading away, or is turned upside down for other reasons. The application of tithe for the maintenance of religious doctrine and the upbuilding and support of the Church has mostly been transformed into a sort of private property revenue. The clergyman's office has the character of a living and the duties of it have changed into rights to an income. Apart from the fact that a number of lucrative benefices, [such as] canonries, entail no official duties at all, it is only too well known how common it is for the English clergy to occupy themselves with anything but the functions of their office, with hunting, &c., and idleness of other kinds, to dissipate the rich revenues of their places in foreign travel, and to hand over their official duties to a poor curate for a pittance that hardly saves him from dying of hunger. A comprehensive idea of the connexion between holding a benefice and drawing its revenues on the one hand and the moral conduct and the fulfilment of official duties on the other is afforded by an example that was the subject of court proceedings a few years ago. A motion came before the court against a clergyman named

Frank,[1] to the effect that, on account of insanity, [295] he was incapable of managing his property and that it should be put in ward. He had a living of £800 per annum, and other benefices of about £600. But the judicial complaint was brought before the court by his son, as having now reached his majority, in the interests of the family. As a result of many days' [proceedings] and a mass of testimony, the publicly proved demonstration of the alleged lunacy brought to light actions of this clergyman of which, wholly undisturbed by a spiritual authority, he had acknowledged his guilt in the course of years; for example, he was once drawn in broad daylight through the streets and over the bridge of his town with a strumpet from a house of ill fame on each arm and pursued by a lot of sneering street-arabs. Still more scandalous were the stories, likewise confirmed by witnesses, of his relations with his own wife and a lover of hers who lived in the same house. This shamelessness in a clergyman of the English Church was no detriment to his possession of his office or to his enjoyment of the income of his benefices. Examples of this kind bring the Church into contempt, especially because, despite the establishment of an episcopal hierarchy, the Church does not itself check corruption of this kind and the scandal it entails. This contempt, like the greed of other clergy in the collection of their tithes, makes its own contribution towards diminishing the respect demanded of the English people for the Church's property rights. Such property, being destined for religious purposes, has a totally different character from that of private property which can be disposed of at will; this difference is the basis of a different [kind of] right, and the enjoyment of these goods is tied up with duties as conditions of their possession; and in Protestant states it is religious purposes which fundamentally justify the state in taking steps for the fulfilment of these purposes and the duties connected with the revenues; considerations of this kind seem to be altogether foreign and unknown to English heads [296]. But in this matter, to stick to the abstract outlook of private rights is far too much to the advantage of the class with the preponderating influence in Parliament. Therefore this class hangs together with the Ministry, which has the chief and most lucrative benefices in its gift, and has an interest in providing with livings of this sort younger sons or brothers who

---

[1] This case does not appear in *The Annual Register*. But for another clerical scandal not wholly dissimilar, see N. Gash, op. cit., p. 375.

are left without capital because landed property in England generally goes to the eldest son. This same class is to retain and even increase its place in Parliament under the Reform Bill. Therefore it is very doubtful if it has anything to fear for its interest so far as the wealth of the Church and its patronage are concerned.

Fears of a reform of such a state of affairs in the English Church have every reason to extend especially to its establishment in Ireland, which has been so heavily attacked for many years, principally in the cause of furthering Catholic emancipation—in itself only a political matter. It is well known that the majority of the Irish population adheres to the Catholic Church. The property that once belonged to it, the churches themselves, tithes, the obligation of parishioners to keep the church buildings in good repair and to provide furnishings for worship and wages for sextons, &c., all this has been taken away from it by right of conquest and made the property of the Anglican Church. In Germany, for more than 150 years as a result of the Thirty Years War, and in recent times as a result of the advance of reason, every dominion, province, city, or village has retained the property belonging to the church of its inhabitants. The religion of prince and government has not absorbed in its area the ecclesiastical properties belonging to another denomination. Even the Turks have generally left alone the churches of their Christian, Armenian, and Jewish subjects; even where these subjects have been forbidden to repair their churches when dilapidated, they were still allowed leave to buy permission to do so. But the English have taken all the churches away from their conquered Catholic population [297]. The Irish, whose poverty and misery and consequential degradation and demoralization is a standing theme in Parliament, acknowledged by every Ministry, are compelled, out of the few pence they may have, to pay their own priest and construct a place for their services. On the other hand, they have to pay a tenth of all their produce to Anglican clergymen, in whose large incumbencies, comprising two or three or six or more parishes, there are often only very few Protestants, and sometimes the sexton is the only one. They are even forced to pay for the upkeep of the churches that are now Anglican and for providing plate, &c., for the services. The foes of emancipation have urged, as a bugbear, that the reform of such crying injustice would be the probable consequence of emancipation. Its friends, however, and their followers, have on the contrary contented themselves at bottom with the thought that, with emancipation, the demands of the Catholics will be satisfied and the establishment of the English Church in Ireland will be all the more secure. This situation, unprecedented in a civilized and Protestant nation, and its legal title, are supported by self-interest and up to now have held out against what must be presumed to be the religious temper of the Anglican clergy and against the rationality of the English people and its Members of Parliament. True, the Reform Bill does assign a few more seats in the Commons to the Irish, and the Catholics may occupy them. But this might be more than counterbalanced by the provision in the same Bill for increasing the number of members drawn from that class whose interest is linked with the present position of the Anglican Church in Ireland.

There is likewise an apprehension that the reform will in due course extend to *manorial rights*. For long past these rights have not merely brought the agricultural class into subjection; they press as heavily on the bulk of that class as villeinage did, indeed they bring it down to an indigence worse than a villein's. In England itself, though incapacitated for the possession [298] of property in land and reduced to the status of tenants or day labourers, this class does find work to some extent in times of prosperity, England being generally opulent and possessed, in particular, of prodigious manufactures; but what really keeps it from the consequences of extreme indigence is the poor law which imposes on every parish the obligation of looking after its poor. In Ireland, on the other hand, this protection is not available to the class which lives on agriculture and is generally propertyless. The descriptions of travellers, as well as documented parliamentary reports, picture the general condition of the Irish peasants as so miserable that it is not easy to find a parallel example in small and poor districts of continental countries, even in those of them that are backward in civilization. The propertylessness of the agricultural class has its origin in the circumstances and the legislation of the old feudal system, which, in the form in which it still exists in many states, does at least assure to the peasant a subsistence from the soil that he cultivates and to which he is bound. But while the Irish villeins do possess personal freedom, the lords of the manor have got property into their own hands so completely that they have cut themselves free from any obligation to look after the subsistence of the people who till their soil for them. This is the justification of the fact that, if landowners find more profitable a mode of cultivation which needs fewer labourers, then those who cultivated the ground hitherto and who were tied to it for their subsistence, just as villeins were, and whose families had lived there in huts for centuries, cultivating the soil, are driven in hundreds, even thousands, from the huts which they lived in but did not own. Those who already own nothing are deprived of their birthplace and their hereditary means of livelihood—in the name of justice. And this too is justice, that the landowners have the huts burnt so as to make sure of getting the peasants off the ground and cut off their chance of delaying their departure or creeping in under shelter again.

These cankers in Ireland[1] are laid before Parliament year in year out. How many speeches are made on them! How many committees have sat! How many witnesses have been examined! [299] How many sound reports have been drawn up! How many remedies have been proposed which appear either unsatisfactory or impracticable! The proposed withdrawal of the surplus poor by colonization would have had to take away at least a million inhabitants if it was to be likely to have any effect. How could this be achieved? For another thing, the empty space thus produced would very quickly be filled in the same way as before if laws and circumstances remained otherwise the same. An Act of Parliament (the Sub-letting Act)[2] which was meant to restrict division into small tenancies, the method of accommodating a fertile class of beggars in Ireland, and their breeding-ground, was shown to be so little adapted to remedy the evil that it had to be repealed recently after a few experimental years. The moment of transition from feudal tenure to property has slipped by without giving the farmer class the chance to own land; a chance of achieving this might have been afforded by altering rights of inheritance, introducing an equal distribution of patrimony between the children, allowing distraint and the sale of property for the payment of debts, and in general altering that legal character of property in land which carries with it who can say what formalities and costs in connexion with

---

[1] Hegel writes 'England'.

[2] 7 Geo. IV, xxix (1826). On 18 March 1831 Melbourne introduced in the House of Lords a Bill to repeal this Act, but the object was to frame new legislation to secure more effectually the object of the earlier Act.

alienation, &c. But English legislation about property in these and other respects has got too far away from the freedom enjoyed in this matter by continental countries; every private relationship is caught too deeply in these fetters. Moreover, to alter the law in order to open for the class that works the land the possibility of acquiring property in land would only be in the highest degree insignificant in relation to the whole situation. The power of the Crown is too weak to see to this transition. Moreover, under the Reform Bill, parliamentary legislation remains in the hands of that class which has its interest, and still more its fixed habits, in the hitherto existing law of property. Hitherto its aim has always been to remedy the results of the system, when need and misery became too crying, by direct action and so by palliatives (like the Sub-letting Act) or by pious aspirations (that the Irish land-owners should take up residence in Ireland, &c.).

[300] The *Game Laws*, again, are mentioned as a matter that might be open to reform. To touch it is to cut to the heart numerous English Members of Parliament and their connexions, but the nuisance and the mischief have become too great for the urging of a change in these laws not to have become inevitable. Universal attention has been drawn in particular to the increase in the number of gamekeepers assaulted and murdered by poachers, to the increasing loss of game suffered by landed proprietors on their estates, especially to the increase in the crimes of poaching coming before the courts, though they are only a small proportion of those actually committed, and furthermore to the disproportionately harsh punishments prescribed by law and actually inflicted for the infringement of game laws, because it is just the aristocrats, who possess these rights, who made the laws and who then sit in court in their capacity as magistrates and jurymen. The interest of the hunting fraternity is likewise engrossed by the great extension of hunting rights in open country. A squire's son has hunting rights and every parson counts as a squire, so that the son may have this privilege which his father, unless himself a squire's son, does not possess, &c. For many years past a Bill has been introduced annually into Parliament for amending these laws, but no such Bill has yet had the luck to be passed in face of the privileged interest of sportsmen.[1] A Bill of this kind is before the

---

[1] By the existing game laws only those persons were permitted to take or sell game who were duly qualified. The ordinary qualification was ownership of

present Parliament. It must be regarded as very much of a problem
to assess the amount of influence the projected Reform Bill would
inevitably have on the legislation about hunting rights, on the
reduction of punishments, on the restriction of personal hunting
rights, and especially, in the interest of the agricultural class, on
the right of hunting stags, hares, foxes with a string of hounds and
twenty, thirty, or more riders and with still more on foot through
sown fields and all cultivated unenclosed land. In many German
provinces a standing article in the grievances of the Estates long
ago was the damage caused by game, the havoc caused in fields by
hunting, and the consumption of crops and fruit by game [301].
Up till now English freedom has put no restriction on these rights
which princes in Germany have long ago renounced in the interest
of their subjects.

The extensive jumble of English private law, which even Englishmen master their pride in their freedom sufficiently to call an
Augean stable, might well afford grounds for hoping for some
tidying up. The little that Robert Peel carried through a few years
ago is regarded as most valuable and has won universal praise.[1]
More comprehensive proposals for the reform of justice, advanced
later by the present Lord Chancellor, Brougham, in a seven-hour
speech, and heard with great acceptance,[2] did give rise to the
appointment of committees but so far have remained without
further result. What has been achieved in Germany for more than
a century by the imperceptible work of scientific education, the
wisdom of princes and their love of justice, the English nation has
not acquired from its popular representation; and in the new Bill
there are just not contained those special features which would
provide a preponderance to profound insight and true knowledge
over the crass igorance of fox-hunters and landed gentry, over an
education acquired simply in social gatherings or through newspapers and parliamentary debates, or over the adroitness of lawyers,
which is generally acquired solely through routine. The qualifications required in Germany, even from the well born and from
wealthy landowners if they are to take part in public administration

---

lands of £100 yearly value: but others could be qualified, such as the sons of
esquires or persons of higher degree. A parson with a life interest in his living
worth £150 per annum would be qualified. These restrictions were removed by
1 and 2 William IV, c. 32.

[1] See N. Gash, *Mr. Secretary Peel*, Chapters 9 and 14.

[2] 1828 in H. of C. See F. Hawes, *Henry Brougham* (London, 1957), p. 201.

or politics either in general or in special spheres, namely theoretical study, scientific education, practice and experience in
affairs—are to be found as little in the new Bill as in the organization existing hitherto, as qualifications of members of an assembly
in whose hands lies the most extensive power of government and
administration. Nowhere more than in England is the prejudice so
fixed and so naïve that if birth and wealth give a man office they
also give him brains.[1] [302] Even the new Bill contains no condition of this kind: it sanctions the principle that a free income of
£10 drawn from property in land is a full qualification for the task
of judging and deciding on a man's capacity for the business of
government and financial administration which lies with Parliament. The idea of a board of examiners drawn from intelligent
men, experienced in the duties of office, instead of a mass of
individuals qualified only by the £10 income, like the idea of
demanding proofs of capacity from candidates for the legislature
and political administration, is of course an idea far too far away
from the idea of the unconditional sovereignty of those entitled to
decisions on this matter.

Those material changes demanded by rational law which have
been touched upon above, and others as well, have been secured
already in many civilized continental states, especially in the German countries, but the need for them seems almost to have gone
to sleep in England. Thus the necessity of reform has not been
shown up as a result of experiencing the little or nothing done by
Parliament in this matter during the persistence of the sort of rights
to the patronage of parliamentary seats that has existed hitherto;
England is in agreement with what the Duke of Wellington said
recently in the House of Lords, that 'from the year 1688' (the year
of the Revolution which drove from the throne the House of
Stuart with its Catholic mentality) 'until now the country's affairs
have been conducted in the best and most glorious way through
the union of the wealth, talents, and innumerable skills which have
represented the great interests of the kingdom'.[2] National pride in
any case keeps the English back from studying and understanding
the progress made by other nations in the development of their
legal institutions. The pomp and display of the formal freedom to

[1] Cf. *Ph.d.R.*, Preface, Eng. tr., p. 8.
[2] *Duke of Wellington's Speeches in Parliament*, vol. i, p. 410 (28 March 1831).
Hegel apparently quotes from a newspaper report which is textually different.

discuss public business in Parliament, and in other assemblies of all classes and groups, and to settle these matters in Parliament, as well as the title to do so without any qualifications, inhibits in England [303] or at least does not encourage quiet reflection on and penetration into the essence of legislation and government. Few European nations are dominated by such dexterity of reasoning in terms of their prejudices and by such shallowness of principle. Fame and wealth [in England] make it superfluous to go back to the foundations of existing rights, a process to which external need, and the need of reason thereby aroused, has driven peoples who have felt existing rights oppressive.

[3. OUTLOOK FOR PARLIAMENTARY REFORM]

We return to the less material points more immediately connected with the present Reform Bill. One point of great importance, also stressed by the opponents of the Bill, is that in Parliament the various great interests of the nation ought to be represented and [the question is] what alteration this representation would now suffer as a result of this Bill.

Views on this matter seem to differ. The Duke of Wellington says[1] that, under the Bill in question, the greater part of the electors would consist of shopkeeprs, and that thus the interests of trade would seem to gain advantage; but there is a general view, on which great stress in laid in the Bill's favour, that landowners and the agricultural interest will not only lose nothing of their influence, but will more likely gain a relative increase, because the proposal in relation to the electoral rights that are to be cancelled[2] is to give to the big cities or to the trading interest only twenty-five members, while the other eighty-one are to go to counties or the landed interest together with the smaller burghs, where into the bargain the influence of the landed proprietor usually prevails. In this matter it is especially remarkable that a number of commercial people, namely the leading bankers in London who are connected with the East India Company and the Bank of England, have declared themselves against the Bill [304]. Their reason is that, while this measure aims at establishing the representation of the kingdom on the great foundation of property and at extending this foundation, it would close the chief avenues whereby the moneyed,

[1] *Duke of Wellington's Speeches in Parliament*, vol. i, p. 411.
[2] 'Transferred' would be more accurate than 'cancelled'.

trading, shipping, and colonial interests have been represented in Parliament along with all other interests throughout the country and in all its foreign possessions down to the remotest corner.

These avenues are the places and small boroughs where a seat in Parliament is directly available for purchase. Consequently it was hitherto possible by the route of ordinary trade to arrange with certainty that bank directors, like directors of the East India Company, had seats in Parliament, just as the great plantation owners in the West Indies and other business men, who dominate equally great branches of trade, likewise confidently expected seats too, so that attention would be paid to their interests and those of their associates, which in any case are of course so important for the national interest in England. From the last Parliament the Bank Director Manning, who had sat there for many years, was expelled on the ground that his opponent had proved that he had used bribery in his election.[1] That the different great interests of the realm should be represented in its great deliberative assembly is a characteristic point of view in England, and in its own way it has been a fundamental article in the constitution of the older Imperial and local Estates in all the European monarchies, just as, for example in the Swedish constitution, it is still the basis of membership of the Diet. This is opposed to the modern principle in accordance with which only the abstract will of individuals as such is to be represented. It is true that in England it is the subjective whim of noblemen and others with electoral privileges that constitutes the basis of nomination to seats, and therefore the representation of interests is left to chance. But still this subjective whim counts with such importance and so momentously that the most eminent bankers are not ashamed to embark on the corruption involved in the sale of parliamentary seats and to complain in a public declaration to Parliament that these great interests would [305] find closed to them by the Bill this route for their representation in Parliament, this route which, being via bribery, was not exposed to accident. Moral considerations weaken such an important point of view, but it is a defect in a constitution to leave to chance what is necessary and to compel people to attain

---

[1] There is some confusion here. W. Manning was elected M.P. for Penryn (a rotten borough) in 1826. A petition was brought against his return. The House of Commons found that there had been bribery but that he was not concerned in it. He was the father of Cardinal Manning.

the necessary end by way of the corruption which morality condemns. The interests divided organically into classes, as they are in the cited example of Sweden into the classes of the nobility, the clergy, the *bourgeois*, and the peasants, no longer correspond completely with the situation in most states since the time when, as in England, the other interests mentioned above have become powerful. This discrepancy would nevertheless be easy to set aside if the earlier basis of inner constitutional law were understood once more, i.e. if the real basic constituents of the life of the state, granted that they be really distinct, and granted that substantial consideration must be given by government and administration to their distinctive worth, were to be consciously and expressly brought to the fore, recognized, and, when they were to be discussed or when decisions were to be taken about them, allowed to speak for themselves without this being left to chance. Napoleon, in a constitution which he gave to the kingdom of Italy, divided the right of representation in the sense of this outlook between *Possidenti*, *Dotti*, and *Merchanti*.

In the earlier parliamentary debates on proposals for very incomplete reforms, a principal reason raised against them, and adduced now too, was that all great interests were represented in hitherto existing [arrangements for] parliamentary seats, and that affairs, not individuals as such, should have an opportunity to express themselves and make themselves prevail. This argument is not pursued in further detail, but there seems to enter into it a point which the Duke of Wellington earnestly pressed on the Lords in his last speech, as a point overlooked alike there and in the Commons, namely that what they had to create was a legislative assembly, not a corporation of the enfranchised, a House of Commons and not a new system for its constituents.[1] If it were not a matter of the right to enfranchisement and therefore of [306] who were to be the constituents, but of the result, the creation of a legislative assembly and a Lower House, it might of course be said that such a House was constituted already in accordance with the hitherto existing law on representation. Indeed in the course of his speech the Duke cites the evidence of a friend[2] of the Reform Bill to the effect that the present House of Commons is so formed that no better could be elected. And in fact there lies in the Reform Bill itself no further guarantee that a House elected in accordance

---

[1] *Duke of Wellington's Speeches in Parliament*, vol. i, p. 406.
[2] Lord Lansdowne, ibid., p. 407.

with its provisions and in transgression of the previously existing positive rights would be any more excellent.

These rights the Duke put in his speech on the same footing as the right on the strength of which he could as little lose his seat in the Upper House as the Prime Minister, Earl Grey, could be deprived of his properties in Yorkshire.[1] In any case the Bill contains the new principle that the privileged franchise is no longer placed in the same category with strict property rights. From this point of view we must recognize as correct that charge made by opponents of the Bill, namely that precisely in virtue of this new principle itself the Bill is downright illogical. A more personal and more offensive charge[2] lies in the statement that the line of demarcation by which electoral rights were to be left to privileged smaller towns was drawn in such a way as to leave untouched the boroughs belonging to the Duke of Bedford, whose brother, Lord John Russell, had introduced the Bill in the Commons. In fact the Bill is a hotchpotch of the old privileges and the general principle of the equal entitlement of all citizens (except for the external limitation of a freehold of £10)[3] to vote for those by whom they are to be represented. Thus the Bill contains an internal contradiction between positive rights and an abstract and theoretical principle. Therefore the illogicality of what is derived from the basis of the old feudal law is shown up in a cruder light than if all entitlements to voting had been put on one and the same footing of positive rights.

This principle does in itself open the way for an infinity [307] of claims on which Parliament can indeed prima facie impose limits; carried out logically it would produce a revolution rather than a mere reform. But that such further claims may not be pressed very energetically so soon is the inference from the fact that the middle and lower classes in the three kingdoms seem to be very generally satisfied with the Bill. The so-called practical sense of the British people, its concentration on gain, subsistence, wealth, does not seem yet to have been much touched by needs for the

---

[1] Ibid., p. 406, not Grey but Brougham, and there is no reference to Yorkshire. In any case Grey's seat was in Northumberland, but Hegel may confuse that county with Yorkshire. See below, p. 316, n. 4.

[2] Croker and others made this charge in the debate on leave to introduce the Reform Bill, 1–9 March 1831.

[3] The basis of *borough* franchise laid down in the Bill was occupation, whether as owner or tenant, of property of £10 annual value. Hegel is mistaken here.

above-mentioned material rights. Still less efficacious in Britain is the purely formal principle of equality. The fanaticism of principles like that is foreign to the British mind. Indeed this British practical sense is involved in an immediate loss because a great mass of people lose the gain from bribes because of the rise in the voting qualification from forty shillings to two hundred.[1] If this higher class[2] has hitherto derived a cash advantage from its votes, it will not lose it. An M.P. elected for Liverpool has just been excluded from Parliament because the voters have been proved to have taken bribes. The electors in this city are very numerous, and it is a wealthy place; so one would expect that amongst the bribed a number of well-to-do people will have been found as well. Further, just as the big landowners knew how to make out that hundreds and thousands of their propertyless tenants were owners of a forty-shilling freehold, so this peculiar method of creating votes will operate again under the new qualification, and these same dependants will appear in the disguise of £10 freeholders. Equally unlikely, [308] despite the elevation of the qualifying freehold, is the disappearance of the numerous weeks of feasting and drinking in which the English masses, with their unbounded bestiality, were encouraged to indulge and in which they got their pay.[3] At the last election but one it was stated that in the populous county of York £80,000 sterling had been disbursed for the election of a landowner there, Beaumont.[4] In parliamentary debates it has been alleged that the election expenses have gradually become all too high; thus the question arises of how the people are to regard the fact that the rich will make savings at their expense. It is still undecided how it will stand with this matter of material advantage,

---

[1] There is further confusion here. While the borough franchise was based on the £10 householder, the county franchise of 40s. freehold still remained. This confusion persists in what follows. Hegel seems to have confused the provisions of the English Reform Bill with those of the Irish Bill which accompanied Catholic emancipation. In the latter the franchise qualification was elevated everywhere from 40s. to £10.

[2] This higher class of £10 freeholders has recently been stigmatized by the name of 'paupers' in the Upper House. [H.]

[3] Reading Boumann's text.

[4] In one of the last sittings of Parliament £120,000 was quoted as the expenditure on the Liverpool election mentioned above. [H.] T. W. Beaumont was a wealthy landowner elected for his County of Northumberland in 1818 and 1820. Defeated in 1826 he was elected again in 1830 in a contested election. County elections were expensive, if contested, as they rarely were. The Yorkshire election of 1826 was estimated to have cost £150,000.

and what new combinations the tireless speculation of agents concerned with the trade in parliamentary seats will produce; it would be too soon to make conjectures about the change which confronts this interest.

But a higher interest seems to be afforded by the franchise itself by the very fact that of itself it awakens a desire and a demand for its more general distribution. Nevertheless experience proves that the exercise of the right to vote is not so attractive as to provoke strong claims or the movements to which they give rise. On the contrary, what seems to prevail in the electorate is great indifference, despite the associated interest derived from the receipt of bribes. From the large class of those who lose their votes because of the raising of the electoral qualification[1] or whose rights are weakened because their votes are cast [along with those of] the general mass of voters in the county, no petitions against a Bill so disadvantageous to them have come forward. On the other hand, the protests that have been raised come from those whose certainty or probability of election to a seat in Parliament has been impaired or altogether lost. By an Act of Parliament a year ago the freehold qualification for a vote in Ireland was raised and as a result 200,000 persons lost their votes, [309] without their making any complaint about this loss of their qualification for participating [as voters] in affairs of state and government. In any event, the electors see in their right a property which accrues to the benefit of those alone who wish to be elected to Parliament and on the altar of whose personal opinion, whim, and interest everything implicit in this right of participating in government and legislation is to be sacrificed.

The chief election job for which candidates recruit agents acquainted with localities and personalities, as well as with the way of handling them, is to hunt out electors and bring them forward, especially by bribery, to cast their votes in favour of their patrons. The great landowners get their crowds of tenants herded to the poll, some of them, as was said above, being disguised for the moment as owners of the requisite freehold. Brougham humorously described a scene at his former election where tenants were camped in courtyards with fires, pudding, and porter and, to withdraw

---

[1] Once again the same confusion between the Irish Bill and the English. Under the latter only non-resident voters were disqualified; in other instances the franchise was continued to possessors during their lifetime.

them from the influence of the opposition, locked up until the very moment when they had to cast their obedient vote. This indifference to the franchise and its exercise is in the highest degree in contrast with the fact that it is in this right that there lies the right of the people to participate in public affairs and in the highest interests of the state and the government. The exercise of this right is a lofty duty, because there rests on it the constituting of an essential part of the public authority, i.e. the representative assembly, because indeed this right and its exercise is, as the French say, the act, the sole act, of the 'sovereignty of the people'. From this indifference to the franchise we can easily draw an indictment against a people on the score of its political obtuseness or corruption, just as we can from the custom of bribery when the right to vote is exercised. Yet this harsh judgement must be softened if we ponder what must obviously contribute to such lukewarmness: namely, the sense that amongst the many thousands of votes cast at an election a single vote is actually insignificant. [310] Out of the approximately 658 members who are to be elected to the House of Commons or the 430 to be elected to the French Chamber (the forthcoming changes to be made in these figures do not matter here) it is only one member who is to be chosen [in a given constituency] and this is a very inconsiderable fraction of the total number: but the single vote is an even more insignificant fraction of the total of 100 or 1,000 votes which secure *one* member's election. The number of voters to be on the roll under the new French electoral law is assessed at 200,000; the number of members to be elected is given in round figures as 450. It follows that one vote is a two-hundred-thousandth part of the total voting power and the ninety-millionth part of one of the three branches of the legislative power.

The individual scarcely brings to mind in figures like these the triviality of his effectiveness, but nevertheless he has a definite inkling of this quantitative insignificance of his vote, and the quantitative consideration, the number of votes, is here what in practice is alone decisive. Of course the qualitatively[1] high considerations of freedom, duty, exercise of sovereign rights, participation in general affairs of state, may be emphasized against indolence. [But] sound common sense is glad to stop at what is effective. If

---

[1] Reading *qualitativen* with Boumann. Lasson and Hoffmeister both read *quantitativen*, but this must be a misprint or a *lapsus calami* of Hegel's.

the individual has brought before him the usual story that, if *everyone* thought so indolently, the state's existence and, above all, freedom itself would be jeopardized, he is bound to remind himself just as much of the principle on which his duty and his whole right to freedom is built, namely that he should let himself be guided not by considering what others do but solely by his own will, and that what is finally decisive for him, what is even duly acknowledged as his sovereign, is his own individual volition.

In any case this influence, in itself so trivial, is restricted to [influence on the choice of] *persons*, and it becomes infinitely more trivial by reason of the fact that it has no bearing on the *thing*; indeed the latter is expressly excluded [from popular influence]. Only in the French democratic constitution of the year III under Robespierre—a constitution adopted by the whole people but of course all the less [311] carried into effect—was it prescribed that *laws* on public affairs were to be brought before individual citizens for confirmation.

Further, the electors are not even constituents giving instructions to their delegates. The programmes which the members of the National Assembly took with them from their election were at once cast aside and forgotten by both parties. It counts as one of the most fundamental constitutional principles in England and France that members, once elected, are just as sovereign in casting their parliamentary votes as their electors were when they cast *their* votes. In both countries members in their deliberations and resolutions on public business do not have the character of officials and they share with the King what is sanctioned for him, namely answerability to no one for the fulfilment of their duties.

In consequence of the feeling of the actually trivial influence of an individual and his sovereign choice (which is tied up with the franchise), experience teaches that elections are not in general attended by many. The numbers, that we sometimes find in newspapers, of those legally entitled to vote and of those who actually cast a vote at an election have usually been obviously very different from one another in the turbulent days of Charles X's[1] last years on the throne. In the most recent election held in the centre of political interest, i.e. in Paris, where the parties seem to have shown no lack of zeal in summoning the electors to cast their votes, it was stated that of about 1,750 voters some 600 did not put in an

---

[1] King of France, 1824–30.

appearance. In this connexion it might be interesting to get to know the average proportion of voters to votes actually cast in other areas where all the citizens are enfranchised and where the franchise affects a much nearer interest of theirs, e.g. in elections for choosing town councillors in Prussia.

In the earlier years of the French Revolution the zeal and the behaviour of the Jacobins at elections disgusted peaceful and decent citizens and even made it dangerous for them to cast their votes. So faction alone held the field.

While [312] the great political bodies which are now making decisions about the franchise think that they are fulfilling a duty of high justice by enlarging the external qualifications for this privilege and granting it to a larger number of people, they do not reflect that they are thereby diminishing the influence of the individual, weakening his idea of its importance and consequentially his interest in exercising this right. Still less do they ask themselves how any political power at all comes to dispose of this right of the citizens by taking into consideration fifty or a hundred francs or so many pounds sterling and altering this right in accordance with amounts like these. This right in its essential character is accepted as sovereign, elementary, inalienable; in short as the opposite of something which can be bestowed or taken away.

The so well-reputed sound common sense of the English people makes individuals feel the insignificance of the influence they exercise on public affairs by their single votes. Moreover, this same common sense gives them a proper sense of their general ignorance and their slender capacity for judging the talents, acquaintance with business, skill, and education required in high officers of state. Is it to be supposed that such a great increase in capacity is involved in possessing a freehold of forty shillings or ten pounds or paying two hundred francs in direct taxes (whether the additional centimes are reckoned in or not)? The rigidity of the French Chambers in disregarding any qualification except that which is supposed to lie in the 200 francs (with or without the additional centimes), and ascribing this qualification solely to members of the Institute, is characteristic enough. The formalism of respecting the 200 francs has obliterated respect for the capacity and good will of prefects, councillors, doctors, advocates, &c., who do not pay so much in taxes.

Moreover, the voters know that, on the strength of their sovereign right, they are exempt from having to have in advance a judgement on, or indeed an examination [313] of, the candidates and that they have to decide without anything of this kind. Thus it is no wonder at all that in England a great number of individuals—no matter whether a majority of them—require to be stimulated by the candidates before they will take what is to them the trifling trouble of voting, and for their trouble, which advantages the candidates, they have to be compensated by them with badges, roasts, beer, and a few guineas. The French are newer in this political path, and they have not yet sunk so far into this sort of compensation, doubtless through the pressure of the vital interests of their situation which has not yet been deeply consolidated and which indeed has become one of the most deadly danger. But since they have been roused to take things and their share in them more seriously, they have seized a share in things for themselves in insurrections, clubs, associations, &c., and have thus gained a right and found compensation for the triviality of the part which their individual sovereignty plays in public affairs.

[4. THE DIVISION OF THE POWERS OF GOVERNMENT]

The peculiarity, which has just been touched on, of one power in England which is supposed to be subordinate and whose members yet make decisions on the whole of the affairs of state without being instructed, without accountability, without being officials, is the basis of a relationship with the monarchical part of the constitution. Mention must be made of the influence which the Reform Bill may have on this relationship and on the governing power in general. For considering this matter it is necessary first to recall the most immediate consequence of the peculiarity which has been referred to, namely that in England the power of the Crown and the power of government are very different from one another. To the power of the Crown there belong the most important branches of the supreme control of the state, especially those with a bearing on [314] other states, the authority to make war and peace, control of the army, the appointment of Ministers (though it has become etiquette for the monarch to appoint directly the Prime Minister only, while the latter puts together the rest of the Cabinet), the appointment of army commanders and officers, of ambassadors, &c. Yet it is to Parliament that there belongs the sovereign decision on the budget (including even the sum allowed for the maintenance of the King and his family), i.e. on the entire range of the means for making war and peace and having an army, ambassadors, &c. Moreover, a Ministry can only govern, i.e. exist, in so far as it falls in with the views and the will of Parliament. Thus the share of the monarch in the power of government is more illusory than real and the substance of this power lies with Parliament. Siéyès had a great reputation for deep insights into the organization of free constitutions. At least, at the transition from the directorial to the consular constitution, Siéyès was able to extract from his papers the plan which was to give France the enjoyment of his experience and profound reflection; it is well known that this plan put at the pinnacle of the state a head to whom was to accrue the pomp of representation in other countries and the appointment of the supreme state counsellor and the responsible Ministers as well as their subordinate officials.[1] Thus the supreme power of government was entrusted to this state counsellor while the *Proclamateur-électeur* was to have no share in it. Napoleon felt himself made master and ruler; we all know his soldier-like judgement on this project for such a chief, in whom he saw only the role of a *cochon à l'engrais de quelques millions*, a role that no man of talent and honour would find himself undertaking. In this project something was genuinely overlooked which in others has been arranged with full awareness and deliberate intention, i.e. that the naming of Ministers and the other officials of the executive is in itself something formal and powerless and that in substance it falls to wherever the power of government effectively is. In England we see this power in Parliament; in the numerous monarchical constitutions created [315] in our experience, the formal separation of the power of government, as the executive, from a power which is *purely* legislative and judiciary is explicitly declared, and the former power is even set out with pomp and distinction. But the nomination of the Ministry has always been the centre of dispute and contention, despite the unconditional ascription to the Crown of this right of nomination; and the so-called 'purely' legislative power has carried off the victory. Even in the latest French constitution the government has soon seen itself compelled to transfer

[1] 9 Nov. 1799. In 1797 Siéyès had drawn up a constitution in which he proposed a Grand Elector who was to reside in state at Versailles and represent the country to foreign powers but have no immediate authority except that of nominating the two Consuls who were to exercise the actual powers of government.

its headquarters to the Chamber of Deputies, where it has been brought even to the point of having to enter into public disputes with its subordinate officials.

Connected above all with the fact that the power of government lies in Parliament is an argument advanced by the opponents of the Reform Bill on behalf of the boroughs through whose possession many parliamentary seats rest with single individuals or families, namely that it was by means of this fact that England's most distinguished statesmen had found their way to Parliament and thence to the Ministry. It may well be a fact that a remarkable and profound talent has often before now been recognized by private friendship and is in the position of being able only through some individual's generosity to attain the due place which otherwise it could not achieve in view of the deficient resources and family connexions of the mass of the citizens in a town or county. But examples of this kind may be ascribed to the realm of chance where one probability may easily be set against another, and a possible advantage against a possible disadvantage.

Connected with this is another ostensible consequence of great importance to which the Duke of Wellington drew attention. (He has not the look of an orator because he lacks what has given many Members of Parliament such a great reputation for eloquence, namely an easy-flowing loquacity continuing for hours at a time and remarkably rich in self-display. But the Duke's speeches with their disjointed sentences, for which he has been reproached, are not lacking in substance or in points that go to the root of the matter.) He expresses his fear that, in the place of those to whom the care of the public interest is now entrusted in Parliament, [316] altogether different men will arrive, and he asks once again whether, as was quoted above, the shopkeepers, of whom in his view the great majority of the voters will consist as a result of the new Bill, are the people who ought to elect the members of the great national council which has to make decisions on domestic and foreign affairs, on the interests of agriculture, manufacture, and colonies.

The Duke speaks from observation of the English Parliament where above the mass of members who are incompetent and ignorant, with a veneer of current prejudices and a culture drawn from conversation and often not even that, there stands a number of brilliant men wholly devoted to political activity and the interest of the state. To the majority of the latter a parliamentary seat is guaranteed partly by their own wealth and the influence which they themselves or their family have in a borough, city, or county, and partly through the influence of the Ministry and then through their party friends.

To this class there belongs a number of men who make political activity the business of their life. This may be because it is their predilection and they have private means, or because they occupy public positions which they have obtained through a connexion with parliamentary influence. Even if they have obtained them by other means, still, either because of their official position or because of their general inner vocation, they cannot neglect attaching themselves to a party and to the class of politicians. Where the service of the state is not tied to other qualifications, for example a degree, passing a government examination, undergoing a course of preliminary training in affairs, &c., a man must be incorporated into this class; he has to create some importance for himself there; he is carried by its influence, just as correspondingly his influence accrues to it. There are a few anomalous cases of individuals isolated from any party connexion, e.g. Hunt,[1] but when they come into Parliament they do not fail to make a strange figure there.

Other bonds of the political class—family connexions, political conversations and speeches at dinners, &c., the endless and world-wide [317] exchange of political correspondence, even the social gadding about to country seats, horse-races, fox-hunting, &c.—will of course not be disturbed. But one chief element in the power of this class, namely the disposal of a number of parliamentary seats, does suffer through the Reform Bill an important modification which may well have the effect which the Duke mentions, i.e. many other individuals will appear in place of those belonging to the present circle of those devoted to the interest of the national government; but this is likely to bring as its sequel a disturbance of the uniformity of the maxims and considerations of that class, and these constitute the brains of Parliament. To be sure it does not appear that Hunt, for example, despite his isolation, goes beyond the usual notions of the oppression of the people by taxes, sinecures, &c., but, as a result of reform, the route to Parliament may be open to ideas which are opposed to the interest of this class and which therefore have not yet entered its head. Ideas, I mean, which make up the foundations of a real freedom and which affect

[1] Henry ('Orator') Hunt, 1773–1835, M.P. for Preston, 1830–3.

the matters above-mentioned—ecclesiastical property and organization, duties of the clergy—as well as the manorial and other bizarre
rights and property restrictions derived from feudalism, and
further sections of the chaos of English laws. In France these ideas
have been intermixed with many further abstractions and bound up
with the violent upheavals familiar to us all. But unalloyed, they
have for long past in Germany become fixed principles of inner
conviction and public opinion, and have brought about the actual
peaceful, gradual, and legal transformation of the [old feudal] rights.[1]
The result is that here we have already made great progress with
the institutions of real freedom; the most important of them we
have established and enjoy already, while the governing power of
[the English] Parliament has scarcely yet brought them seriously
to mind. From the pressing claims of these principles and from
the demand for their immediate realization England might indeed
have to fear an extreme shattering of the bonds of its social and
political life. In England the contrast between prodigious wealth
and utterly embarrassed penury is enormous; just as great, perhaps
still greater, is that between, on the one hand, the privileges [318]
of its aristocracy and in general the institutions of its positive law
and, on the other, the rights and laws as reconstituted in the
civilized states of the Continent and the principles which, being
grounded on universal reason, cannot always remain so foreign,
even to the English understanding, as they have been hitherto.

The *novi homines* who, the Duke of Wellington fears, will worm
their way into the place of the present statesmen may well find in
these principles the strongest supports of their ambition and their
attainment of popularity. In England it is impossible for these
principles to be adopted and carried into effect by the government,
which has hitherto been in the hands of the privileged class. Consequently their advocates would inevitably come on the scene only
as an opposition to the government and the existing order of things;
and the principles themselves would have to appear not in their
practical truth and application, as in Germany, but in the dangerous
form of French abstractions. The antithesis between *hommes d'état*
and *hommes à principes* which appeared in France at the beginning

---

[1] Hegel thinks of reforms and codifications of law, abolition of serfdom, grant
of self-government to Estates, &c., which took place in Germany after 1789.
These reforms were French-inspired, but they were the work of absolute princes
and their officials and not of representative bodies. See G. P. Gooch, *Germany
and the French Revolution* (London, 1920), pp. 515 ff.

of the Revolution in just as sharp a form has not yet set foot in England; but it may well be introduced as a result of opening a broader way to seats in Parliament. The new class may all the more easily get a footing, since the principles as such are simple in nature and so can be quickly grasped by the ignorant. Since in addition, on the strength of their universality, these principles have a claim to adequacy for everything, they suffice in a man of a certain slenderness of talent, and a certain energy of character and ambition, for the requisite all-attacking rhetoric, and they exercise a blinding effect on the reason of the masses who are just as inexperienced in these matters. On the other hand, the knowledge, experience, and business routine of *hommes d'état* cannot be so easily procured, and these qualities are just as necessary for applying rational principles and introducing them to life as it is lived.

However, the introduction of such a new element would not only disturb the class whose members have the state's business in their hands; it is the power of government [319] which would be thrown off the rails. This power, as has been said, lies in Parliament; however much it is divided into parties and however great the passion with which they confront one another, still equally so little are they factions. They stand within the same general interest, and hitherto a change of Ministry has had important consequences rather in relation to foreign affairs, to war and peace, than in relation to domestic affairs. The principle of monarchy, on the other hand, has little to lose in England. The resignation of Wellington's Ministry is well known to have been brought about as a result of the minority in which it found itself on the motion[1] about the adjustment of the Crown's Civil List—an occurrence of special interest because it affected one of the few things left to the monarchical principle in England.[2] The remains of the Crown lands, which yet had the same character of family property, the private property of the royal family, as the properties of families of dukes, earls, and barons in England, were handed over to the exchequer in the last century, and in compensation a fixed sum corresponding to their revenues was set aside in the budget voted for other purposes annually by the House of Commons. This

---

[1] Actually to refer the Civil List to a committee of the House of Commons.
[2] Here Hegel's political knowledge and insight fail him. He knew that the King's appointment of Ministers was only formal (see above [314]), but he does not seem to have known of the conventions about votes on the Civil List.

landed property, the miserable remains of the earlier great wealth of the throne which was so seriously diminished by extravagance, especially through purchasing troops and baronial support in civil wars, had not been split into what was to remain family property and what was to be spent for the general purposes of the state. Now the characteristic of family and private property which belonged to one part of that remaining wealth had already been altered, at least in form, as a result of that property's having changed from land into a compensating sum included in the annual parliamentary budget. Nevertheless there still remained an appearance of monarchical influence on this small part of the annual British expenditure, even though this influence was subject to the Cabinet. Even this relic of regal control has been abolished by Parliament's recent decision to separate one part which is set aside under the King's control for expenditure on himself and his family and to leave the rest, hitherto already spent on national purposes, to disposal by Parliament. [320] In this connexion it must not be overlooked that the majority which was strong enough on a monarchical matter to bring about the resignation of Wellington's Ministry[1] was, as is well known, a majority of only *one* at the second reading of the Reform Bill[2] which is directed against the prerogatives of the aristocracy.

What can be regarded as characteristic for the position of the monarch in the constitution is the reproach cast at the Ministry in connexion with the Catholic Emancipation Bill as well as in debates on the Reform Bill, namely that it had allowed the King's partly given consent to these measures to become public. There was no question of the exercise of monarchical omnipotence or of a so-called *coup d'état*. What is found improper is only the authority or influence which a personal remark of the King could exercise. On the one hand by its action the Ministry vindicated its delicacy by avoiding in the management of a Bill the embarrassment of going contrary to the King's will. But the situation equally clearly implies that even in the matter of the initiative accruing to the monarchical element, the throne, Parliament wishes to deal solely with a Ministry dependent on and incorporated with that element, and strictly only with its members, since only in that capacity can

[1] Nov. 1830; a motion for a committee to examine the Civil List was carried against the government by a majority of 29.
[2] 22 March 1831. 302 for, 301 against.

Ministers move a Bill. Thus the right accruing to the King, as the third branch of the legislative power, of confirming or rejecting a Bill accepted by both Houses becomes all the more illusory in that the Cabinet is once again the same Ministry embodied in Parliament. Earl Grey has said,[1] in reply to that reproach, that the Ministry's introduction of the Bill did have the King's agreement in advance, but that the Ministry was exonerated from the blame of saying outright that the King's agreement had been secured, simply by the fact that this statement had not come from Ministers but from elsewhere.

Thus the special dissension which might be introduced into Parliament by the presence of *novi homines* would not be the struggle with which each of the numerous French constitutions began every time about whether the power of government was actually to be given to the King and his Ministers, these being those [321] to whom it was ascribed in words. In the English political administration as it exists there has been settled very long ago what in France has always first needed a decisive and authentic interpretation through the insurrection and violence of an insurgent people. Thus the reintroduction of the Reform Bill can only touch the effective power of government established in Parliament. On the situation existing hitherto, this power suffers purely superficial variations appearing as changes of Ministries, and no genuine dissension on principles. A new Ministry belongs itself to the same class of interests and the same group of statesmen as its predecessor. The necessary preponderant strength that it needs as a party it gains partly through the number of members who count as independent and who on the whole take the side of the Ministry, feeling that a government there must be, but also partly through the influence it may be able to exercise on appointments to a number of parliamentary seats. Now even if the so-called agricultural interest seems to have declared that it will find its account in the mode of election which is to be newly introduced, and even if a great part of the former patronage of parliamentary seats and the combinations for their purchase retain their position, still there is no escaping the fact that the class that has hitherto dominated Parliament, the class that afforded to every Ministry ready-made material for [maintaining] the existing system of social life, will suffer modification as a result of introducing new men and different

[1] 28 March 1831 in the House of Lords.

principles. The Reform Bill in itself encroaches on this system, i.e. on the principle of purely positive rights which secures the possession of privileges, no matter what relation, if any, they may have to the rights of real freedom. When claims of a new kind, which hitherto have scarcely come to halting and involuntary expression and have been not so much demanded as vaguely feared, come to be increasingly discussed in Parliament, the opposition changes its character: the parties have an object other than that of getting the Ministry.

If we grasp this hitherto different character of an opposition as it appears in its extreme in France, it is most distinctively expressed in [322] the surprise, expressed recently in France at every change of Ministry, that individuals coming out of opposition into power now acted on almost the same maxims as their supplanted predecessors. In French opposition newspapers we read naïve complaints that so many excellent individuals become backsliders as a result of their progress through office and become false to the left to which they belonged earlier, i.e. that, while of course they had previously granted *in abstracto* that there had to be a government they have now learnt what government really is and that something more is needed for it than principles. These, as we all know, consist of general ideas about freedom, equality, the people, its sovereignty, &c. For men of principles, national legislation is in essence more or less exhausted by the *droits de l'homme et du citoyen*, framed by Lafayette and the model for the earlier French constitutions. A more fully detailed legislation, an organization of the powers of the state and the hierarchy of administrative officials, and the subordination of the people to these public authorities, was of course accepted as necessary and was drawn up. But instead of that activity of institutions in which public order and genuine freedom consists, recourse was had once more to these generalities which, by what they demand in the way of freedom, make constitutional law self-contradictory from the start. Obedience to law is granted to be necessary, but when demanded by the authorities, i.e. by individuals, it is seen to run counter to freedom. The right to command, the difference arising from this right, the general difference between commanding and obeying, is contrary to equality. A multitude of men can call itself a 'people', and rightly, because 'people' is just this indefinite multitude; but authorities and officials, in general the members of the organized power of the

state, are different from the 'people', and they are therefore to be
in the wrong; they have forsaken equality and they stand over
against the 'people' which has the infinite advantage of being
recognized as the sovereign will. In the circle of this extreme contradiction a nation revolves once it has been dominated by these
abstract categories. [323] The members of the English Parliament
under the existing system, and Englishmen in general, have a more
practical political sense and they have an idea of what government
and governing is. Yet it also lies in the character of their constitution that the government as good as does not encroach at all on
the particular circles of social life, on the administration of counties,
cities, &c., on ecclesiastical and educational establishments, and
even on other public concerns such as road-making. This freer
and more concrete condition of civil life may add to the probability
that abstract principles of freedom will not so soon find in the class
above the lower one (which in England is of course extremely
numerous and which in general is most open to these abstractions)
the welcome which the opponents of the Reform Bill represent as
threatening immediately.

But should the Bill, on account of its principle rather than of its
terms, open the way to Parliament, and so into the heart of the
power of government, for principles opposed to the system existing hitherto, these principles might appear there with greater
influence than radical reformers have been able to gain up till now.
If so, the battle would threaten to be all the more dangerous, in
that between the interests of positive privilege and the demands
for more real freedom there stands no higher mediating power to
restrain and adjust the dispute. In England the monarchical element
in the constitution lacks the power which in other states has earned
gratitude to the Crown for the transition from a legal system based
purely on positive rights to one based on the principles of real
freedom, a transition wholly exempt from earthquake, violence,
and robbery. The people would be a power of a different kind; and
an opposition which, erected on a basis hitherto at variance with
the stability of Parliament, might feel itself no match for the
opposite party in Parliament, could be led to look for its strength
to the people, and then introduce not reform but revolution.

INDEX

[The index, for which the translator is responsible, supplements the table of contents. The references are all to the pages of this book.]

ISBN 0–19–	Author	Title
8143567	ALFÖLDI A.	The Conversion of Constantine and Pagan Rome
6286409	ANDERSON George K.	The Literature of the Anglo-Saxons
8228813	BARTLETT & MacKAY	Medieval Frontier Societies
8114222	BROOKS Kenneth R.	Andreas and the Fates of the Apostles
8148348	CAMPBELL J.B.	The Emperor and the Roman Army 31 BC to 235 AD
826643X	CHADWICK Henry	Priscillian of Avila
826447X	CHADWICK Henry	Boethius
8219393	COWDREY H.E.J.	The Age of Abbot Desiderius
8148992	DAVIES M.	Sophocles: Trachiniae
825301X	DOWNER L.	Leges Henrici Primi
8143109	FRAENKEL Edward	Horace
8201540	GOLDBERG P.J.P.	Women, Work and Life Cycle in a Medieval Economy
8140215	GOTTSCHALK H.B.	Heraclides of Pontus
8266162	HANSON R.P.C.	Saint Patrick
8224354	HARRISS G.L.	King, Parliament and Public Finance in Medieval England to 1369
8581114	HEATH Sir Thomas	Aristarchus of Samos
8140444	HOLLIS A.S.	Callimachus: Hecale
8212968	HOLLISTER C. Warren	Anglo-Saxon Military Institutions
8223129	HURNARD Naomi	The King's Pardon for Homicide – before AD 1307
8140401	HUTCHINSON G.O.	Hellenistic Poetry
8142560	JONES A.H.M.	The Greek City
8218354	JONES Michael	Ducal Brittany 1364–1399
8271484	KNOX & PELCZYNSKI	Hegel's Political Writings
8225253	LE PATOUREL John	The Norman Empire
8212720	LENNARD Reginald	Rural England 1086–1135
8212321	LEVISON W.	England and the Continent in the 8th century
8148224	LIEBESCHUETZ J.H.W.G.	Continuity and Change in Roman Religion
8141378	LOBEL Edgar & PAGE Sir Denys	Poetarum Lesbiorum Fragmenta
8152442	MAAS P. & TRYPANIS C.A .	Sancti Romani Melodi Cantica
8148178	MATTHEWS John	Western Aristocracies and Imperial Court AD 364–425
8223447	McFARLANE K.B.	Lancastrian Kings and Lollard Knights
8226578	McFARLANE K.B.	The Nobility of Later Medieval England
8148100	MEIGGS Russell	Roman Ostia
8148402	MEIGGS Russell	Trees and Timber in the Ancient Mediterranean World
8142641	MILLER J. Innes	The Spice Trade of the Roman Empire
8147813	MOORHEAD John	Theoderic in Italy
8264259	MOORMAN John	A History of the Franciscan Order
8116020	OWEN A.L.	The Famous Druids
8143427	PFEIFFER R.	History of Classical Scholarship (vol 1)
8111649	PHEIFER J.D.	Old English Glosses in the Epinal-Erfurt Glossary
8142277	PICKARD–CAMBRIDGE A.W.	Dithyramb Tragedy and Comedy
8269765	PLATER & WHITE	Grammar of the Vulgate
8213891	PLUMMER Charles	Lives of Irish Saints (2 vols)
820695X	POWICKE Michael	Military Obligation in Medieval England
8269684	POWICKE Sir Maurice	Stephen Langton
821460X	POWICKE Sir Maurice	The Christian Life in the Middle Ages
8225369	PRAWER Joshua	Crusader Institutions
8225571	PRAWER Joshua	The History of The Jews in the Latin Kingdom of Jerusalem
8143249	RABY F.J.E.	A History of Christian Latin Poetry
8143257	RABY F.J.E.	A History of Secular Latin Poetry in the Middle Ages (2 vols)
8214316	RASHDALL & POWICKE	The Universities of Europe in the Middle Ages (3 vols)
8148380	RICKMAN Geoffrey	The Corn Supply of Ancient Rome
8141076	ROSS Sir David	Aristotle: Metaphysics (2 vols)
8141092	ROSS Sir David	Aristotle: Physics
8264178	RUNCIMAN Sir Steven	The Eastern Schism
814833X	SALMON J.B.	Wealthy Corinth
8171587	SALZMAN L.F.	Building in England Down to 1540
8218362	SAYERS Jane E.	Papal Judges Delegate in the Province of Canterbury 1198–1254
8221657	SCHEIN Sylvia	Fideles Crucis
8148135	SHERWIN WHITE A.N.	The Roman Citizenship
8642040	SOUTER Alexander	A Glossary of Later Latin to 600 AD
8222254	SOUTHERN R.W.	Eadmer: Life of St. Anselm
8251408	SQUIBB G.	The High Court of Chivalry
8212011	STEVENSON & WHITELOCK	Asser's Life of King Alfred
8212011	SWEET Henry	A Second Anglo-Saxon Reader—Archaic and Dialectical
8148259	SYME Sir Ronald	History in Ovid

8143273	SYME Sir Ronald	Tacitus (2 vols)
8200951	THOMPSON Sally	Women Religious
8201745	WALKER Simon	The Lancastrian Affinity 1361–1399
8161115	WELLESZ Egon	A History of Byzantine Music and Hymnography
8140185	WEST M.L.	Greek Metre
8141696	WEST M.L.	Hesiod: Theogony
8148542	WEST M.L.	The Orphic Poems
8140053	WEST M.L.	Hesiod: Works & Days
822799X	WHITBY M. & M.	The History of Theophylact Simocatta
8114877	WOOLF Rosemary	The English Religious Lyric in the Middle Ages
8119224	WRIGHT Joseph	Grammar of the Gothic Language